OMAMORI HIMARI

1

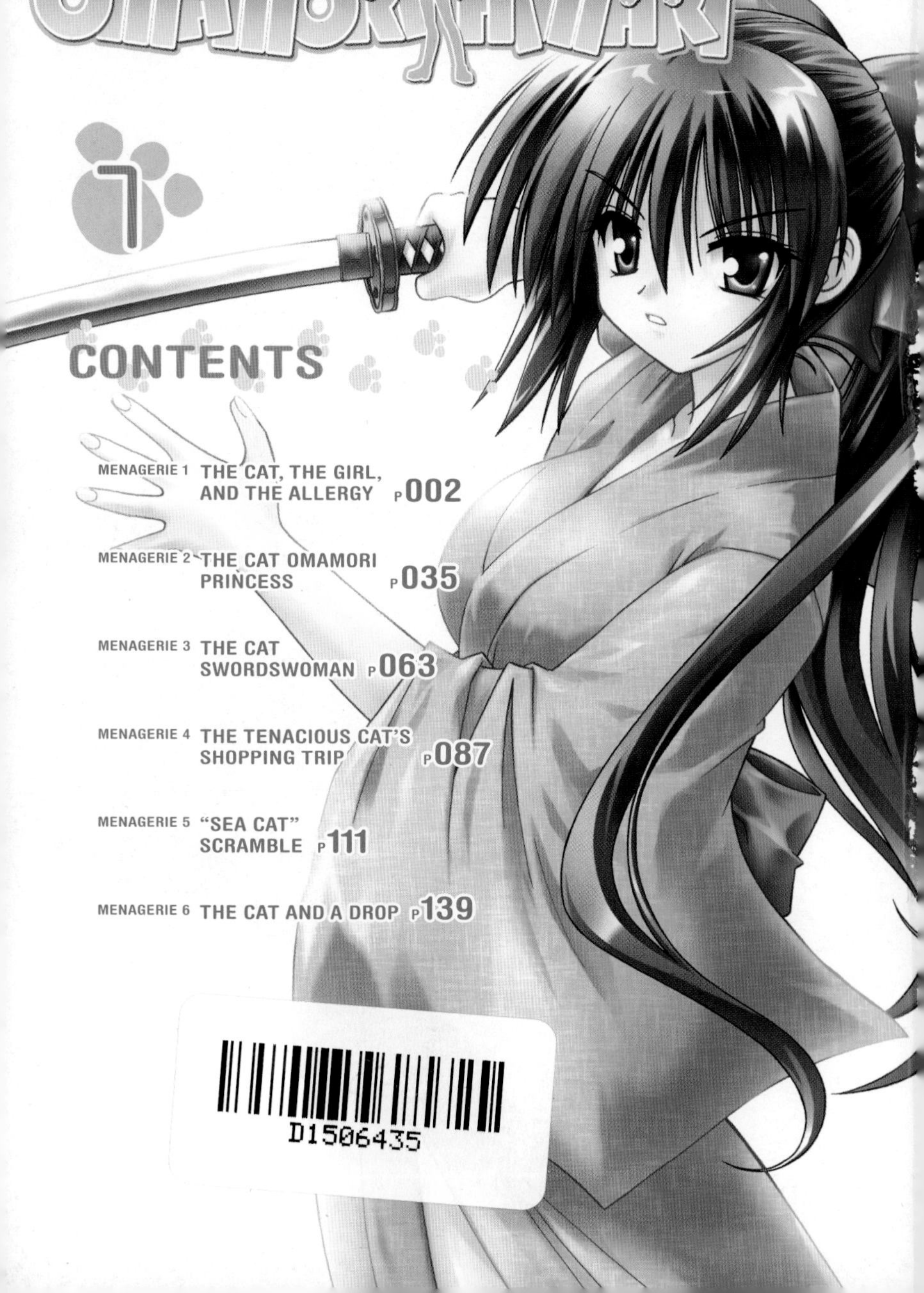

CONTENTS

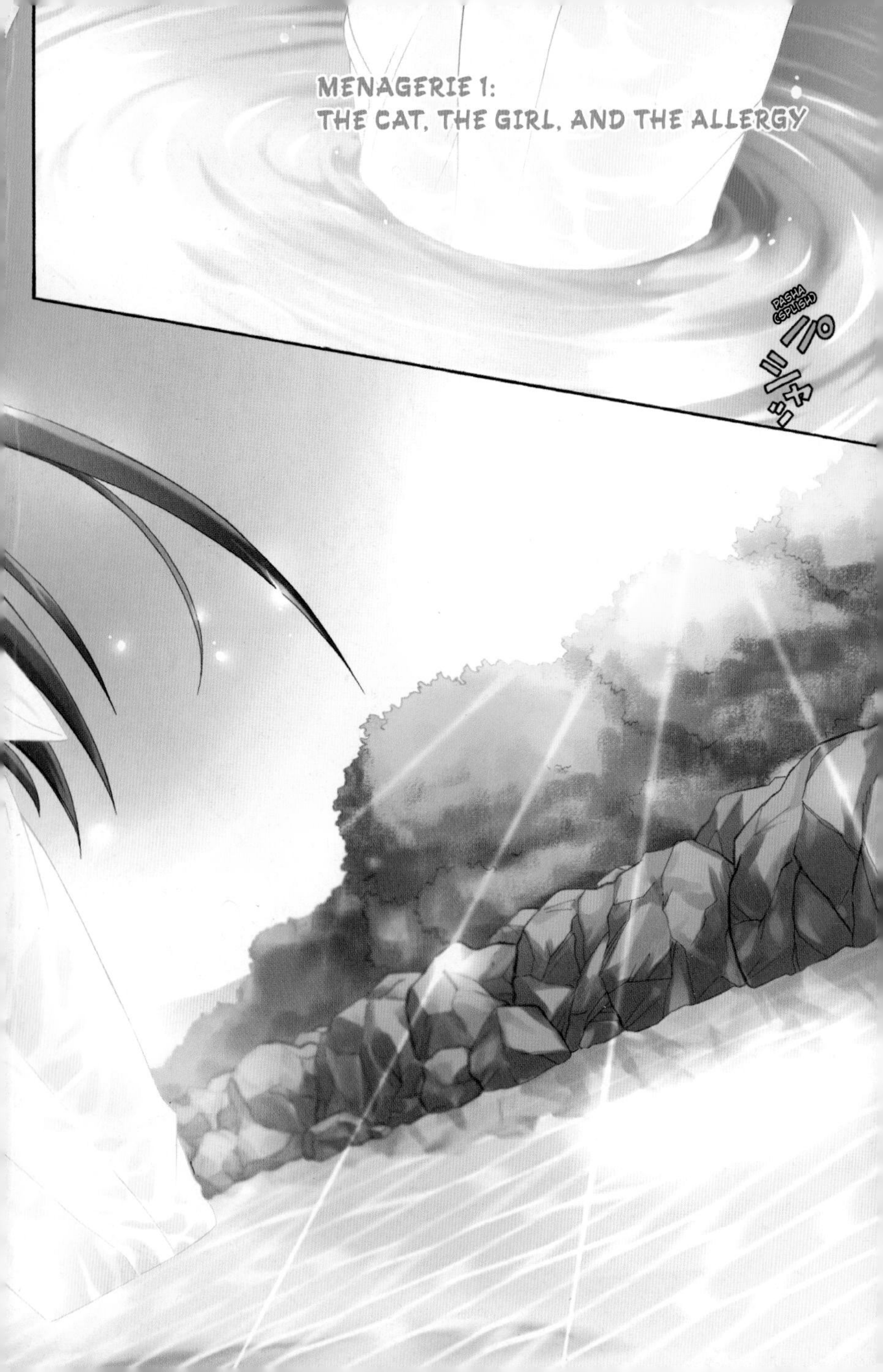
MENAGERIE 1:
THE CAT, THE GIRL, AND THE ALLERGY
PASHA (SPLISH)

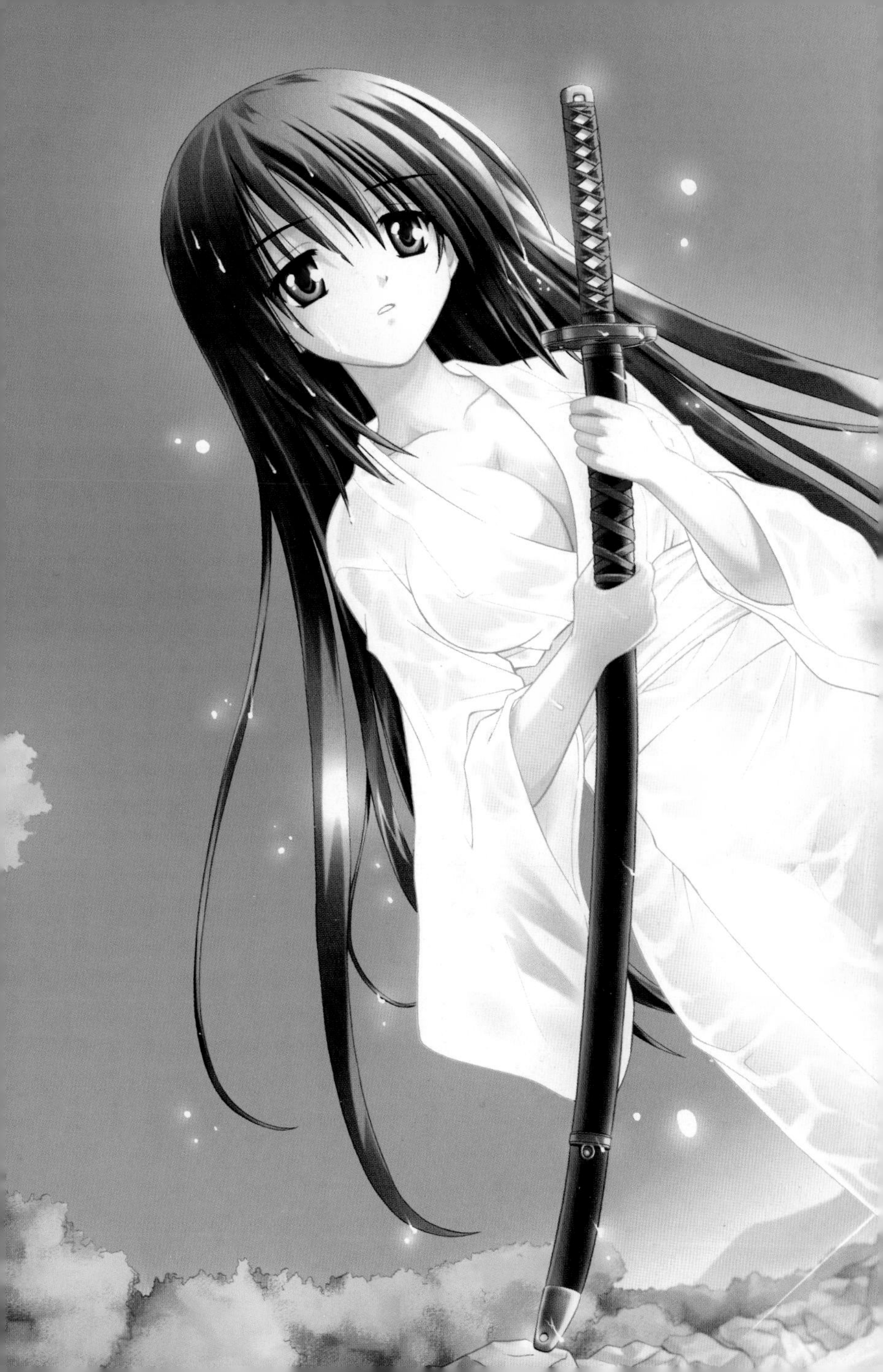

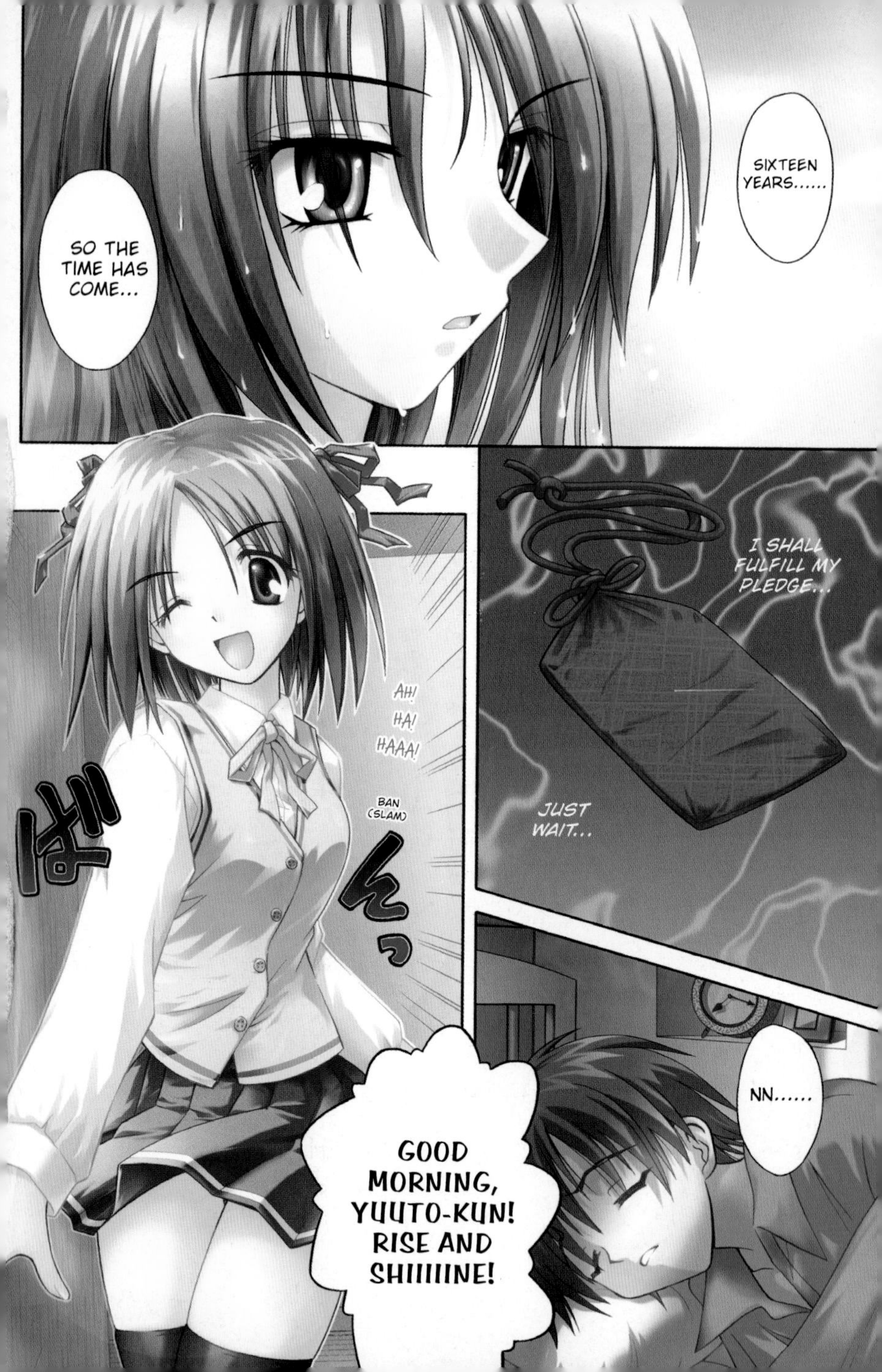
SIXTEEN YEARS......
SO THE TIME HAS COME...
I SHALL FULFILL MY PLEDGE...
JUST WAIT...
NN......
AH! HA! HAAA!
BAN (SLAM)
ばんっ
GOOD MORNING, YUUTO-KUN! RISE AND SHIIIIINE!

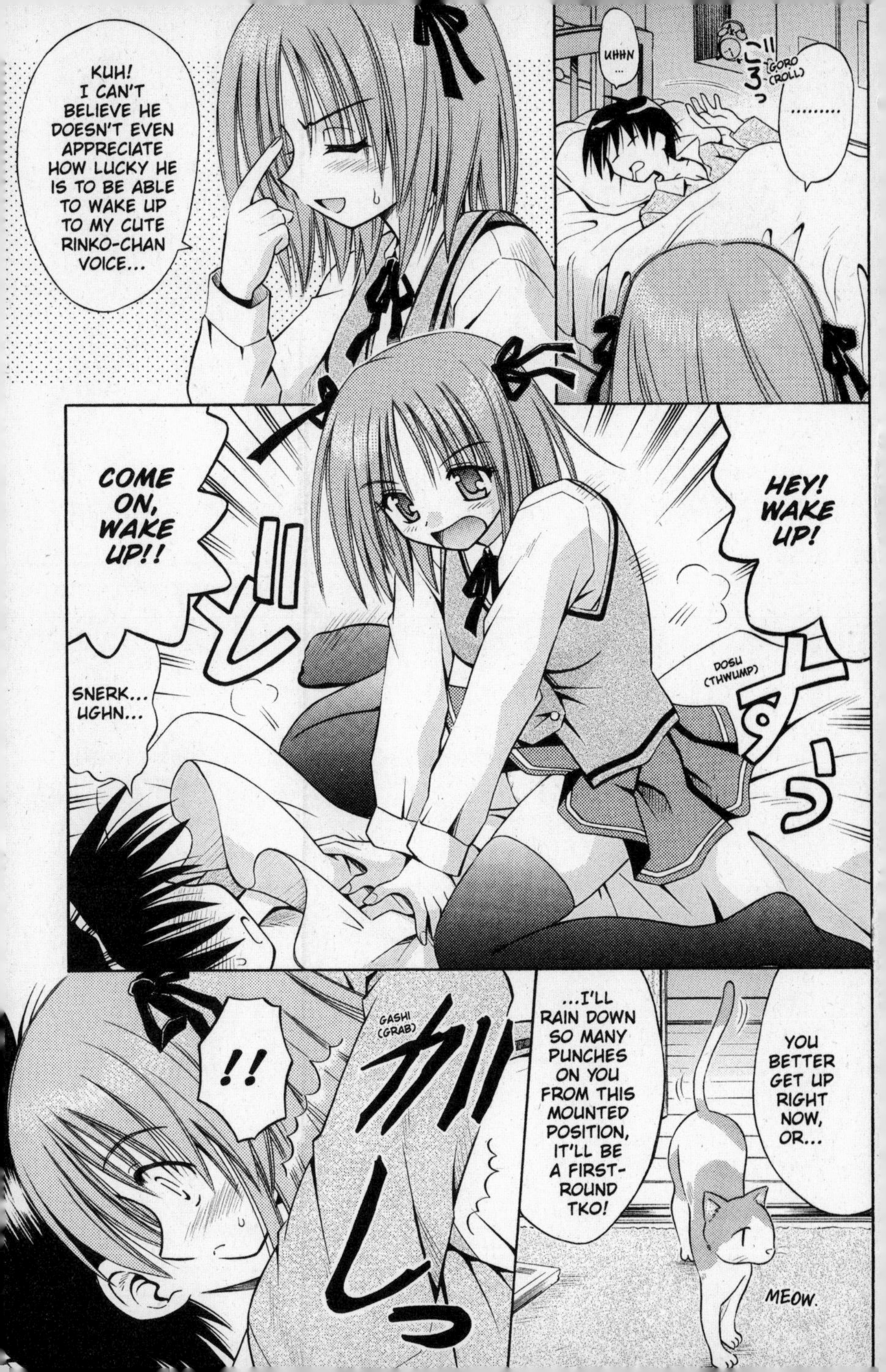
UHHN...
GORO (ROLL)
....
KUH! I CAN'T BELIEVE HE DOESN'T EVEN APPRECIATE HOW LUCKY HE IS TO BE ABLE TO WAKE UP TO MY CUTE RINKO-CHAN VOICE...
HEY! WAKE UP!
DOSU (THWUMP)
COME ON, WAKE UP!!
SNERK... UGHN...
YOU BETTER GET UP RIGHT NOW, OR...
...I'LL RAIN DOWN SO MANY PUNCHES ON YOU FROM THIS MOUNTED POSITION, IT'LL BE A FIRST-ROUND TKO!
MEOW.
GASHI (GRAB)
!!

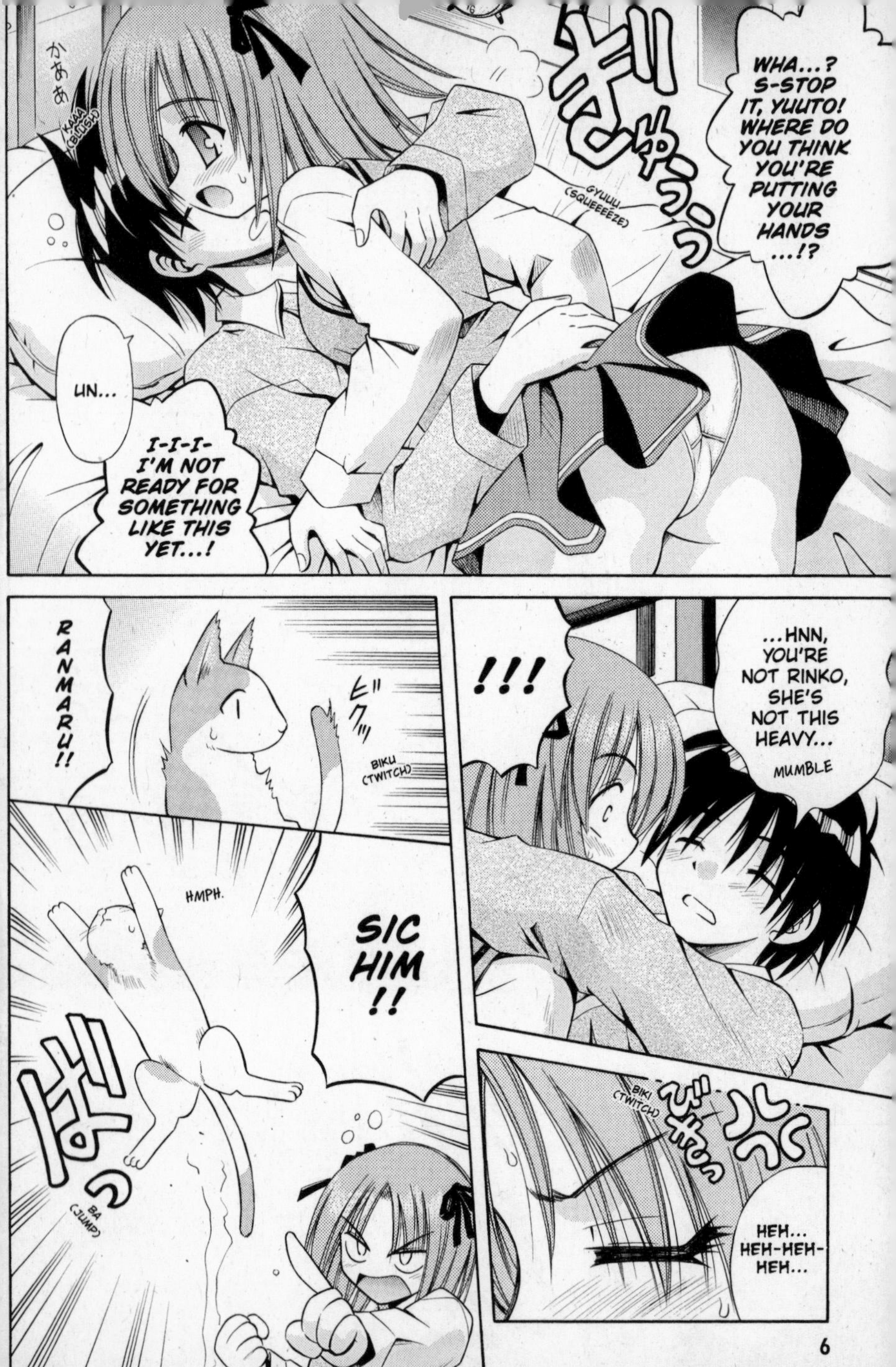
WHA...? S-STOP IT, YUUTO! WHERE DO YOU THINK YOU'RE PUTTING YOUR HANDS ...!?
ぎゅううう
GYUUU (SQUEEEEZE)
かあぁ
KAAA (BLUSH)
UN...
I-I-I-I'M NOT READY FOR SOMETHING LIKE THIS YET...!
...HNN, YOU'RE NOT RINKO, SHE'S NOT THIS HEAVY...
MUMBLE
!!!
びきっ
BIKI (TWITCH)
HEH... HEH-HEH-HEH...
RANMARU!!
ビクッ
BIKU (TWITCH)
HMPH.
SIC HIM!!
ばっ
BA (JUMP)

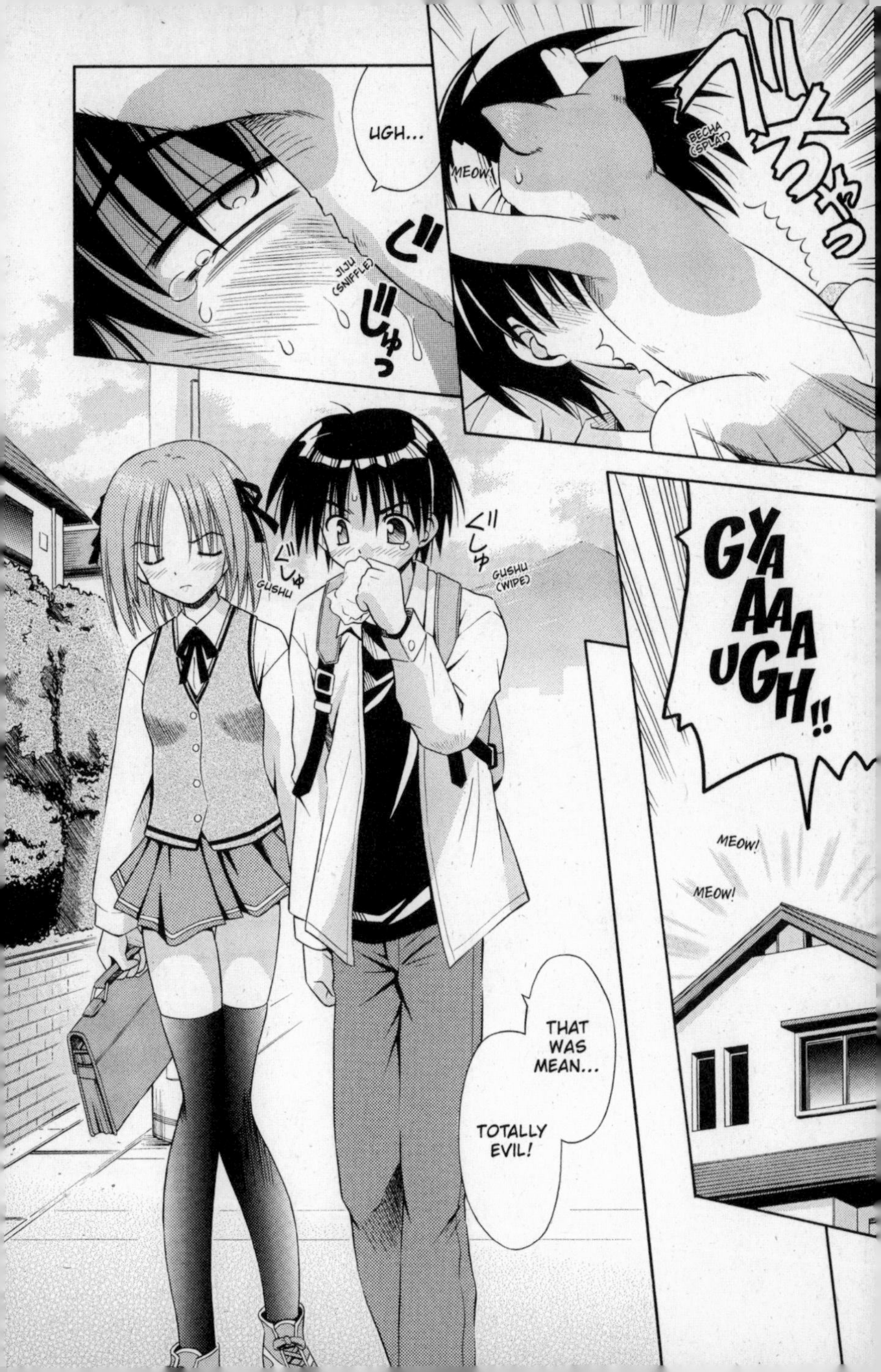
BECHA (SPLAT)
MEOW!
UGH...
JIJU (SNIFFLE)
GYAAAAUGH!!
MEOW!
MEOW!
GUSHU (WIPE)
GUSHU
THAT WAS MEAN...
TOTALLY EVIL!

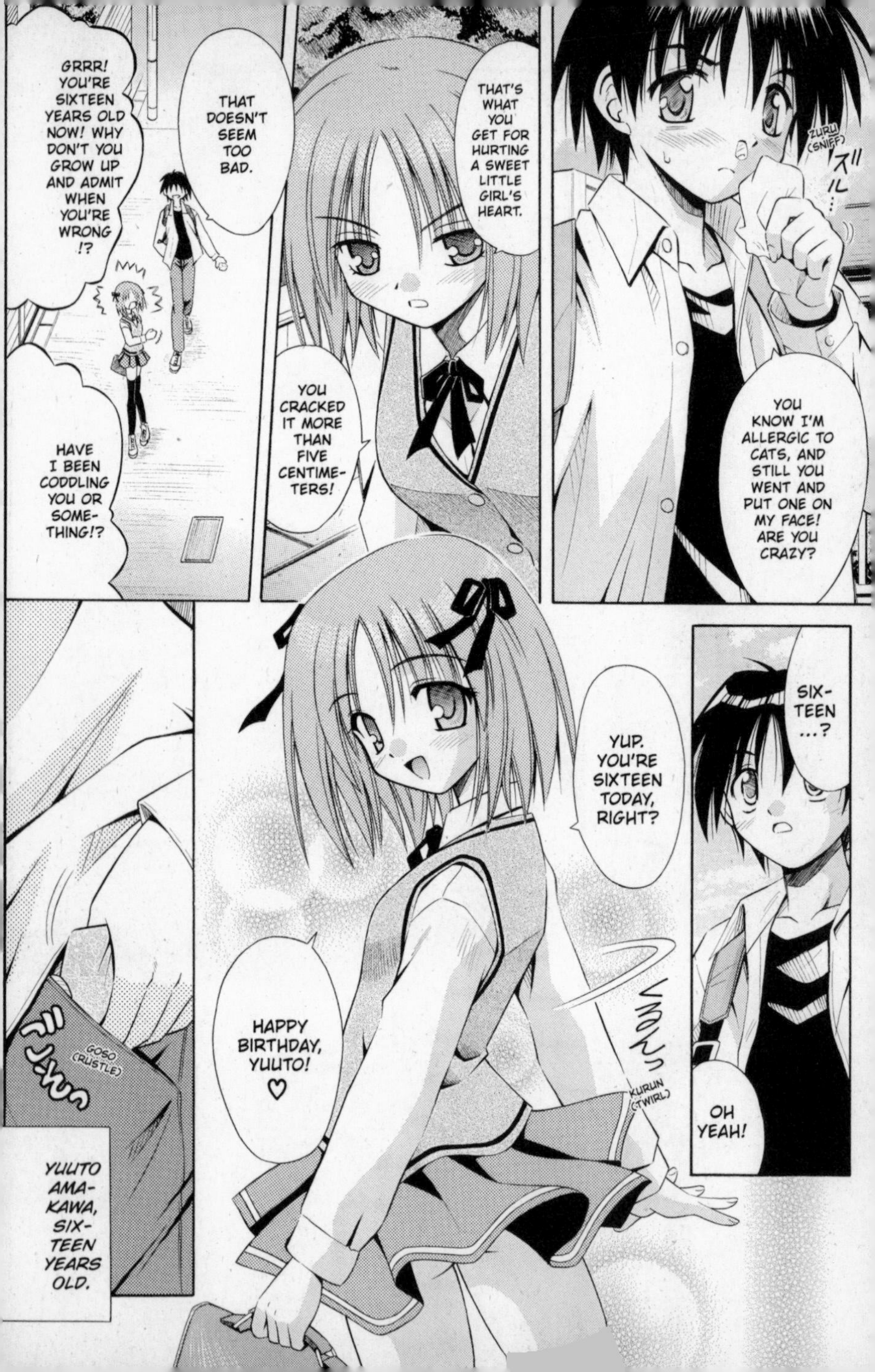
ZURU (SNIFF)
ズル…
YOU KNOW I'M ALLERGIC TO CATS, AND STILL YOU WENT AND PUT ONE ON MY FACE! ARE YOU CRAZY?
THAT'S WHAT YOU GET FOR HURTING A SWEET LITTLE GIRL'S HEART.
YOU CRACKED IT MORE THAN FIVE CENTIMETERS!
THAT DOESN'T SEEM TOO BAD.
GRRR! YOU'RE SIXTEEN YEARS OLD NOW! WHY DON'T YOU GROW UP AND ADMIT WHEN YOU'RE WRONG!?
HAVE I BEEN CODDLING YOU OR SOMETHING!?
SIX-TEEN ...?
OH YEAH!
YUP. YOU'RE SIXTEEN TODAY, RIGHT?
KURUN (TWIRL)
HAPPY BIRTHDAY, YUUTO! ♡
GOSO (RUSTLE)
YUUTO AMAKAWA, SIXTEEN YEARS OLD.

*AN OMAMORI IS AN AMULET OFTEN SOLD AT SHRINES AND TEMPLES, USED TO BRING GOOD LUCK OR PROTECT AGAINST EVIL.

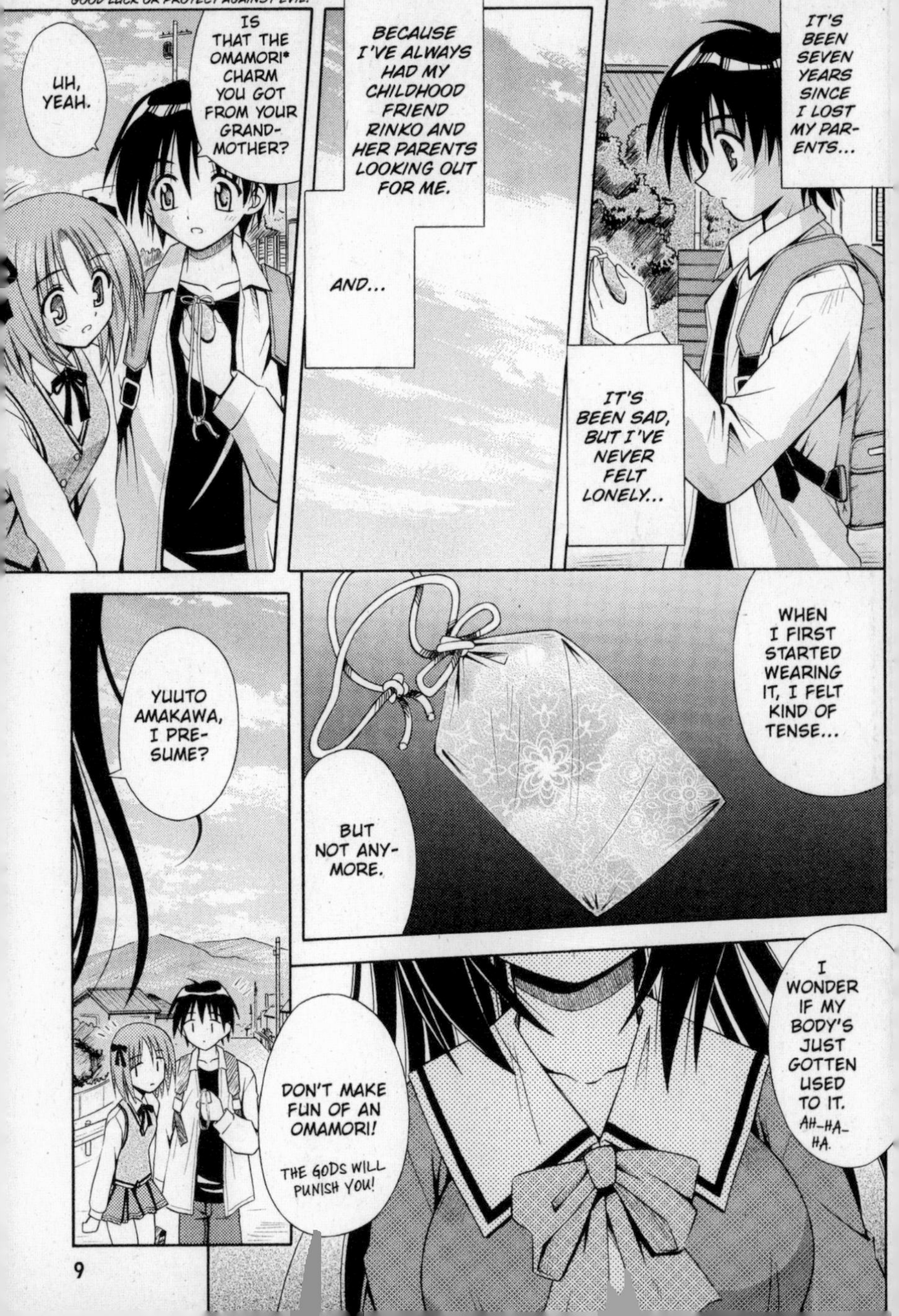
IT'S BEEN SEVEN YEARS SINCE I LOST MY PARENTS...
IT'S BEEN SAD, BUT I'VE NEVER FELT LONELY...
BECAUSE I'VE ALWAYS HAD MY CHILDHOOD FRIEND RINKO AND HER PARENTS LOOKING OUT FOR ME.
AND...
IS THAT THE OMAMORI* CHARM YOU GOT FROM YOUR GRANDMOTHER?
UH, YEAH.
WHEN I FIRST STARTED WEARING IT, I FELT KIND OF TENSE...
BUT NOT ANYMORE.
I WONDER IF MY BODY'S JUST GOTTEN USED TO IT. AH-HA-HA.
DON'T MAKE FUN OF AN OMAMORI!
THE GODS WILL PUNISH YOU!
YUUTO AMAKAWA, I PRESUME?

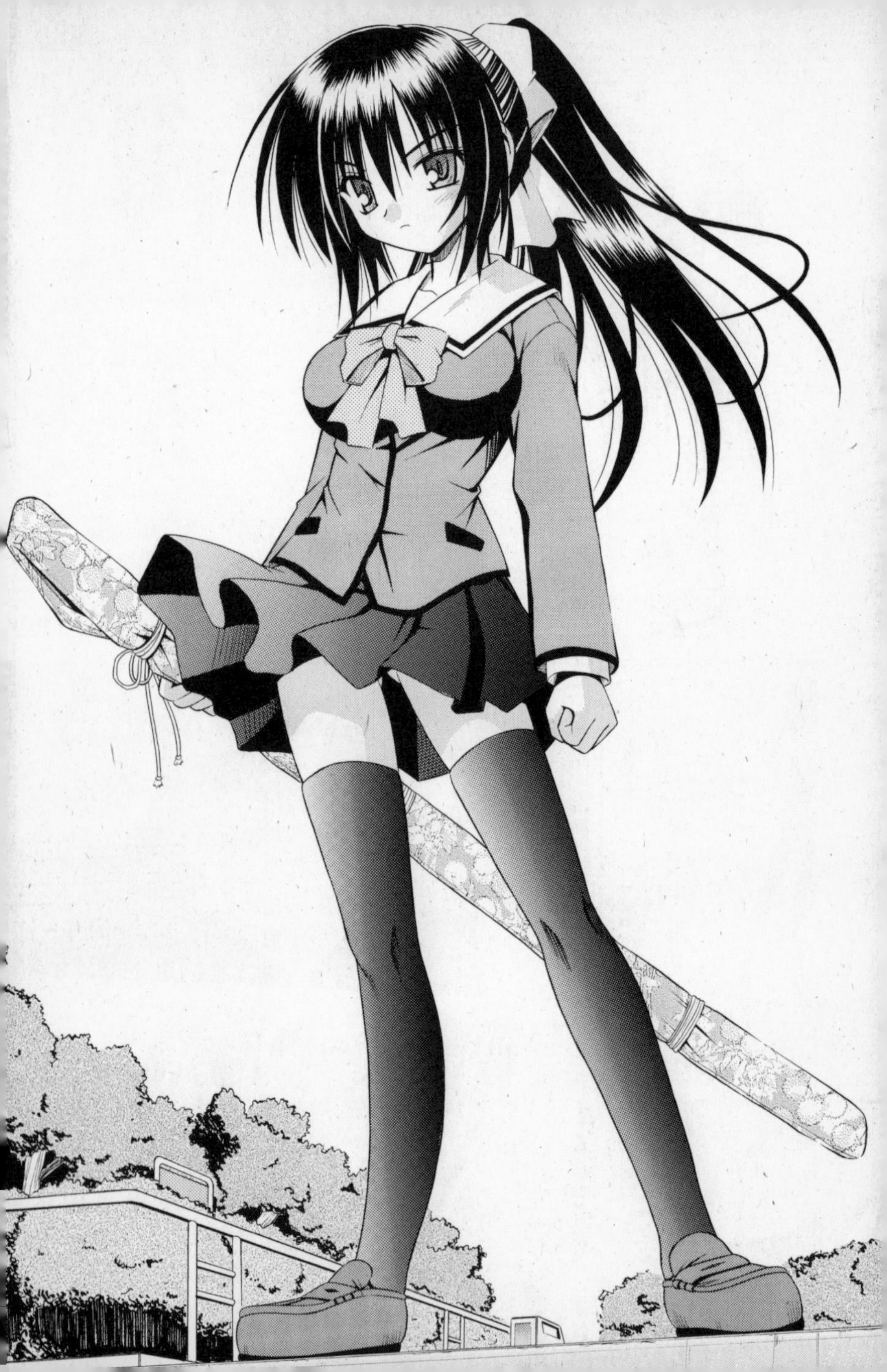

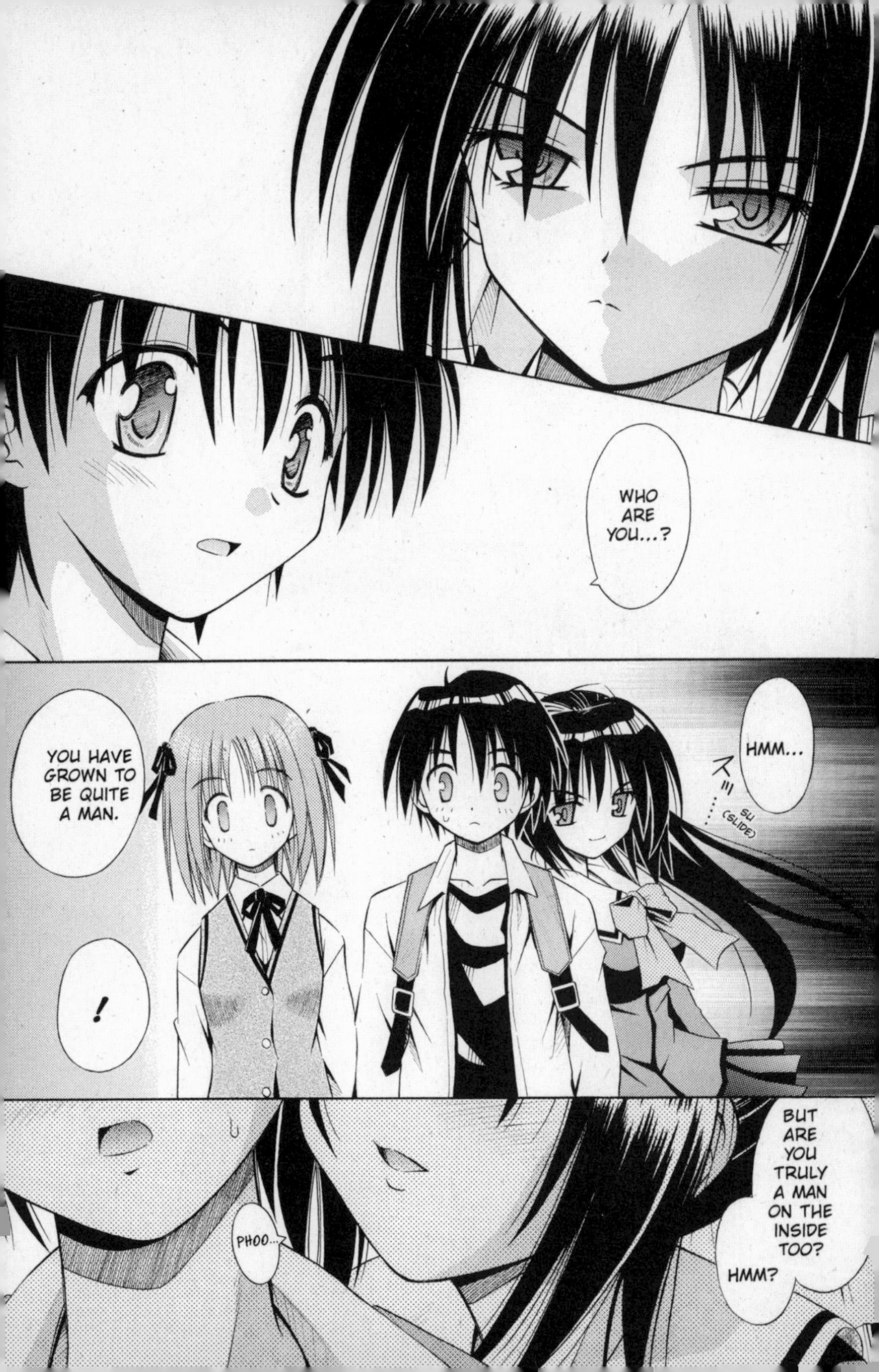
WHO ARE YOU...?
HMM...
スッ...
SU (SLIDE)
YOU HAVE GROWN TO BE QUITE A MAN.
!
BUT ARE YOU TRULY A MAN ON THE INSIDE TOO?
HMM?
PHOO...

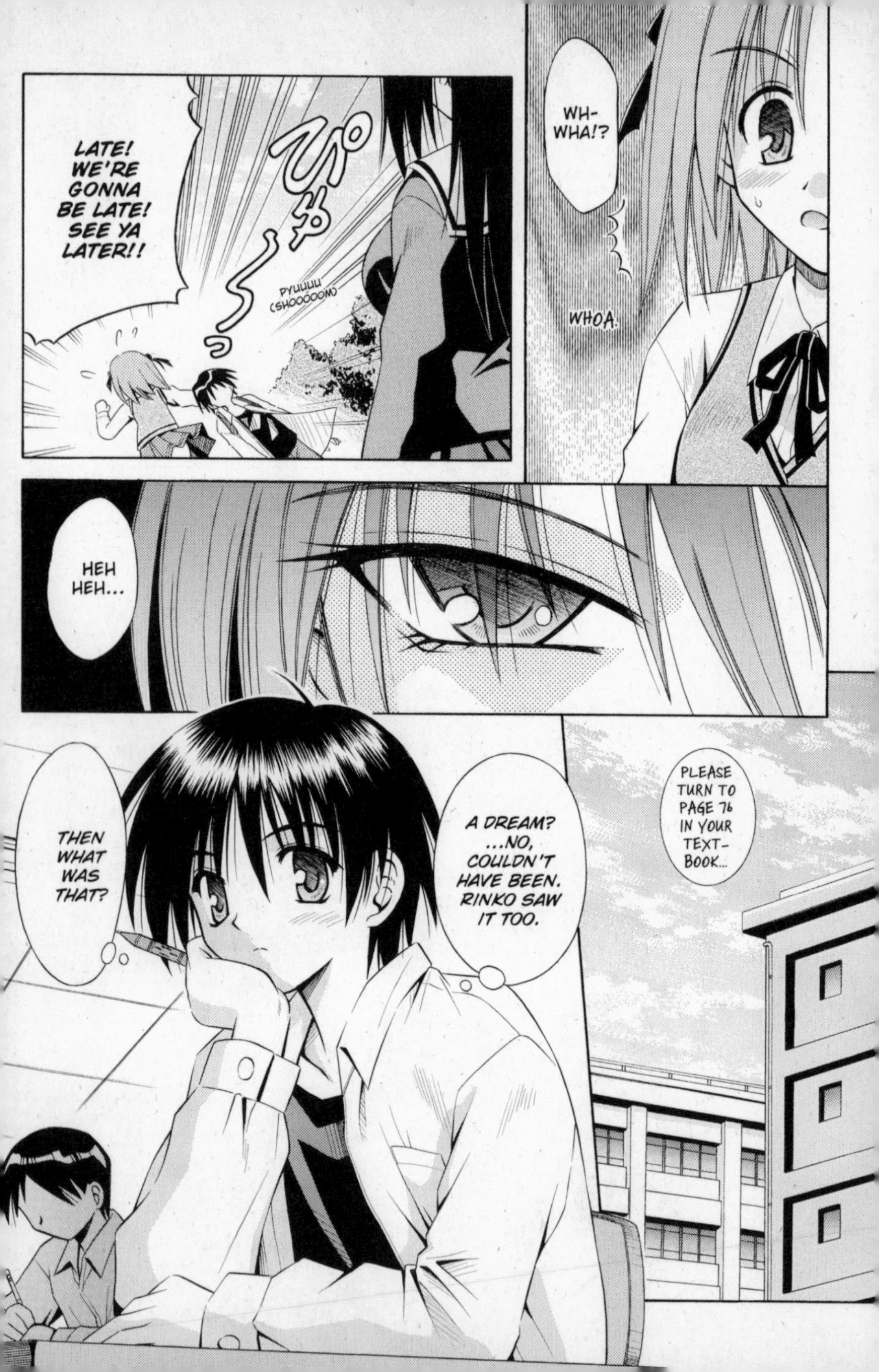
WH-WHA!?
WHOA.
LATE! WE'RE GONNA BE LATE! SEE YA LATER!!
PYUUUU (SHOOOOOM)
HEH HEH...
PLEASE TURN TO PAGE 76 IN YOUR TEXT-BOOK...
A DREAM? ...NO, COULDN'T HAVE BEEN. RINKO SAW IT TOO.
THEN WHAT WAS THAT?

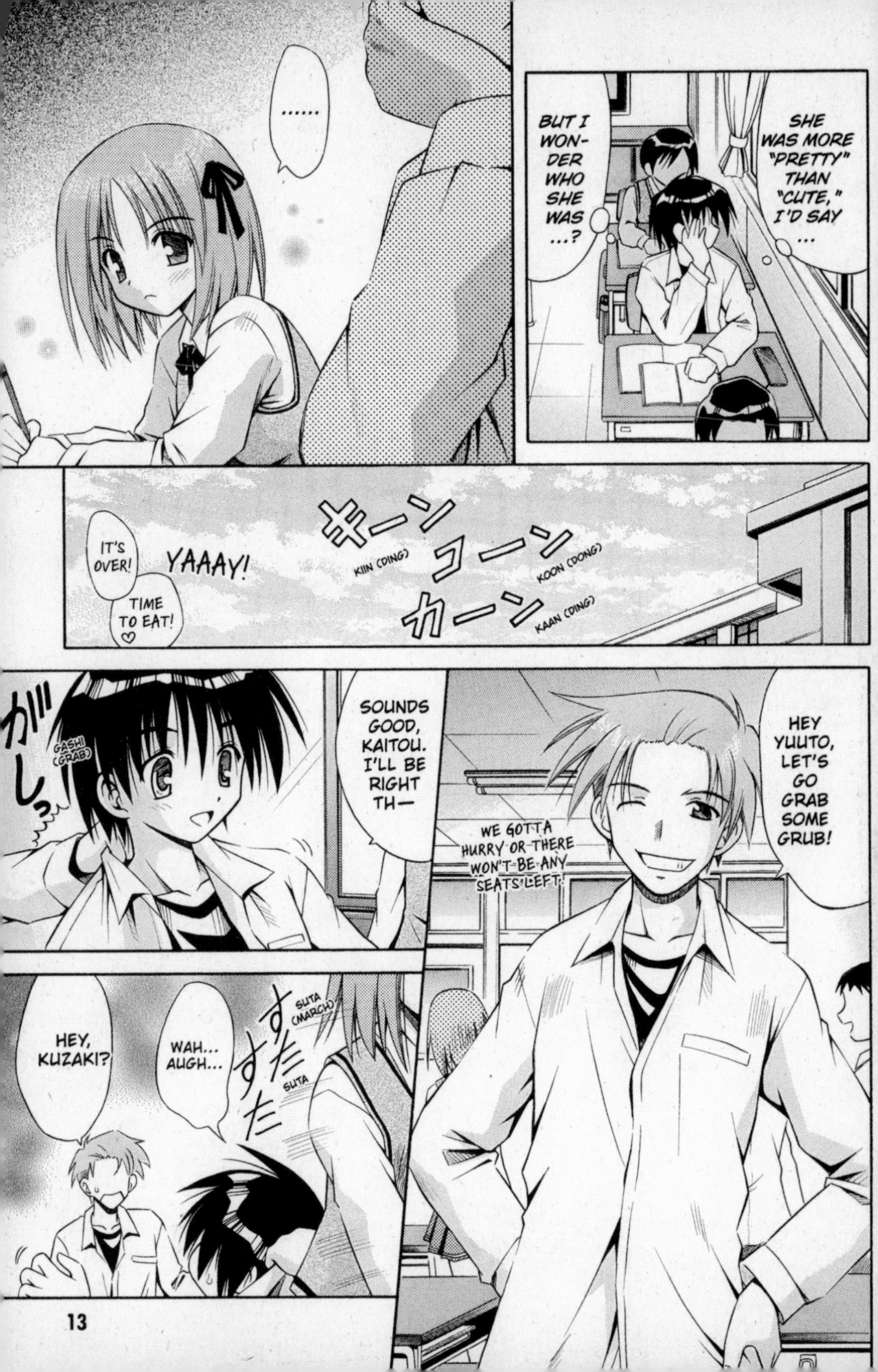
SHE WAS MORE "PRETTY" THAN "CUTE," I'D SAY ...
BUT I WONDER WHO SHE WAS ...?
......
キーン
KIIN (DING)
コーン
KOON (DONG)
カーン
KAAN (DING)
YAAAY!
IT'S OVER!
TIME TO EAT! ♡
HEY YUUTO, LET'S GO GRAB SOME GRUB!
WE GOTTA HURRY OR THERE WON'T BE ANY SEATS LEFT.
SOUNDS GOOD, KAITOU. I'LL BE RIGHT TH—
がしっ
GASHI (GRAB)
すた
SUTA (MARCH)
すた
SUTA
WAH... AUGH...
HEY, KUZAKI?

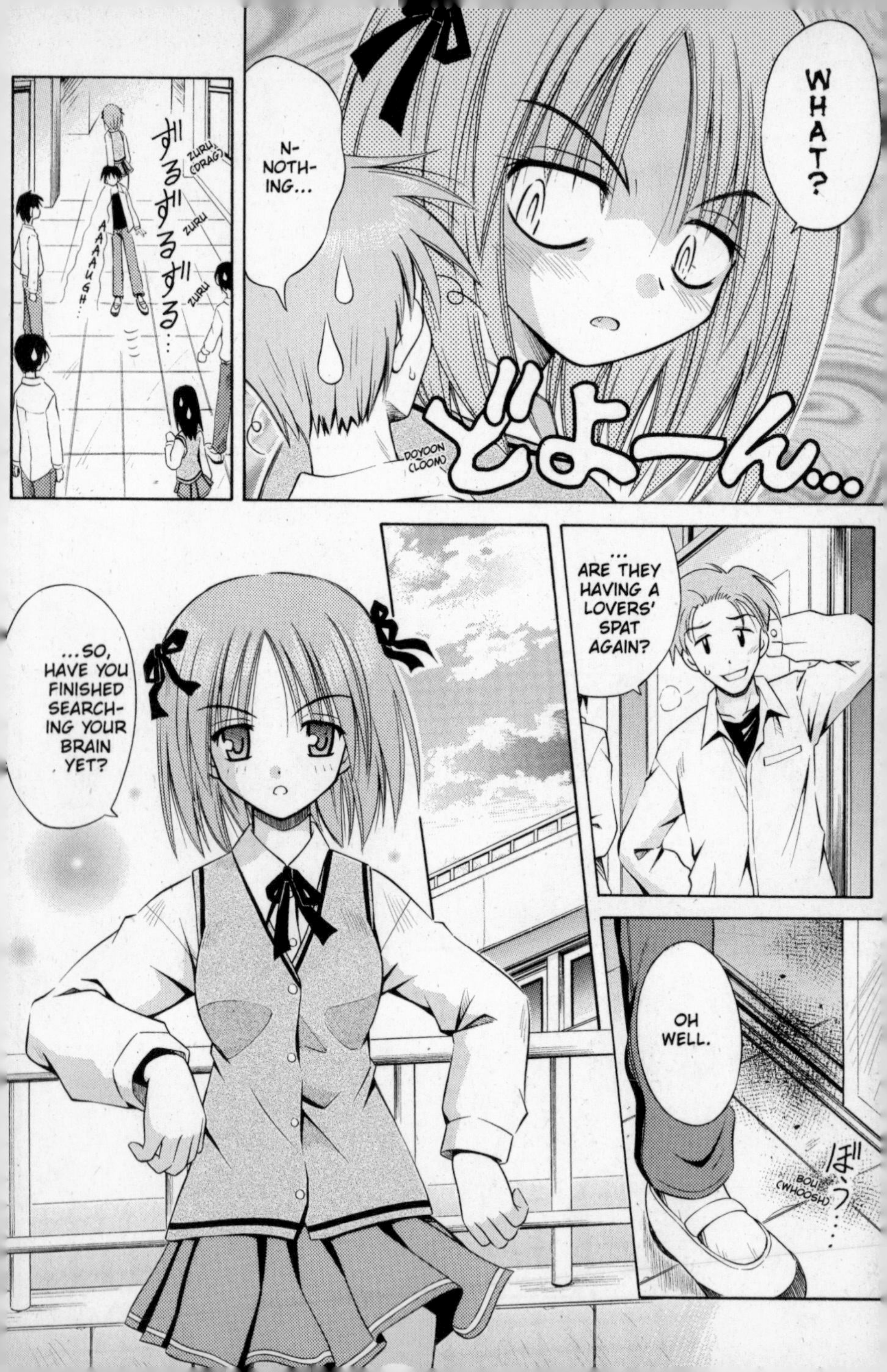
WHAT?
N-NOTHING...
どよーん...
DOYOON (LOOM)
ずるずるずるずる...
ZURU (DRAG)
ZURU
ZURU
AAAAUGH...
... ARE THEY HAVING A LOVERS' SPAT AGAIN?
OH WELL.
ぼっ...
BOU (WHOOSH)
...SO, HAVE YOU FINISHED SEARCHING YOUR BRAIN YET?

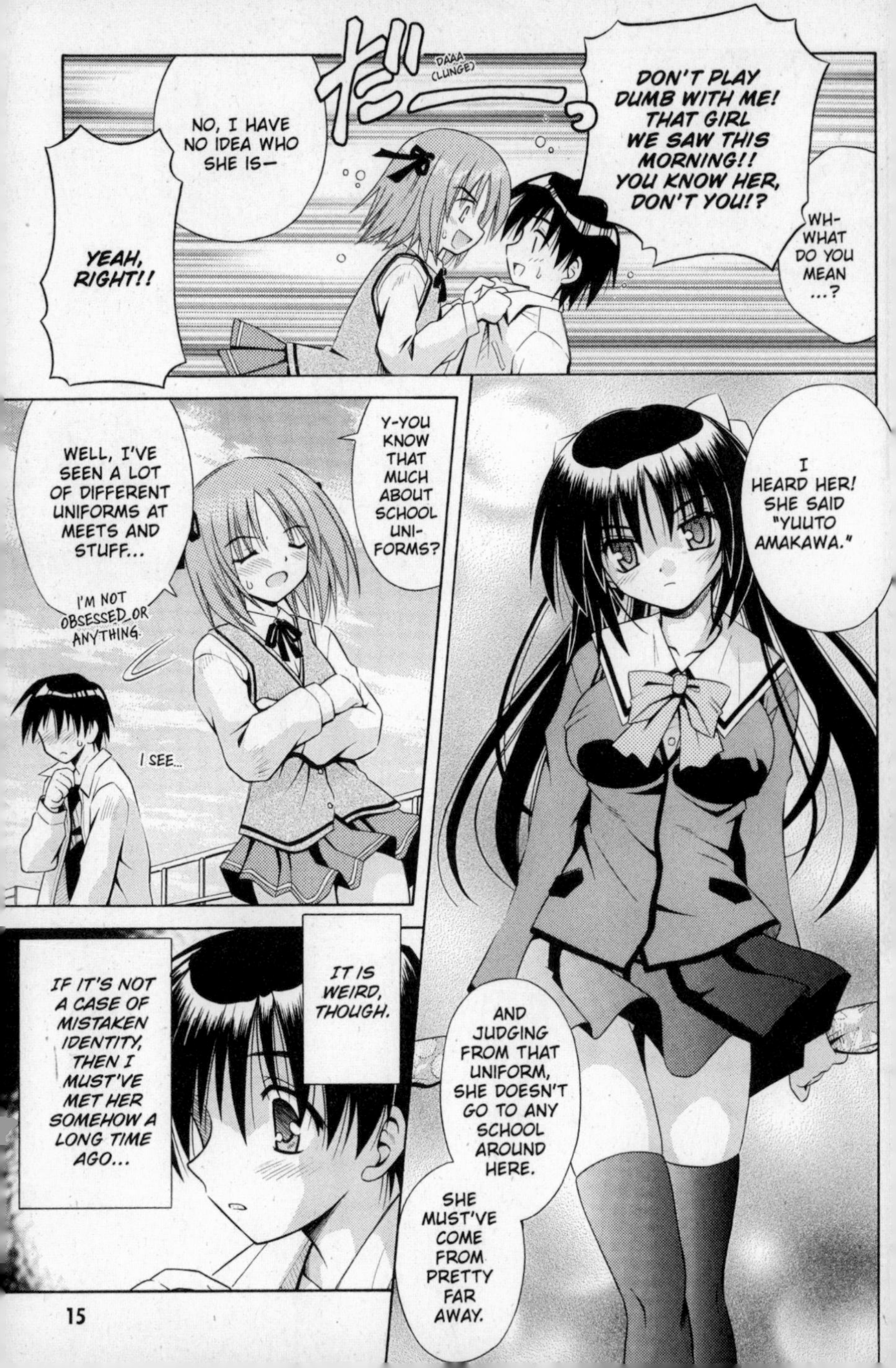

DON'T PLAY DUMB WITH ME! THAT GIRL WE SAW THIS MORNING!! YOU KNOW HER, DON'T YOU!?
WH-WHAT DO YOU MEAN ...?
DAAA (LUNGE)
NO, I HAVE NO IDEA WHO SHE IS—
YEAH, RIGHT!!
I HEARD HER! SHE SAID "YUUTO AMAKAWA."
AND JUDGING FROM THAT UNIFORM, SHE DOESN'T GO TO ANY SCHOOL AROUND HERE.
SHE MUST'VE COME FROM PRETTY FAR AWAY.
Y-YOU KNOW THAT MUCH ABOUT SCHOOL UNI-FORMS?
WELL, I'VE SEEN A LOT OF DIFFERENT UNIFORMS AT MEETS AND STUFF...
I'M NOT OBSESSED OR ANYTHING.
I SEE...
IT IS WEIRD, THOUGH.
IF IT'S NOT A CASE OF MISTAKEN IDENTITY, THEN I MUST'VE MET HER SOMEHOW A LONG TIME AGO...

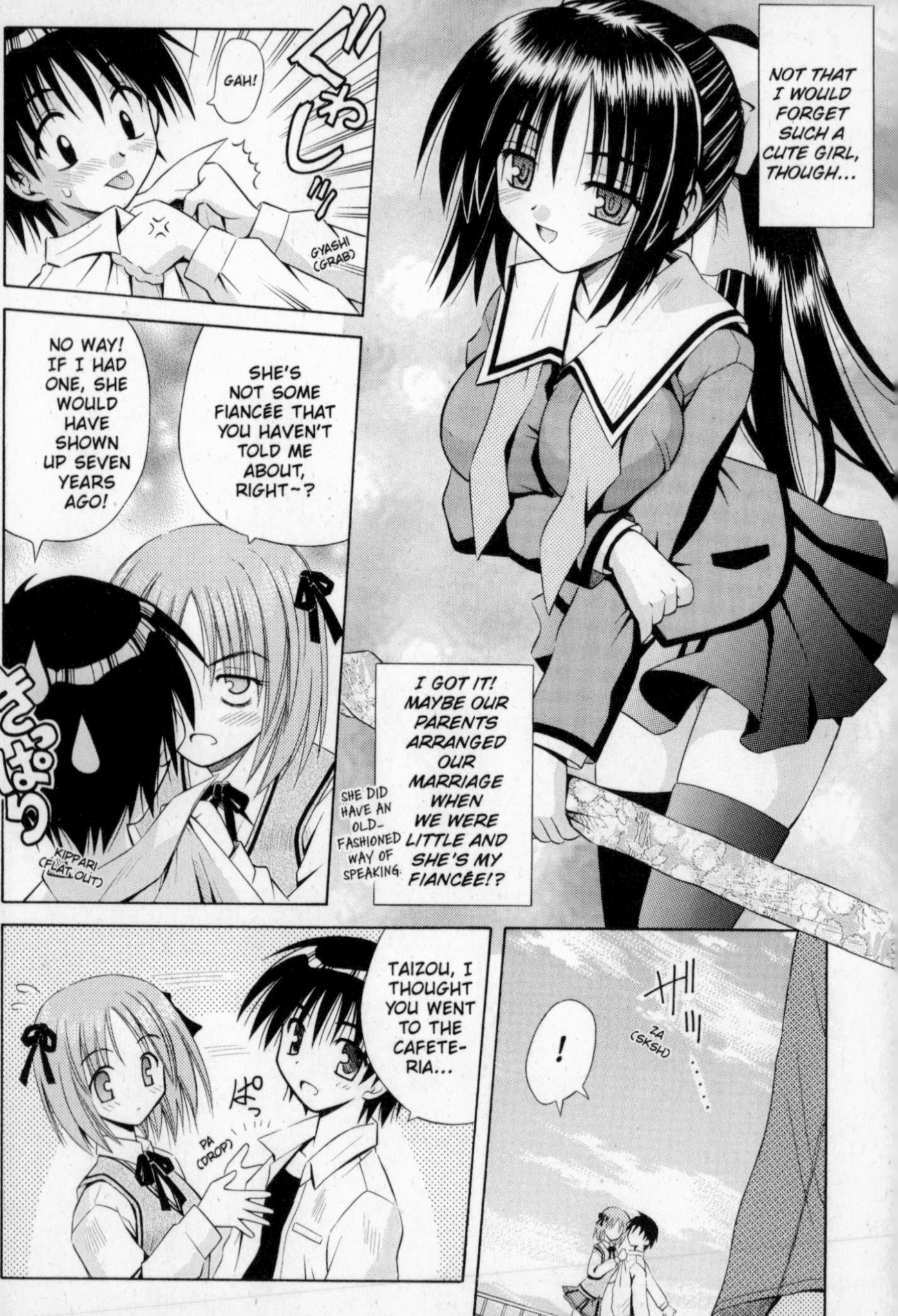
NOT THAT I WOULD FORGET SUCH A CUTE GIRL, THOUGH...
I GOT IT! MAYBE OUR PARENTS ARRANGED OUR MARRIAGE WHEN WE WERE LITTLE AND SHE'S MY FIANCÉE!?
SHE DID HAVE AN OLD-FASHIONED WAY OF SPEAKING.
GAH!
GYASHI (GRAB)
SHE'S NOT SOME FIANCÉE THAT YOU HAVEN'T TOLD ME ABOUT, RIGHT~?
NO WAY! IF I HAD ONE, SHE WOULD HAVE SHOWN UP SEVEN YEARS AGO!
KIPPARI (FLAT OUT)
!
ZA (SKSH)
TAIZOU, I THOUGHT YOU WENT TO THE CAFETE-RIA...
PA (DROP)

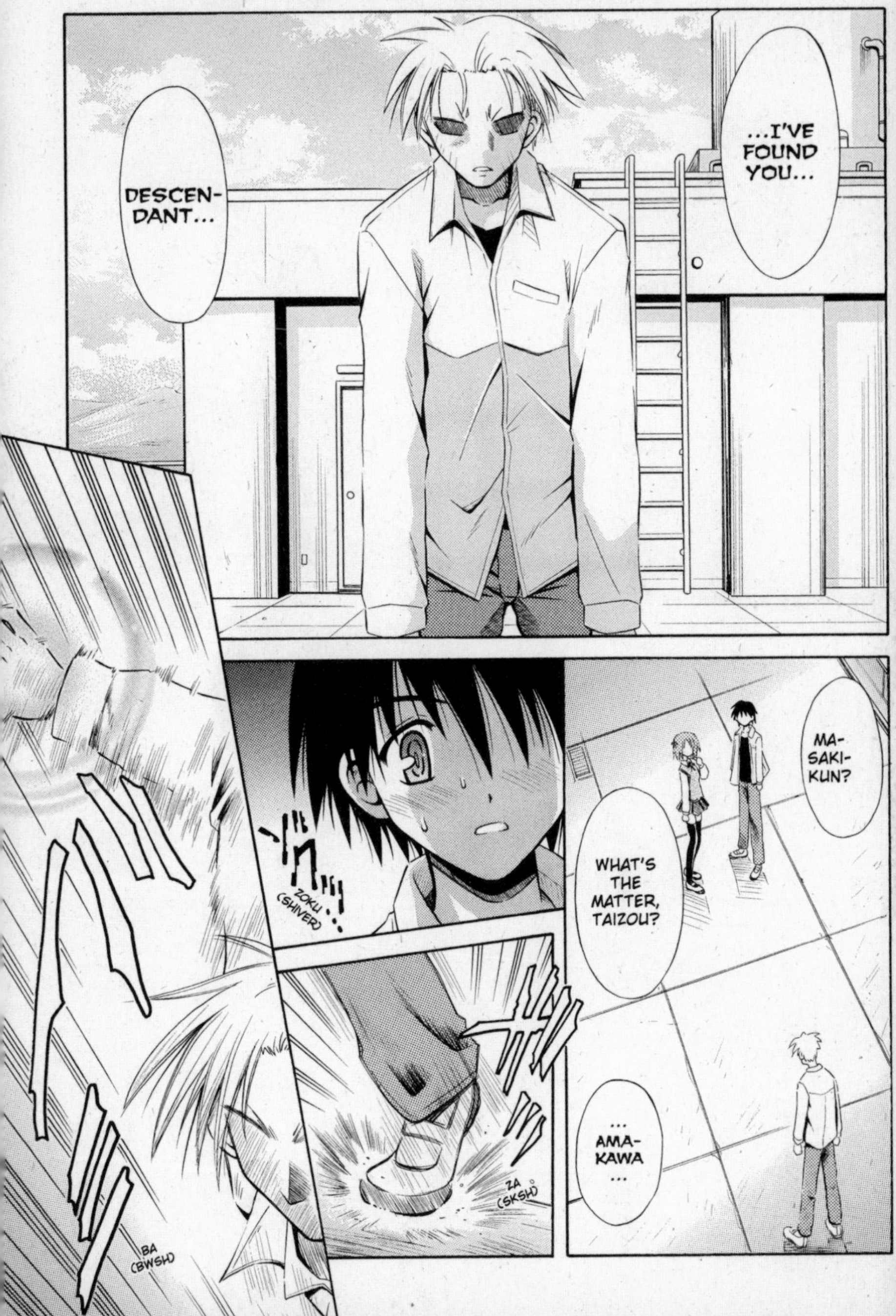
...I'VE FOUND YOU...
DESCEN-DANT...
MA-SAKI-KUN?
WHAT'S THE MATTER, TAIZOU?
... AMA-KAWA ...
ZOKU (SHIVER)
ZA (SKSH)
BA (BWSH)

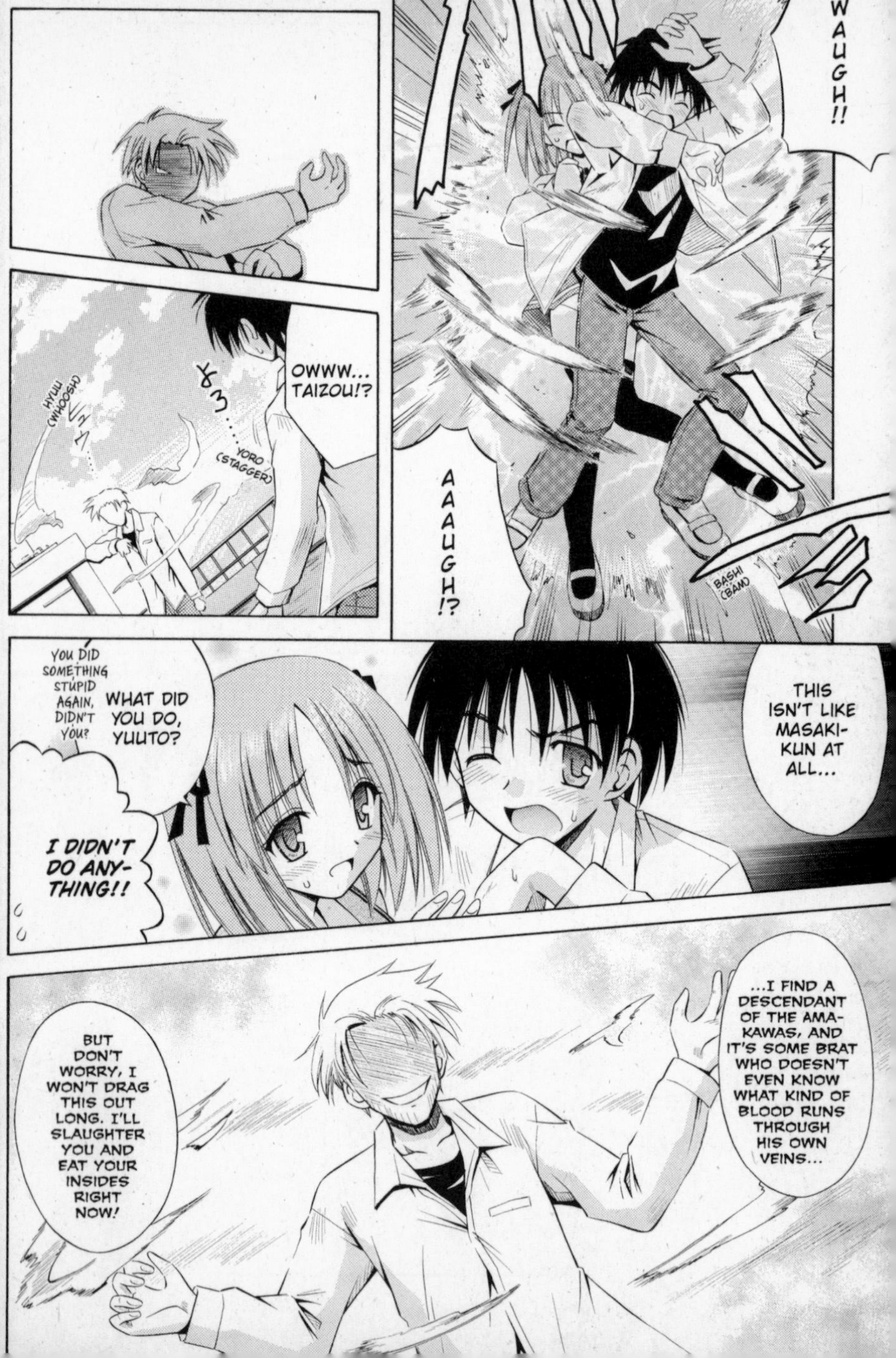
WAUGH!!
AAAUGH!?
BASHI (BAM)
OWWW... TAIZOU!?
YORO (STAGGER)
HYUU (WHOOSH)
THIS ISN'T LIKE MASAKI-KUN AT ALL...
WHAT DID YOU DO, YUUTO?
YOU DID SOMETHING STUPID AGAIN, DIDN'T YOU?
I DIDN'T DO ANYTHING!!
...I FIND A DESCENDANT OF THE AMAKAWAS, AND IT'S SOME BRAT WHO DOESN'T EVEN KNOW WHAT KIND OF BLOOD RUNS THROUGH HIS OWN VEINS...
BUT DON'T WORRY, I WON'T DRAG THIS OUT LONG. I'LL SLAUGHTER YOU AND EAT YOUR INSIDES RIGHT NOW!

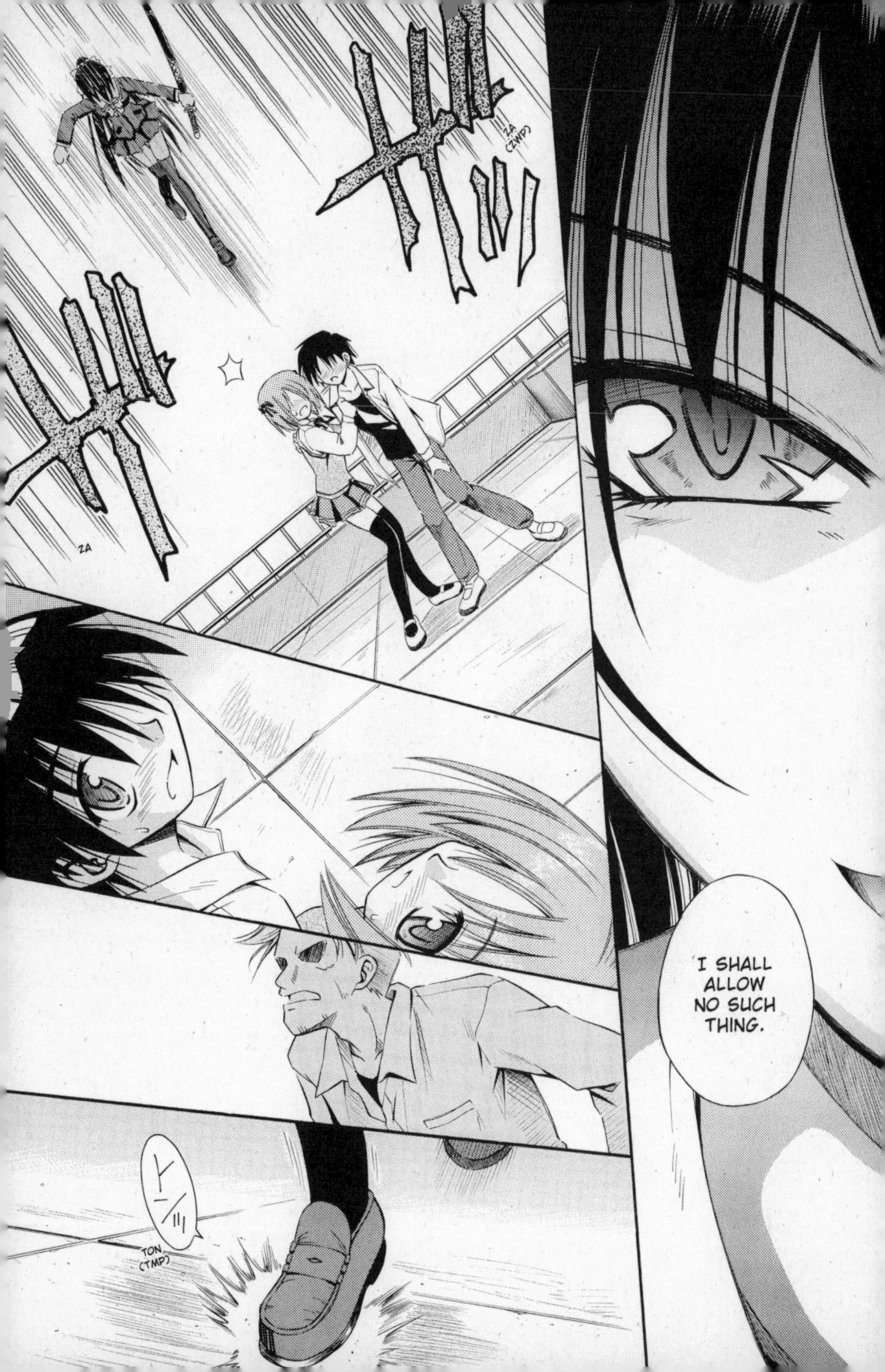
I SHALL ALLOW NO SUCH THING.
ZA (ZWIP)
ZA
TON (TMP)

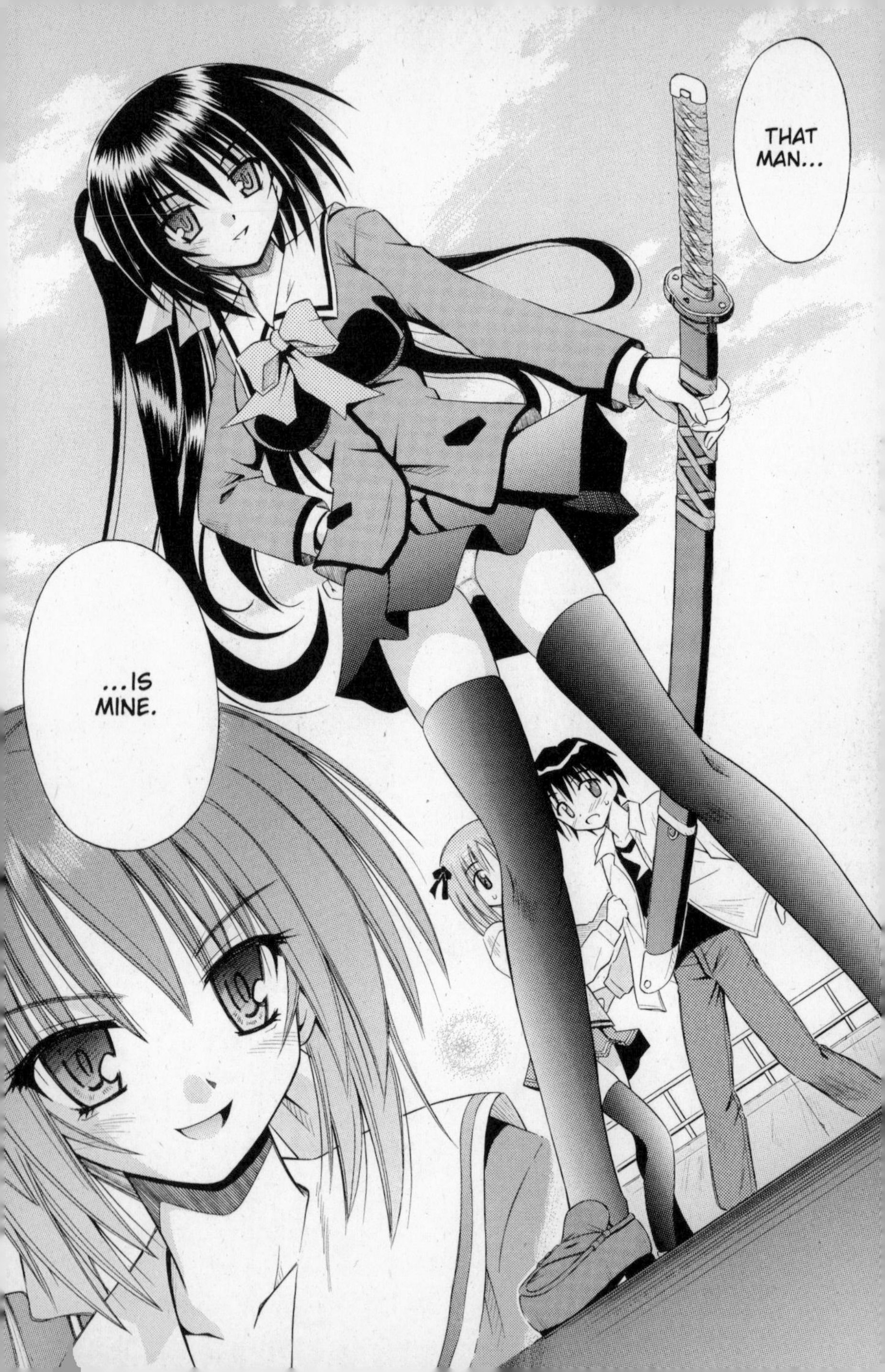
THAT MAN...
...IS MINE.

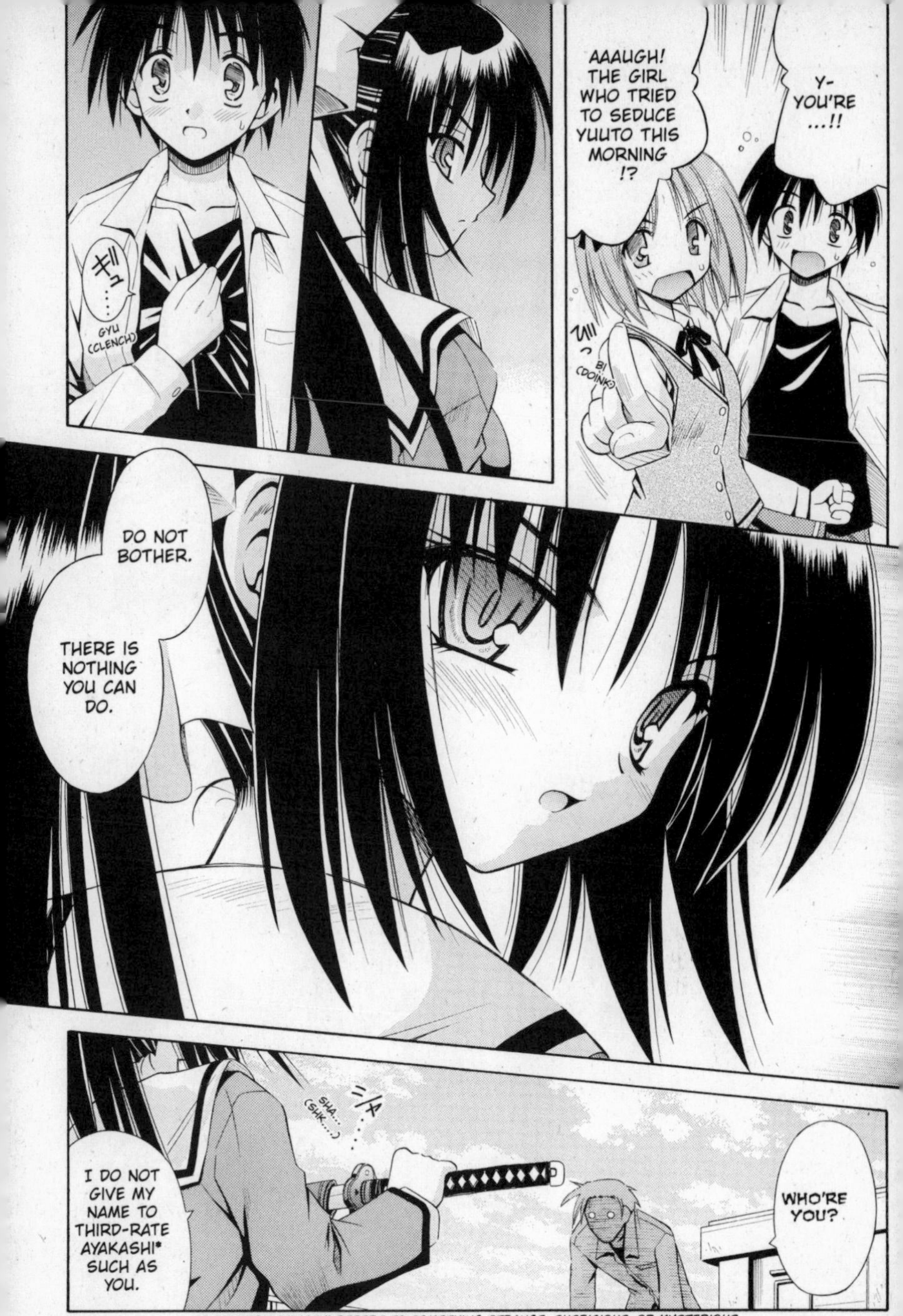
Y-YOU'RE ...!!
AAAUGH! THE GIRL WHO TRIED TO SEDUCE YUUTO THIS MORNING !?
BI (DOINK)
GYU (CLENCH)
DO NOT BOTHER.
THERE IS NOTHING YOU CAN DO.
WHO'RE YOU?
SHA... (SHK...)
I DO NOT GIVE MY NAME TO THIRD-RATE AYAKASHI* SUCH AS YOU.

*THE TERM AYAKASHI REFERS TO SOMETHING STRANGE, SUSPICIOUS, OR MYSTERIOUS, SUCH AS A SPIRIT, GHOST, SPECTER, DEMON, OR SUPERNATURAL CREATURE.

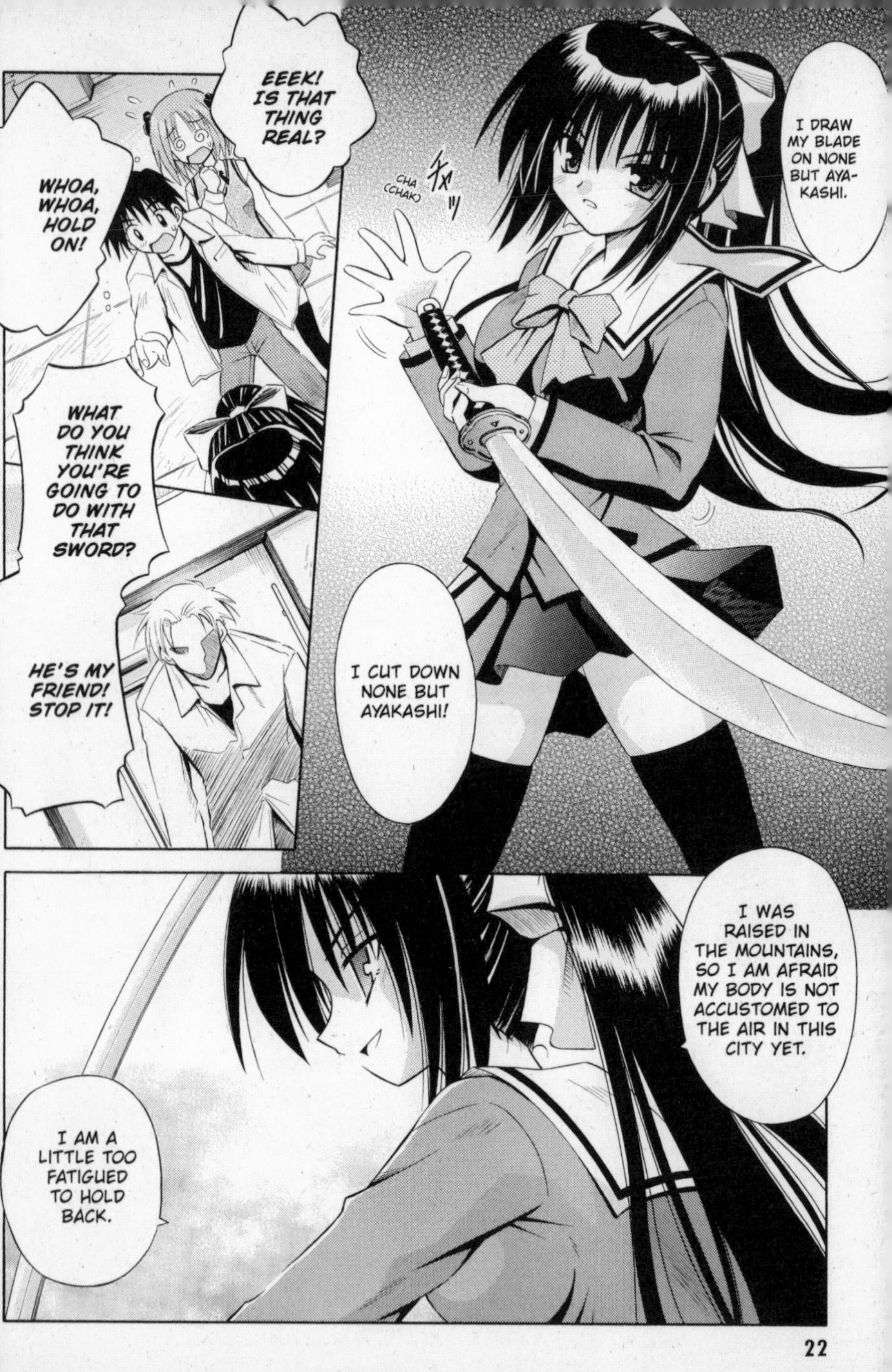
I DRAW MY BLADE ON NONE BUT AYA-KASHI.
CHA (CHAK)
I CUT DOWN NONE BUT AYAKASHI!
EEEK! IS THAT THING REAL?
WHOA, WHOA, HOLD ON!
WHAT DO YOU THINK YOU'RE GOING TO DO WITH THAT SWORD?
HE'S MY FRIEND! STOP IT!
I WAS RAISED IN THE MOUNTAINS, SO I AM AFRAID MY BODY IS NOT ACCUSTOMED TO THE AIR IN THIS CITY YET.
I AM A LITTLE TOO FATIGUED TO HOLD BACK.

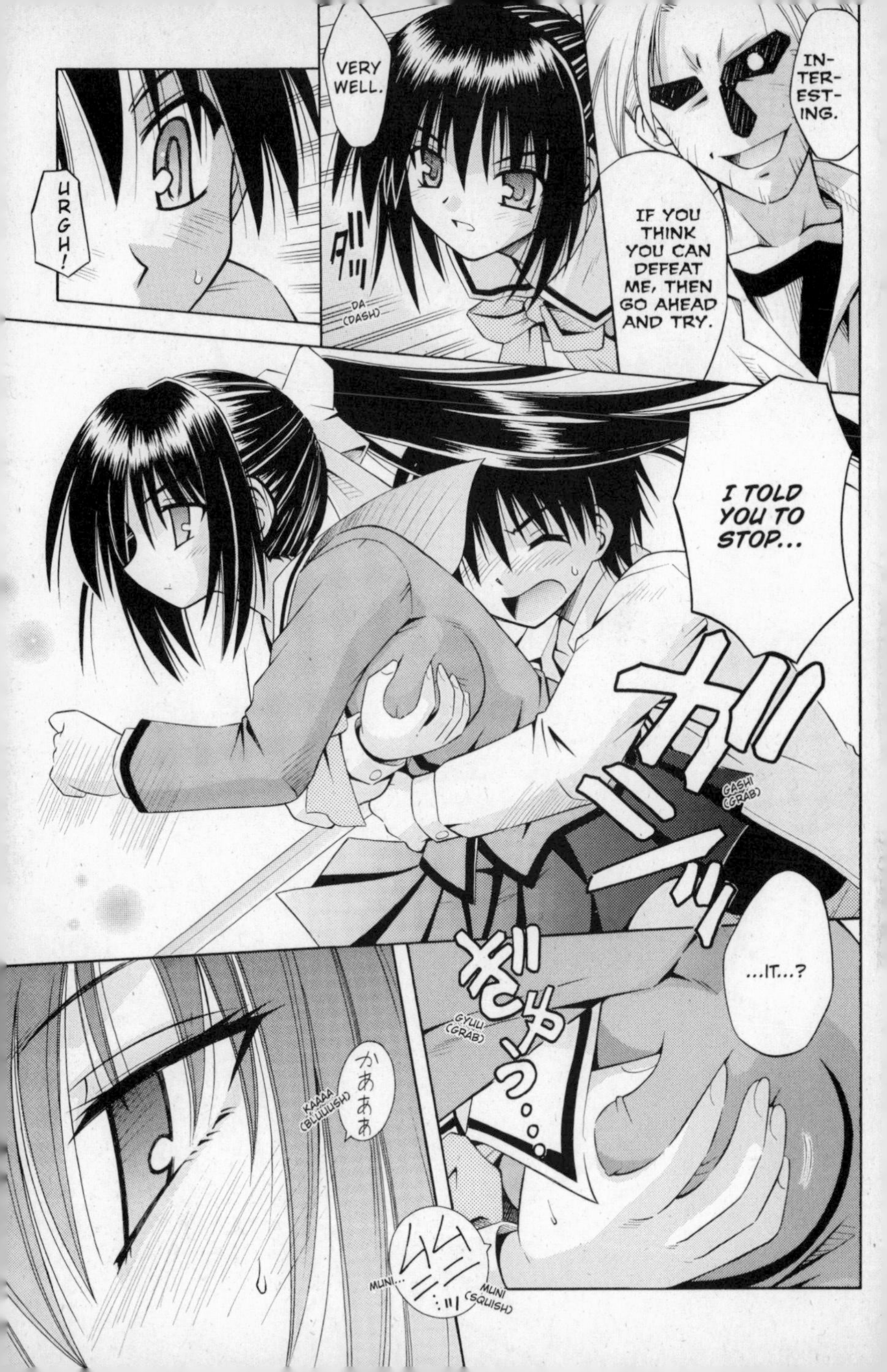
INTER-EST-ING.
IF YOU THINK YOU CAN DEFEAT ME, THEN GO AHEAD AND TRY.
VERY WELL.
ダッ
DA (DASH)
URGH!
I TOLD YOU TO STOP...
GASHI (GRAB)
...IT...?
GYUU (GRAB)
かあああ
KAAAA (BLUUUSH)
MUNI...
MUNI (SQUISH)

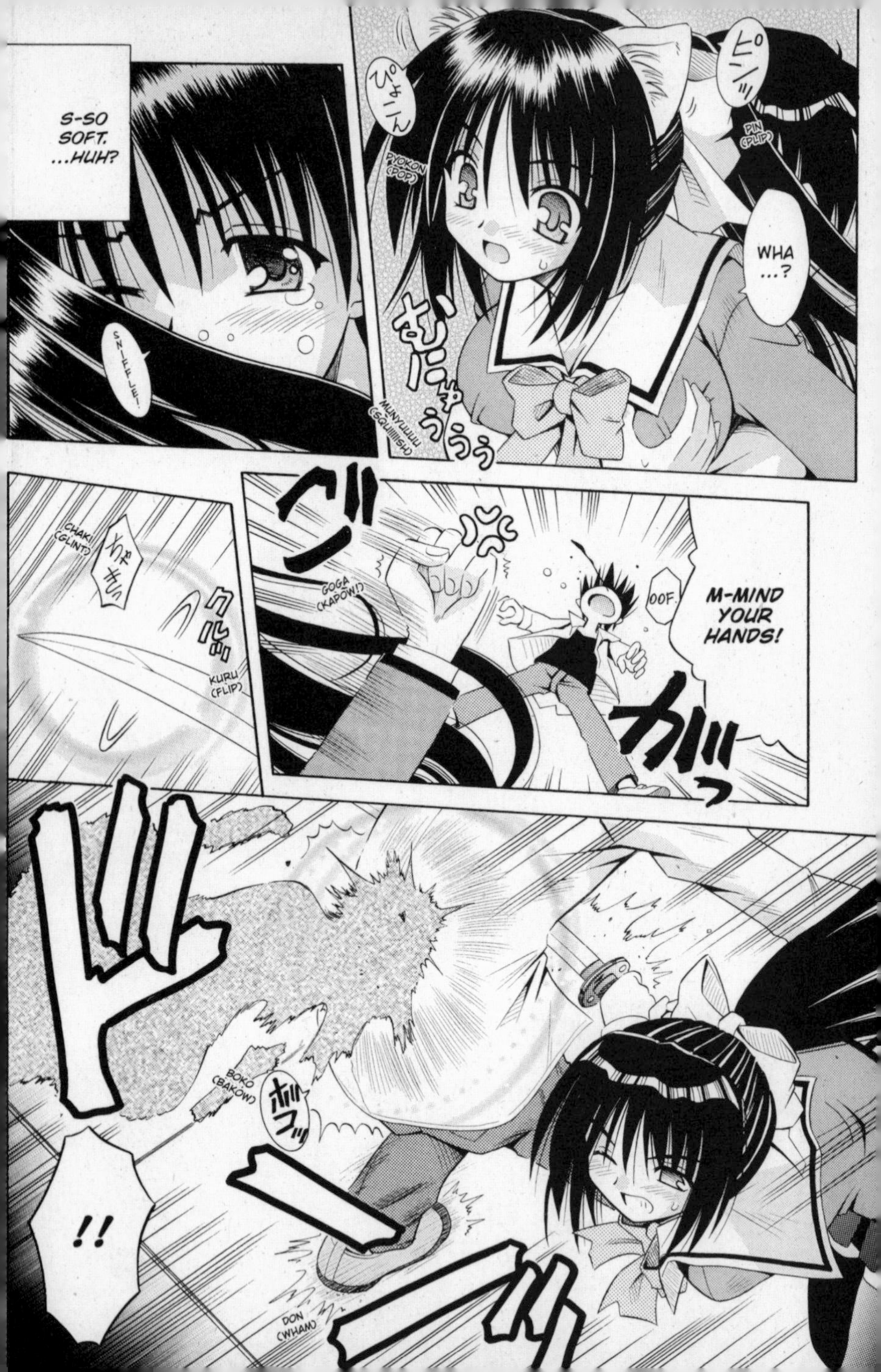
PIN (PLIP)
PYOKON (POP)
WHA...?
MUNYUUUU (SQUIIIISH)
S-SO SOFT. ...HUH?
SNIFFLE!
M-MIND YOUR HANDS!
OOF.
GOGA (KAPOW!)
CHAKI (GLINT)
KURU (FLIP)
BOKO (BAKOW)
!!
DON (WHAM)

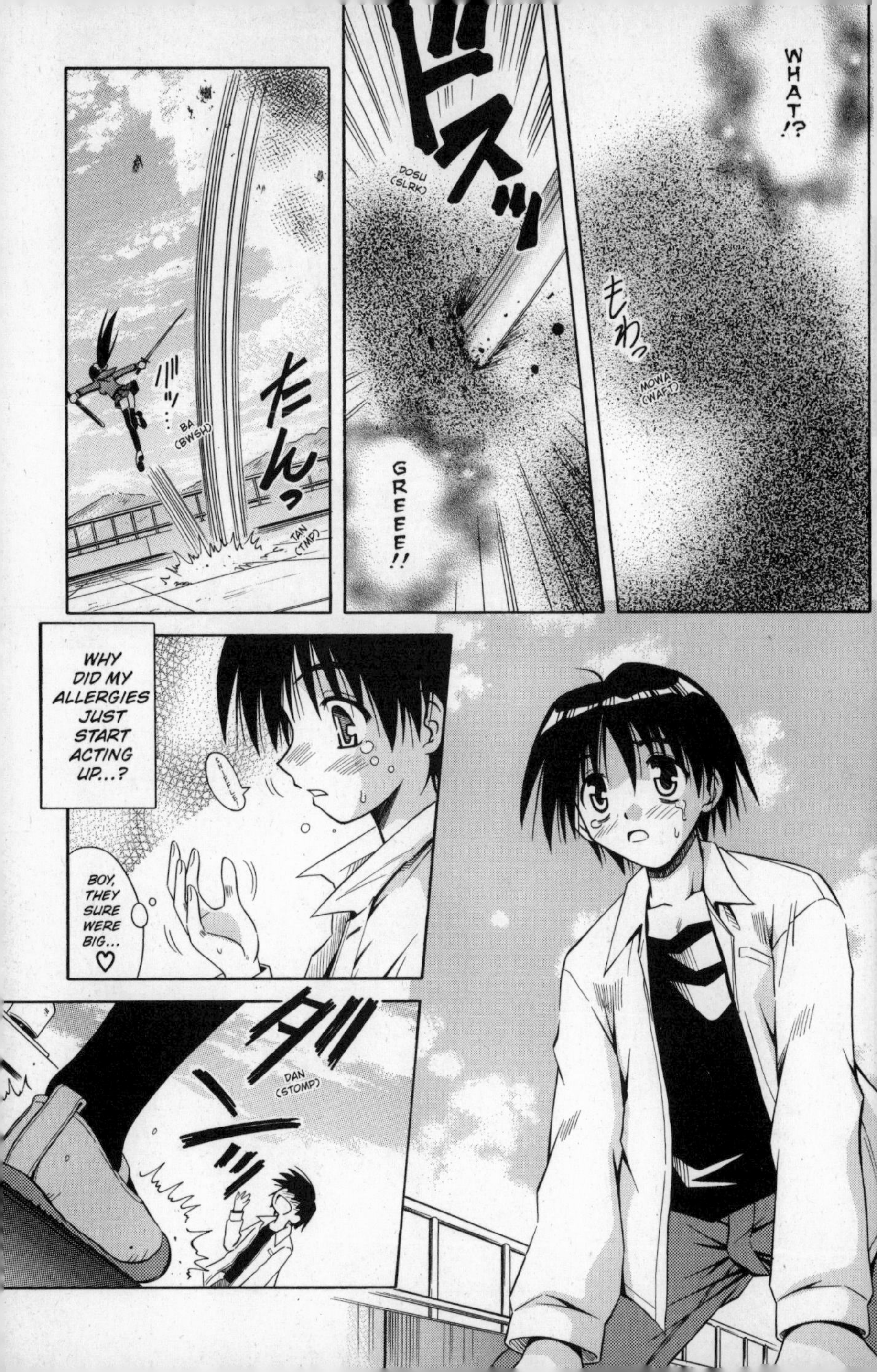
WHAT!?
もわっ
MOWA (WAFT)
ドスッ
DOSU (SLRK)
GREEE!!
バッ
BA (BWSH)
たんっ
TAN (TMP)
WHY DID MY ALLERGIES JUST START ACTING UP...?
SNIFFLE!
BOY, THEY SURE WERE BIG... ♡
ダン
DAN (STOMP)

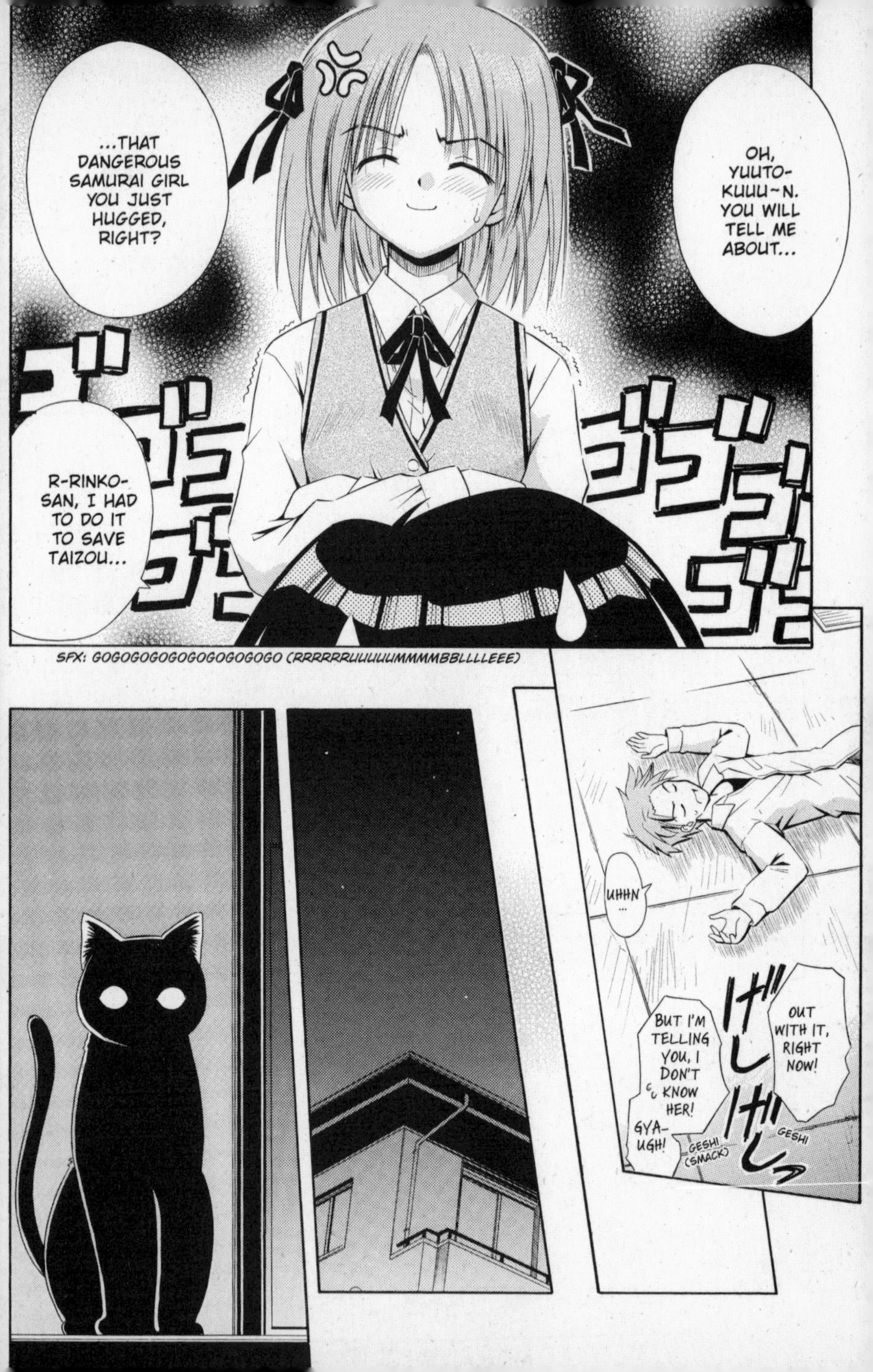
OH, YUUTO-KUUU~N. YOU WILL TELL ME ABOUT...
...THAT DANGEROUS SAMURAI GIRL YOU JUST HUGGED, RIGHT?
R-RINKO-SAN, I HAD TO DO IT TO SAVE TAIZOU...
SFX: GOGOGOGOGOGOGOGOGOGO (RRRRRRUUUUUMMMMBBLLLLEEE)
UHHN ...
OUT WITH IT, RIGHT NOW!
BUT I'M TELLING YOU, I DON'T KNOW HER!
GYA-UGH!
GESHI (SMACK)
GESHI

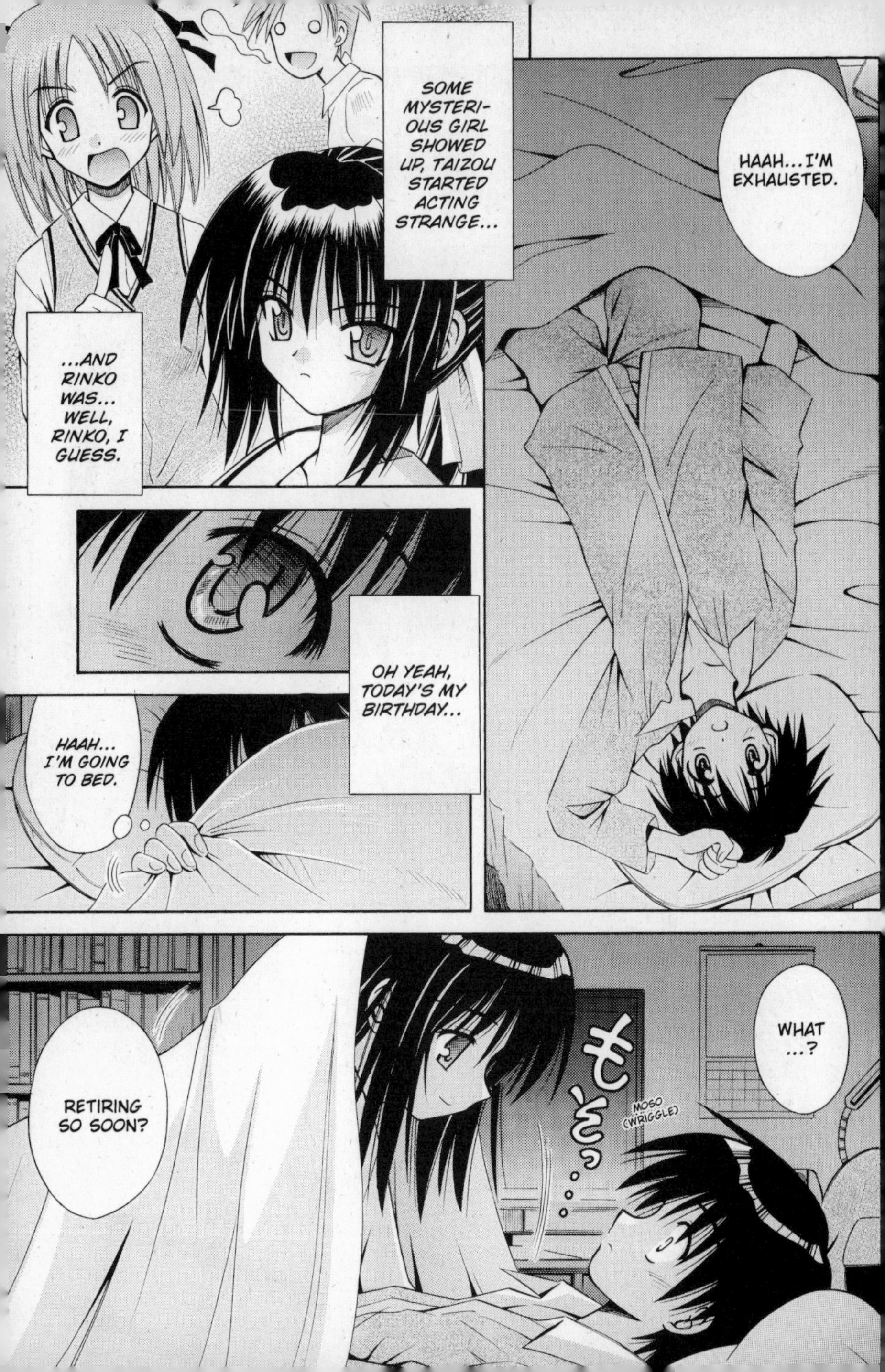
HAAH...I'M EXHAUSTED.
SOME MYSTERIOUS GIRL SHOWED UP, TAIZOU STARTED ACTING STRANGE...
...AND RINKO WAS... WELL, RINKO, I GUESS.
OH YEAH, TODAY'S MY BIRTHDAY...
HAAH... I'M GOING TO BED.
WHAT ...?
もそっ
MOSO (WRIGGLE)
RETIRING SO SOON?

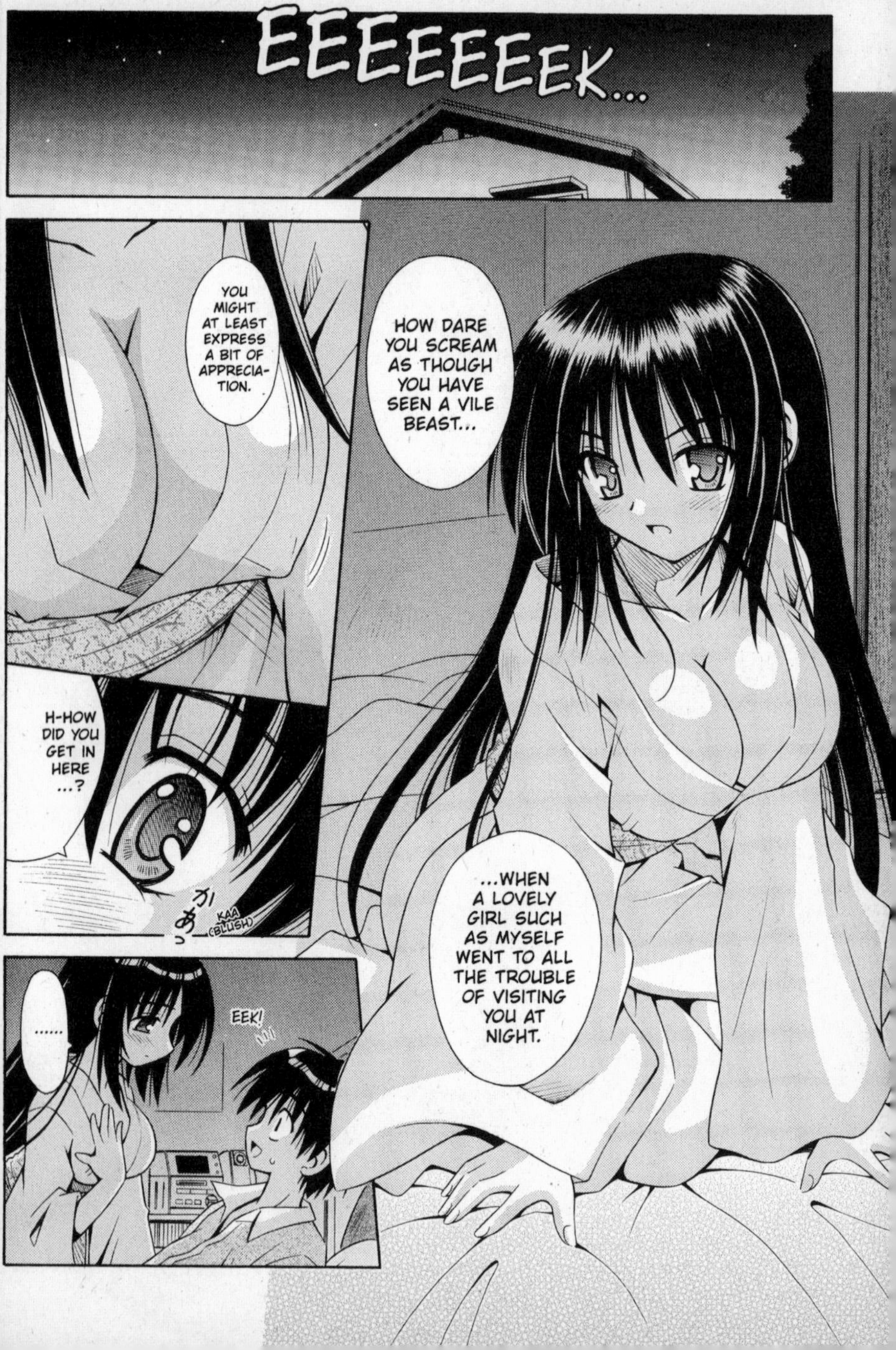
EEEEEEEK...
HOW DARE YOU SCREAM AS THOUGH YOU HAVE SEEN A VILE BEAST...
...WHEN A LOVELY GIRL SUCH AS MYSELF WENT TO ALL THE TROUBLE OF VISITING YOU AT NIGHT.
YOU MIGHT AT LEAST EXPRESS A BIT OF APPRECIA-TION.
H-HOW DID YOU GET IN HERE ...?
かあっ
KAA (BLUSH)
EEK!
......

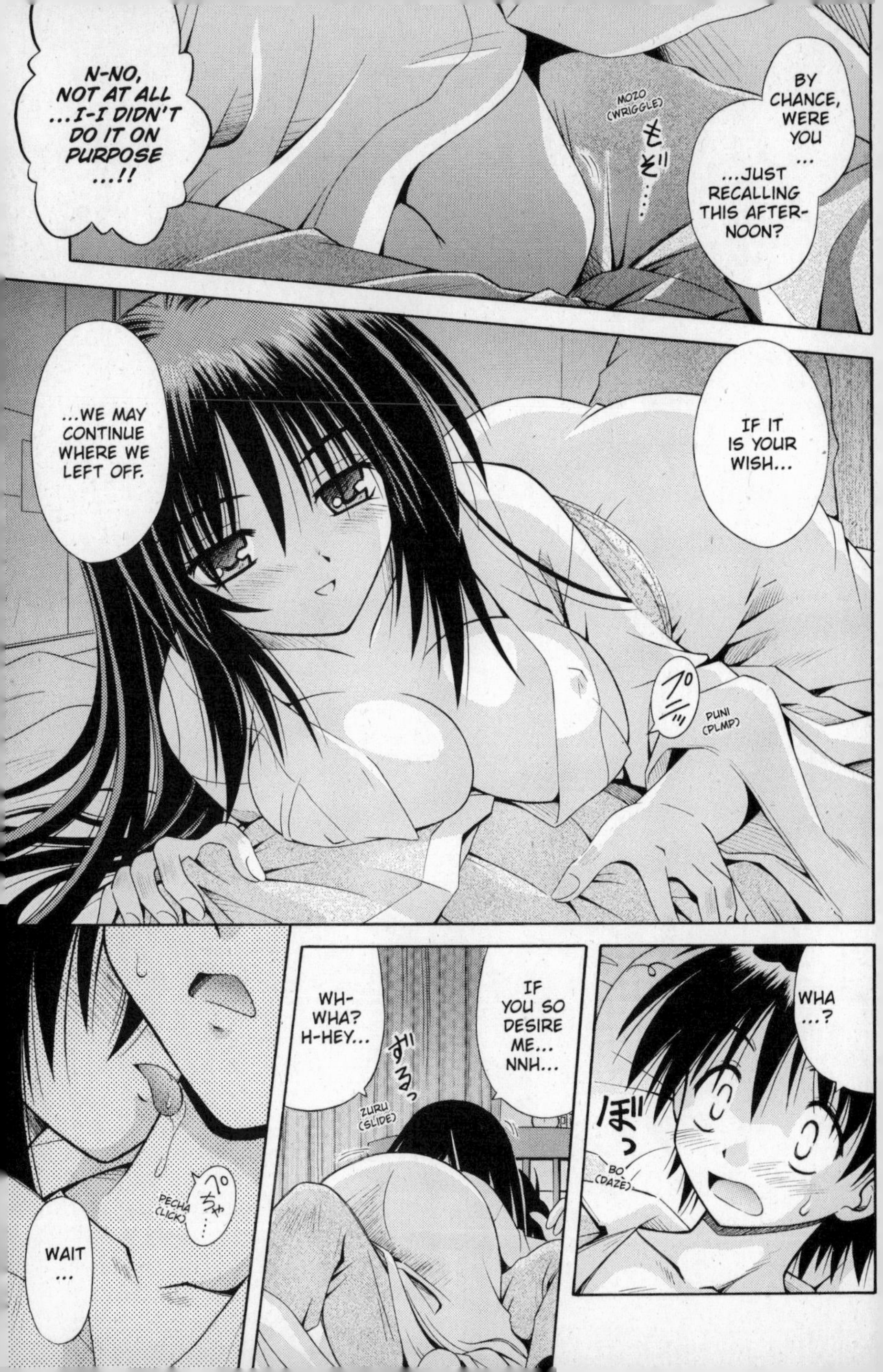
BY CHANCE, WERE YOU ... ...JUST RECALLING THIS AFTERNOON?
もぞ…
MOZO (WRIGGLE)
N-NO, NOT AT ALL ...I-I DIDN'T DO IT ON PURPOSE ...!!
IF IT IS YOUR WISH...
...WE MAY CONTINUE WHERE WE LEFT OFF.
PUNI (PLMP)
WHA ...?
ぼっ
BO (DAZE)
IF YOU SO DESIRE ME... NNH...
WH- WHA? H-HEY...
ずるっ
ZURU (SLIDE)
ぺちゃ…
PECHA (LICK)
WAIT ...

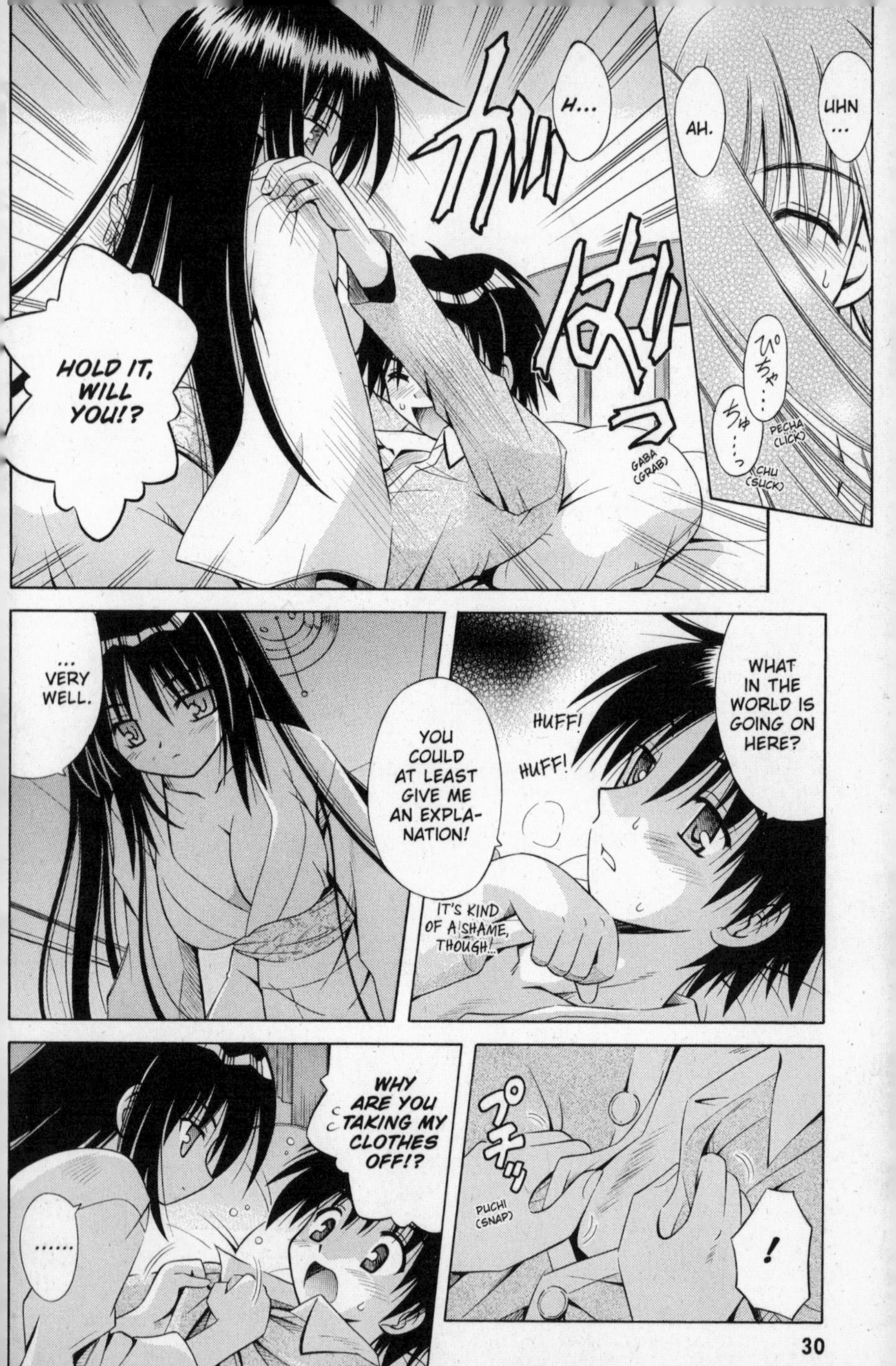
UHN ...
AH.
ぴちゃ...
ちゅ...っ
PECHA (LICK)
CHU (SUCK)
H...
GABA (GRAB)
HOLD IT, WILL YOU!?
WHAT IN THE WORLD IS GOING ON HERE?
HUFF!
HUFF!
YOU COULD AT LEAST GIVE ME AN EXPLANATION!
IT'S KIND OF A SHAME, THOUGH...
... VERY WELL.
PUCHI (SNAP)
!
WHY ARE YOU TAKING MY CLOTHES OFF!?
......

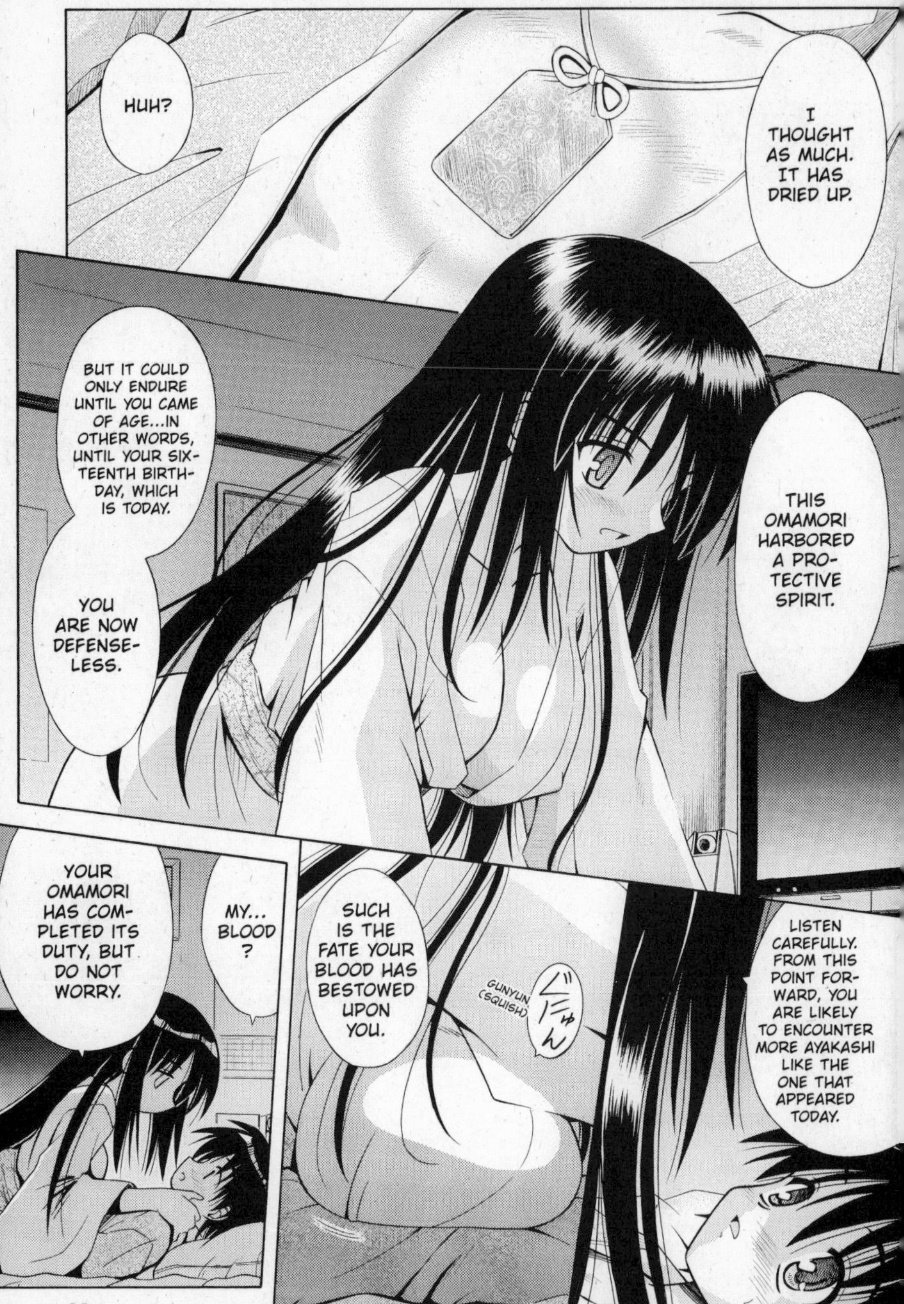
I THOUGHT AS MUCH. IT HAS DRIED UP.
HUH?
THIS OMAMORI HARBORED A PROTECTIVE SPIRIT.
BUT IT COULD ONLY ENDURE UNTIL YOU CAME OF AGE...IN OTHER WORDS, UNTIL YOUR SIXTEENTH BIRTHDAY, WHICH IS TODAY.
YOU ARE NOW DEFENSELESS.
LISTEN CAREFULLY. FROM THIS POINT FORWARD, YOU ARE LIKELY TO ENCOUNTER MORE AYAKASHI LIKE THE ONE THAT APPEARED TODAY.
ぐにゅん
GUNYUN (SQUISH)
SUCH IS THE FATE YOUR BLOOD HAS BESTOWED UPON YOU.
MY... BLOOD?
YOUR OMAMORI HAS COMPLETED ITS DUTY, BUT DO NOT WORRY.

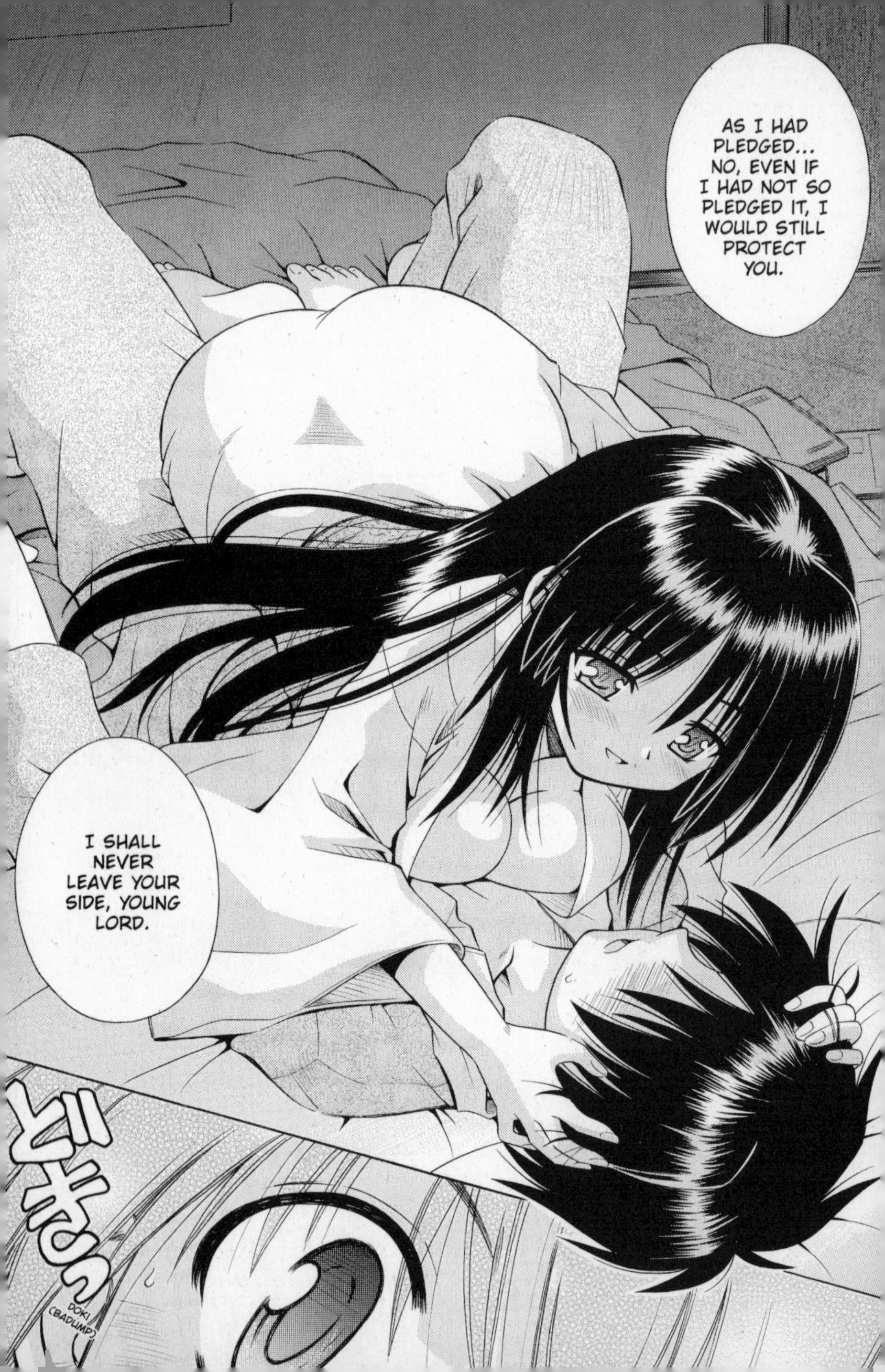
AS I HAD PLEDGED... NO, EVEN IF I HAD NOT SO PLEDGED IT, I WOULD STILL PROTECT YOU.
I SHALL NEVER LEAVE YOUR SIDE, YOUNG LORD.
どきっ
DOKI (BADUMP)

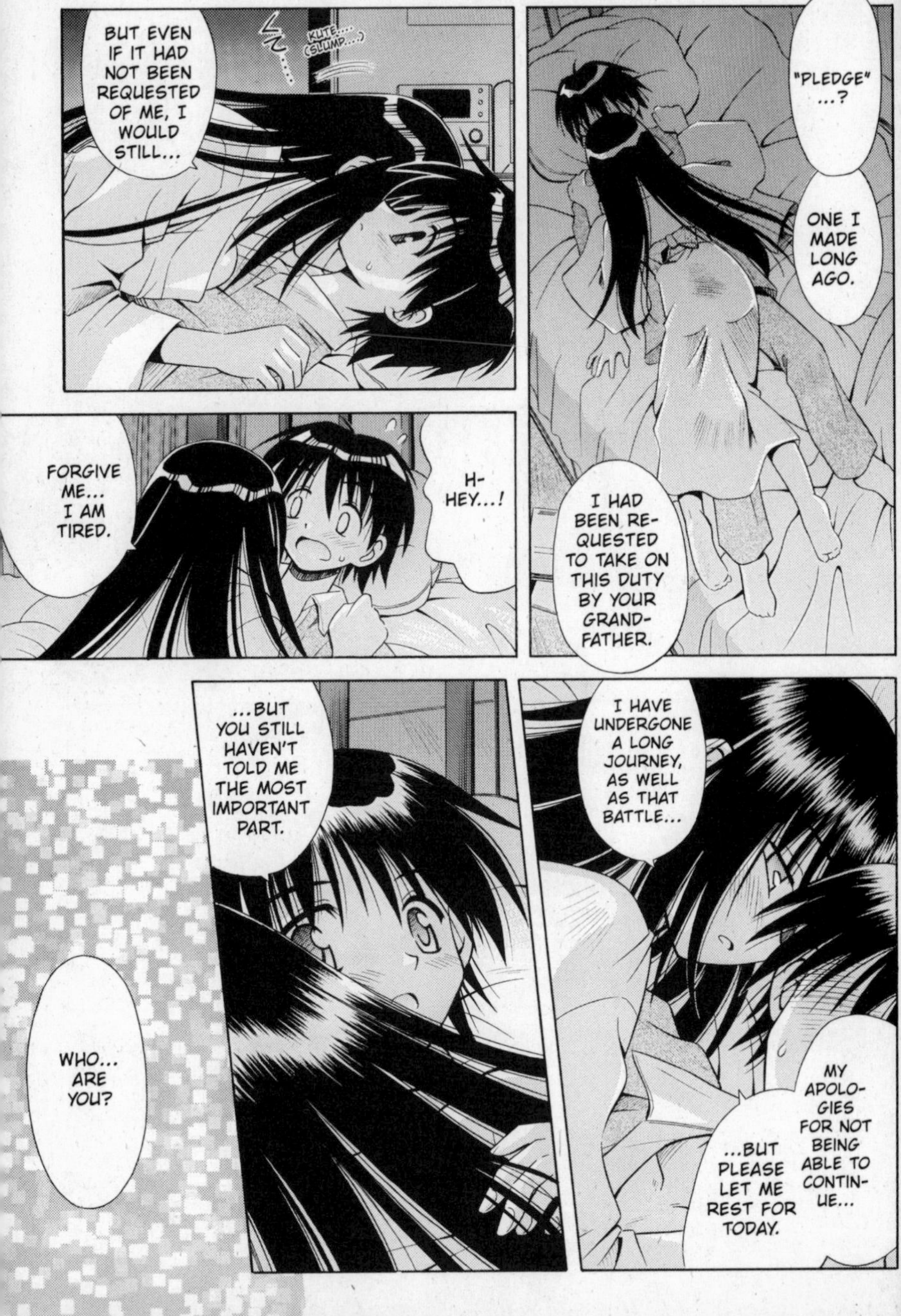
"PLEDGE" ...?
ONE I MADE LONG AGO.
I HAD BEEN REQUESTED TO TAKE ON THIS DUTY BY YOUR GRANDFATHER.
BUT EVEN IF IT HAD NOT BEEN REQUESTED OF ME, I WOULD STILL...
KUTE... (SLUMP...)
H-HEY...!
FORGIVE ME... I AM TIRED.
I HAVE UNDERGONE A LONG JOURNEY, AS WELL AS THAT BATTLE...
MY APOLOGIES FOR NOT BEING ABLE TO CONTINUE...
...BUT PLEASE LET ME REST FOR TODAY.
...BUT YOU STILL HAVEN'T TOLD ME THE MOST IMPORTANT PART.
WHO... ARE YOU?

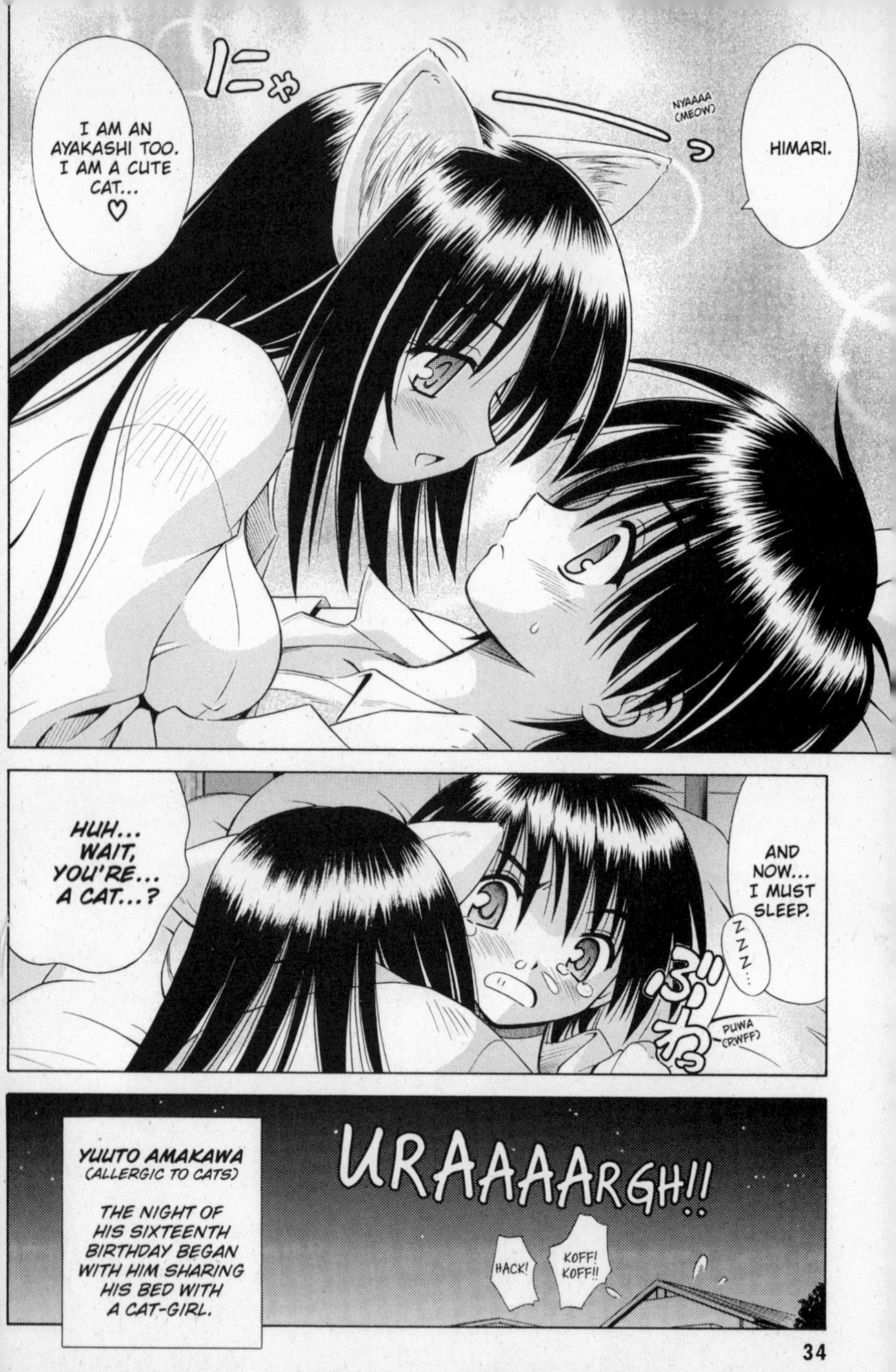
HIMARI.
NYAAAA (MEOW)
I AM AN AYAKASHI TOO. I AM A CUTE CAT... ♡
AND NOW... I MUST SLEEP.
Z Z Z...
PUWA (PWFF)
HUH... WAIT, YOU'RE... A CAT...?
URAAAAARGH!!
KOFF! KOFF!!
HACK!
YUUTO AMAKAWA (ALLERGIC TO CATS)
THE NIGHT OF HIS SIXTEENTH BIRTHDAY BEGAN WITH HIM SHARING HIS BED WITH A CAT-GIRL.

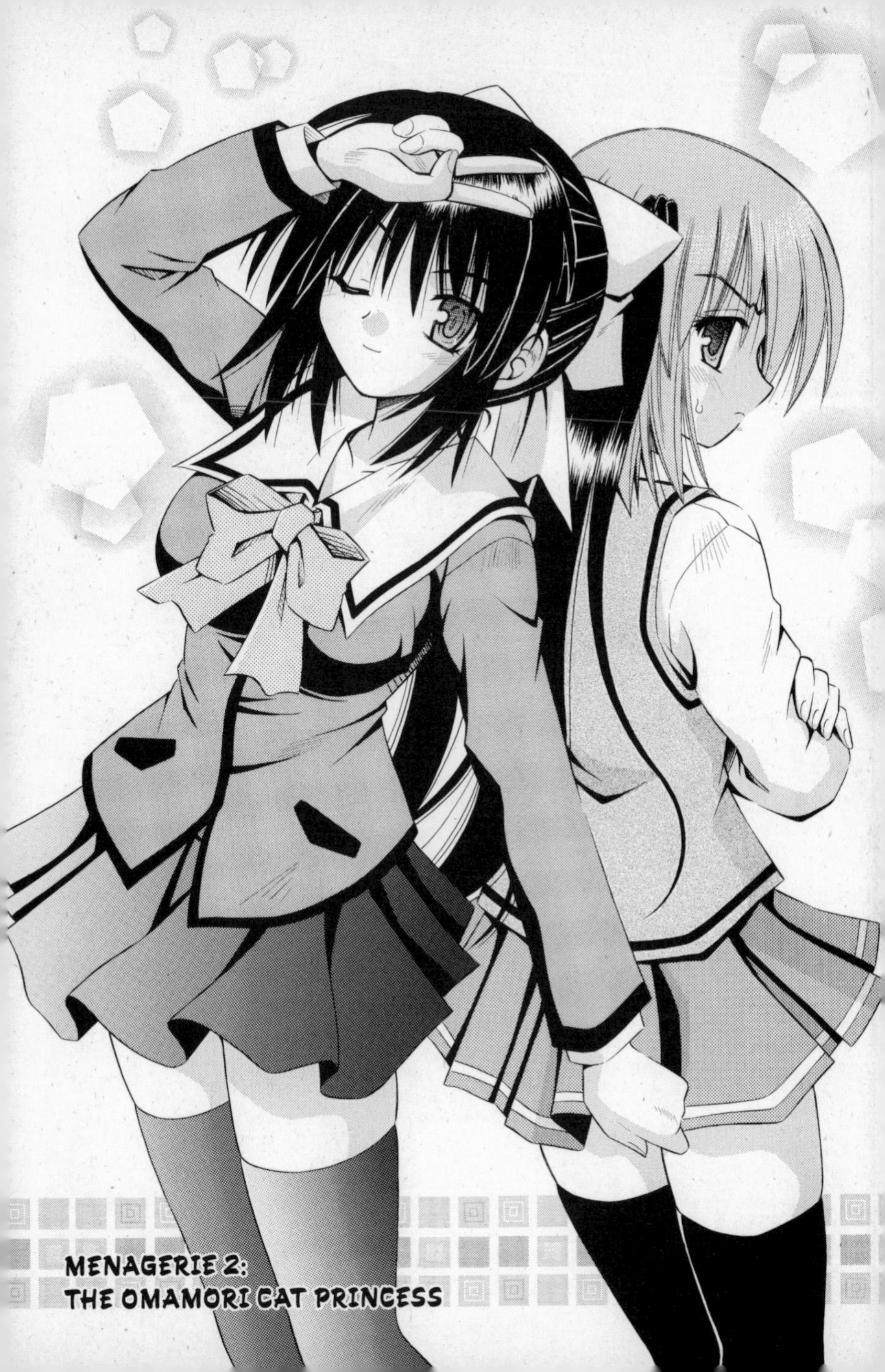

MENAGERIE 2:
THE OMAMORI CAT PRINCESS

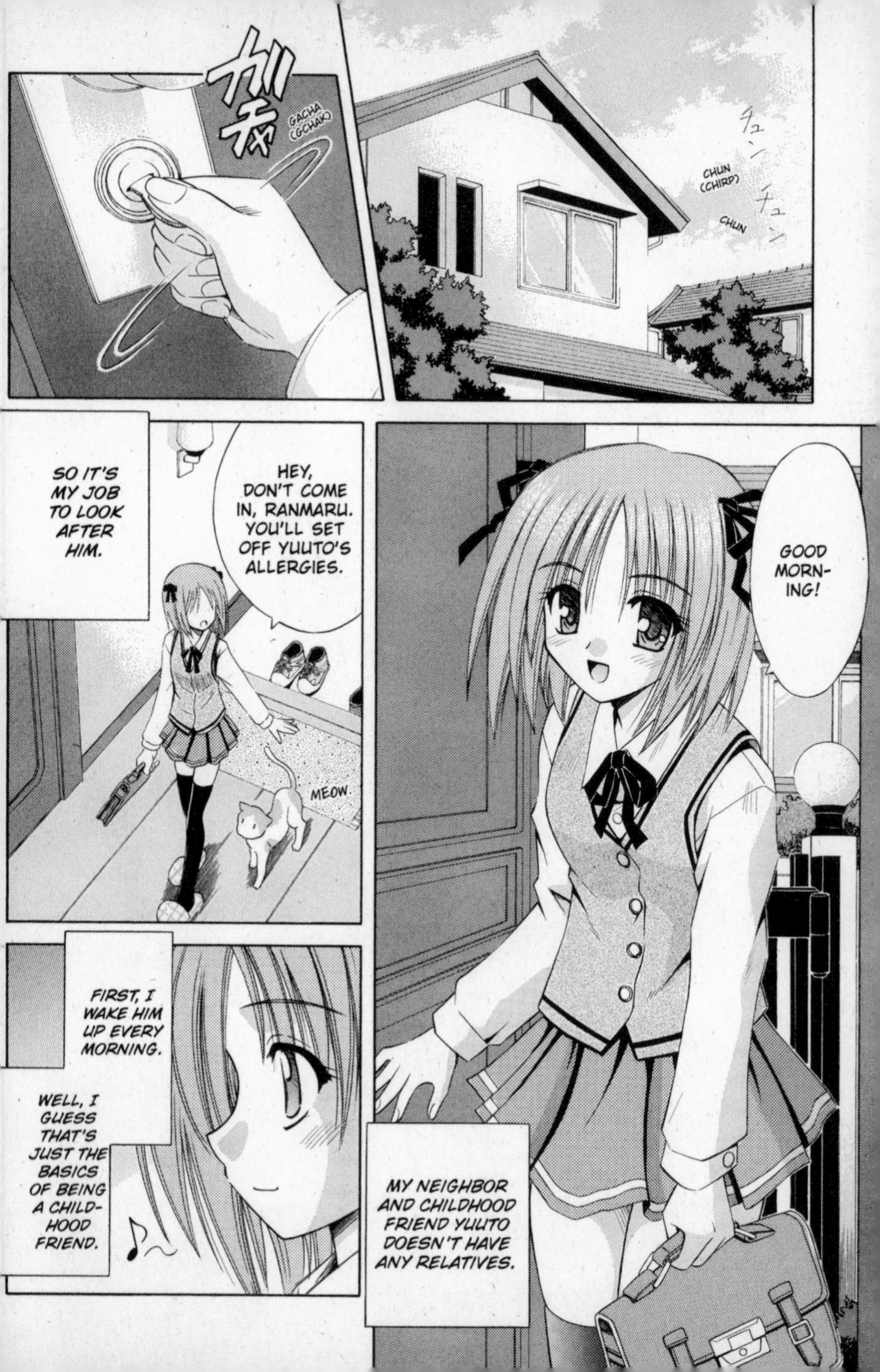
チュン
CHUN (CHIRP)
チュン
CHUN
ガチャ
GACHA (GCHAK)
GOOD MORNING!
MY NEIGHBOR AND CHILDHOOD FRIEND YUUTO DOESN'T HAVE ANY RELATIVES.
HEY, DON'T COME IN, RANMARU. YOU'LL SET OFF YUUTO'S ALLERGIES.
MEOW.
SO IT'S MY JOB TO LOOK AFTER HIM.
FIRST, I WAKE HIM UP EVERY MORNING.
WELL, I GUESS THAT'S JUST THE BASICS OF BEING A CHILD-HOOD FRIEND.
♪~

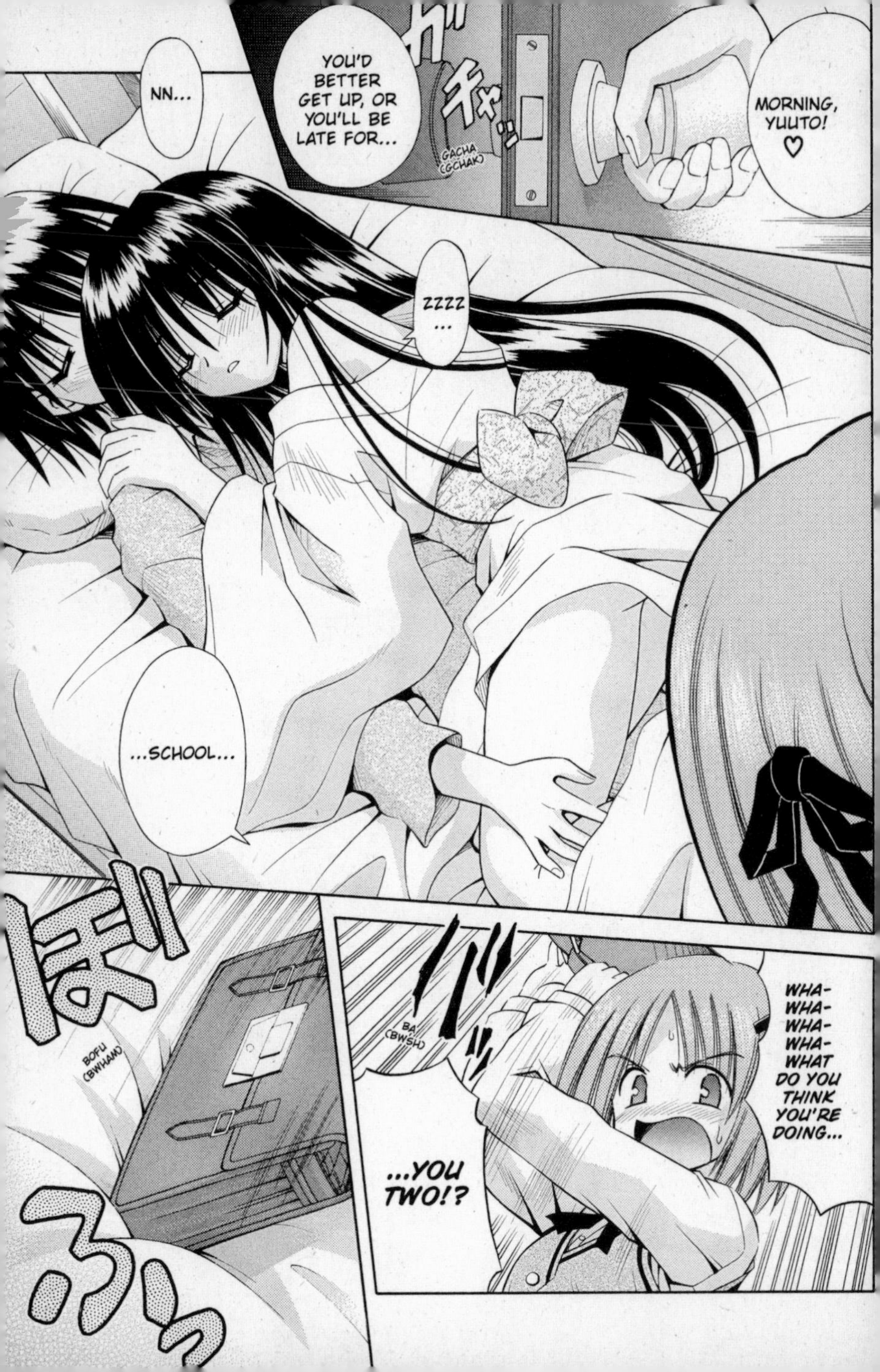
MORNING, YUUTO! ♡
GACHA (GCHAK)
YOU'D BETTER GET UP, OR YOU'LL BE LATE FOR...
NN...
ZZZZ...
...SCHOOL...
BA (BWSH)
WHA-WHA-WHA-WHA-WHAT DO YOU THINK YOU'RE DOING...
...YOU TWO!?
BOFU (BWHAM)

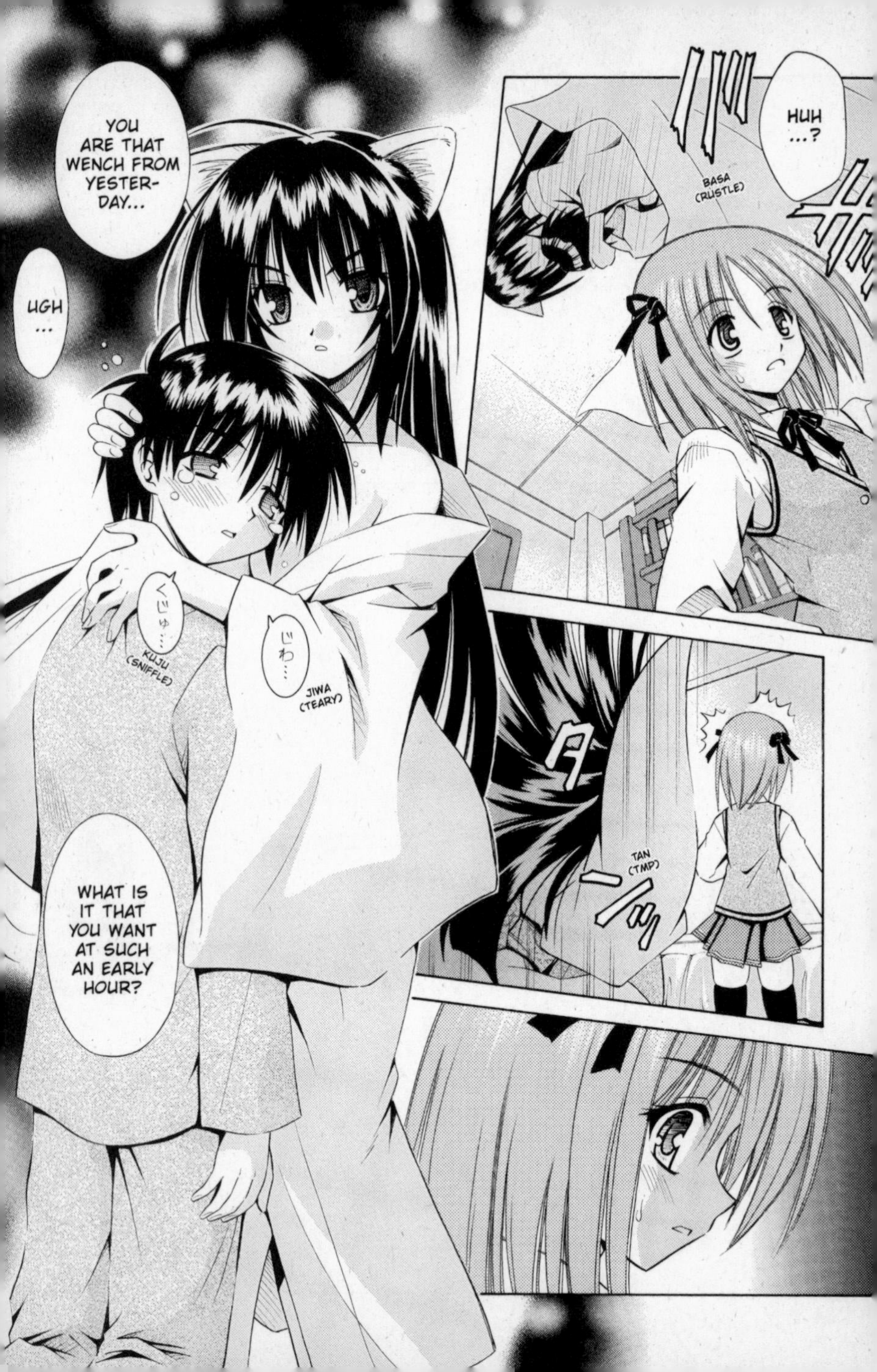
HUH ...?
BASA (RUSTLE)
TAN (TMP)
YOU ARE THAT WENCH FROM YESTER-DAY...
UGH ...
くじゅ…
KUJU (SNIFFLE)
じわ…
JIWA (TEARY)
WHAT IS IT THAT YOU WANT AT SUCH AN EARLY HOUR?

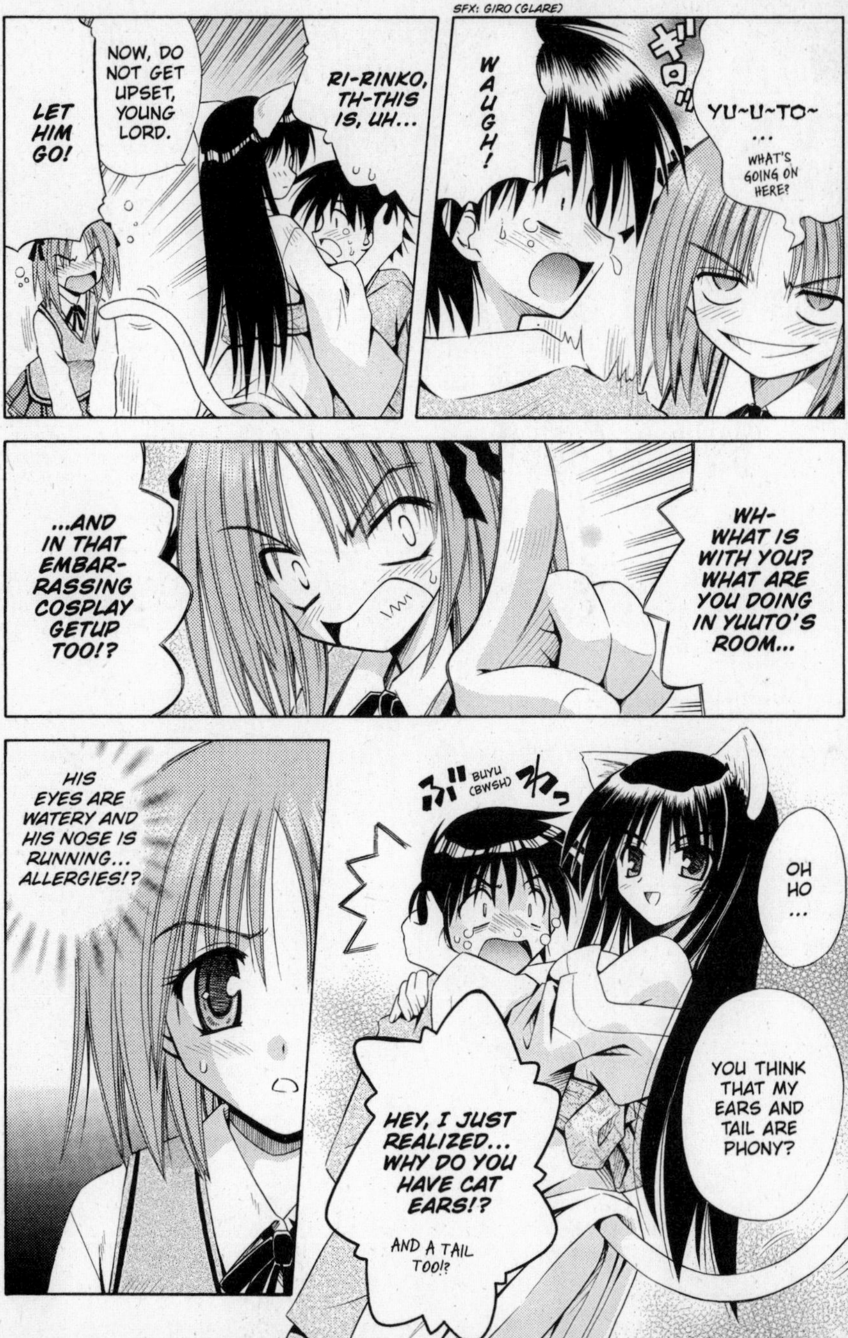
SFX: GIRO (GLARE)
YU~U~TO~ ...
WHAT'S GOING ON HERE?
WAUGH!
RI-RINKO, TH-THIS IS, UH...
NOW, DO NOT GET UPSET, YOUNG LORD.
LET HIM GO!
WH-WHAT IS WITH YOU? WHAT ARE YOU DOING IN YUUTO'S ROOM...
...AND IN THAT EMBARRASSING COSPLAY GETUP TOO!?
BUYU (BWSH)
OH HO ...
YOU THINK THAT MY EARS AND TAIL ARE PHONY?
HEY, I JUST REALIZED... WHY DO YOU HAVE CAT EARS!?
AND A TAIL TOO!?
HIS EYES ARE WATERY AND HIS NOSE IS RUNNING... ALLERGIES!?

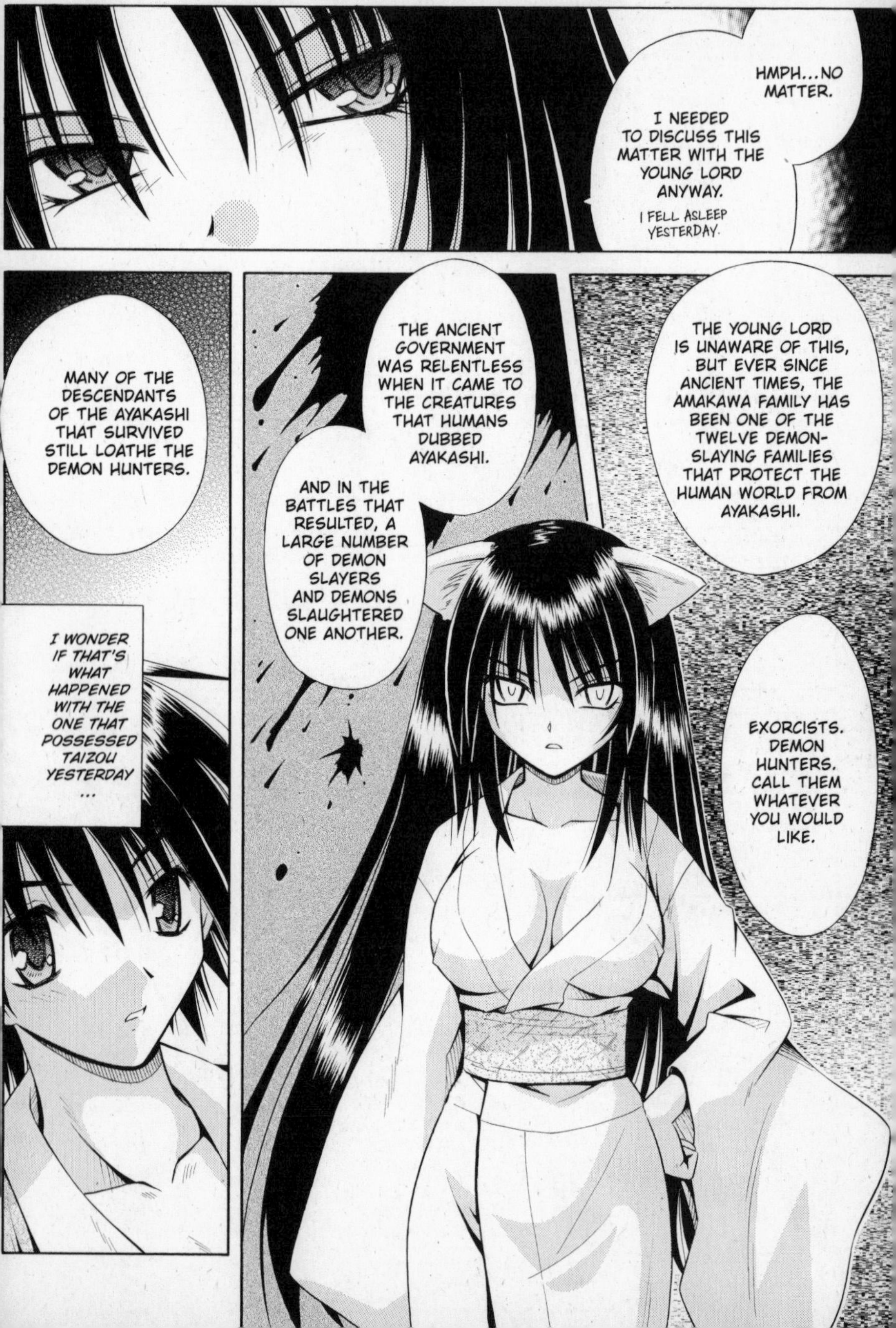
HMPH...NO MATTER.
I NEEDED TO DISCUSS THIS MATTER WITH THE YOUNG LORD ANYWAY.
I FELL ASLEEP YESTERDAY.
THE YOUNG LORD IS UNAWARE OF THIS, BUT EVER SINCE ANCIENT TIMES, THE AMAKAWA FAMILY HAS BEEN ONE OF THE TWELVE DEMON-SLAYING FAMILIES THAT PROTECT THE HUMAN WORLD FROM AYAKASHI.
EXORCISTS. DEMON HUNTERS. CALL THEM WHATEVER YOU WOULD LIKE.
THE ANCIENT GOVERNMENT WAS RELENTLESS WHEN IT CAME TO THE CREATURES THAT HUMANS DUBBED AYAKASHI.
AND IN THE BATTLES THAT RESULTED, A LARGE NUMBER OF DEMON SLAYERS AND DEMONS SLAUGHTERED ONE ANOTHER.
MANY OF THE DESCENDANTS OF THE AYAKASHI THAT SURVIVED STILL LOATHE THE DEMON HUNTERS.
I WONDER IF THAT'S WHAT HAPPENED WITH THE ONE THAT POSSESSED TAIZOU YESTERDAY ...

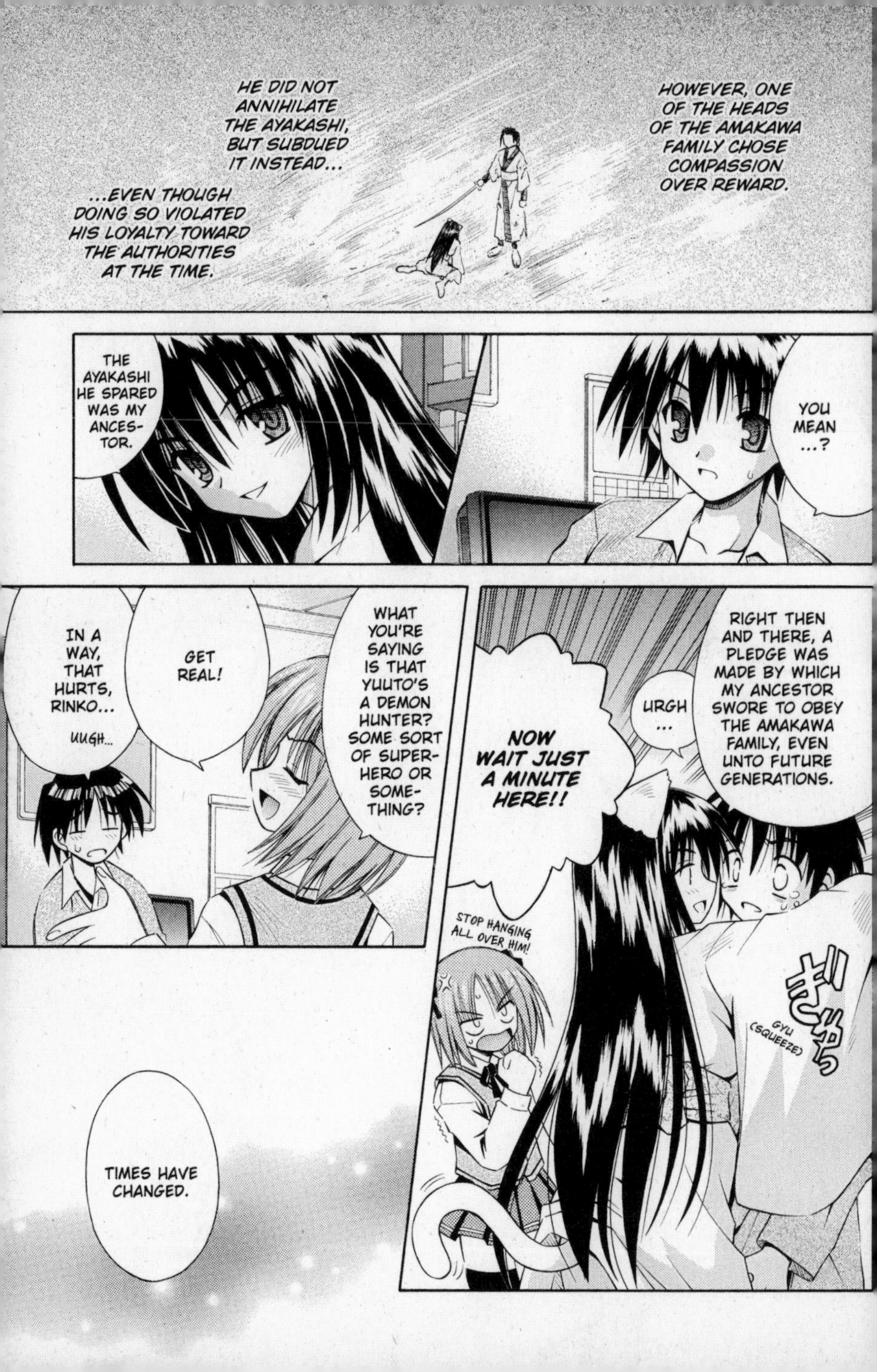
HOWEVER, ONE OF THE HEADS OF THE AMAKAWA FAMILY CHOSE COMPASSION OVER REWARD.
HE DID NOT ANNIHILATE THE AYAKASHI, BUT SUBDUED IT INSTEAD...
...EVEN THOUGH DOING SO VIOLATED HIS LOYALTY TOWARD THE AUTHORITIES AT THE TIME.
YOU MEAN ...?
THE AYAKASHI HE SPARED WAS MY ANCESTOR.
RIGHT THEN AND THERE, A PLEDGE WAS MADE BY WHICH MY ANCESTOR SWORE TO OBEY THE AMAKAWA FAMILY, EVEN UNTO FUTURE GENERATIONS.
URGH ...
NOW WAIT JUST A MINUTE HERE!!
STOP HANGING ALL OVER HIM!
GYU (SQUEEZE)
WHAT YOU'RE SAYING IS THAT YUUTO'S A DEMON HUNTER? SOME SORT OF SUPER-HERO OR SOME-THING?
GET REAL!
IN A WAY, THAT HURTS, RINKO...
UUGH...
TIMES HAVE CHANGED.

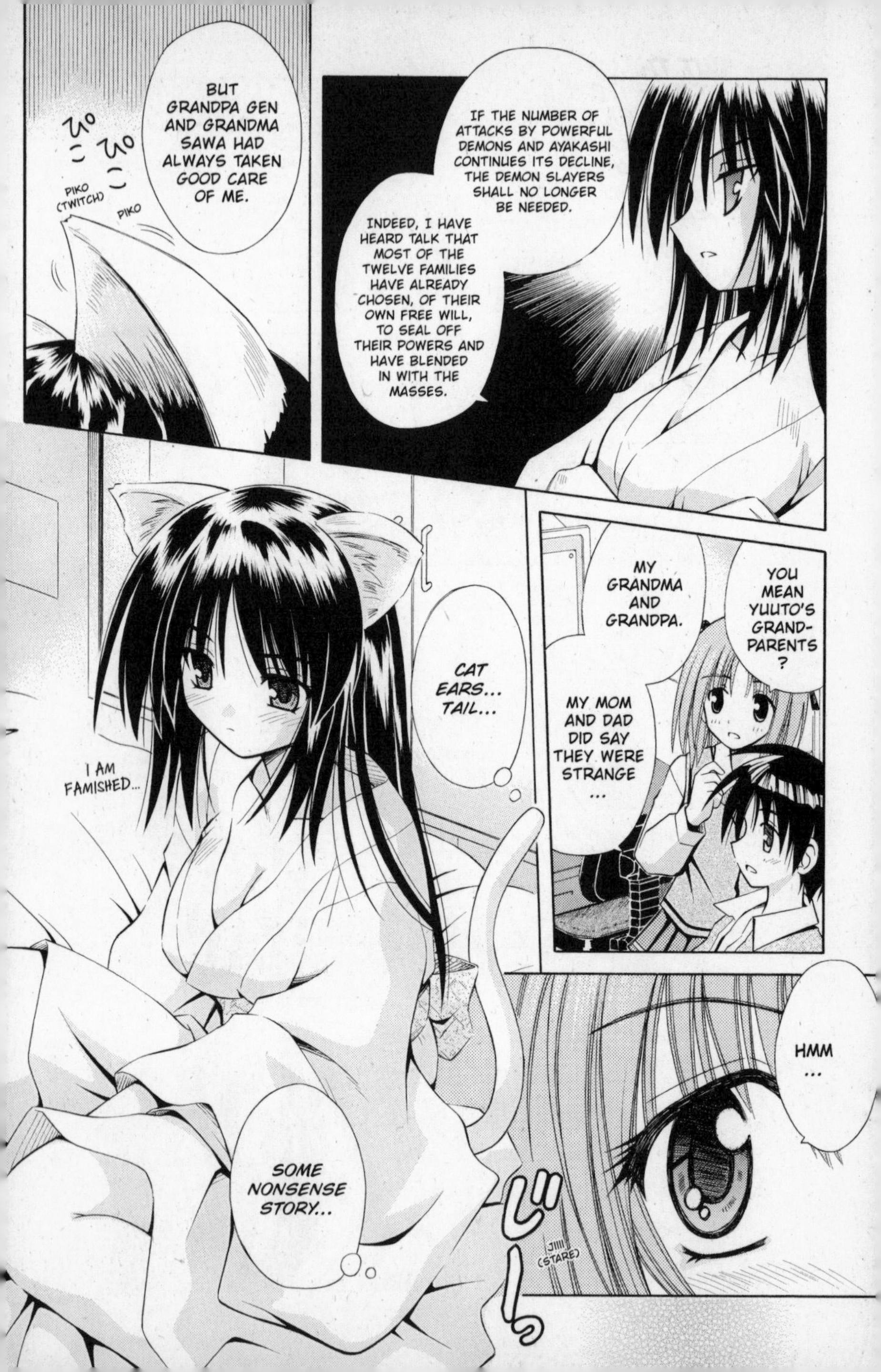
IF THE NUMBER OF ATTACKS BY POWERFUL DEMONS AND AYAKASHI CONTINUES ITS DECLINE, THE DEMON SLAYERS SHALL NO LONGER BE NEEDED.
INDEED, I HAVE HEARD TALK THAT MOST OF THE TWELVE FAMILIES HAVE ALREADY CHOSEN, OF THEIR OWN FREE WILL, TO SEAL OFF THEIR POWERS AND HAVE BLENDED IN WITH THE MASSES.
BUT GRANDPA GEN AND GRANDMA SAWA HAD ALWAYS TAKEN GOOD CARE OF ME.
PIKO (TWITCH)
PIKO
YOU MEAN YUUTO'S GRAND-PARENTS?
MY GRANDMA AND GRANDPA.
MY MOM AND DAD DID SAY THEY WERE STRANGE ...
HMM ...
JIIII (STARE)
CAT EARS... TAIL...
I AM FAMISHED...
SOME NONSENSE STORY...

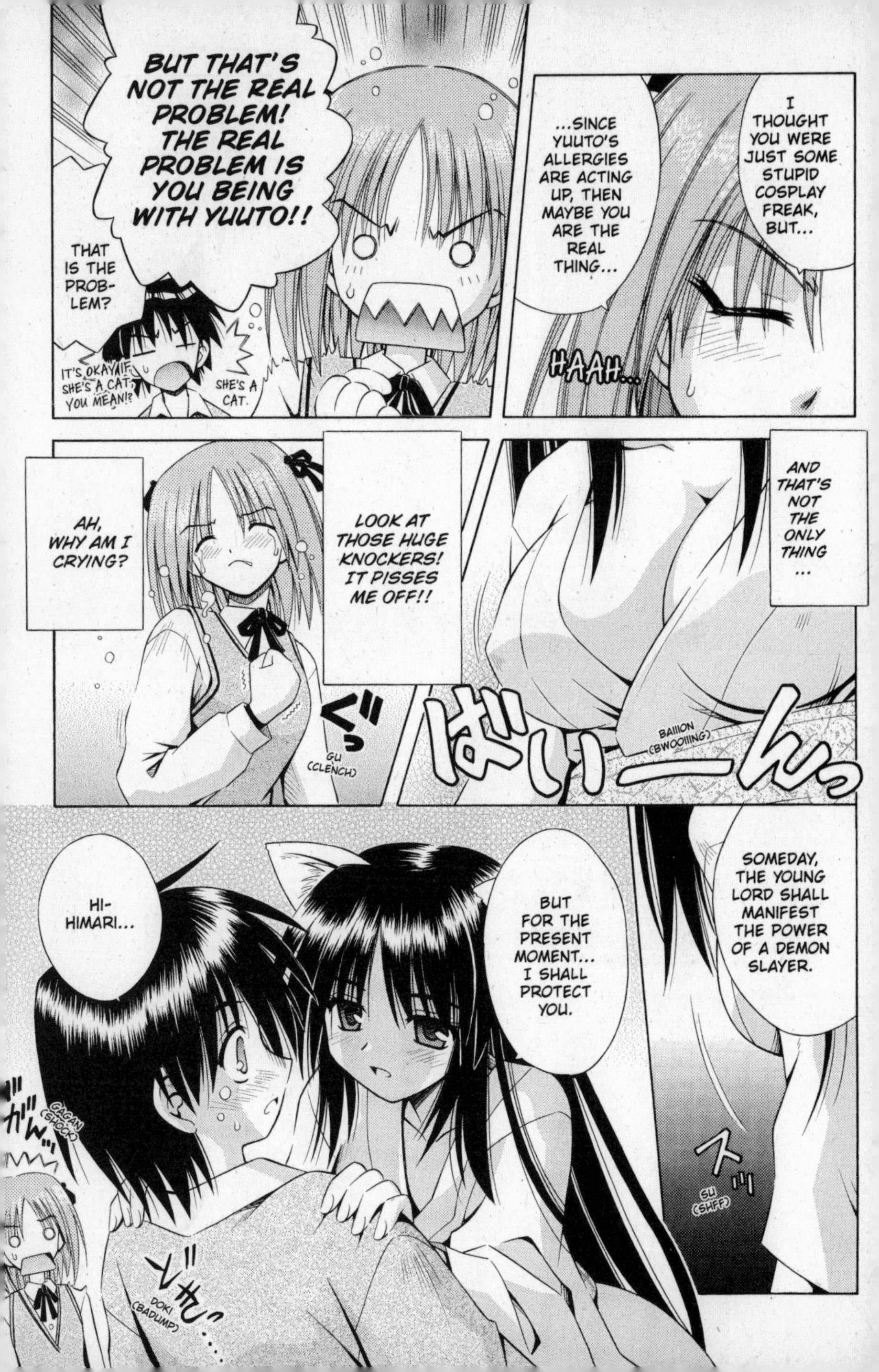
I THOUGHT YOU WERE JUST SOME STUPID COSPLAY FREAK, BUT...
...SINCE YUUTO'S ALLERGIES ARE ACTING UP, THEN MAYBE YOU ARE THE REAL THING...
HAAH...
BUT THAT'S NOT THE REAL PROBLEM! THE REAL PROBLEM IS YOU BEING WITH YUUTO!!
THAT IS THE PROB-LEM?
SHE'S A CAT.
IT'S OKAY IF SHE'S A CAT, YOU MEAN!?
AND THAT'S NOT THE ONLY THING...
BAIIION (BWOOIIING)
LOOK AT THOSE HUGE KNOCKERS! IT PISSES ME OFF!!
AH, WHY AM I CRYING?
GU (CLENCH)
SOMEDAY, THE YOUNG LORD SHALL MANIFEST THE POWER OF A DEMON SLAYER.
SU (SHFF)
BUT FOR THE PRESENT MOMENT... I SHALL PROTECT YOU.
HI-HIMARI...
GAGAN (SHOCK)
DOKI (BADUMP)

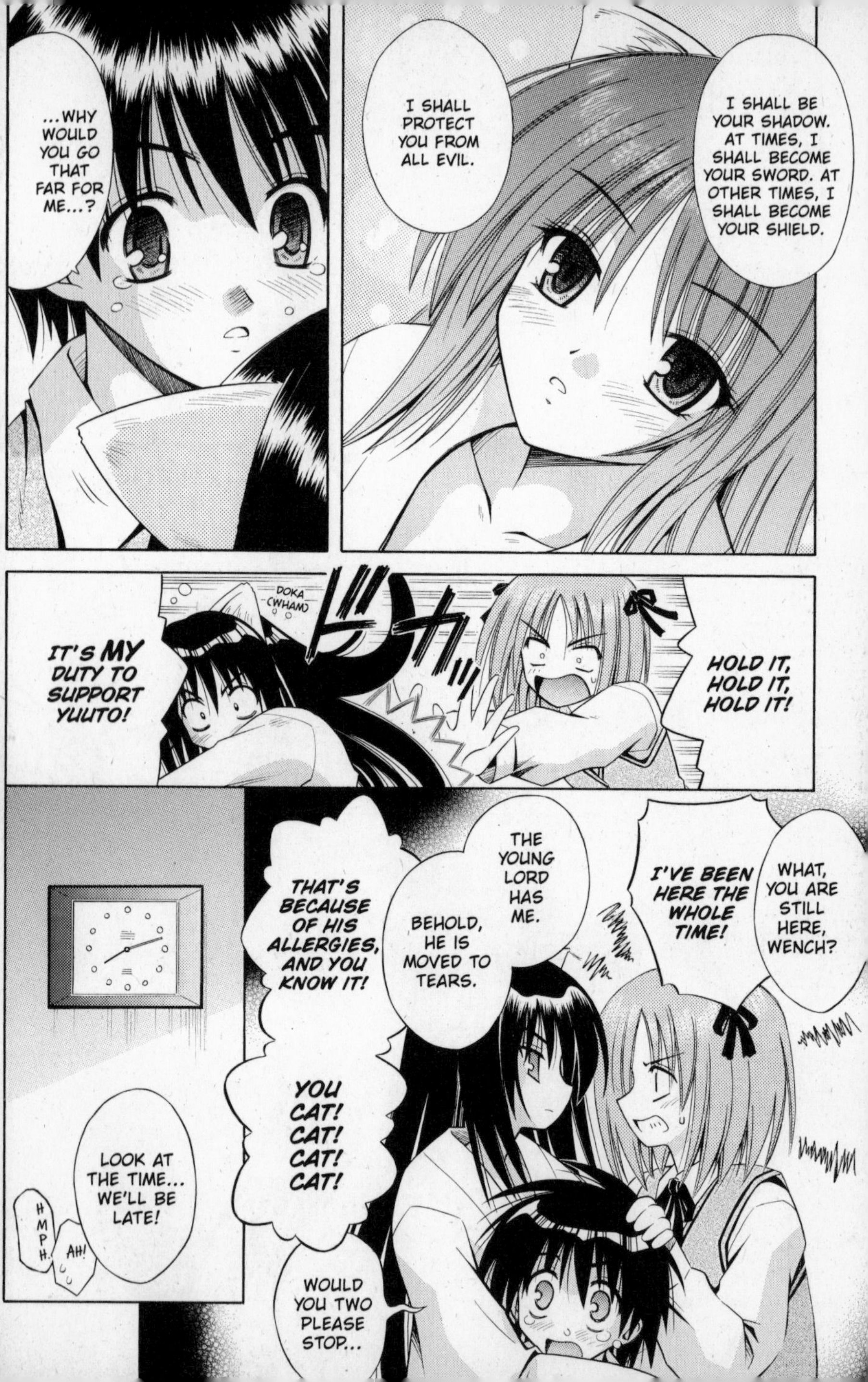
I SHALL BE YOUR SHADOW. AT TIMES, I SHALL BECOME YOUR SWORD. AT OTHER TIMES, I SHALL BECOME YOUR SHIELD.
I SHALL PROTECT YOU FROM ALL EVIL.
...WHY WOULD YOU GO THAT FAR FOR ME...?
HOLD IT, HOLD IT, HOLD IT!
DOKA (WHAM)
IT'S MY DUTY TO SUPPORT YUUTO!
WHAT, YOU ARE STILL HERE, WENCH?
I'VE BEEN HERE THE WHOLE TIME!
THE YOUNG LORD HAS ME.
BEHOLD, HE IS MOVED TO TEARS.
THAT'S BECAUSE OF HIS ALLERGIES, AND YOU KNOW IT!
YOU CAT! CAT! CAT! CAT!
WOULD YOU TWO PLEASE STOP...
LOOK AT THE TIME... WE'LL BE LATE!
AH!
HMPH.

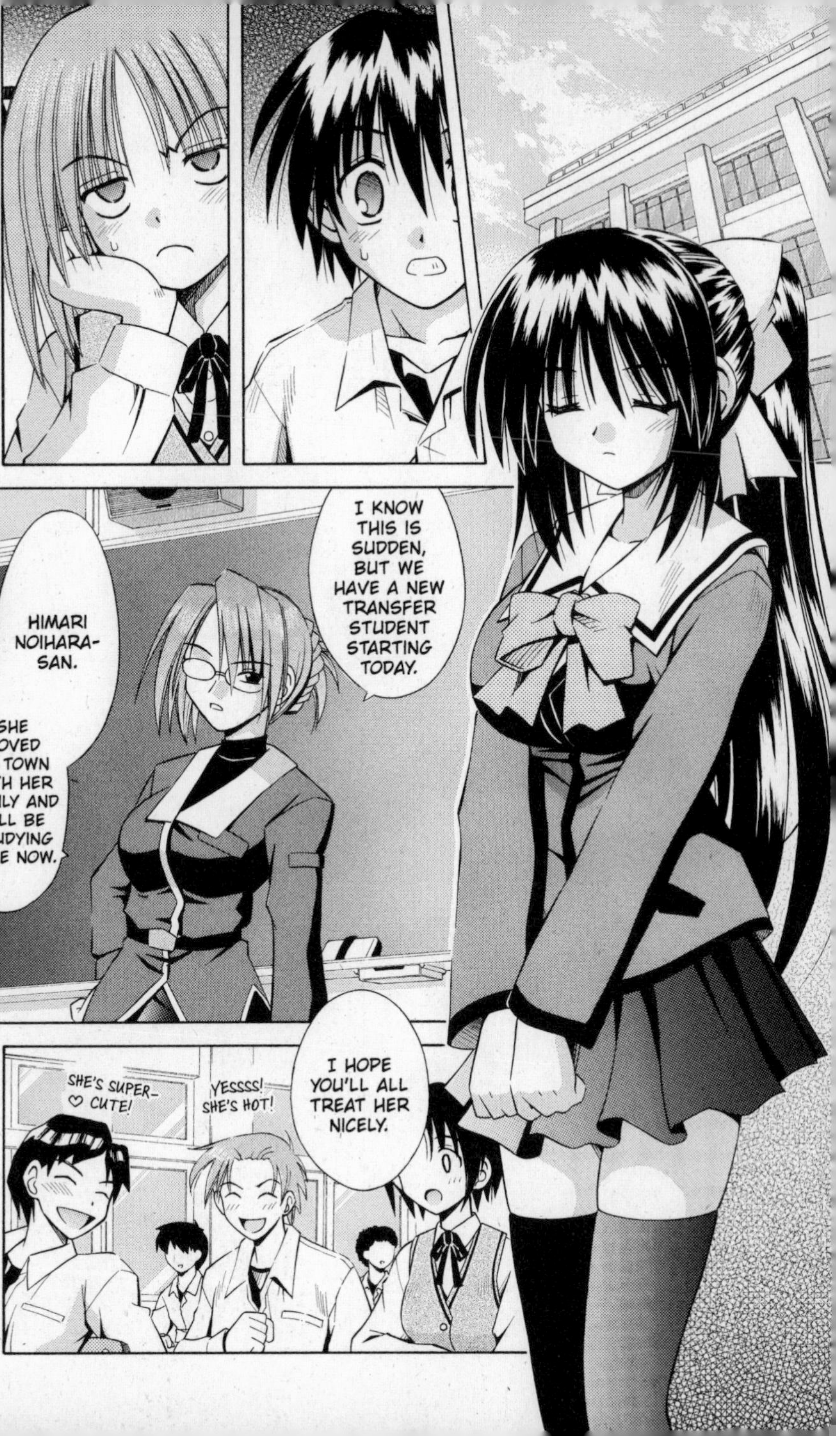
I KNOW THIS IS SUDDEN, BUT WE HAVE A NEW TRANSFER STUDENT STARTING TODAY.
HIMARI NOIHARA-SAN.
SHE MOVED TO TOWN WITH HER FAMILY AND WILL BE STUDYING HERE NOW.
I HOPE YOU'LL ALL TREAT HER NICELY.
YESSSS! SHE'S HOT!
SHE'S SUPER-♡ CUTE!

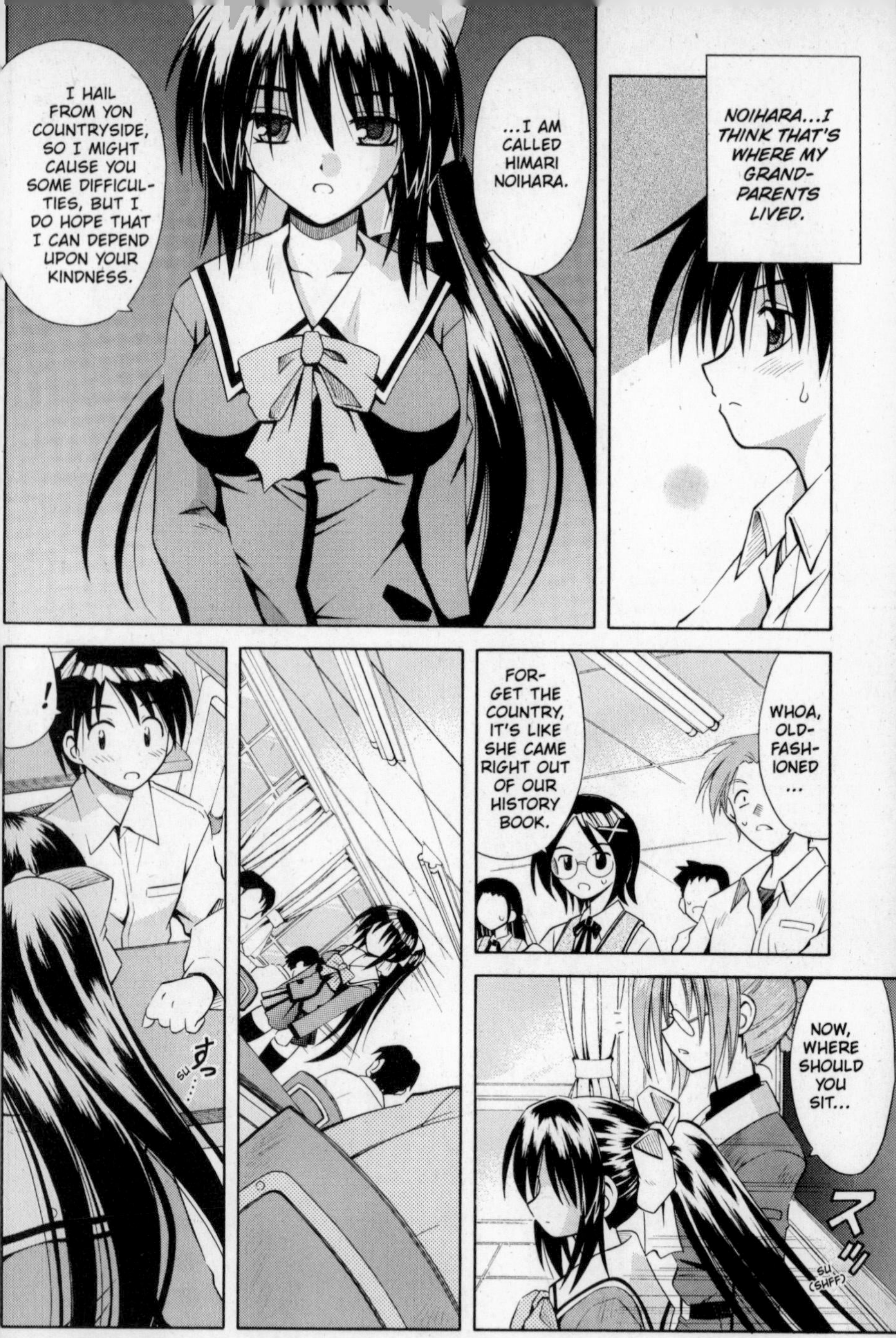
...I AM CALLED HIMARI NOIHARA.
I HAIL FROM YON COUNTRYSIDE, SO I MIGHT CAUSE YOU SOME DIFFICULTIES, BUT I DO HOPE THAT I CAN DEPEND UPON YOUR KINDNESS.
NOIHARA...I THINK THAT'S WHERE MY GRAND-PARENTS LIVED.
WHOA, OLD-FASHIONED...
FOR-GET THE COUNTRY, IT'S LIKE SHE CAME RIGHT OUT OF OUR HISTORY BOOK.
NOW, WHERE SHOULD YOU SIT...
スッ
SU (SHFF)
!
すっ
SU...

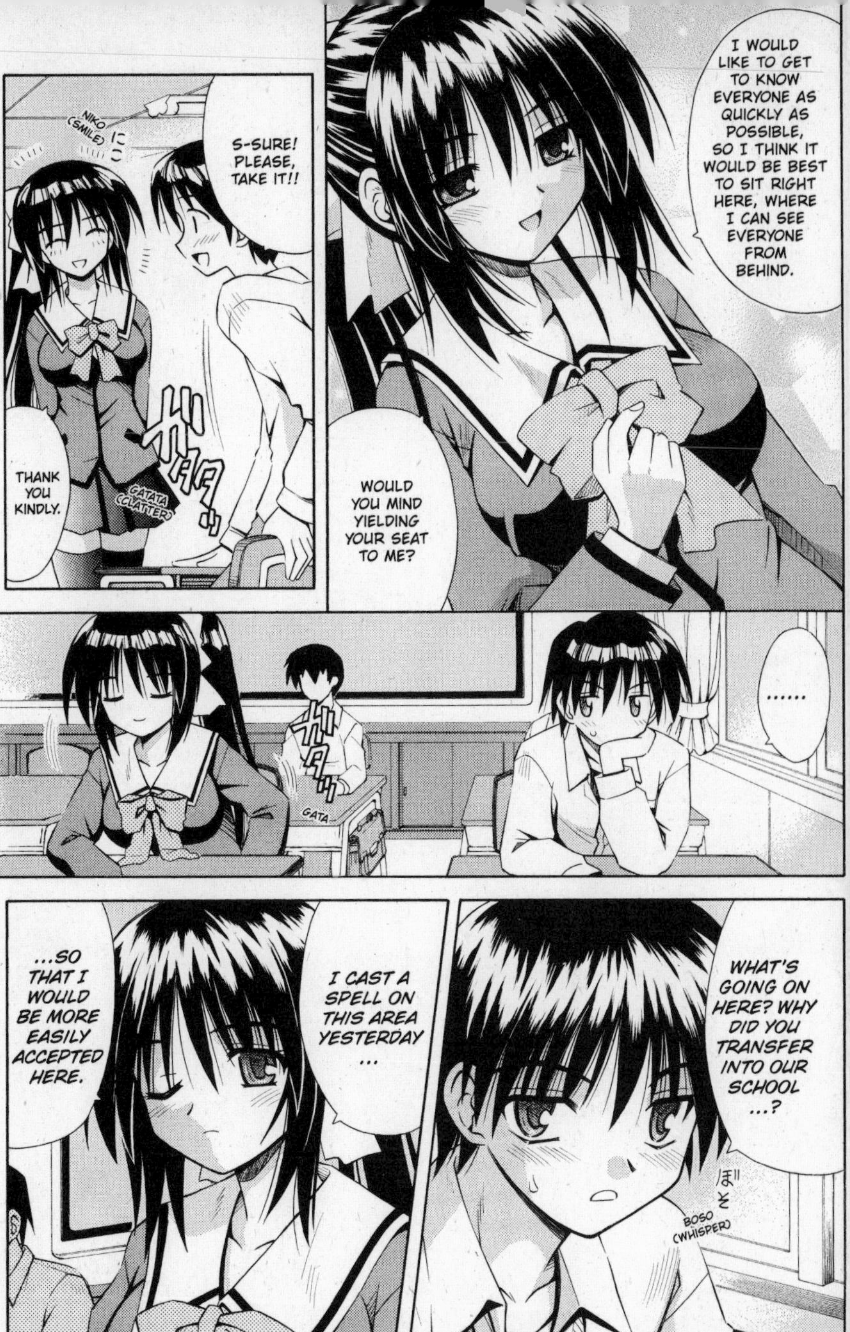
I WOULD LIKE TO GET TO KNOW EVERYONE AS QUICKLY AS POSSIBLE, SO I THINK IT WOULD BE BEST TO SIT RIGHT HERE, WHERE I CAN SEE EVERYONE FROM BEHIND.
WOULD YOU MIND YIELDING YOUR SEAT TO ME?
S-SURE! PLEASE, TAKE IT!!
NIKO (SMILE)
GATATA (CLATTER)
THANK YOU KINDLY.
......
GATA
WHAT'S GOING ON HERE? WHY DID YOU TRANSFER INTO OUR SCHOOL ...?
BOSO (WHISPER)
I CAST A SPELL ON THIS AREA YESTERDAY ...
...SO THAT I WOULD BE MORE EASILY ACCEPTED HERE.

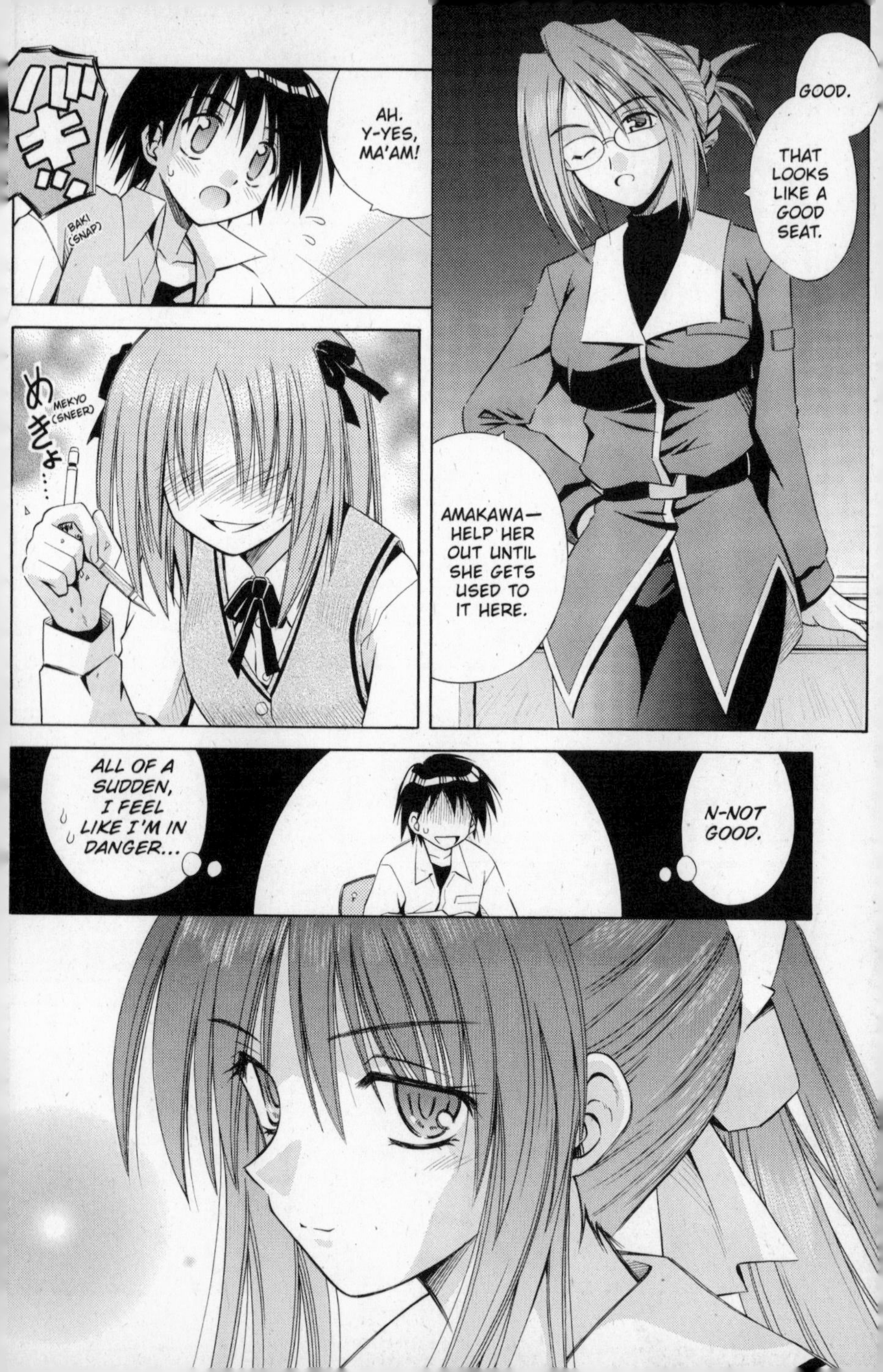
GOOD.
THAT LOOKS LIKE A GOOD SEAT.
AMAKAWA— HELP HER OUT UNTIL SHE GETS USED TO IT HERE.
バキ
BAKI (SNAP)
AH. Y-YES, MA'AM!
めきょ…
MEKYO (SNEER)
N-NOT GOOD.
ALL OF A SUDDEN, I FEEL LIKE I'M IN DANGER...

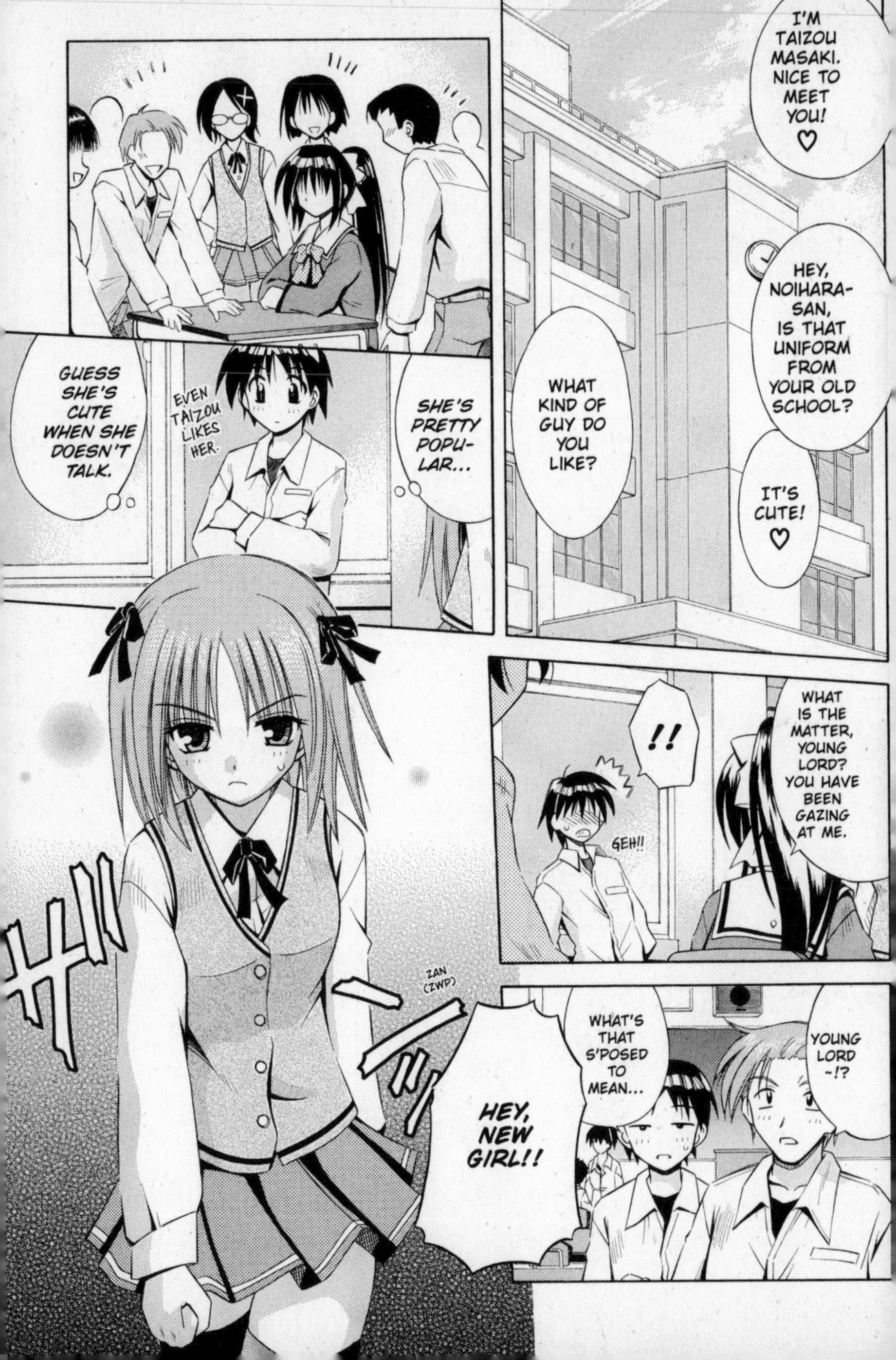
I'M TAIZOU MASAKI. NICE TO MEET YOU! ♡
HEY, NOIHARA-SAN, IS THAT UNIFORM FROM YOUR OLD SCHOOL?
IT'S CUTE! ♡
WHAT KIND OF GUY DO YOU LIKE?
SHE'S PRETTY POPULAR...
EVEN TAIZOU LIKES HER.
GUESS SHE'S CUTE WHEN SHE DOESN'T TALK.
WHAT IS THE MATTER, YOUNG LORD? YOU HAVE BEEN GAZING AT ME.
!!
GEH!!
YOUNG LORD-!?
WHAT'S THAT S'POSED TO MEAN...
HEY, NEW GIRL!!
ZAN (ZWP)

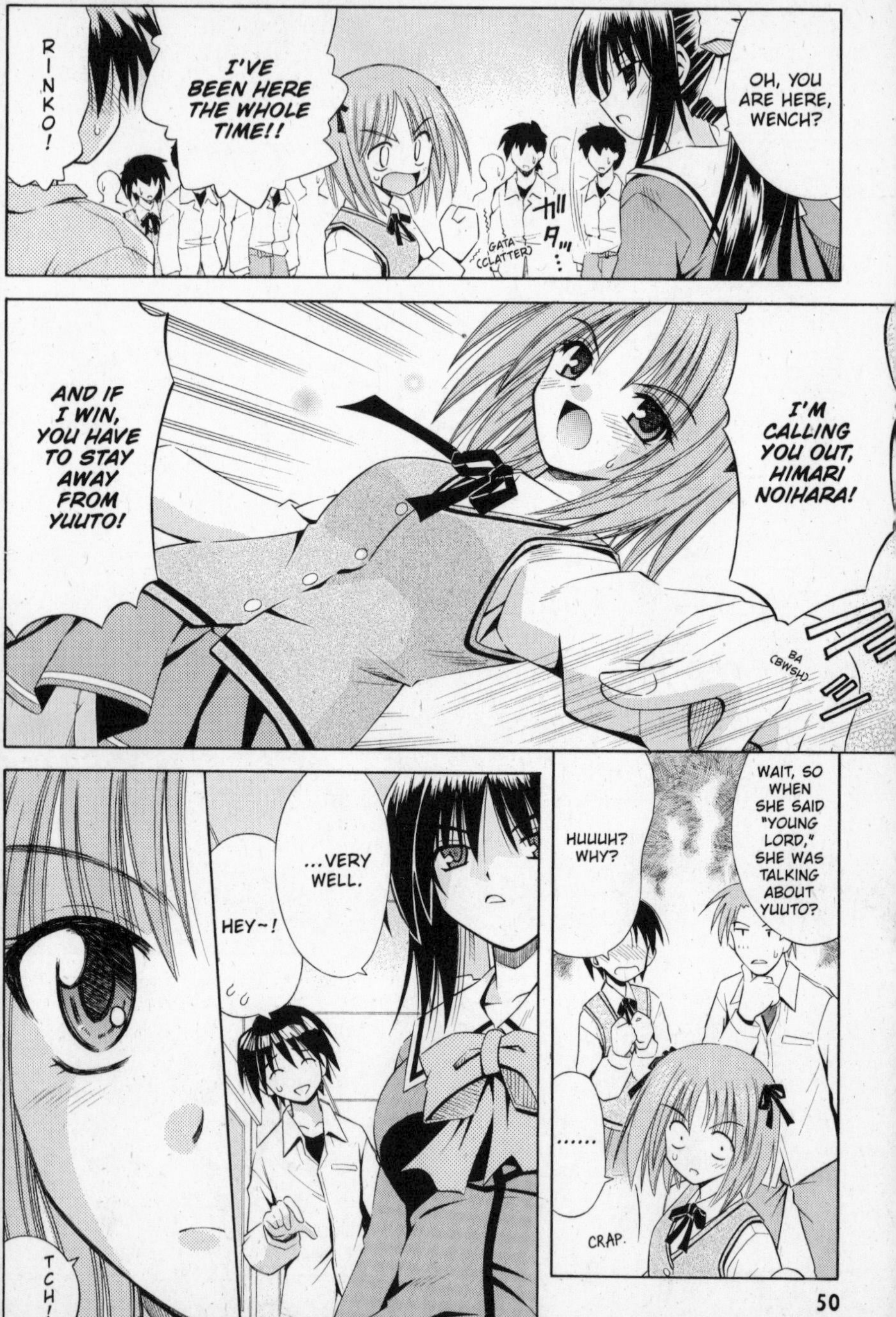
OH, YOU ARE HERE, WENCH?
I'VE BEEN HERE THE WHOLE TIME!!
RINKO!
GATA (CLATTER)
I'M CALLING YOU OUT, HIMARI NOIHARA!
AND IF I WIN, YOU HAVE TO STAY AWAY FROM YUUTO!
BA (BWSH)
WAIT, SO WHEN SHE SAID "YOUNG LORD," SHE WAS TALKING ABOUT YUUTO?
HUUUH? WHY?
......
CRAP.
...VERY WELL.
HEY~!
TCH!

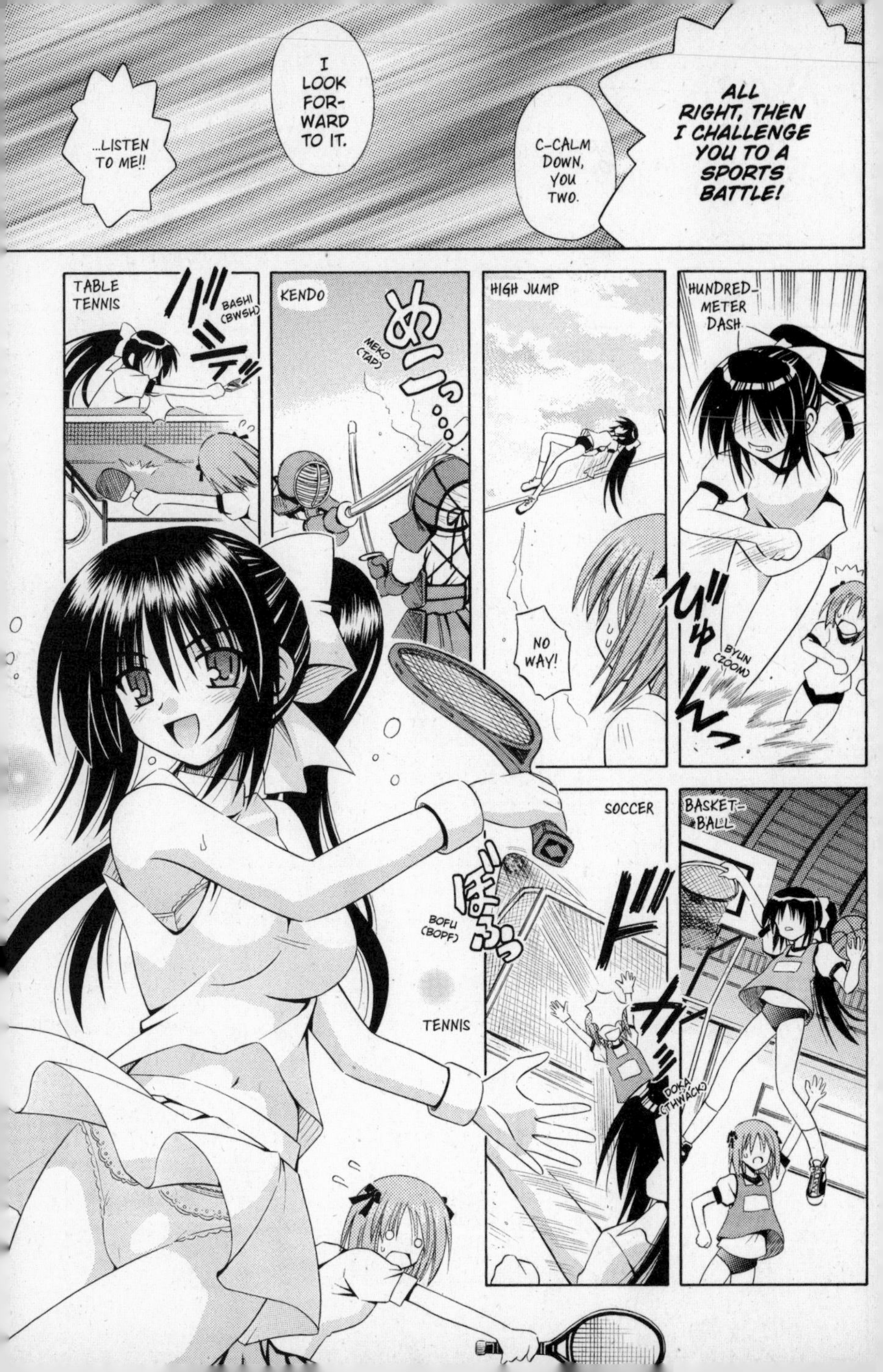
ALL RIGHT, THEN I CHALLENGE YOU TO A SPORTS BATTLE!
C-CALM DOWN, YOU TWO.
I LOOK FOR-WARD TO IT.
...LISTEN TO ME!!
HUNDRED-METER DASH
BYUN (ZOOM)
HIGH JUMP
NO WAY!
KENDO
MEKO (TAP)
TABLE TENNIS
BASHI (BWSH)
BASKET-BALL
DOKA (THWACK)
SOCCER
BOFU (BOPF)
TENNIS

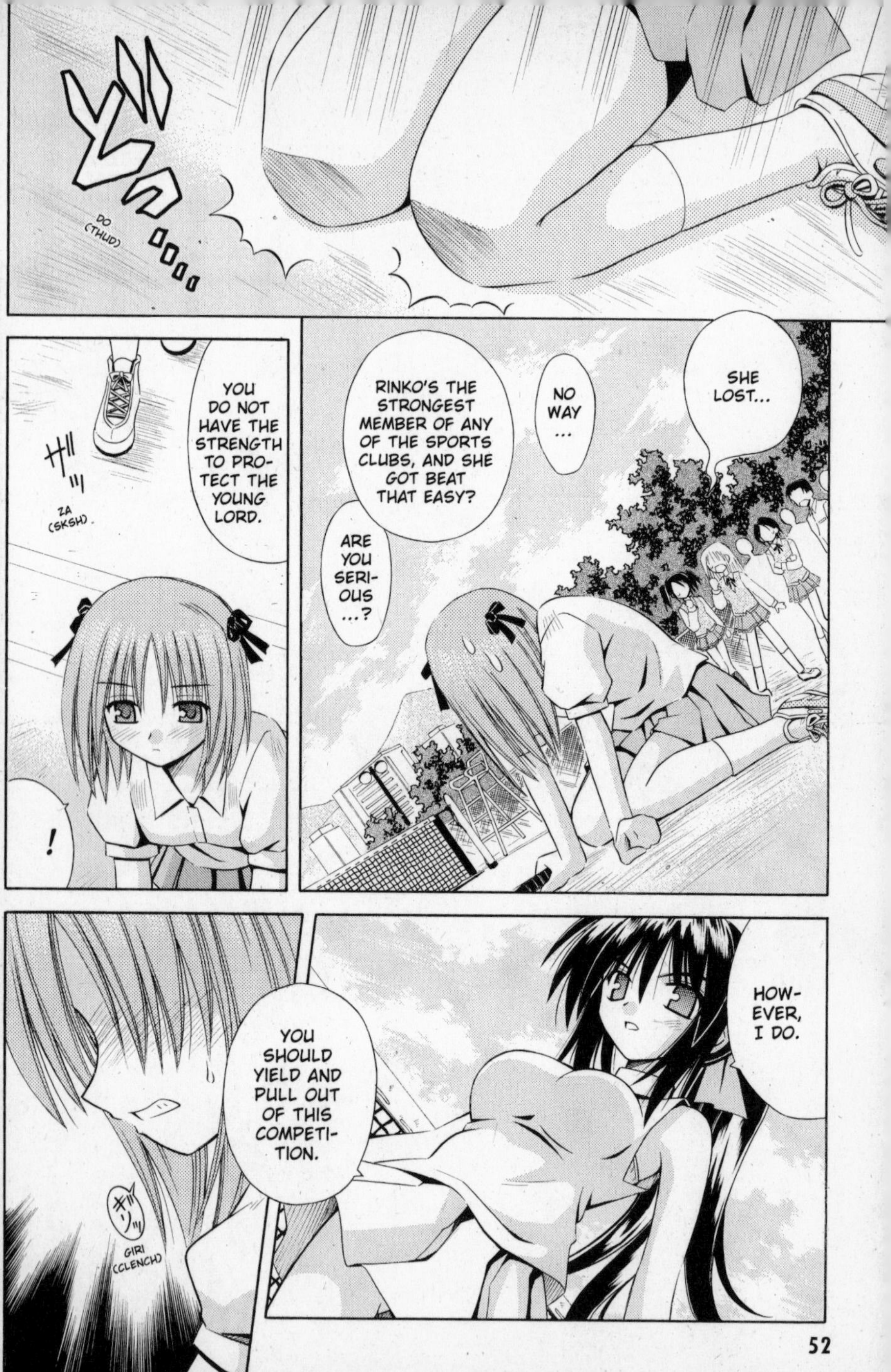
DO (THUD)
SHE LOST...
NO WAY ...
RINKO'S THE STRONGEST MEMBER OF ANY OF THE SPORTS CLUBS, AND SHE GOT BEAT THAT EASY?
ARE YOU SERI-OUS ...?
YOU DO NOT HAVE THE STRENGTH TO PRO-TECT THE YOUNG LORD.
ZA (SKSH)
!
HOW-EVER, I DO.
YOU SHOULD YIELD AND PULL OUT OF THIS COMPETI-TION.
GIRI (CLENCH)

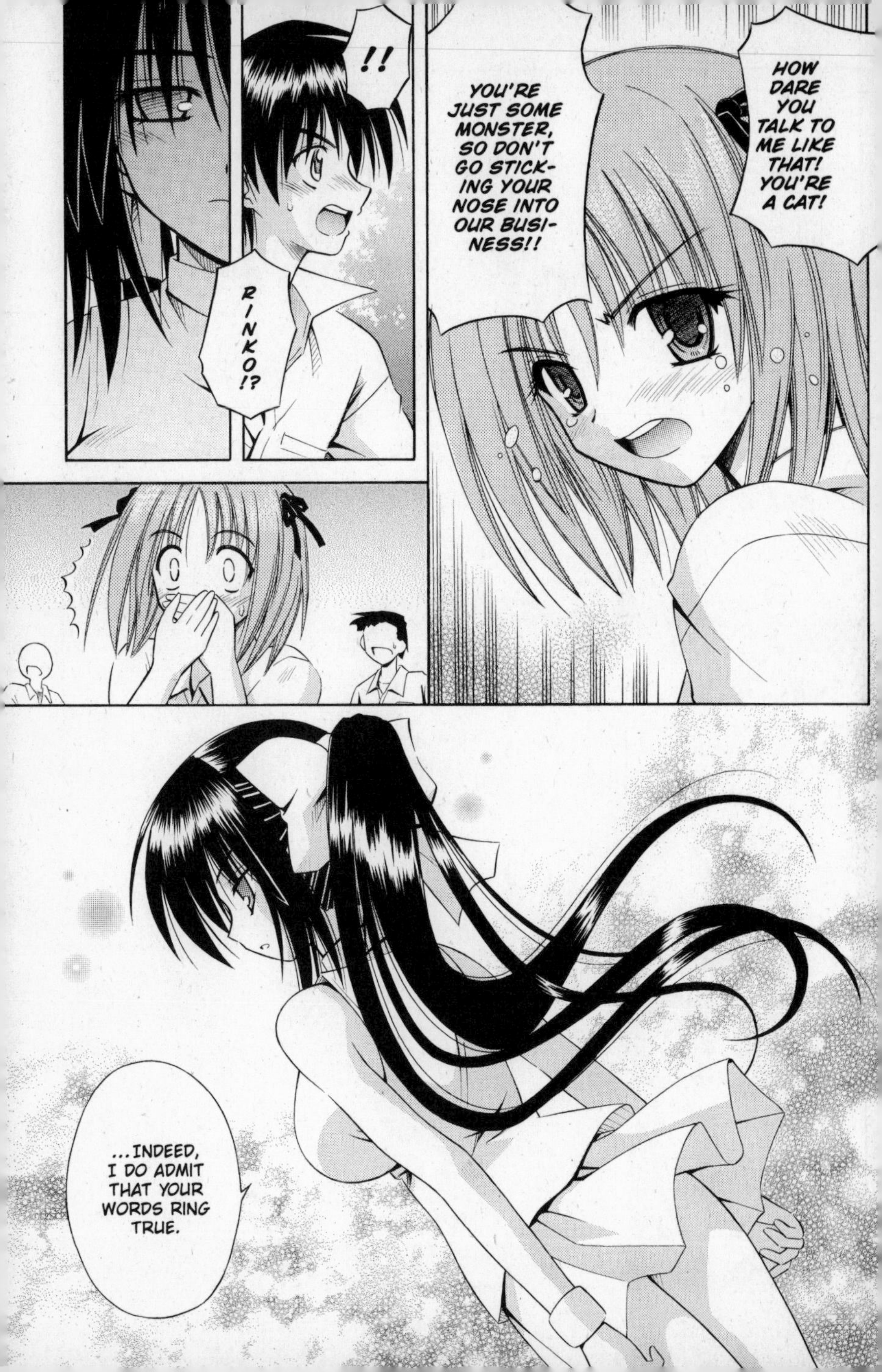
HOW DARE YOU TALK TO ME LIKE THAT! YOU'RE A CAT!
YOU'RE JUST SOME MONSTER, SO DON'T GO STICKING YOUR NOSE INTO OUR BUSINESS!!
!!
RINKO!?
...INDEED, I DO ADMIT THAT YOUR WORDS RING TRUE.

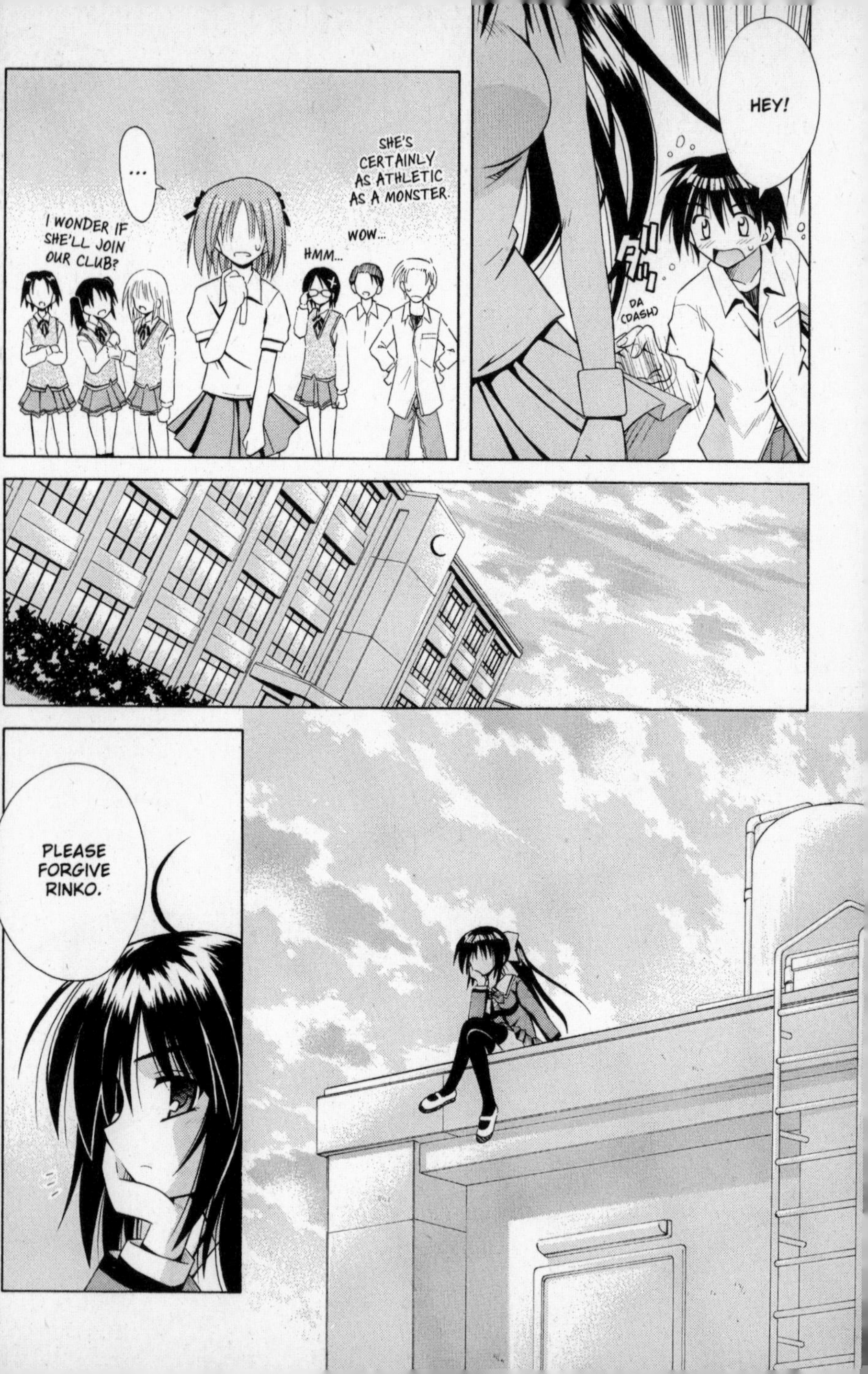
HEY!
DA (DASH)
SHE'S CERTAINLY AS ATHLETIC AS A MONSTER.
...
WOW...
HMM...
I WONDER IF SHE'LL JOIN OUR CLUB?
PLEASE FORGIVE RINKO.

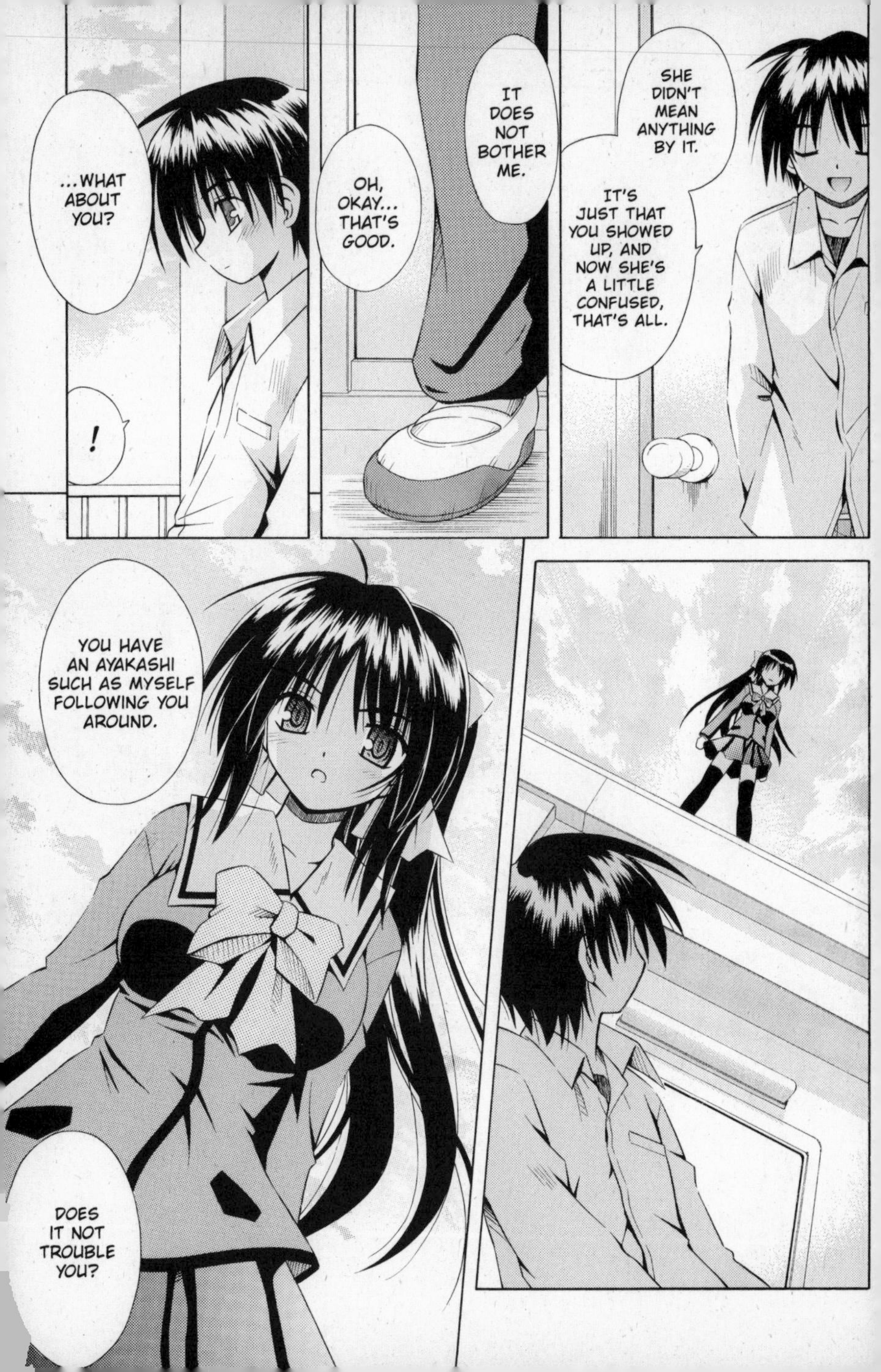
SHE DIDN'T MEAN ANYTHING BY IT.
IT'S JUST THAT YOU SHOWED UP, AND NOW SHE'S A LITTLE CONFUSED, THAT'S ALL.
IT DOES NOT BOTHER ME.
OH, OKAY... THAT'S GOOD.
...WHAT ABOUT YOU?
!
YOU HAVE AN AYAKASHI SUCH AS MYSELF FOLLOWING YOU AROUND.
DOES IT NOT TROUBLE YOU?

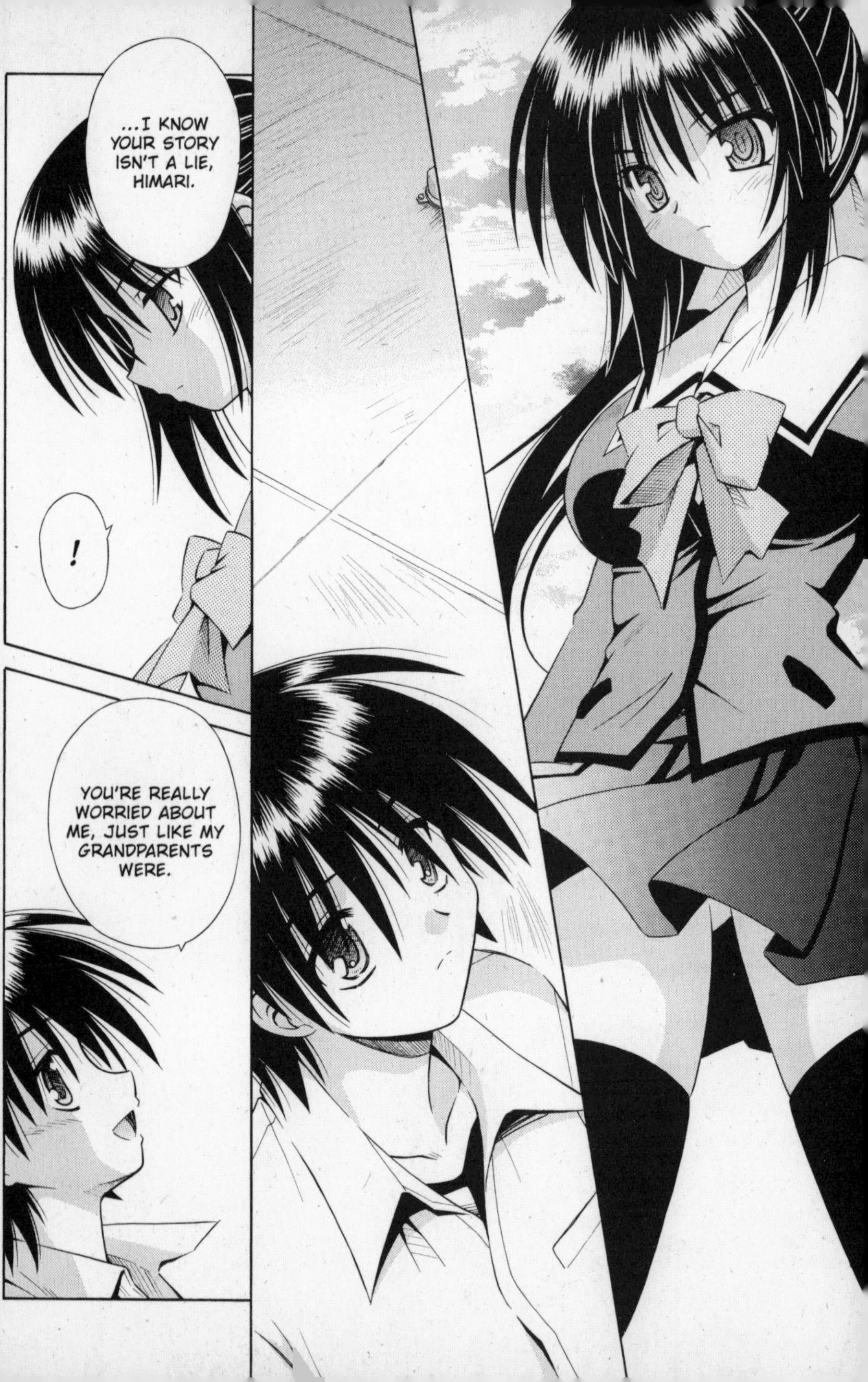
...I KNOW YOUR STORY ISN'T A LIE, HIMARI.
!
YOU'RE REALLY WORRIED ABOUT ME, JUST LIKE MY GRANDPARENTS WERE.

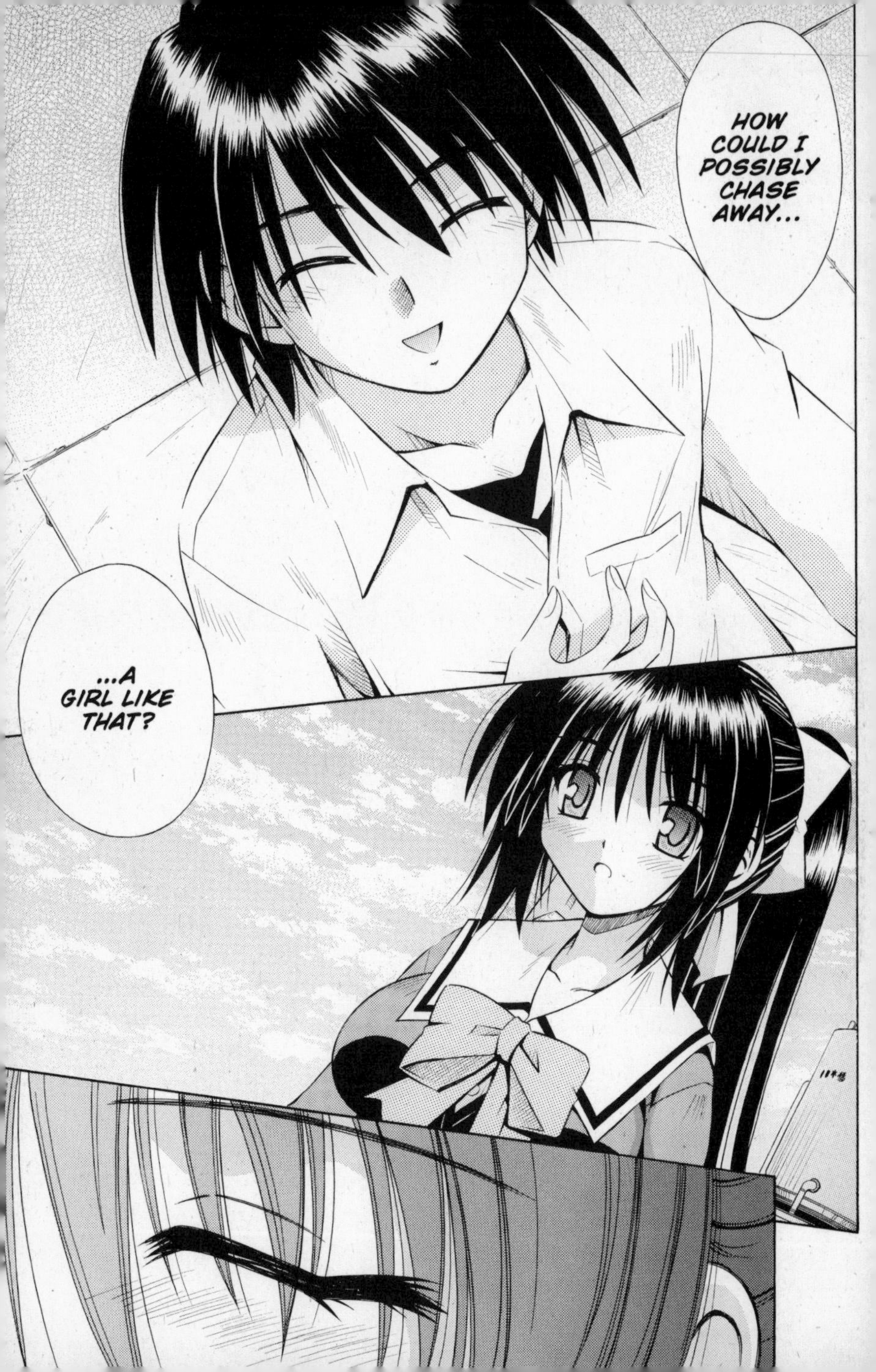
HOW COULD I POSSIBLY CHASE AWAY...
...A GIRL LIKE THAT?

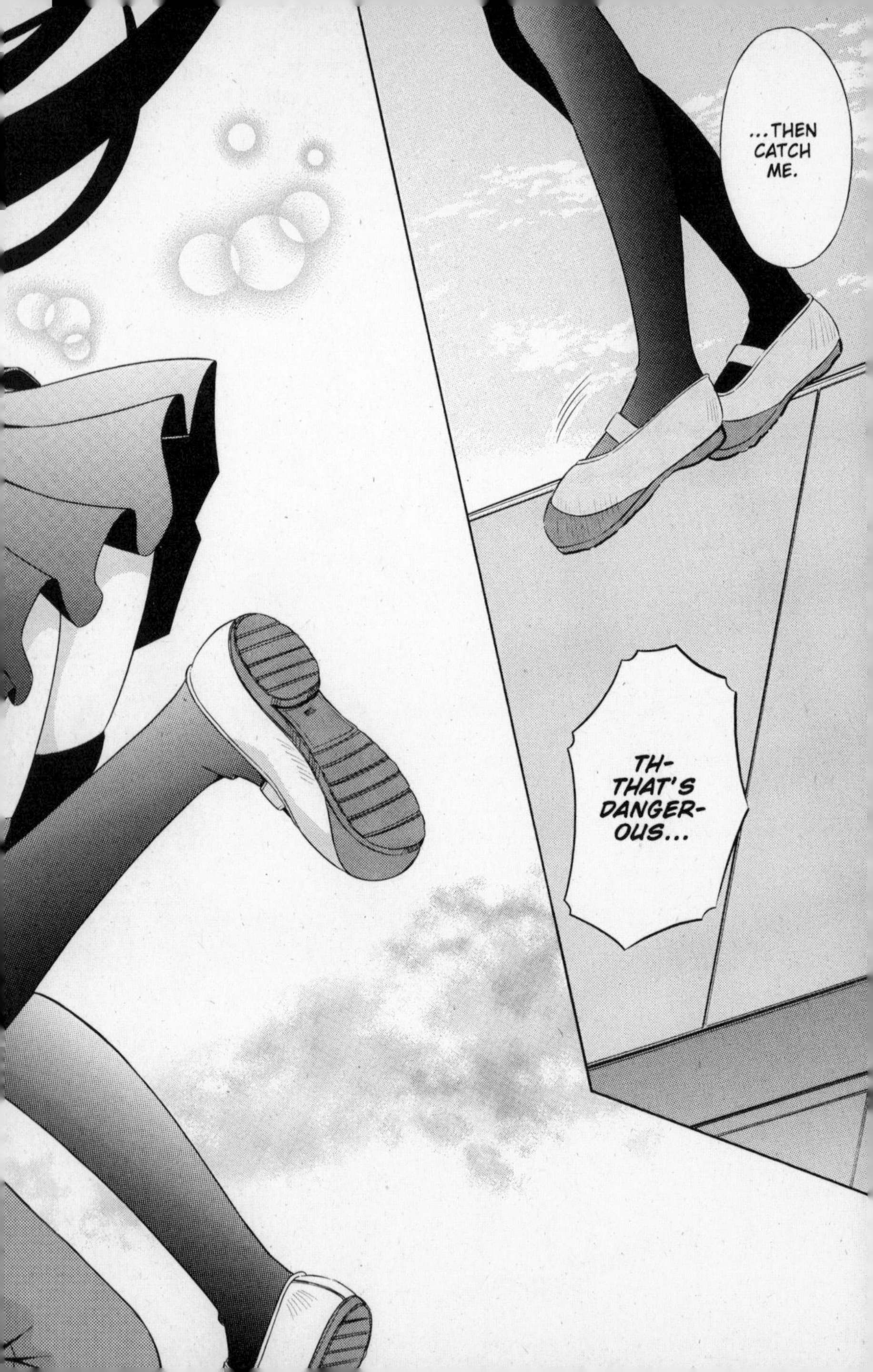
...THEN CATCH ME.
TH- THAT'S DANGER- OUS...

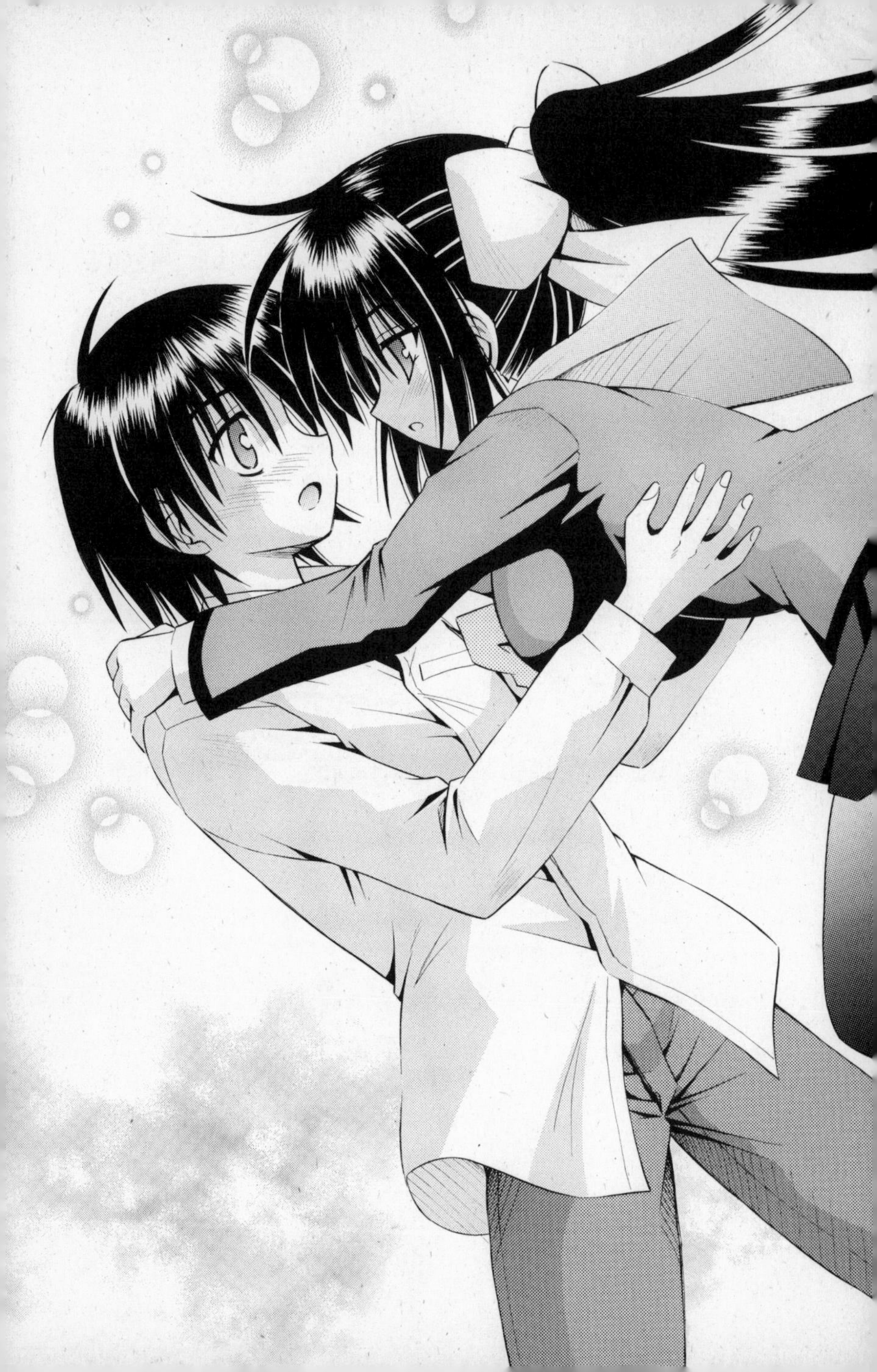

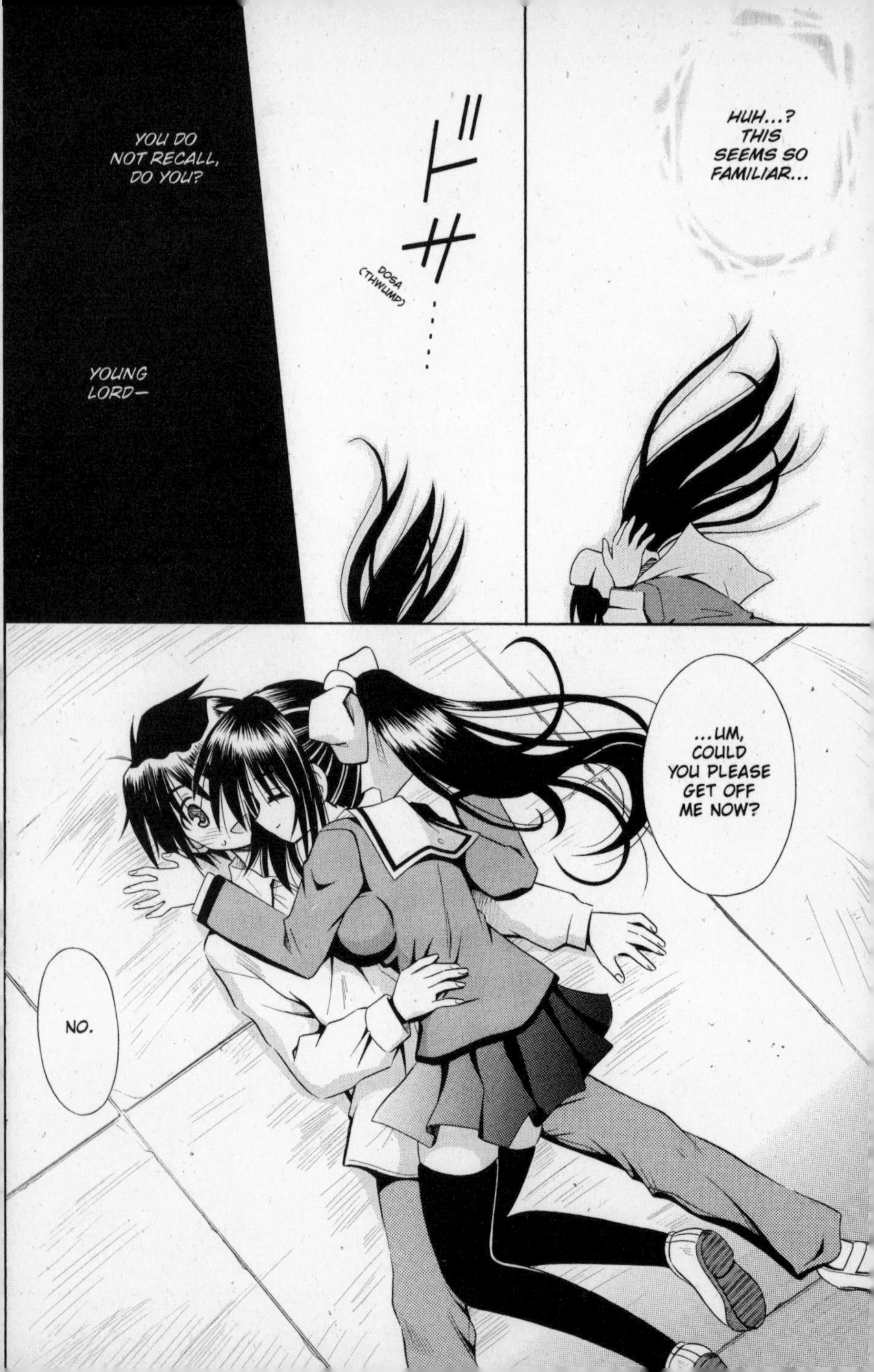
HUH...? THIS SEEMS SO FAMILIAR...
ドサ...
DOSA (THWUMP)
YOU DO NOT RECALL, DO YOU?
YOUNG LORD—
...UM, COULD YOU PLEASE GET OFF ME NOW?
NO.

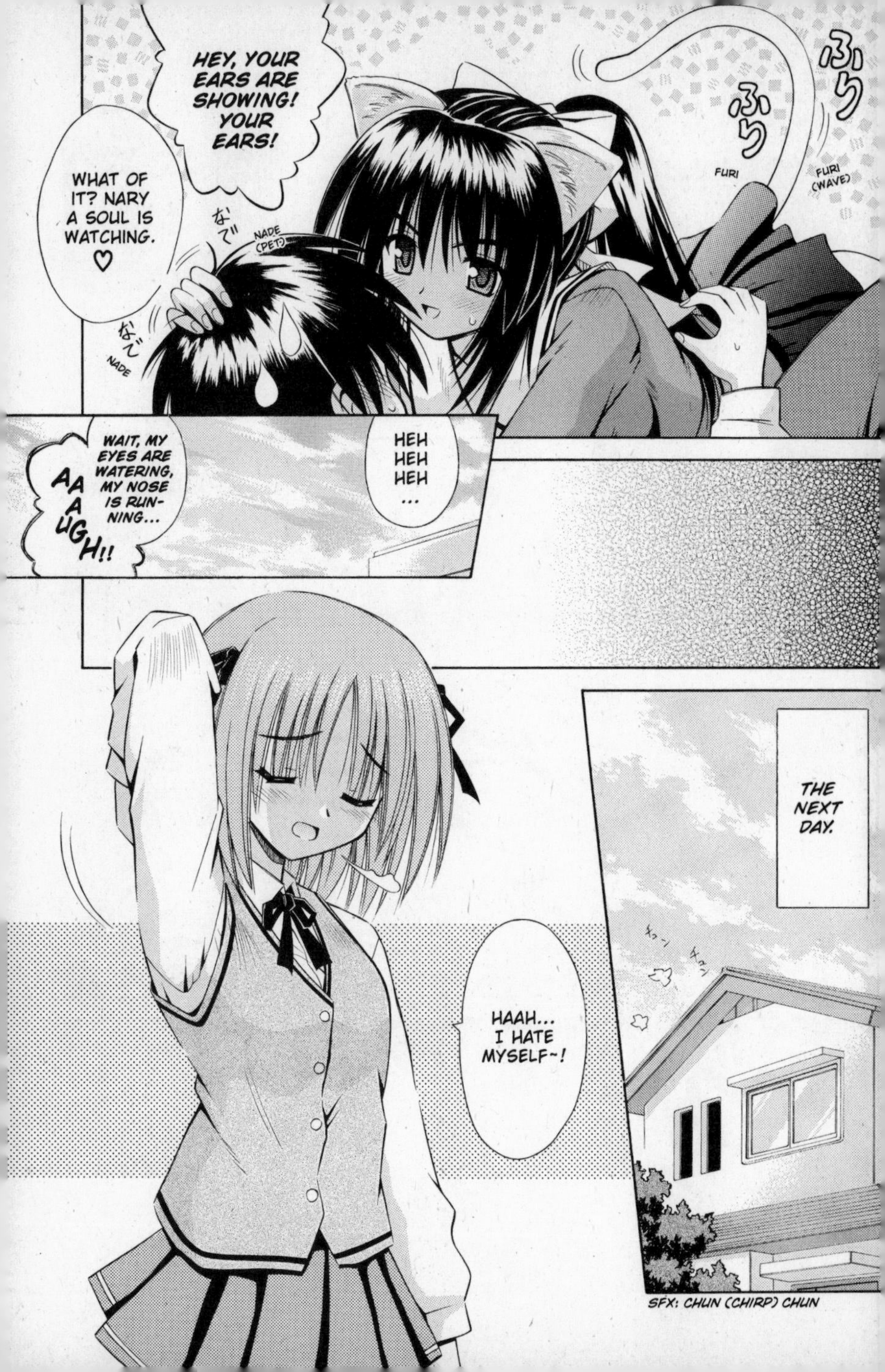
ふり
ふり
FURI (WAVE)
FURI
HEY, YOUR EARS ARE SHOWING! YOUR EARS!
WHAT OF IT? NARY A SOUL IS WATCHING. ♡
なで
NADE (PET)
なで
NADE
HEH HEH HEH ...
WAIT, MY EYES ARE WATERING, MY NOSE IS RUN-NING...
AAAUGH!!
THE NEXT DAY.
SFX: CHUN (CHIRP) CHUN
HAAH... I HATE MYSELF~!

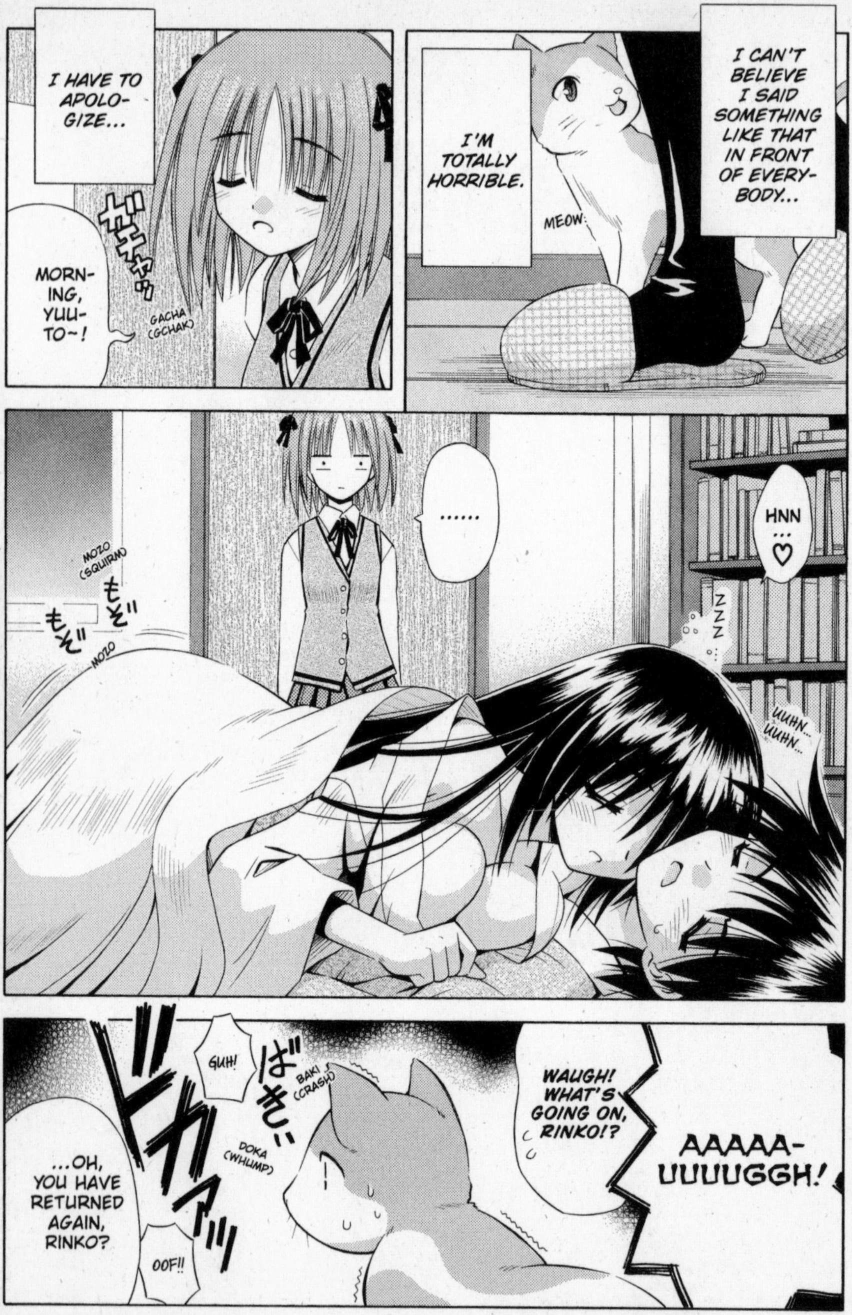
I CAN'T BELIEVE I SAID SOMETHING LIKE THAT IN FRONT OF EVERYBODY...
I'M TOTALLY HORRIBLE.
MEOW
I HAVE TO APOLOGIZE...
GACHA (GCHAK)
MORNING, YUUTO~!
HNN... ♡
ZZZ
UUHN... UUHN...
......
MOZO (SQUIRM)
MOZO
AAAAA-UUUUGGH!
WAUGH! WHAT'S GOING ON, RINKO!?
BAKI (CRASH)
GUH!
DOKA (WHUMP)
OOF!!
...OH, YOU HAVE RETURNED AGAIN, RINKO?

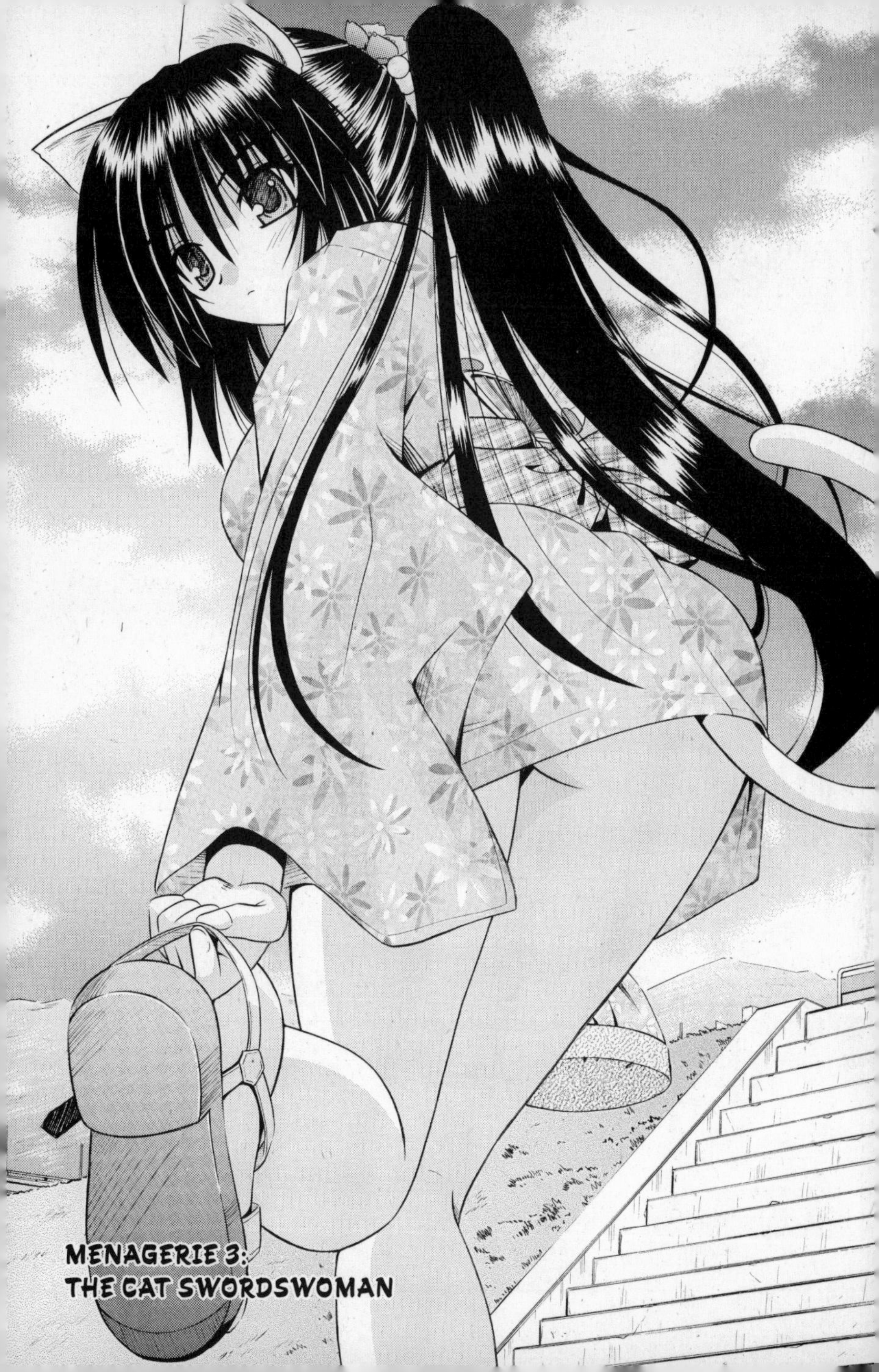
MENAGERIE 3:
THE CAT SWORDSWOMAN

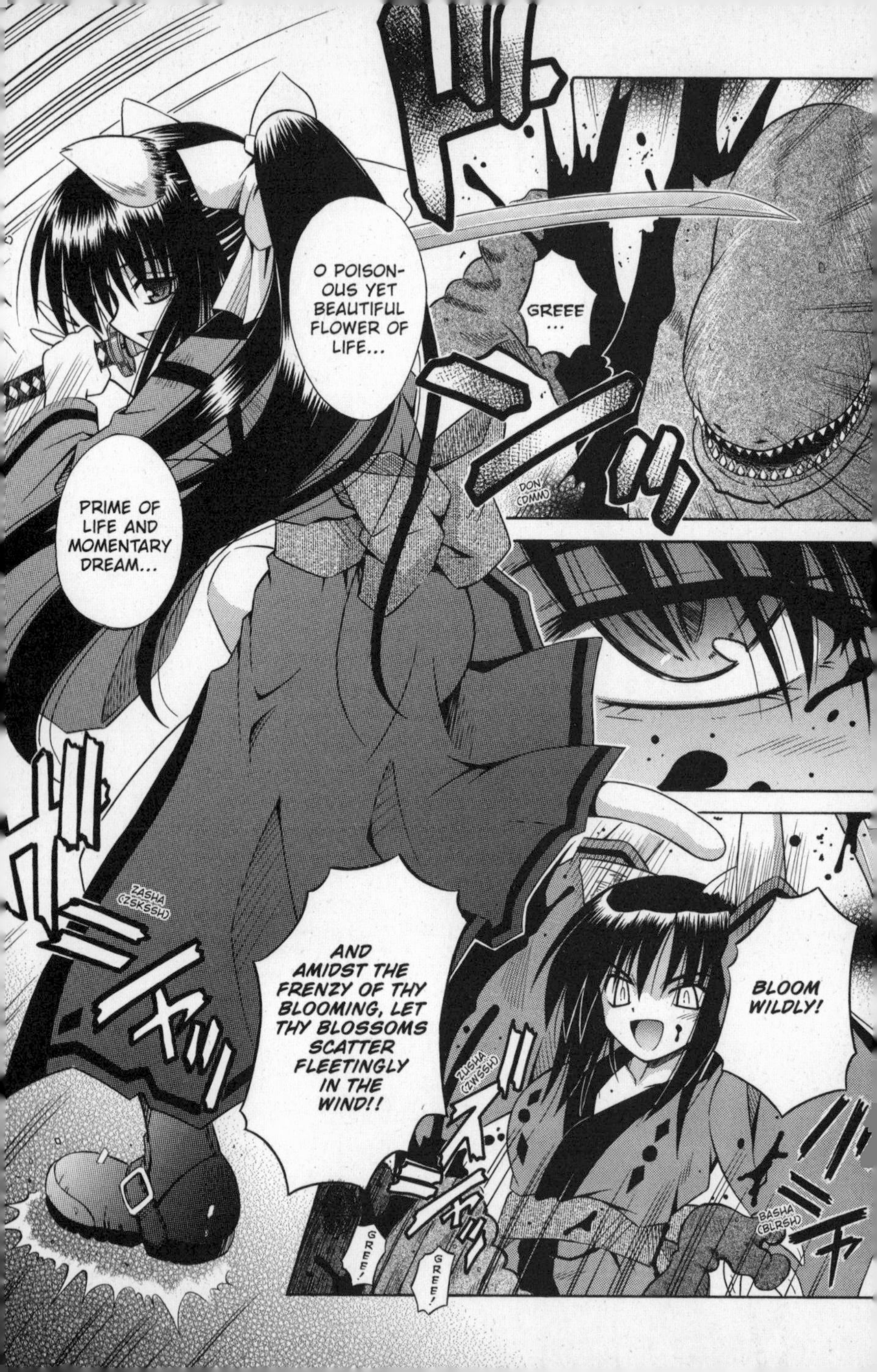

GREEE ...
DON (DMN)
O POISONOUS YET BEAUTIFUL FLOWER OF LIFE...
PRIME OF LIFE AND MOMENTARY DREAM...
ZASHA (ZSKSSH)
AND AMIDST THE FRENZY OF THY BLOOMING, LET THY BLOSSOMS SCATTER FLEETINGLY IN THE WIND!!
BLOOM WILDLY!
ZUSHA (ZWSSH)
BASHA (BLRSH)
GREE!
GREE!

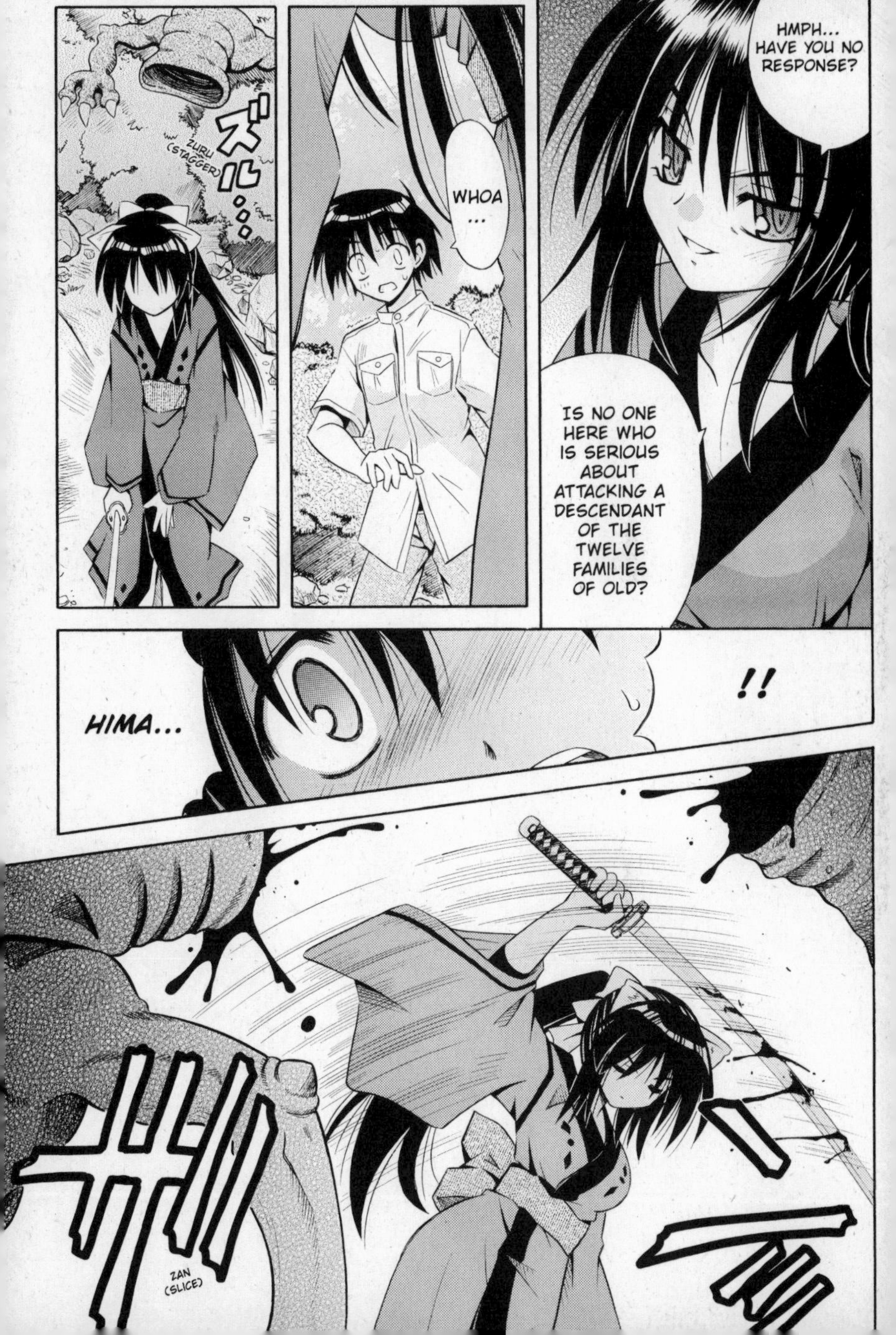
HMPH... HAVE YOU NO RESPONSE?
IS NO ONE HERE WHO IS SERIOUS ABOUT ATTACKING A DESCENDANT OF THE TWELVE FAMILIES OF OLD?
WHOA ...
ズル
ZURU (STAGGER)
!!
HIMA...
ZAN (SLICE)

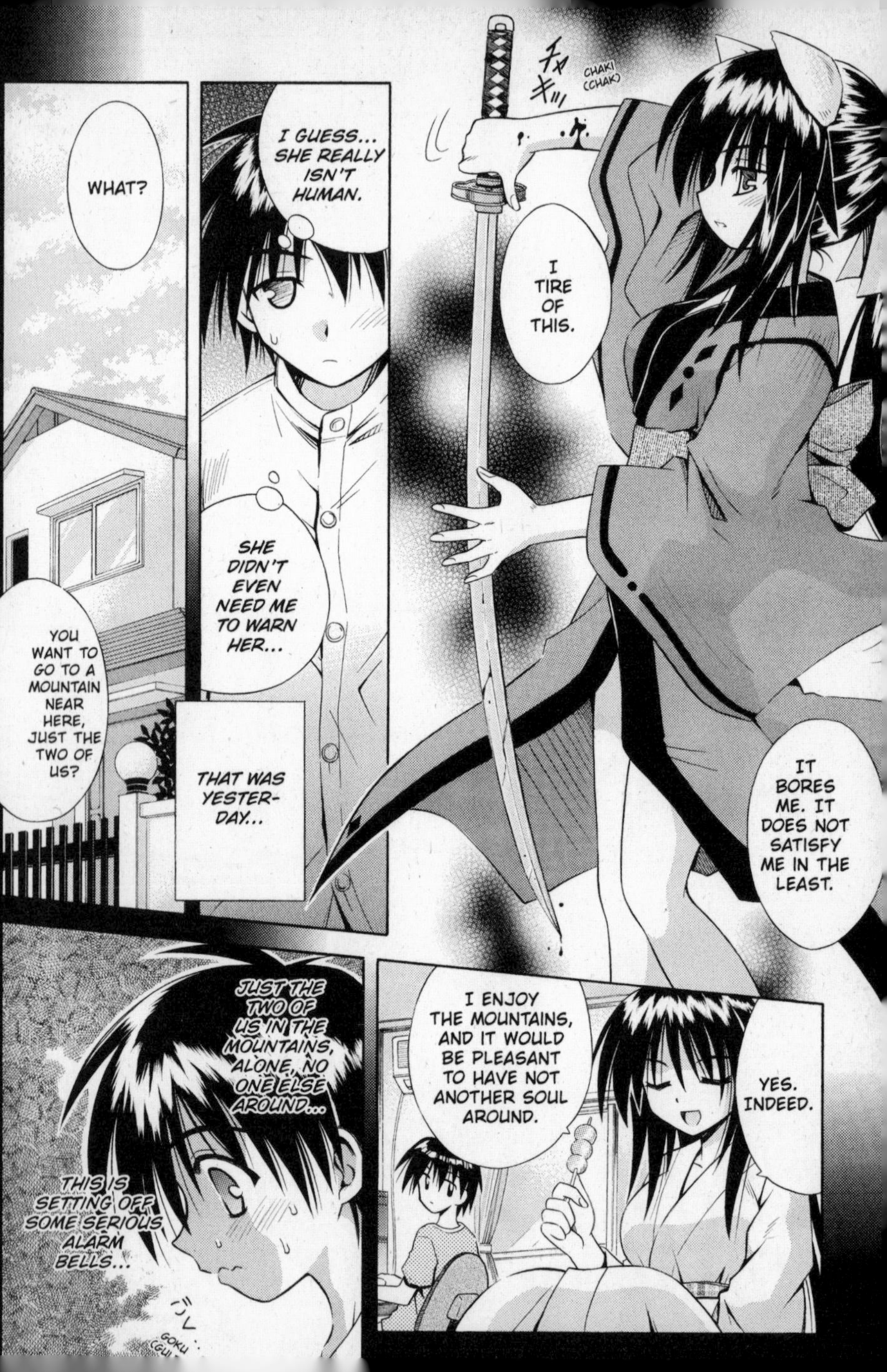
CHAKI (CHAK)
I TIRE OF THIS.
IT BORES ME. IT DOES NOT SATISFY ME IN THE LEAST.
I GUESS... SHE REALLY ISN'T HUMAN.
SHE DIDN'T EVEN NEED ME TO WARN HER...
THAT WAS YESTERDAY...
WHAT?
YOU WANT TO GO TO A MOUNTAIN NEAR HERE, JUST THE TWO OF US?
YES. INDEED.
I ENJOY THE MOUNTAINS, AND IT WOULD BE PLEASANT TO HAVE NOT ANOTHER SOUL AROUND.
JUST THE TWO OF US IN THE MOUNTAINS, ALONE, NO ONE ELSE AROUND...
THIS IS SETTING OFF SOME SERIOUS ALARM BELLS...
GOKU (GULP)

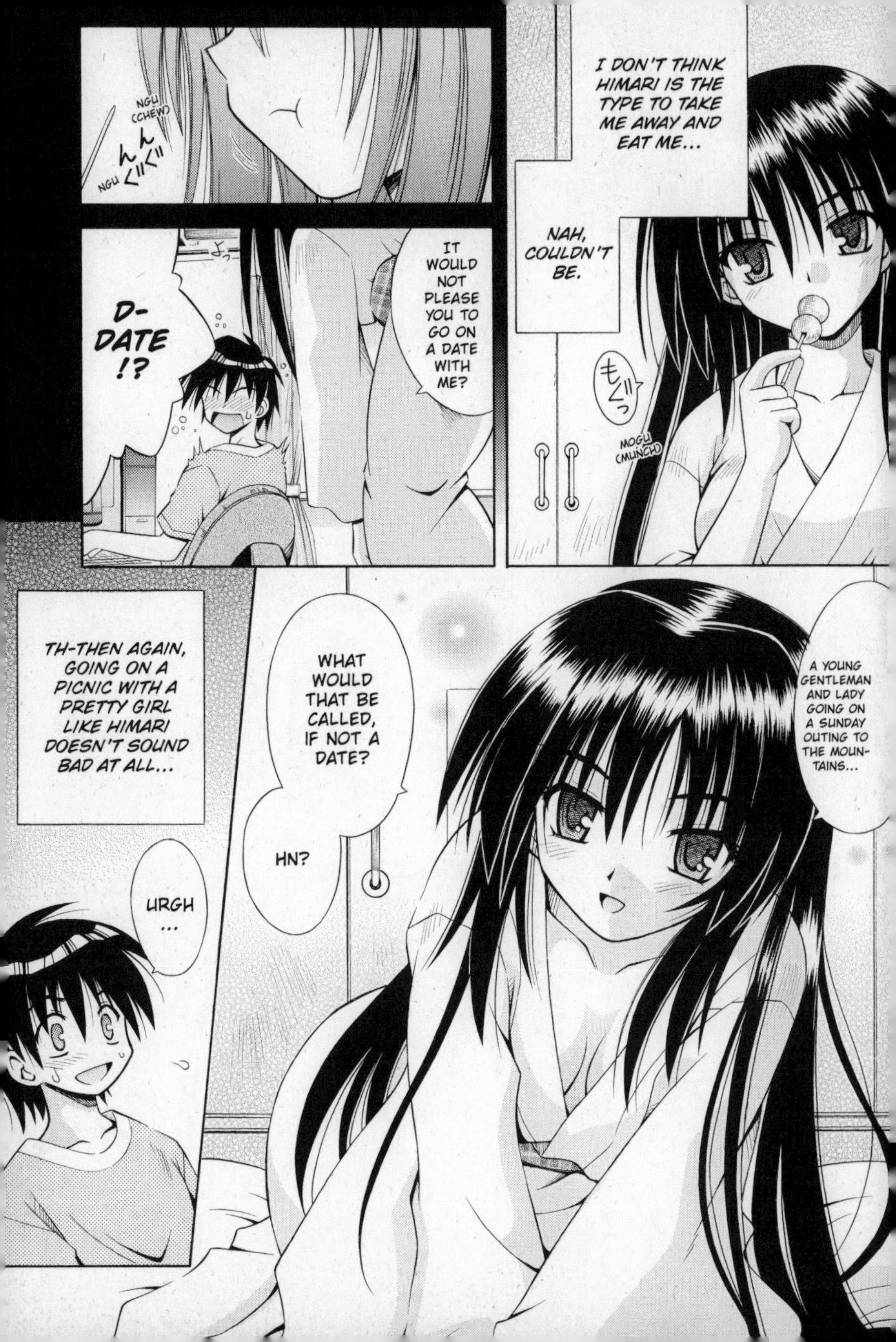
I DON'T THINK HIMARI IS THE TYPE TO TAKE ME AWAY AND EAT ME...
NAH, COULDN'T BE.
MOGU (MUNCH)
NGU (CHEW)
NGU
IT WOULD NOT PLEASE YOU TO GO ON A DATE WITH ME?
D-DATE!?
A YOUNG GENTLEMAN AND LADY GOING ON A SUNDAY OUTING TO THE MOUN-TAINS...
WHAT WOULD THAT BE CALLED, IF NOT A DATE?
HN?
TH-THEN AGAIN, GOING ON A PICNIC WITH A PRETTY GIRL LIKE HIMARI DOESN'T SOUND BAD AT ALL...
URGH...

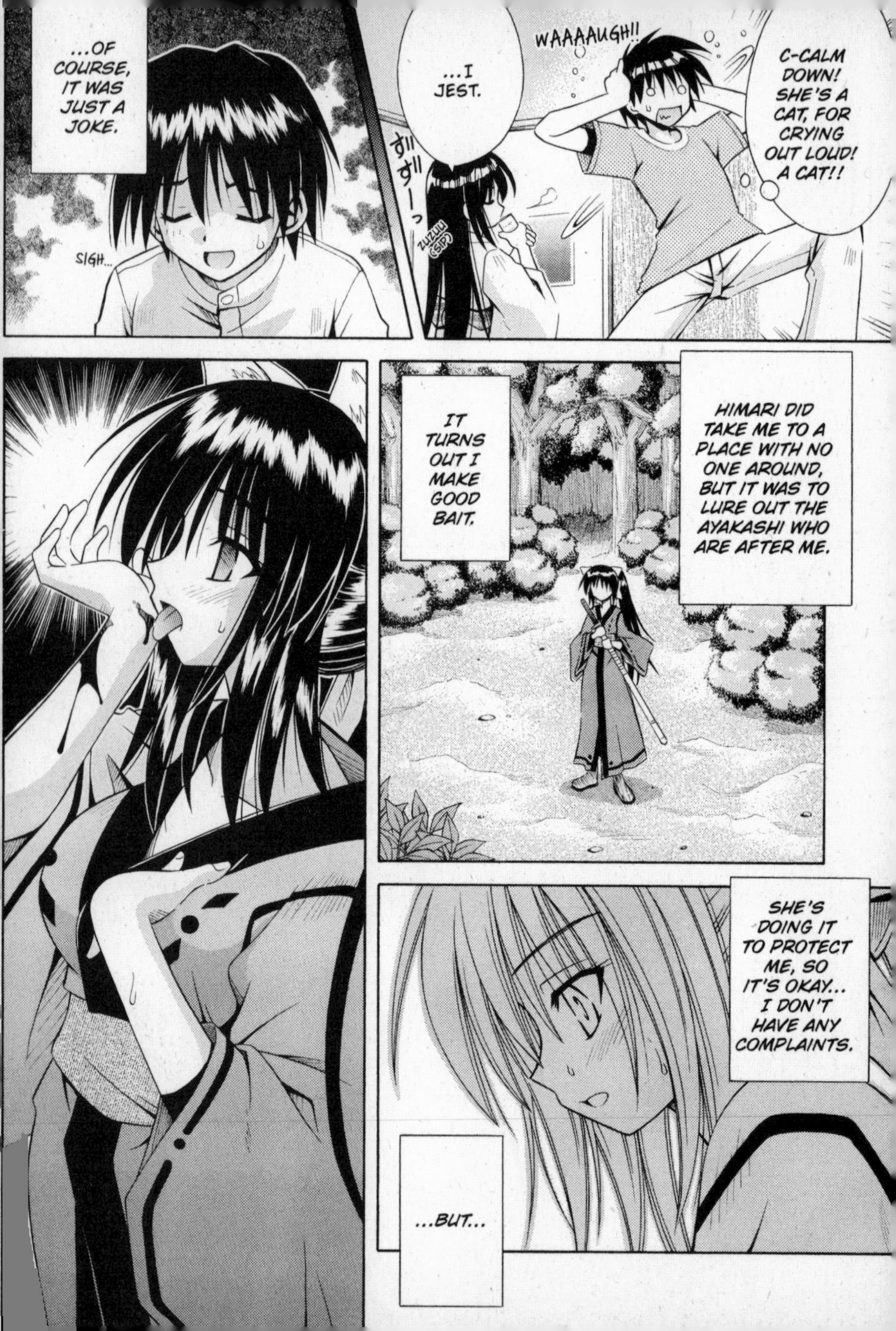
C-CALM DOWN! SHE'S A CAT, FOR CRYING OUT LOUD! A CAT!!
WAAAAUGH!!
...I JEST.
ずずーっ
ZUZUU (SIP)
...OF COURSE, IT WAS JUST A JOKE.
SIGH...
HIMARI DID TAKE ME TO A PLACE WITH NO ONE AROUND, BUT IT WAS TO LURE OUT THE AYAKASHI WHO ARE AFTER ME.
IT TURNS OUT I MAKE GOOD BAIT.
SHE'S DOING IT TO PROTECT ME, SO IT'S OKAY... I DON'T HAVE ANY COMPLAINTS.
...BUT...

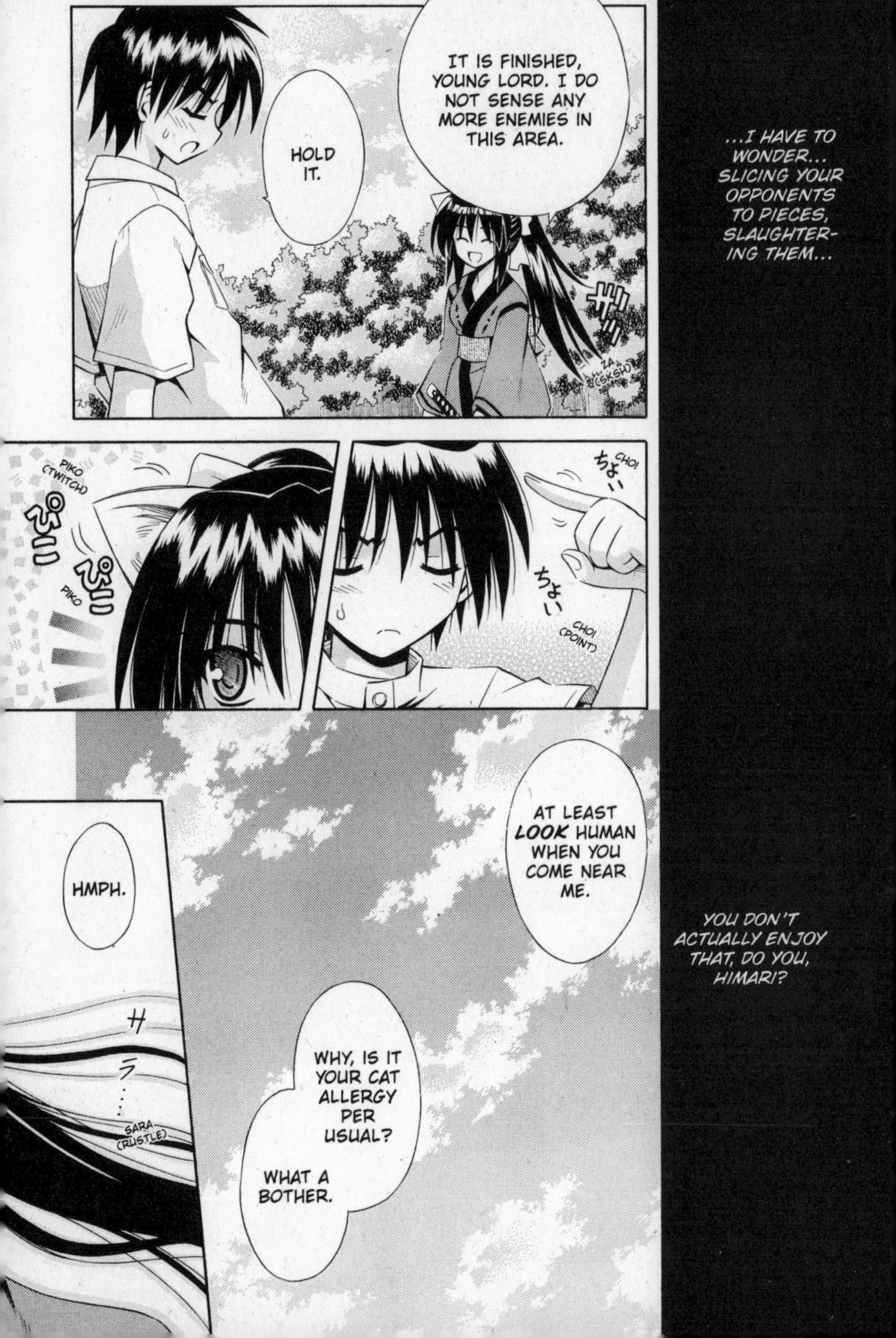
...I HAVE TO WONDER... SLICING YOUR OPPONENTS TO PIECES, SLAUGHTERING THEM...
IT IS FINISHED, YOUNG LORD. I DO NOT SENSE ANY MORE ENEMIES IN THIS AREA.
HOLD IT.
ZA (SKSH)
CHOI (POINT)
CHOI
PIKO (TWITCH)
PIKO
YOU DON'T ACTUALLY ENJOY THAT, DO YOU, HIMARI?
AT LEAST LOOK HUMAN WHEN YOU COME NEAR ME.
HMPH.
WHY, IS IT YOUR CAT ALLERGY PER USUAL?
WHAT A BOTHER.
SARA (RUSTLE)

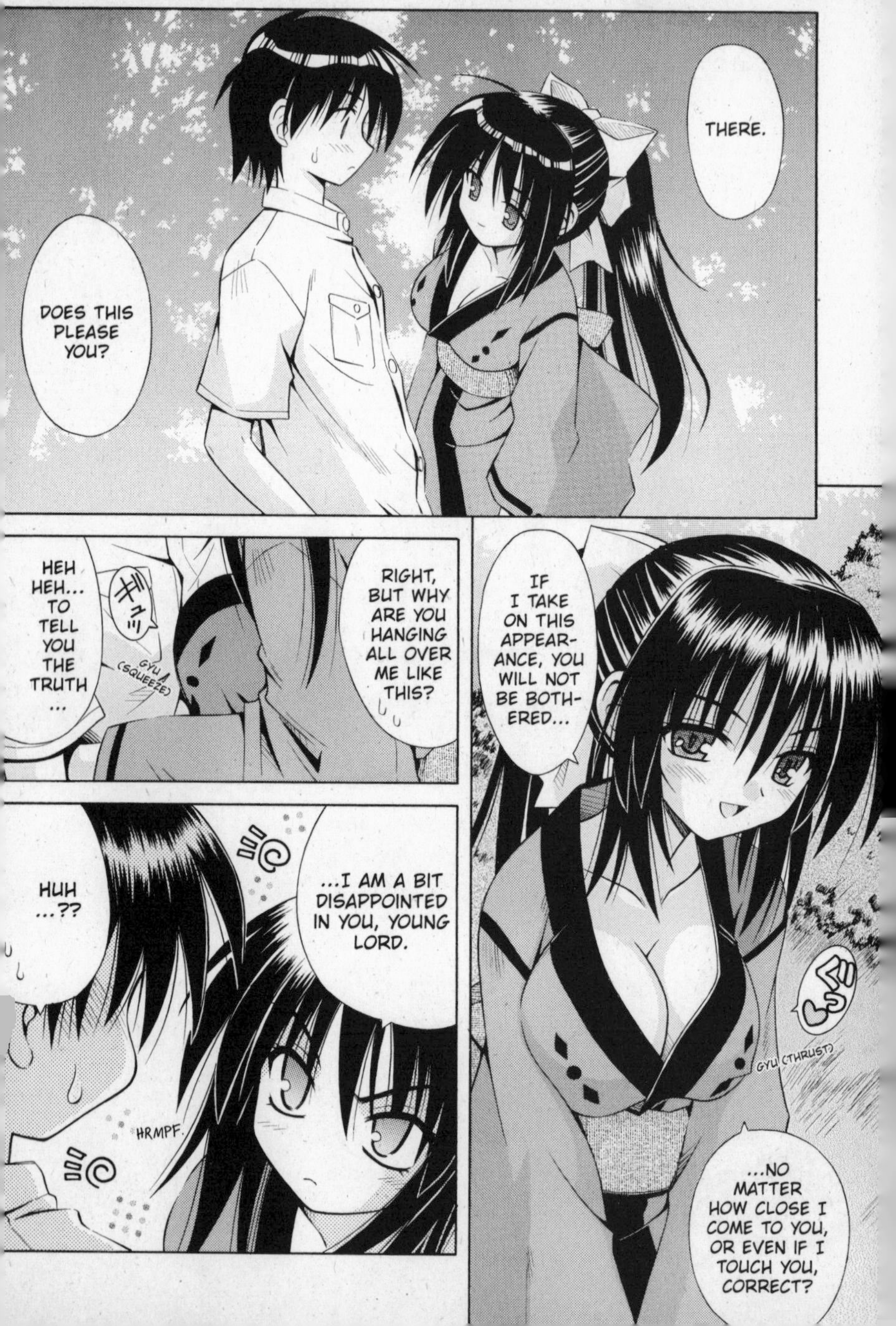
THERE.
DOES THIS PLEASE YOU?
IF I TAKE ON THIS APPEAR-ANCE, YOU WILL NOT BE BOTH-ERED...
GYU (THRUST)
...NO MATTER HOW CLOSE I COME TO YOU, OR EVEN IF I TOUCH YOU, CORRECT?
RIGHT, BUT WHY ARE YOU HANGING ALL OVER ME LIKE THIS?
GYU (SQUEEZE)
HEH HEH... TO TELL YOU THE TRUTH ...
...I AM A BIT DISAPPOINTED IN YOU, YOUNG LORD.
HUH ...??
HRMPF.

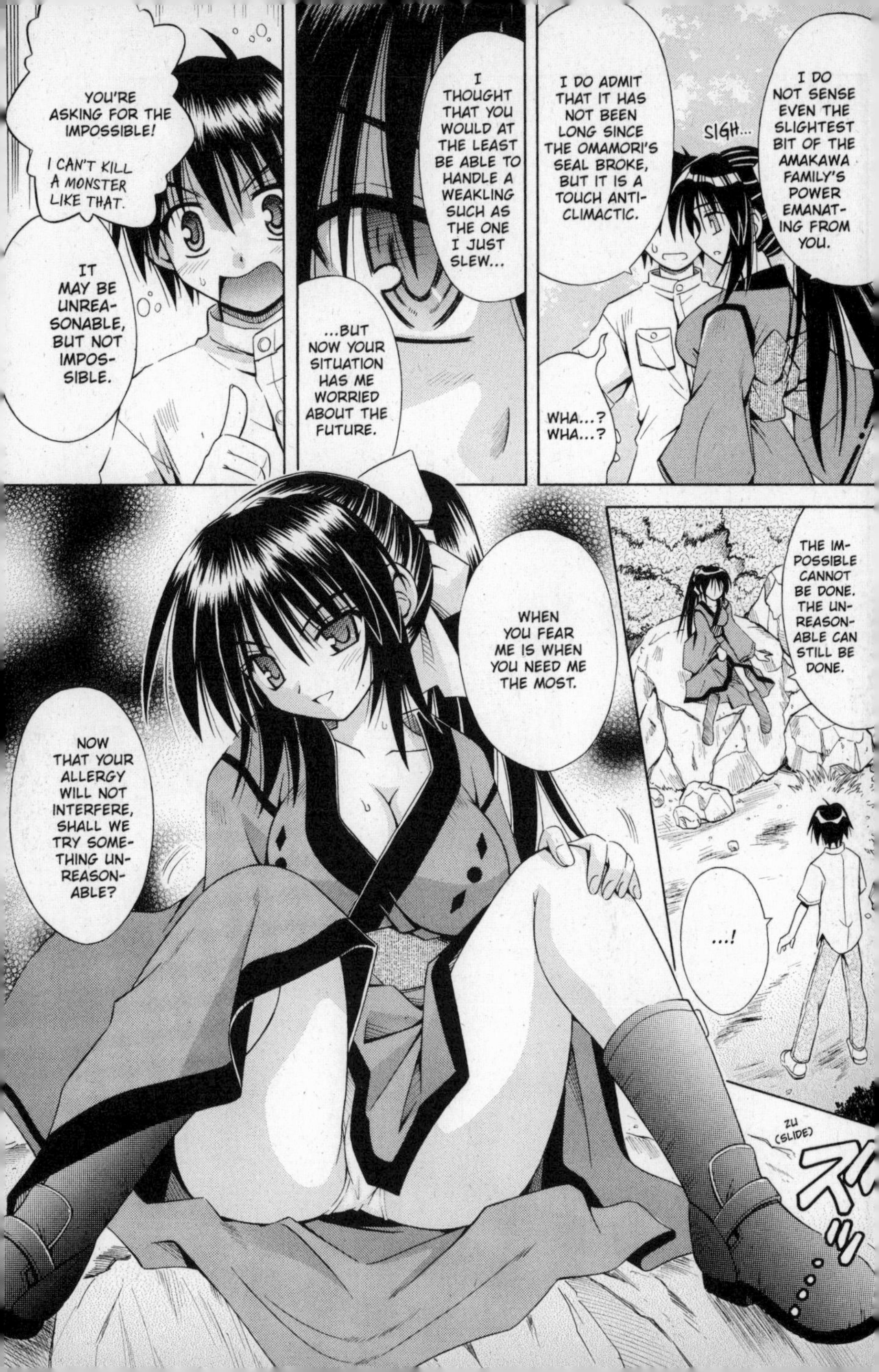
I DO NOT SENSE EVEN THE SLIGHTEST BIT OF THE AMAKAWA FAMILY'S POWER EMANATING FROM YOU.
SIGH...
I DO ADMIT THAT IT HAS NOT BEEN LONG SINCE THE OMAMORI'S SEAL BROKE, BUT IT IS A TOUCH ANTI-CLIMACTIC.
WHA...? WHA...?
I THOUGHT THAT YOU WOULD AT THE LEAST BE ABLE TO HANDLE A WEAKLING SUCH AS THE ONE I JUST SLEW...
...BUT NOW YOUR SITUATION HAS ME WORRIED ABOUT THE FUTURE.
YOU'RE ASKING FOR THE IMPOSSIBLE!
I CAN'T KILL A MONSTER LIKE THAT.
IT MAY BE UNREASONABLE, BUT NOT IMPOSSIBLE.
THE IMPOSSIBLE CANNOT BE DONE. THE UNREASONABLE CAN STILL BE DONE.
...!
ZU (SLIDE)
WHEN YOU FEAR ME IS WHEN YOU NEED ME THE MOST.
NOW THAT YOUR ALLERGY WILL NOT INTERFERE, SHALL WE TRY SOMETHING UNREASONABLE?

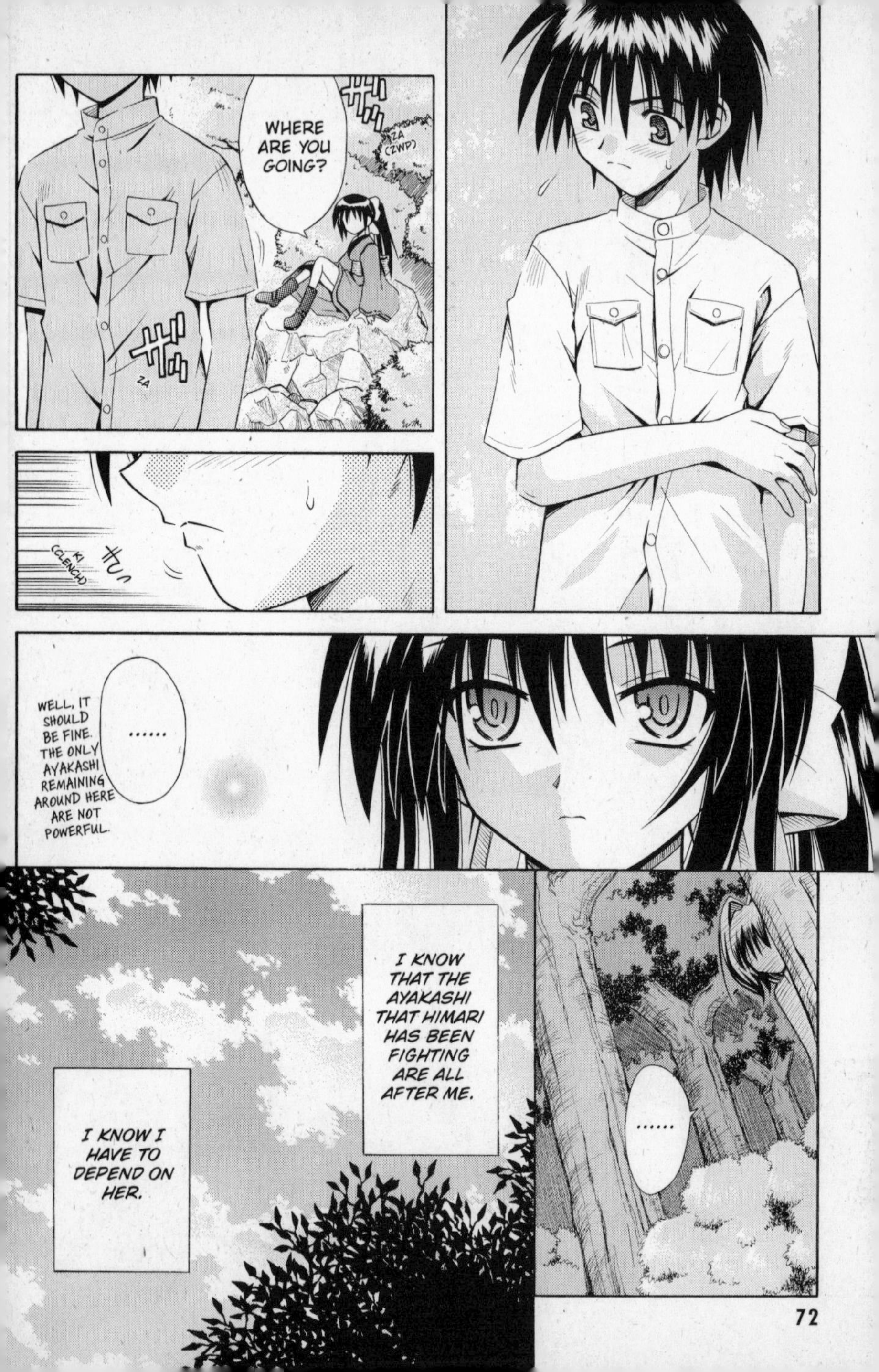
ZA (ZWP)
WHERE ARE YOU GOING?
ZA
KI (CLENCH)
......
WELL, IT SHOULD BE FINE. THE ONLY AYAKASHI REMAINING AROUND HERE ARE NOT POWERFUL.
......
I KNOW THAT THE AYAKASHI THAT HIMARI HAS BEEN FIGHTING ARE ALL AFTER ME.
I KNOW I HAVE TO DEPEND ON HER.

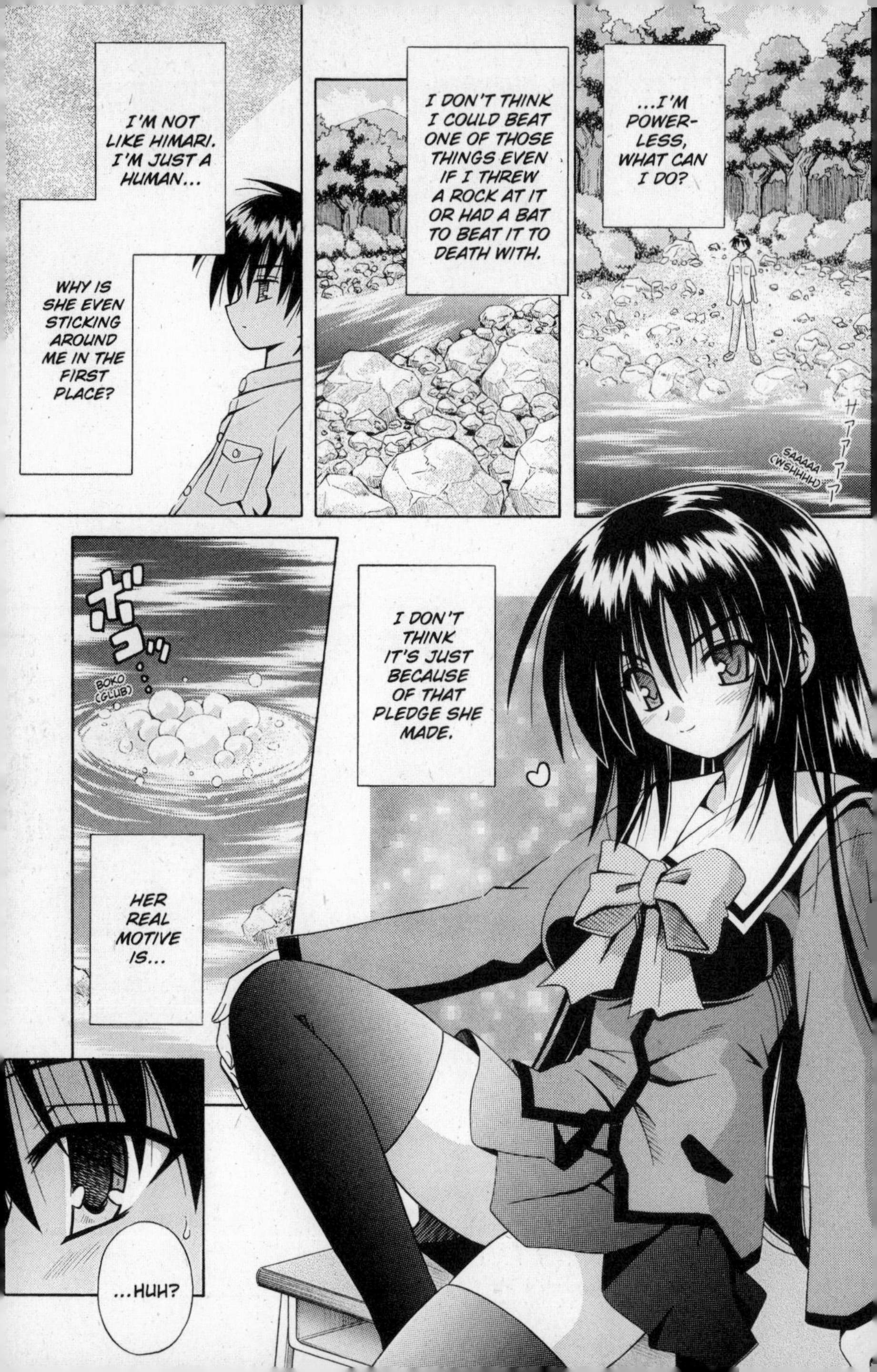
...I'M POWERLESS, WHAT CAN I DO?
SAAAAA (WSHHHH)
I DON'T THINK I COULD BEAT ONE OF THOSE THINGS EVEN IF I THREW A ROCK AT IT OR HAD A BAT TO BEAT IT TO DEATH WITH.
I'M NOT LIKE HIMARI. I'M JUST A HUMAN...
WHY IS SHE EVEN STICKING AROUND ME IN THE FIRST PLACE?
I DON'T THINK IT'S JUST BECAUSE OF THAT PLEDGE SHE MADE.
BOKO (GLUB)
HER REAL MOTIVE IS...
...HUH?

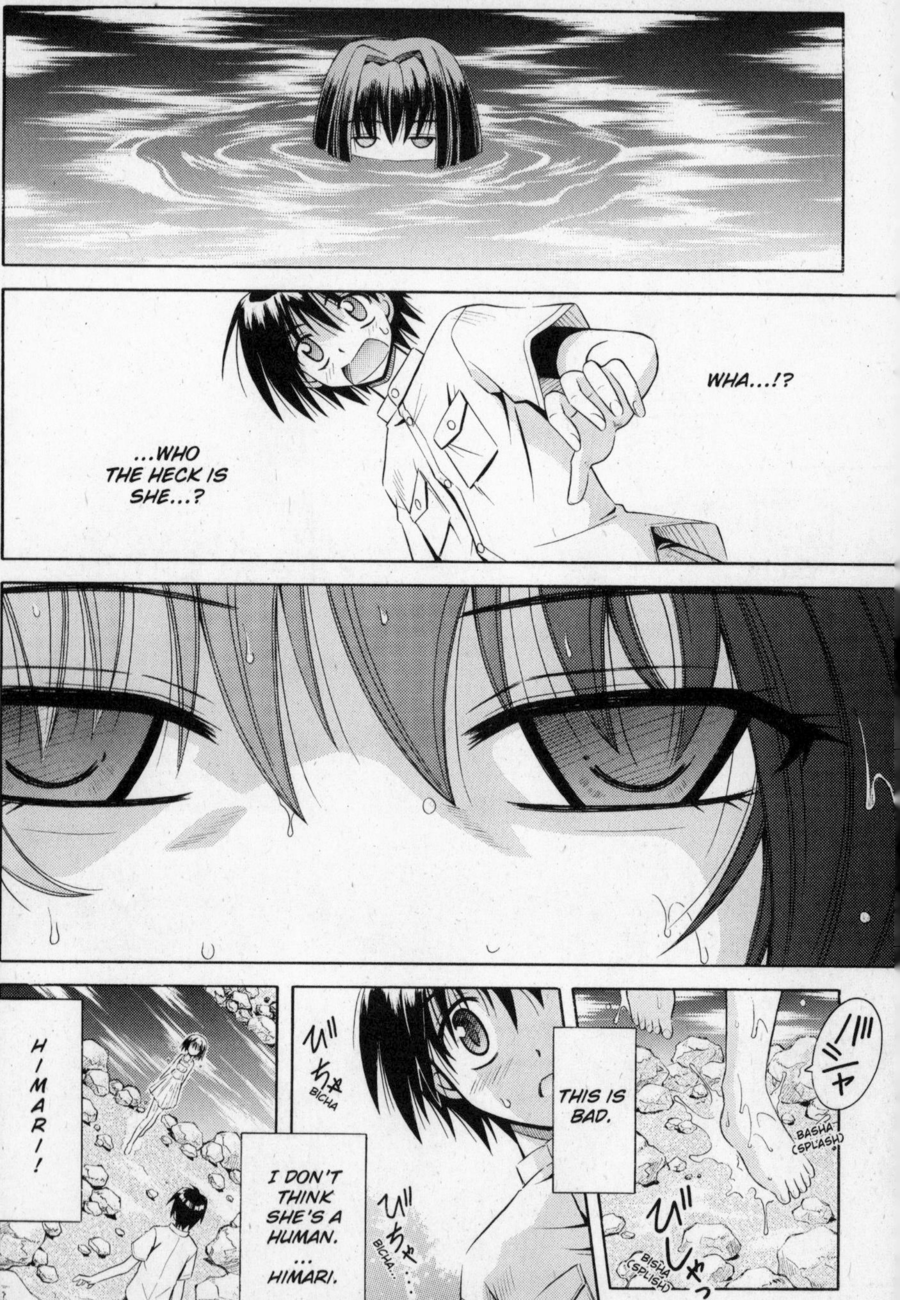

WHA...!?
...WHO THE HECK IS SHE...?
バシャ
BASHA (SPLASH)
びしゃっ
BISHA (SPLISH)
THIS IS BAD.
びちゃ
BICHA
I DON'T THINK SHE'S A HUMAN. ... HIMARI.
びちゃ
BICHA...
HIMARI!

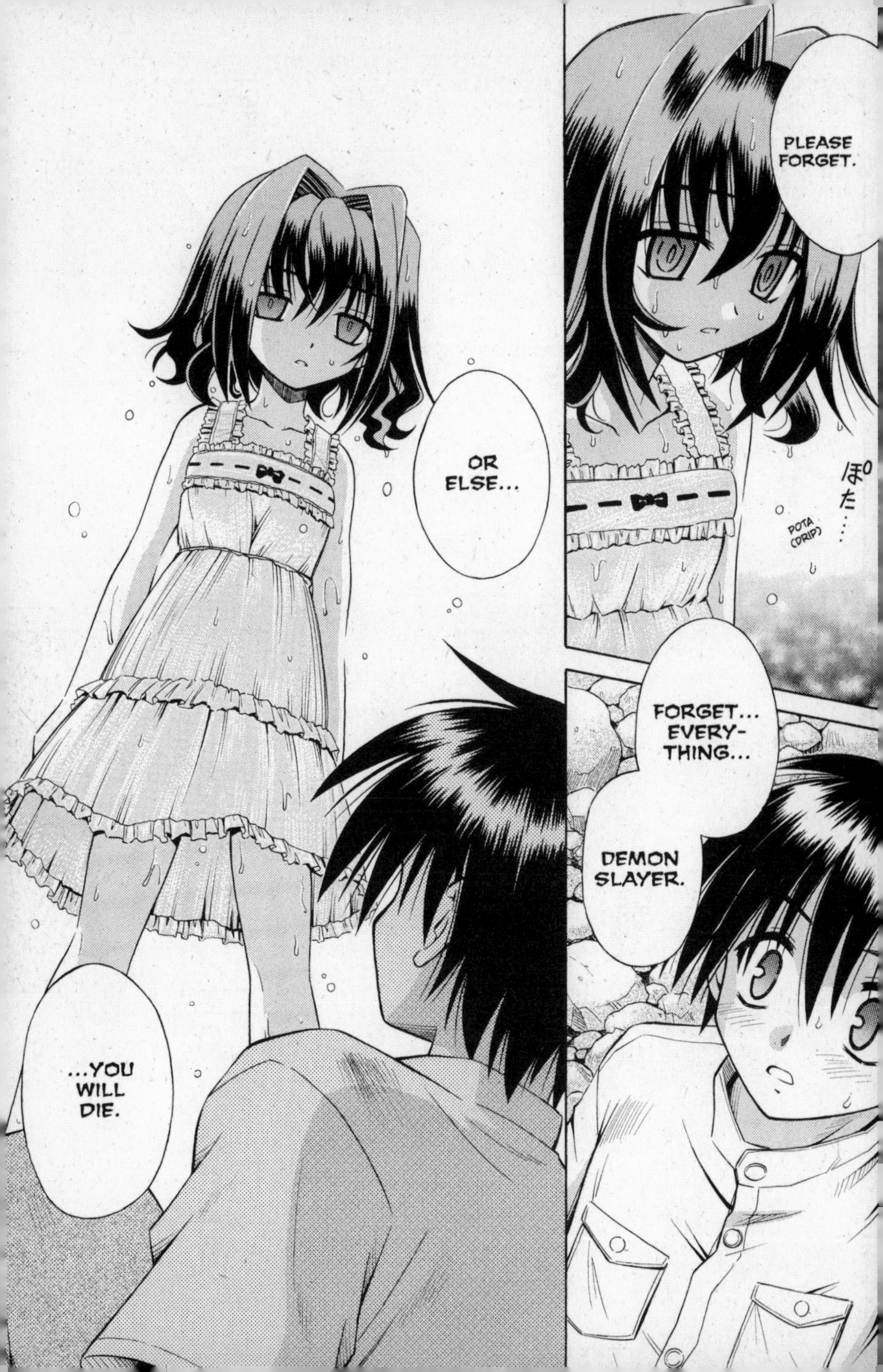
PLEASE FORGET.
ぽた…
POTA (DRIP)
FORGET... EVERY-THING...
DEMON SLAYER.
OR ELSE...
...YOU WILL DIE.

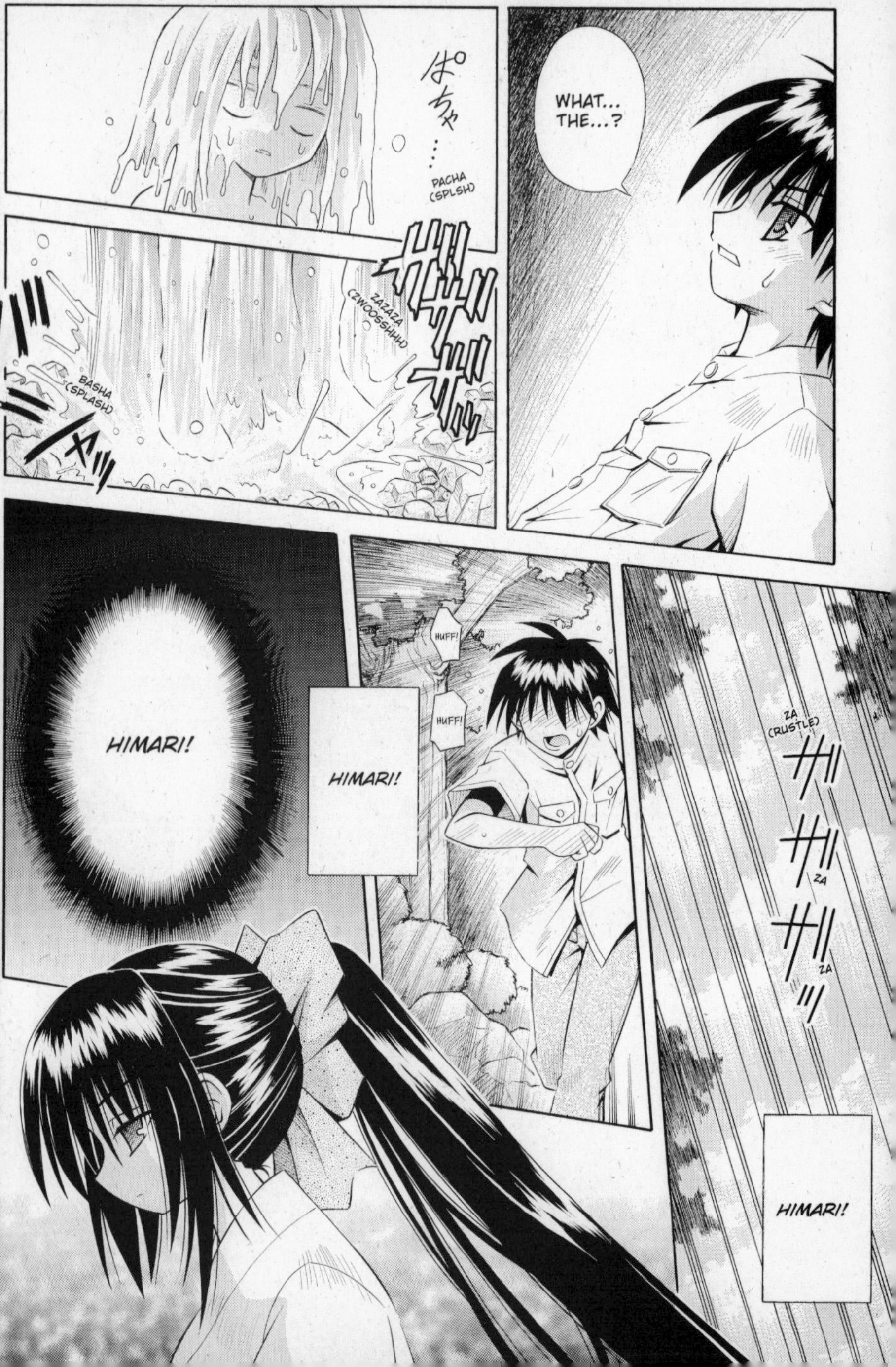
WHAT... THE...?
ぱちゃ…
PACHA (SPLSH)
ZAZAZA (ZWOOSSHHH)
BASHA (SPLASH)
ZA (RUSTLE)
ZA
ZA
HIMARI!
HUFF!
HUFF!
HIMARI!
HIMARI!

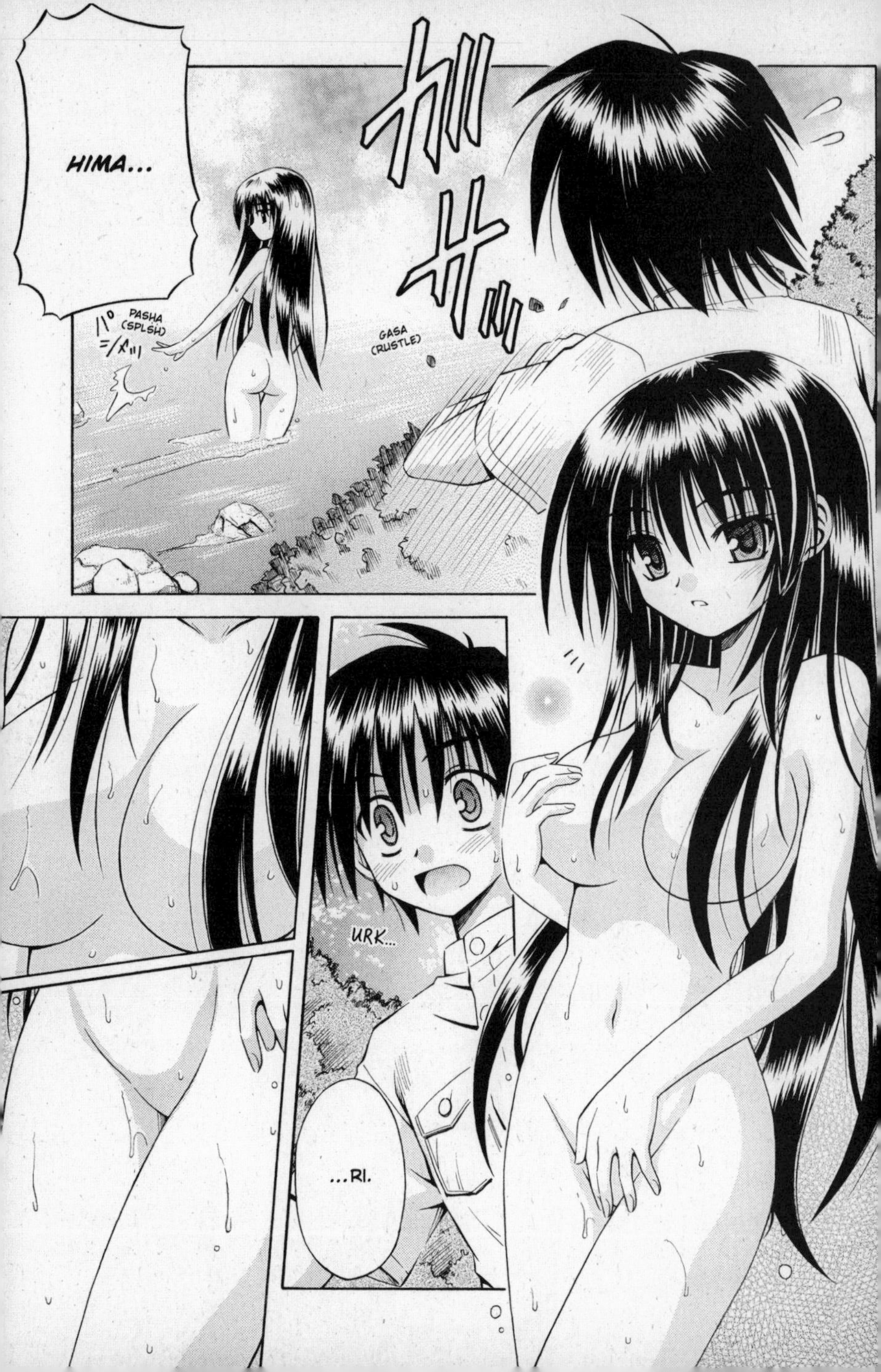
ガサッ
GASA (RUSTLE)
HIMA...
パシャッ
PASHA (SPLSH)
URK...
...RI.

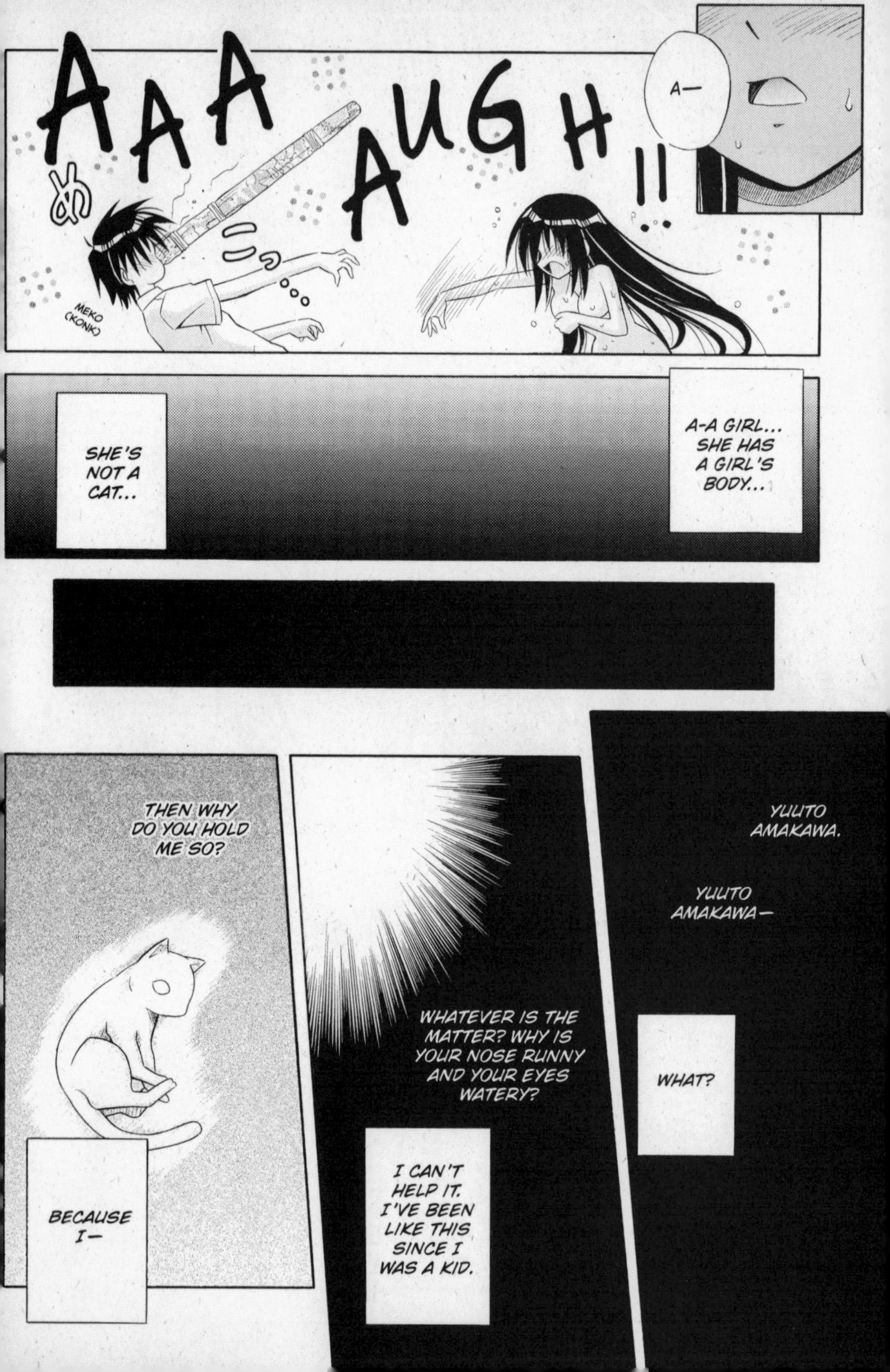
A—
AAAAUGH!!
め
MEKO (KONK)
A-A GIRL... SHE HAS A GIRL'S BODY...
SHE'S NOT A CAT...
YUUTO AMAKAWA.
YUUTO AMAKAWA—
WHAT?
WHATEVER IS THE MATTER? WHY IS YOUR NOSE RUNNY AND YOUR EYES WATERY?
I CAN'T HELP IT. I'VE BEEN LIKE THIS SINCE I WAS A KID.
THEN WHY DO YOU HOLD ME SO?
BECAUSE I—

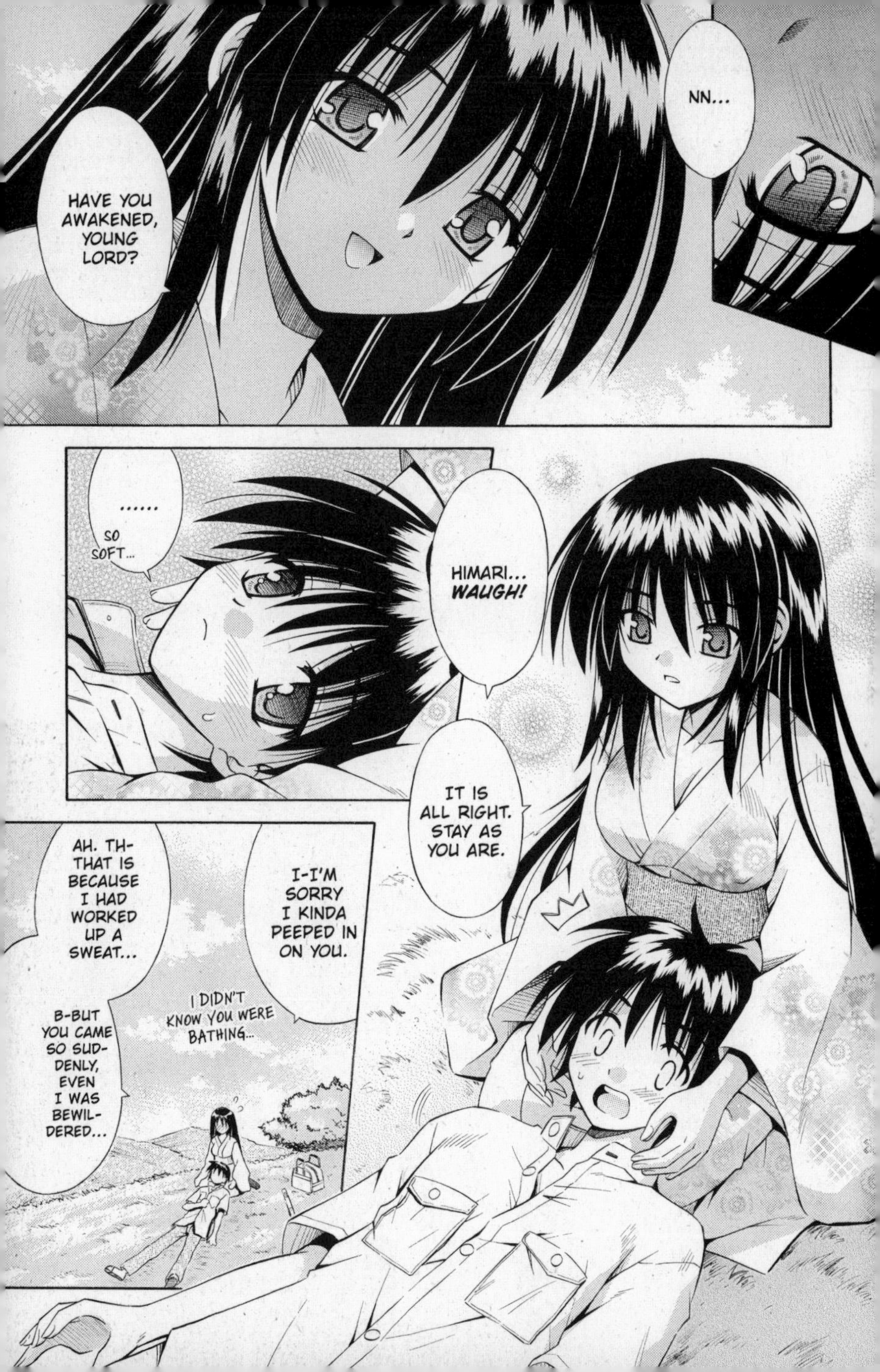
NN...
HAVE YOU AWAKENED, YOUNG LORD?
HIMARI... WAUGH!
IT IS ALL RIGHT. STAY AS YOU ARE.
......
SO SOFT...
I-I'M SORRY I KINDA PEEPED IN ON YOU.
I DIDN'T KNOW YOU WERE BATHING...
AH. TH-THAT IS BECAUSE I HAD WORKED UP A SWEAT...
B-BUT YOU CAME SO SUD-DENLY, EVEN I WAS BEWIL-DERED...

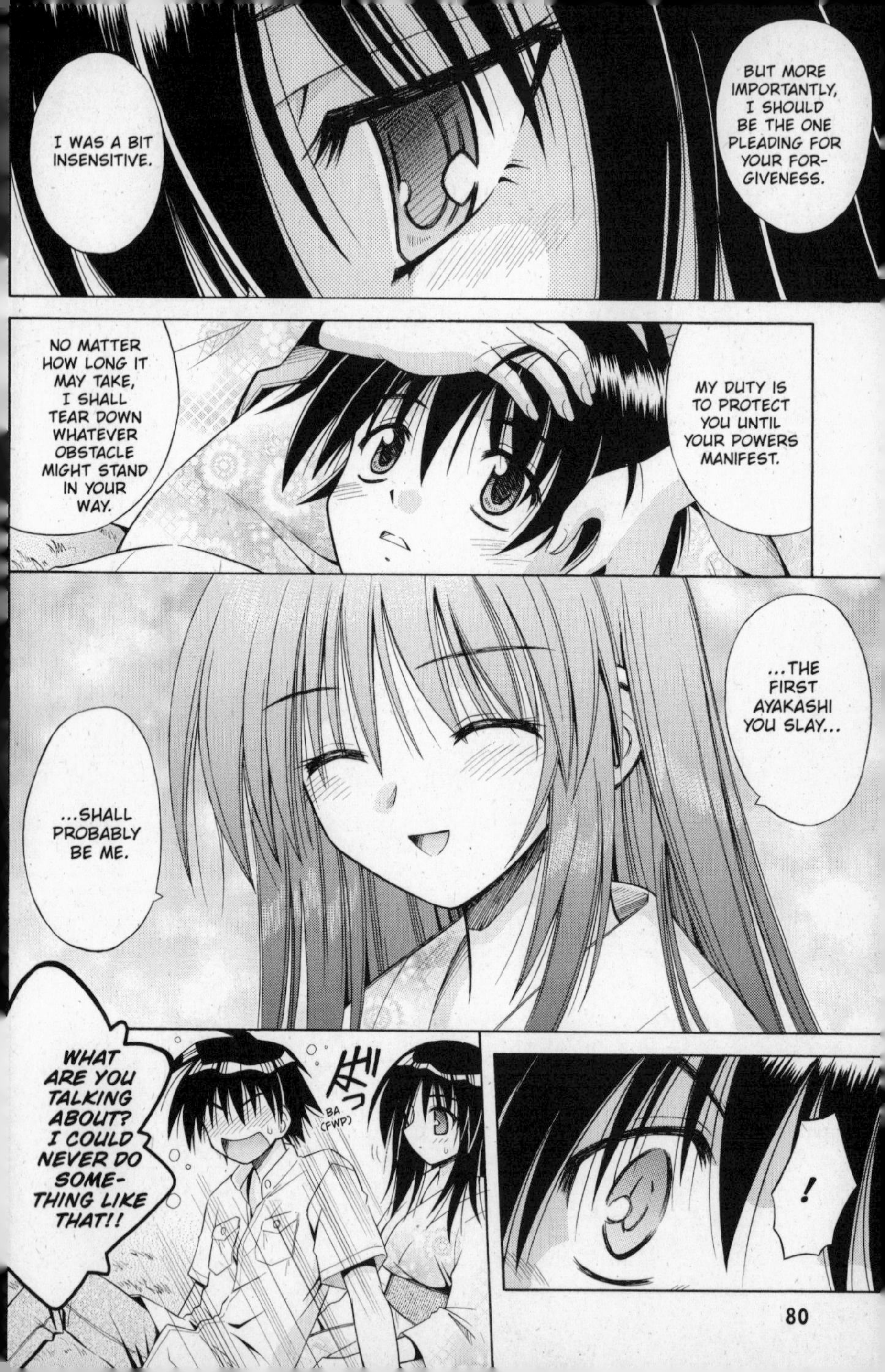
BUT MORE IMPORTANTLY, I SHOULD BE THE ONE PLEADING FOR YOUR FOR-GIVENESS.
I WAS A BIT INSENSITIVE.
MY DUTY IS TO PROTECT YOU UNTIL YOUR POWERS MANIFEST.
NO MATTER HOW LONG IT MAY TAKE, I SHALL TEAR DOWN WHATEVER OBSTACLE MIGHT STAND IN YOUR WAY.
...THE FIRST AYAKASHI YOU SLAY...
...SHALL PROBABLY BE ME.
!
BA (FWP)
WHAT ARE YOU TALKING ABOUT? I COULD NEVER DO SOME-THING LIKE THAT!!

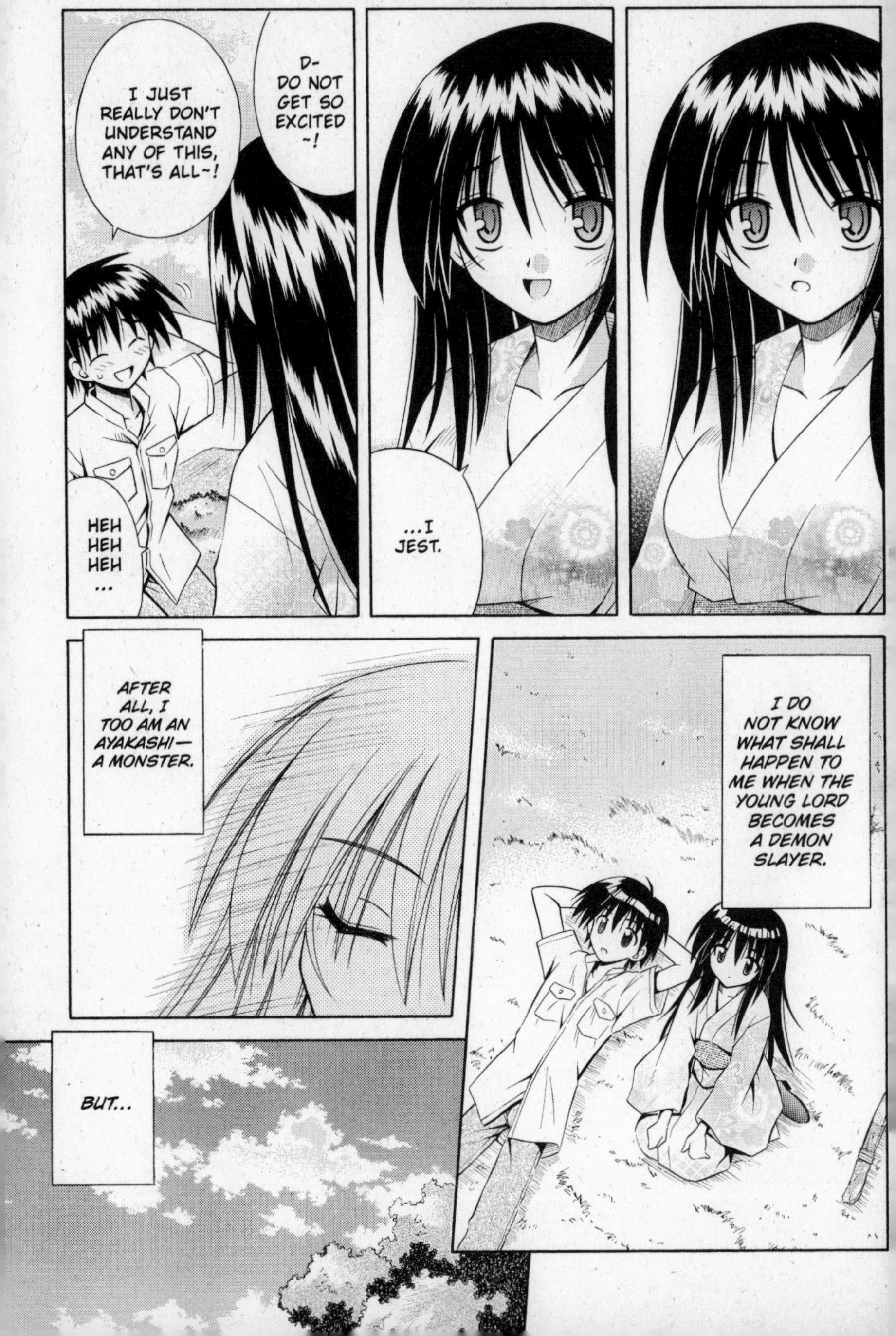
...I JEST.
D- DO NOT GET SO EXCITED ~!
I JUST REALLY DON'T UNDERSTAND ANY OF THIS, THAT'S ALL~!
HEH HEH HEH ...
I DO NOT KNOW WHAT SHALL HAPPEN TO ME WHEN THE YOUNG LORD BECOMES A DEMON SLAYER.
AFTER ALL, I TOO AM AN AYAKASHI— A MONSTER.
BUT...

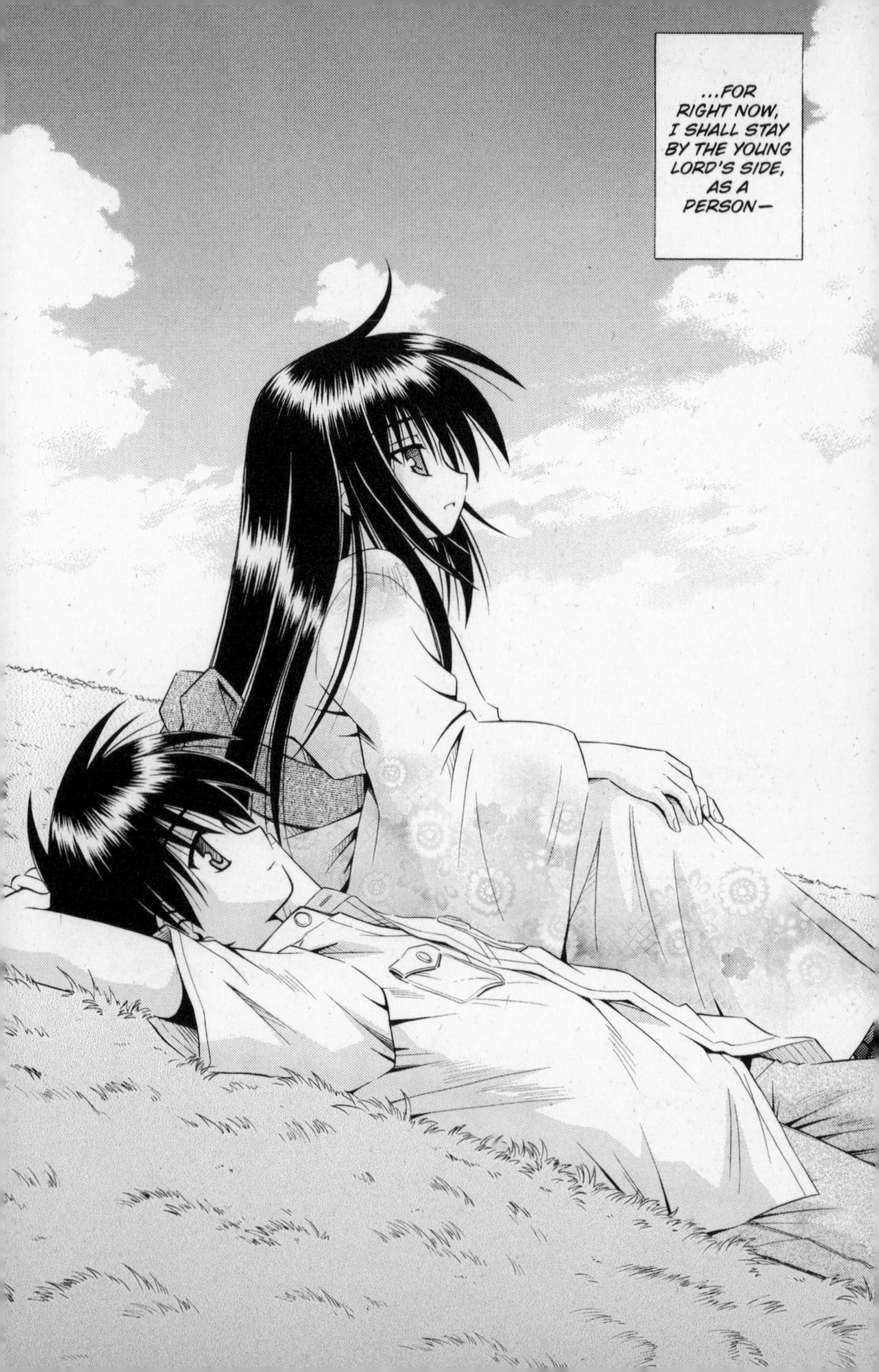
...FOR RIGHT NOW, I SHALL STAY BY THE YOUNG LORD'S SIDE, AS A PERSON—

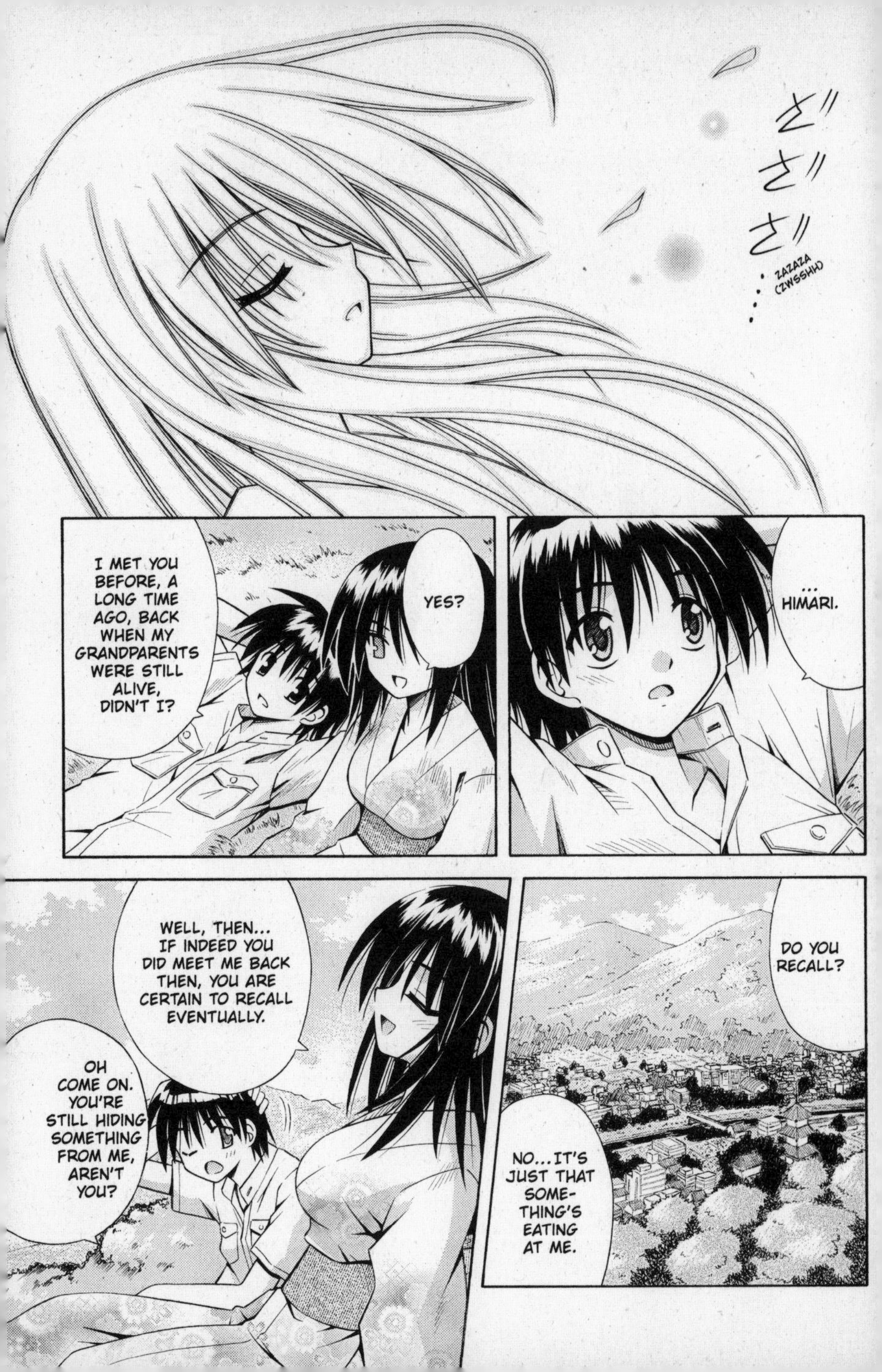
ざざざ
ZAZAZA (ZWSSHH)
...HIMARI.
YES?
I MET YOU BEFORE, A LONG TIME AGO, BACK WHEN MY GRANDPARENTS WERE STILL ALIVE, DIDN'T I?
DO YOU RECALL?
NO...IT'S JUST THAT SOME-THING'S EATING AT ME.
WELL, THEN... IF INDEED YOU DID MEET ME BACK THEN, YOU ARE CERTAIN TO RECALL EVENTUALLY.
OH COME ON. YOU'RE STILL HIDING SOMETHING FROM ME, AREN'T YOU?

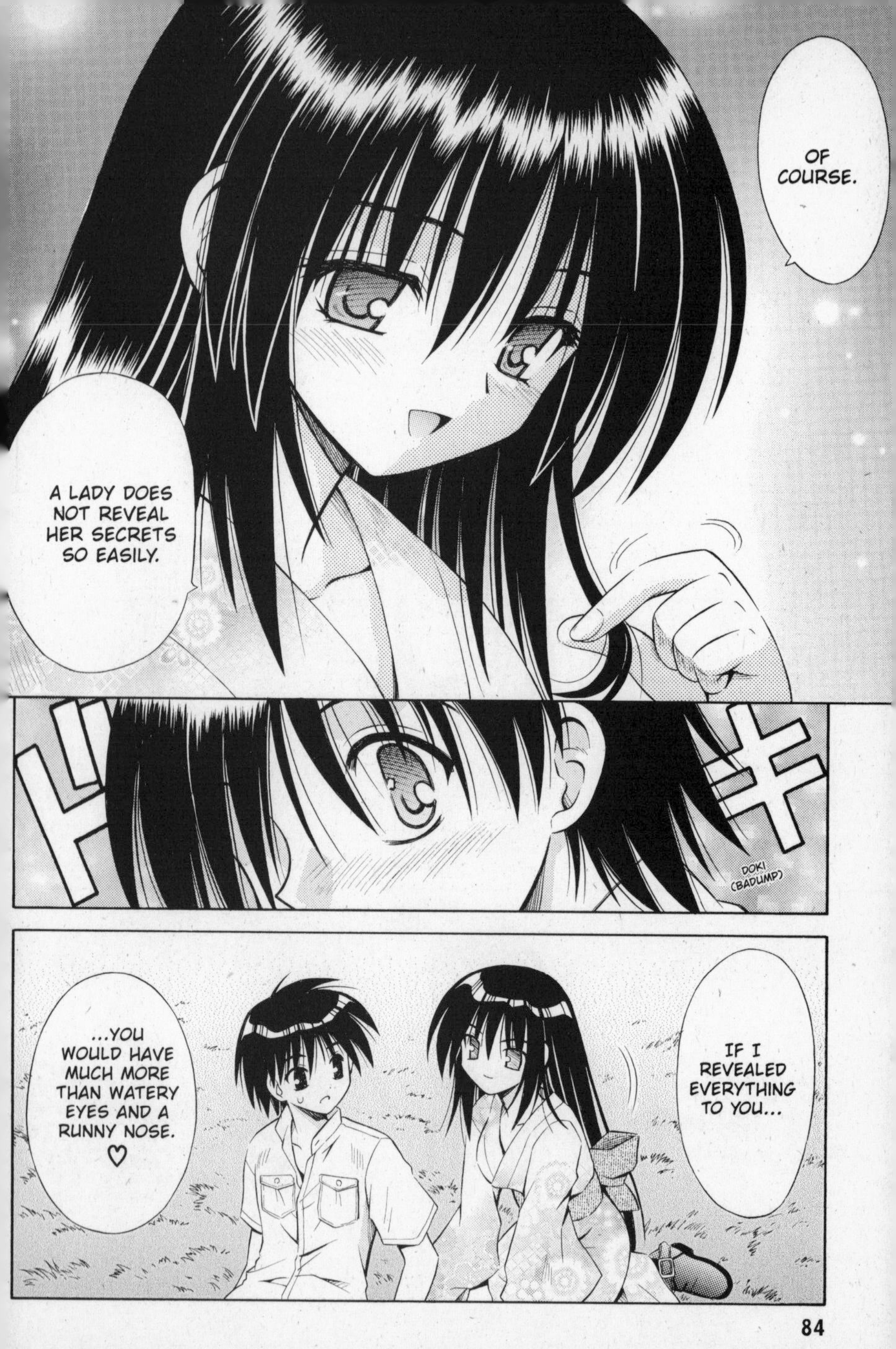
OF COURSE.
A LADY DOES NOT REVEAL HER SECRETS SO EASILY.
DOKI (BADUMP)
IF I REVEALED EVERYTHING TO YOU...
...YOU WOULD HAVE MUCH MORE THAN WATERY EYES AND A RUNNY NOSE. ♥

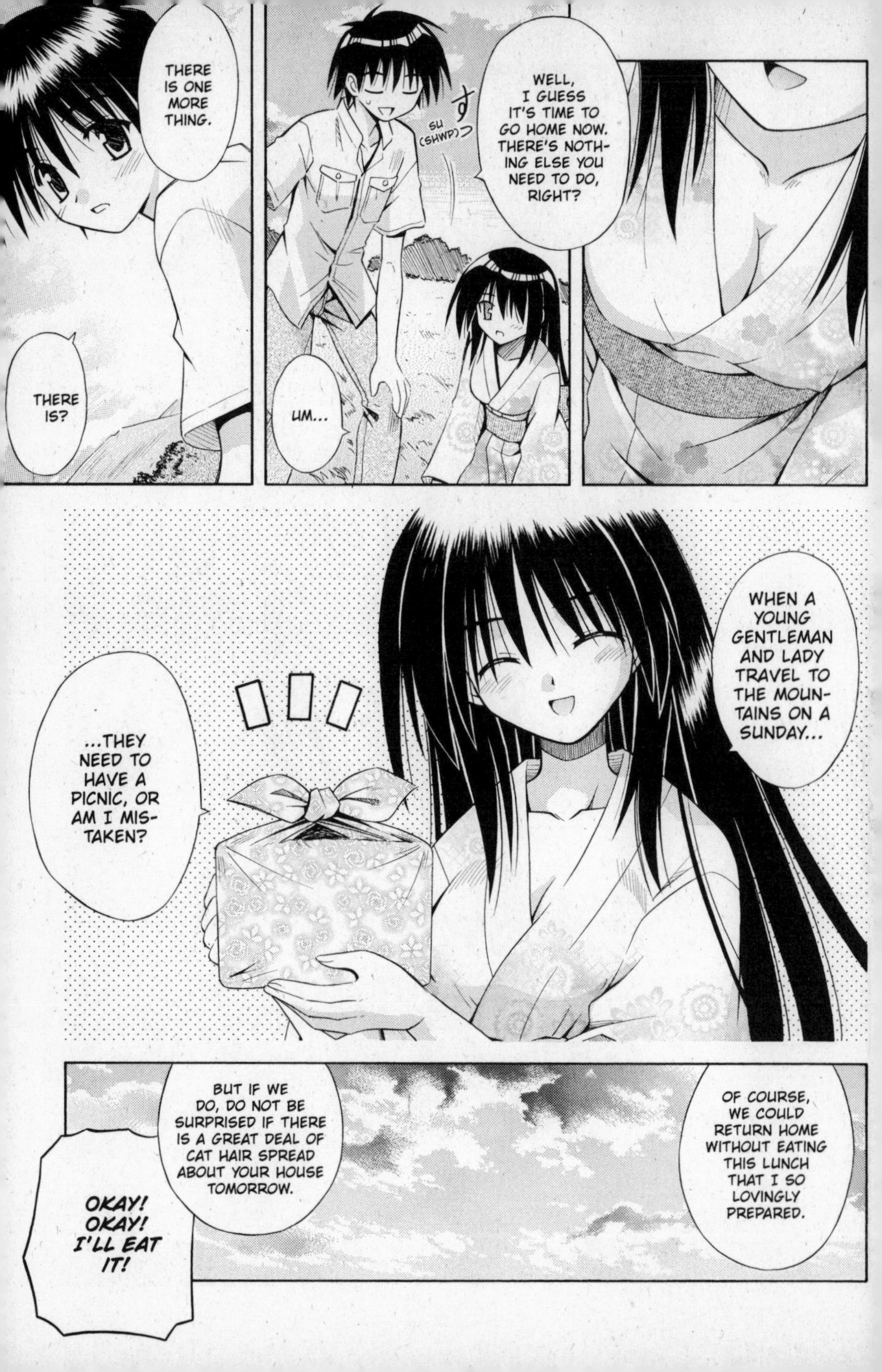
WELL, I GUESS IT'S TIME TO GO HOME NOW. THERE'S NOTHING ELSE YOU NEED TO DO, RIGHT?
す
SU (SHWP)
UM...
THERE IS ONE MORE THING.
THERE IS?
WHEN A YOUNG GENTLEMAN AND LADY TRAVEL TO THE MOUNTAINS ON A SUNDAY...
...THEY NEED TO HAVE A PICNIC, OR AM I MISTAKEN?
OF COURSE, WE COULD RETURN HOME WITHOUT EATING THIS LUNCH THAT I SO LOVINGLY PREPARED.
BUT IF WE DO, DO NOT BE SURPRISED IF THERE IS A GREAT DEAL OF CAT HAIR SPREAD ABOUT YOUR HOUSE TOMORROW.
OKAY! OKAY! I'LL EAT IT!

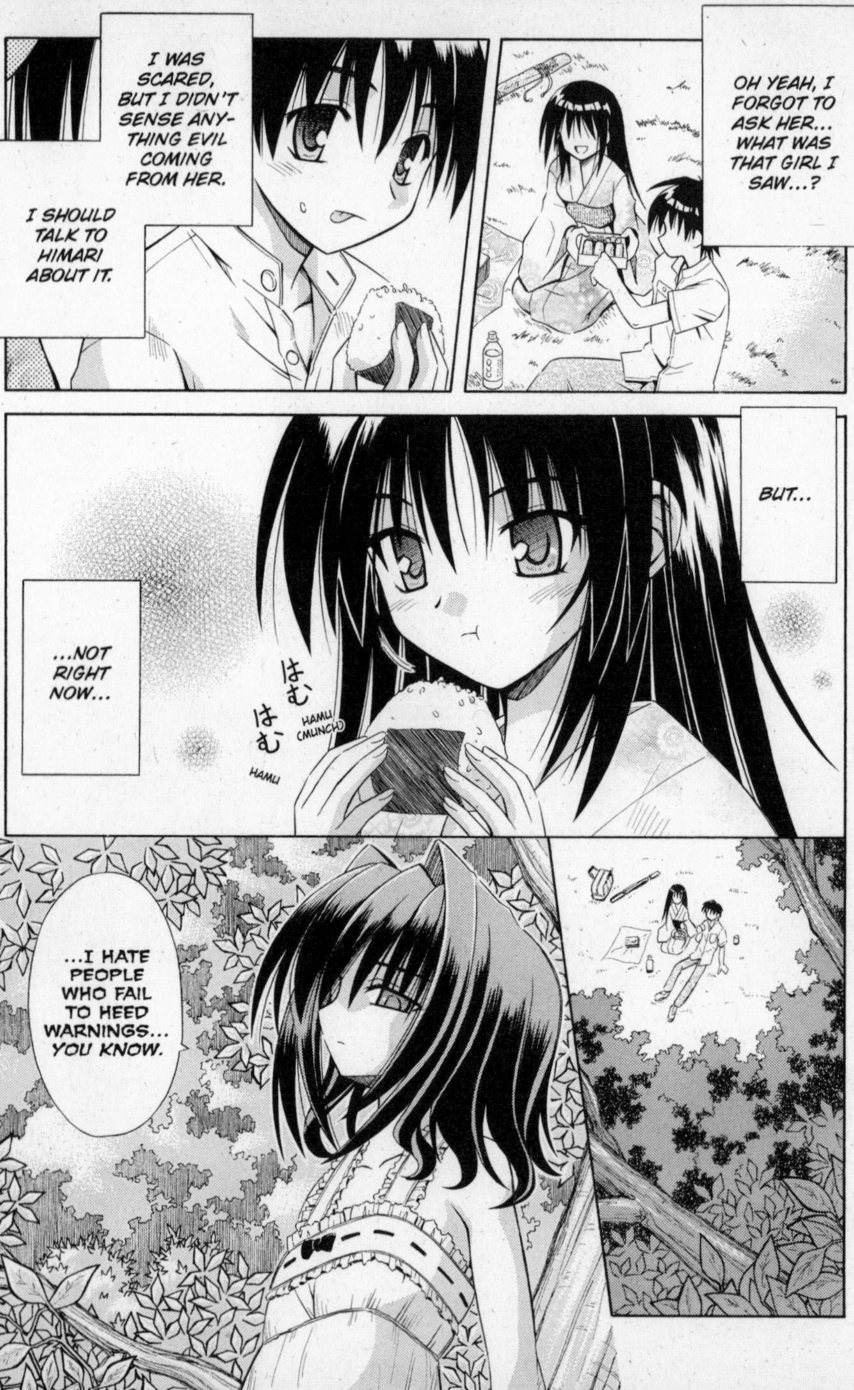
OH YEAH, I FORGOT TO ASK HER... WHAT WAS THAT GIRL I SAW...?
I WAS SCARED, BUT I DIDN'T SENSE ANY-THING EVIL COMING FROM HER.
I SHOULD TALK TO HIMARI ABOUT IT.
BUT...
...NOT RIGHT NOW...
はむ
HAMU (MUNCH)
はむ
HAMU
...I HATE PEOPLE WHO FAIL TO HEED WARNINGS... YOU KNOW.

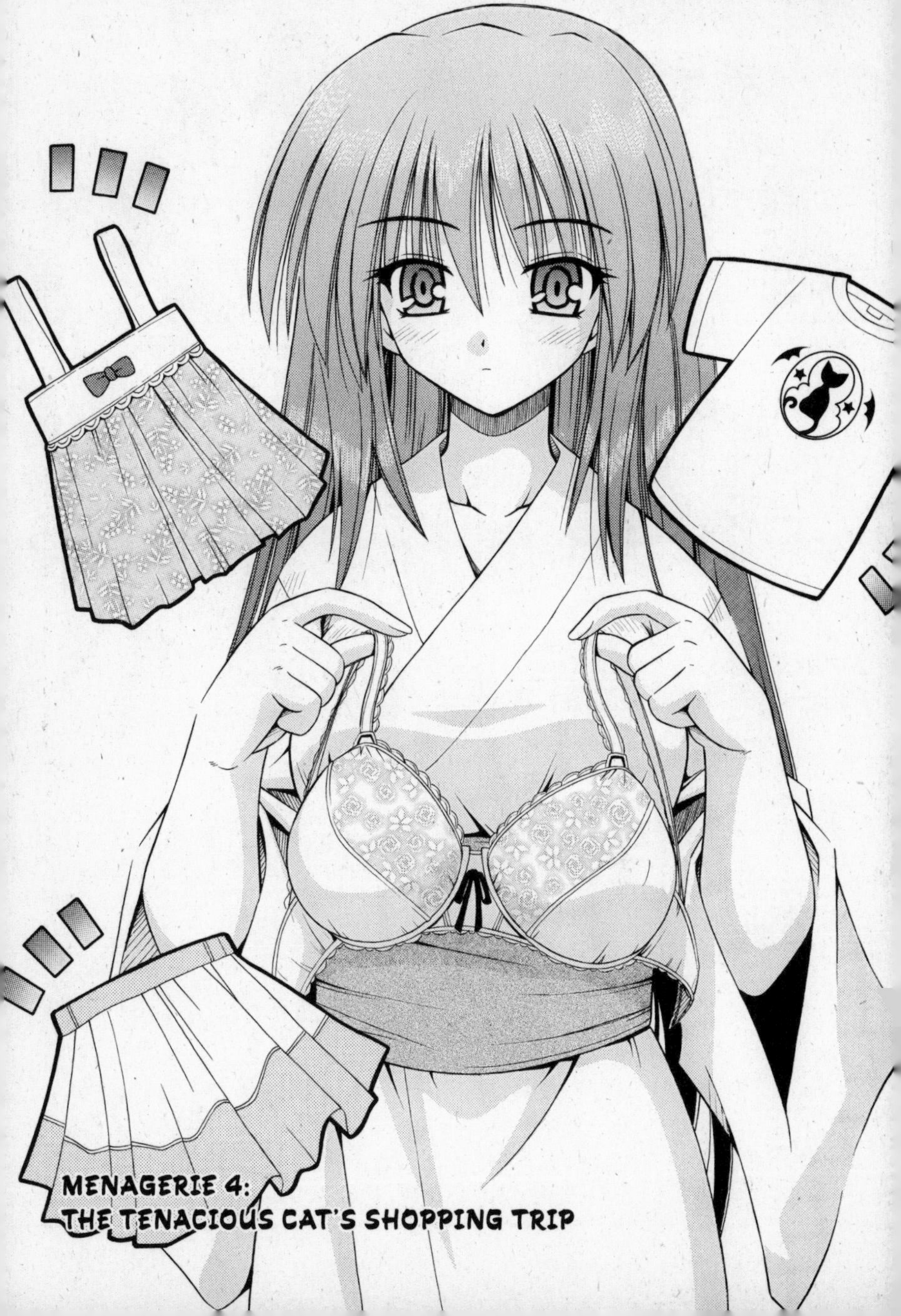

MENAGERIE 4: THE TENACIOUS CAT'S SHOPPING TRIP

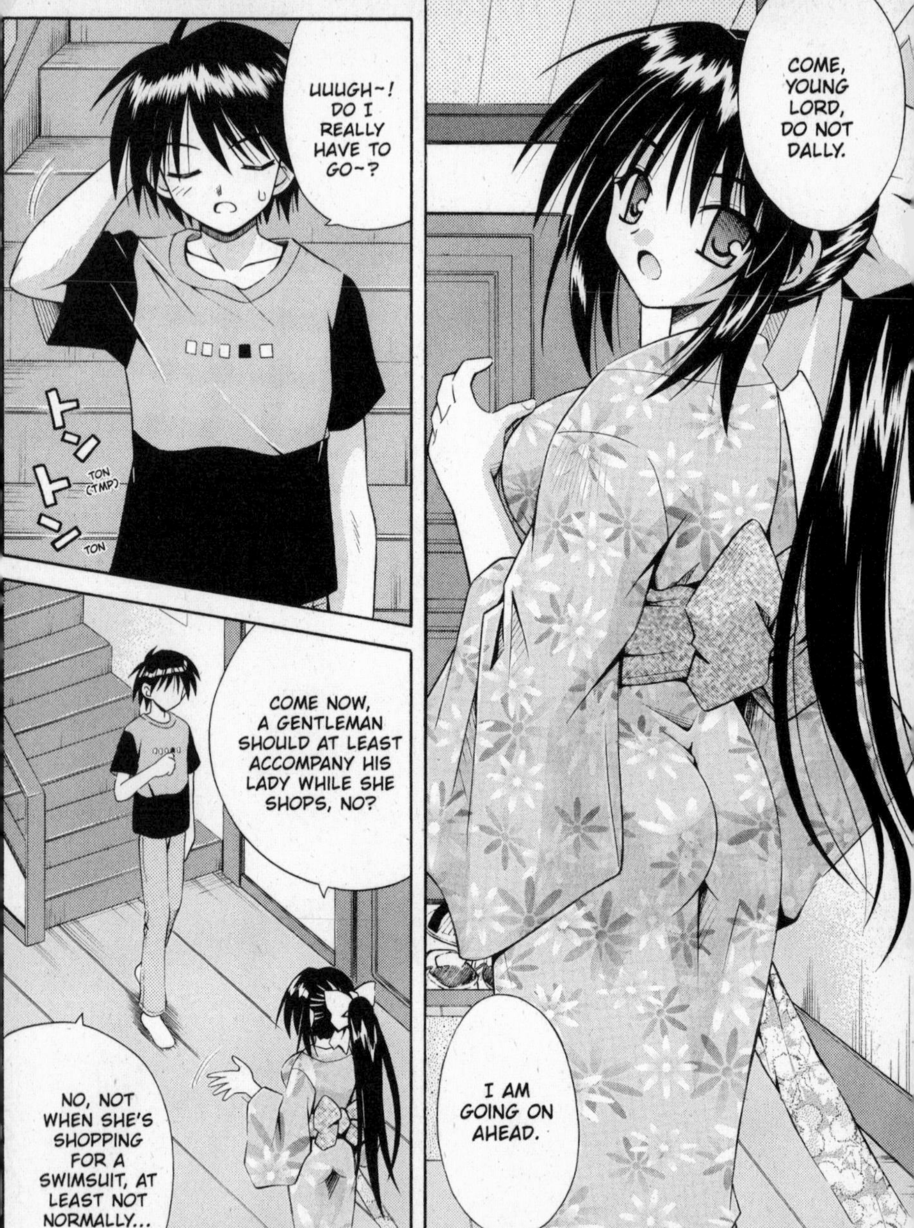
COME, YOUNG LORD, DO NOT DALLY.
I AM GOING ON AHEAD.
UUUGH~! DO I REALLY HAVE TO GO~?
TON (TMP)
TON
COME NOW, A GENTLEMAN SHOULD AT LEAST ACCOMPANY HIS LADY WHILE SHE SHOPS, NO?
NO, NOT WHEN SHE'S SHOPPING FOR A SWIMSUIT, AT LEAST NOT NORMALLY...

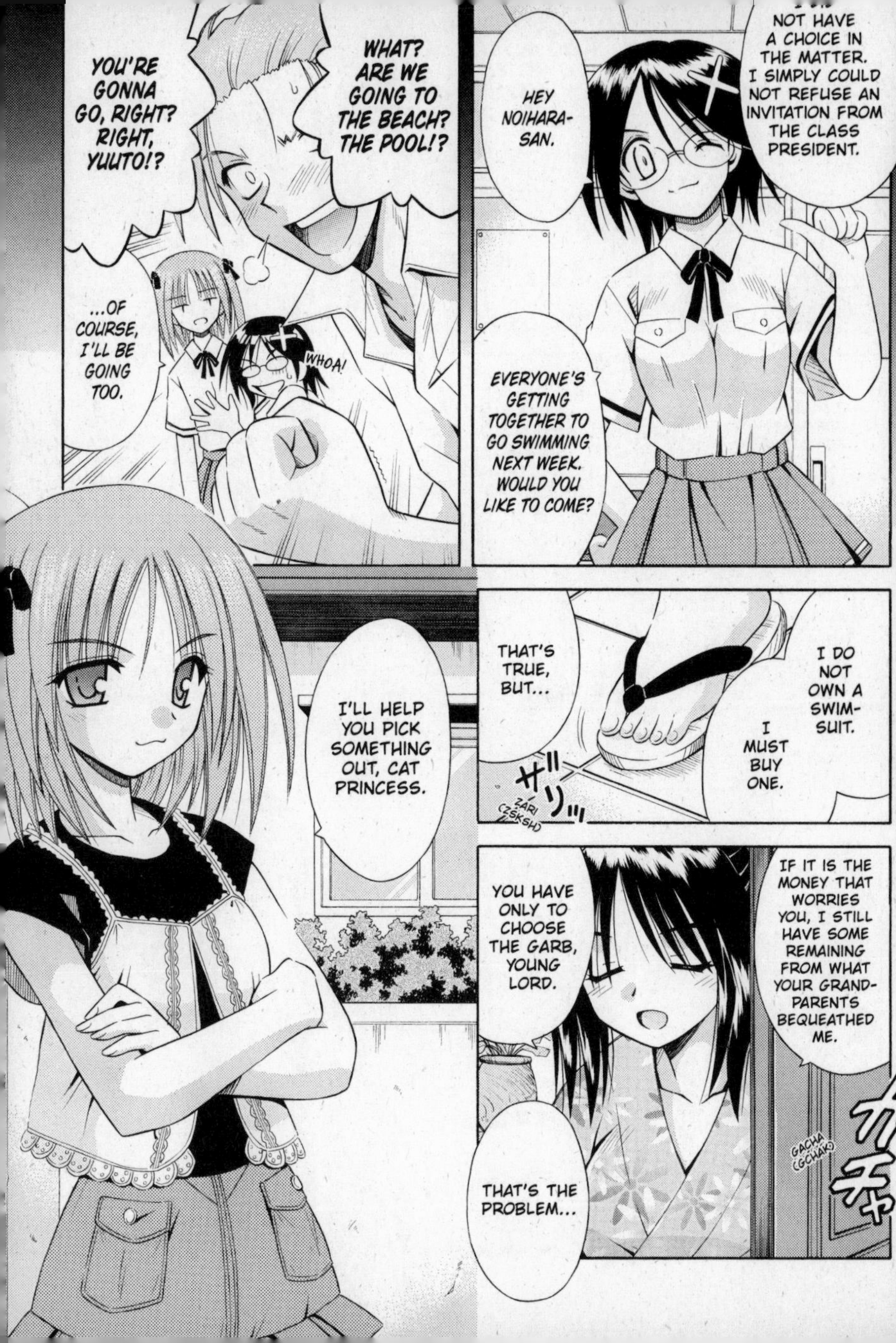
HEY NOIHARA-SAN.
EVERYONE'S GETTING TOGETHER TO GO SWIMMING NEXT WEEK. WOULD YOU LIKE TO COME?
NOT HAVE A CHOICE IN THE MATTER. I SIMPLY COULD NOT REFUSE AN INVITATION FROM THE CLASS PRESIDENT.
WHAT? ARE WE GOING TO THE BEACH? THE POOL!?
YOU'RE GONNA GO, RIGHT? RIGHT, YUUTO!?
WHOA!
...OF COURSE, I'LL BE GOING TOO.
I DO NOT OWN A SWIM-SUIT.
I MUST BUY ONE.
THAT'S TRUE, BUT...
ZARI (ZSKSH)
IF IT IS THE MONEY THAT WORRIES YOU, I STILL HAVE SOME REMAINING FROM WHAT YOUR GRAND-PARENTS BEQUEATHED ME.
YOU HAVE ONLY TO CHOOSE THE GARB, YOUNG LORD.
GACHA (GCHAK)
THAT'S THE PROBLEM...
I'LL HELP YOU PICK SOMETHING OUT, CAT PRINCESS.

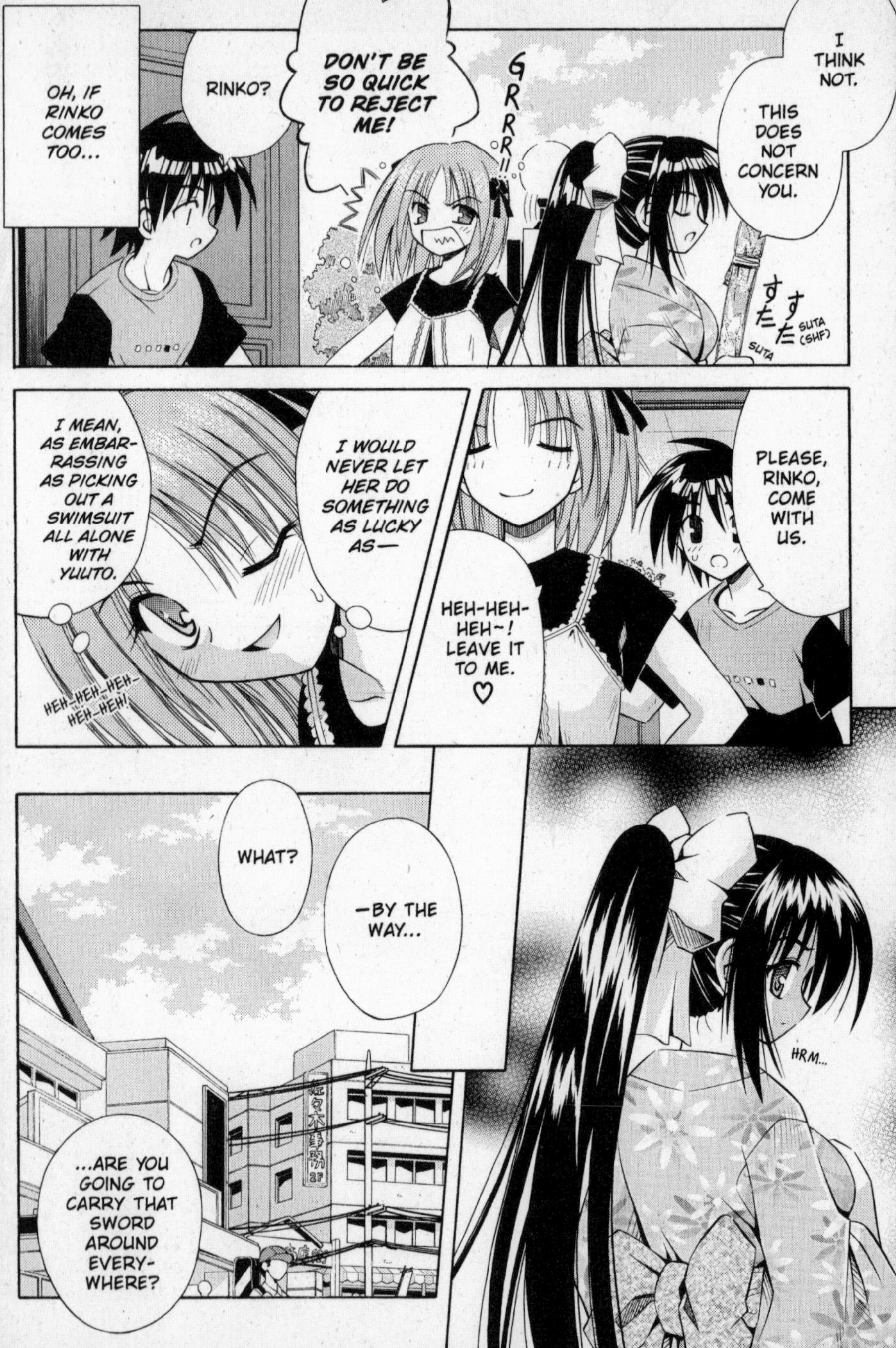
I THINK NOT.
THIS DOES NOT CONCERN YOU.
すた すた
SUTA SUTA (SHF)
GRRR!!
DON'T BE SO QUICK TO REJECT ME!
RINKO?
OH, IF RINKO COMES TOO...
PLEASE, RINKO, COME WITH US.
HEH-HEH-HEH~! LEAVE IT TO ME. ♡
I WOULD NEVER LET HER DO SOMETHING AS LUCKY AS—
I MEAN, AS EMBARRASSING AS PICKING OUT A SWIMSUIT ALL ALONE WITH YUUTO.
HEH-HEH-HEH-HEH-HEH!
HRM...
WHAT?
—BY THE WAY...
...ARE YOU GOING TO CARRY THAT SWORD AROUND EVERYWHERE?

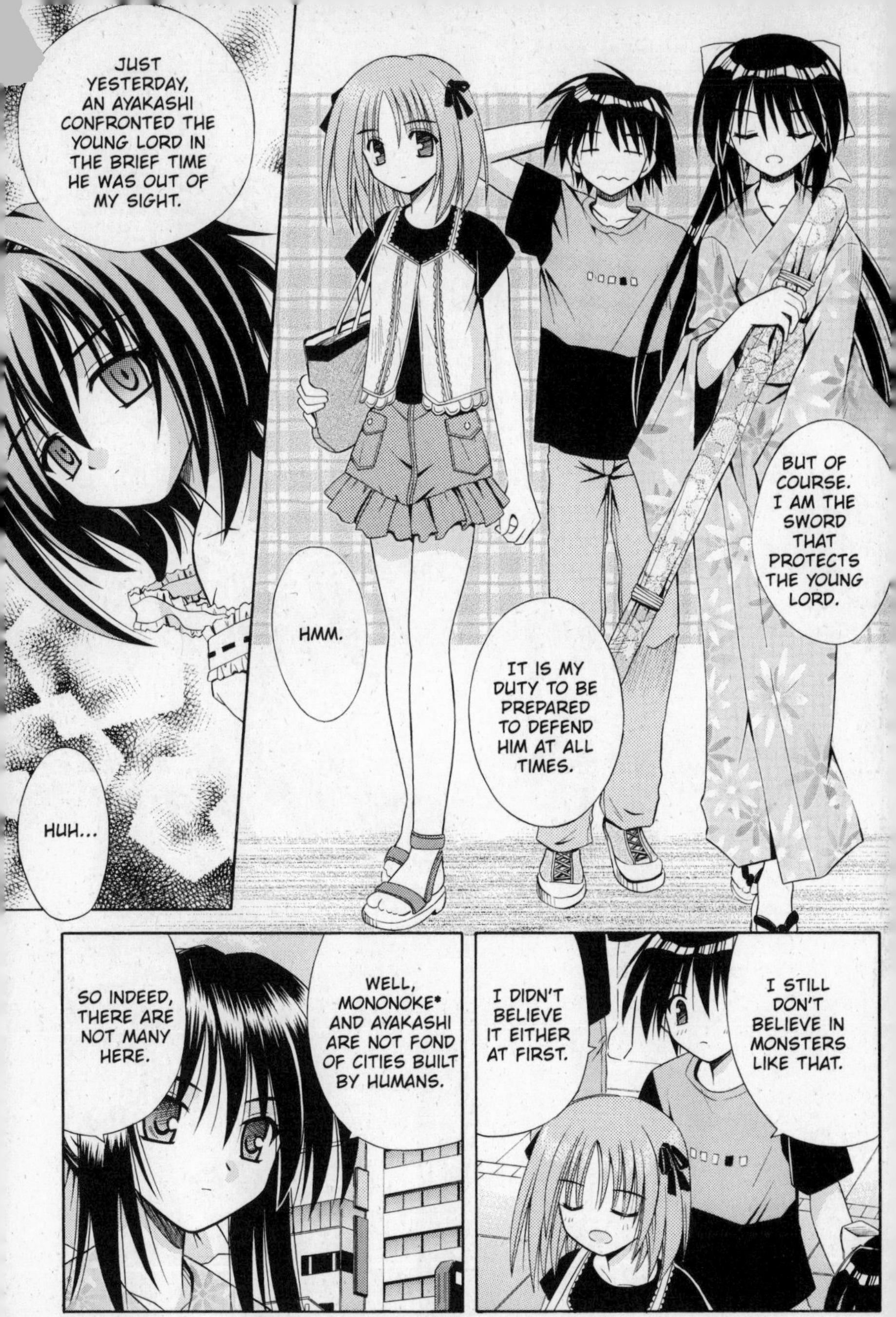
BUT OF COURSE. I AM THE SWORD THAT PROTECTS THE YOUNG LORD.
IT IS MY DUTY TO BE PREPARED TO DEFEND HIM AT ALL TIMES.
HMM.
JUST YESTERDAY, AN AYAKASHI CONFRONTED THE YOUNG LORD IN THE BRIEF TIME HE WAS OUT OF MY SIGHT.
HUH...
I STILL DON'T BELIEVE IN MONSTERS LIKE THAT.
I DIDN'T BELIEVE IT EITHER AT FIRST.
WELL, MONONOKE* AND AYAKASHI ARE NOT FOND OF CITIES BUILT BY HUMANS.
SO INDEED, THERE ARE NOT MANY HERE.

*MONONOKE *ARE VENGEFUL SPIRITS.*

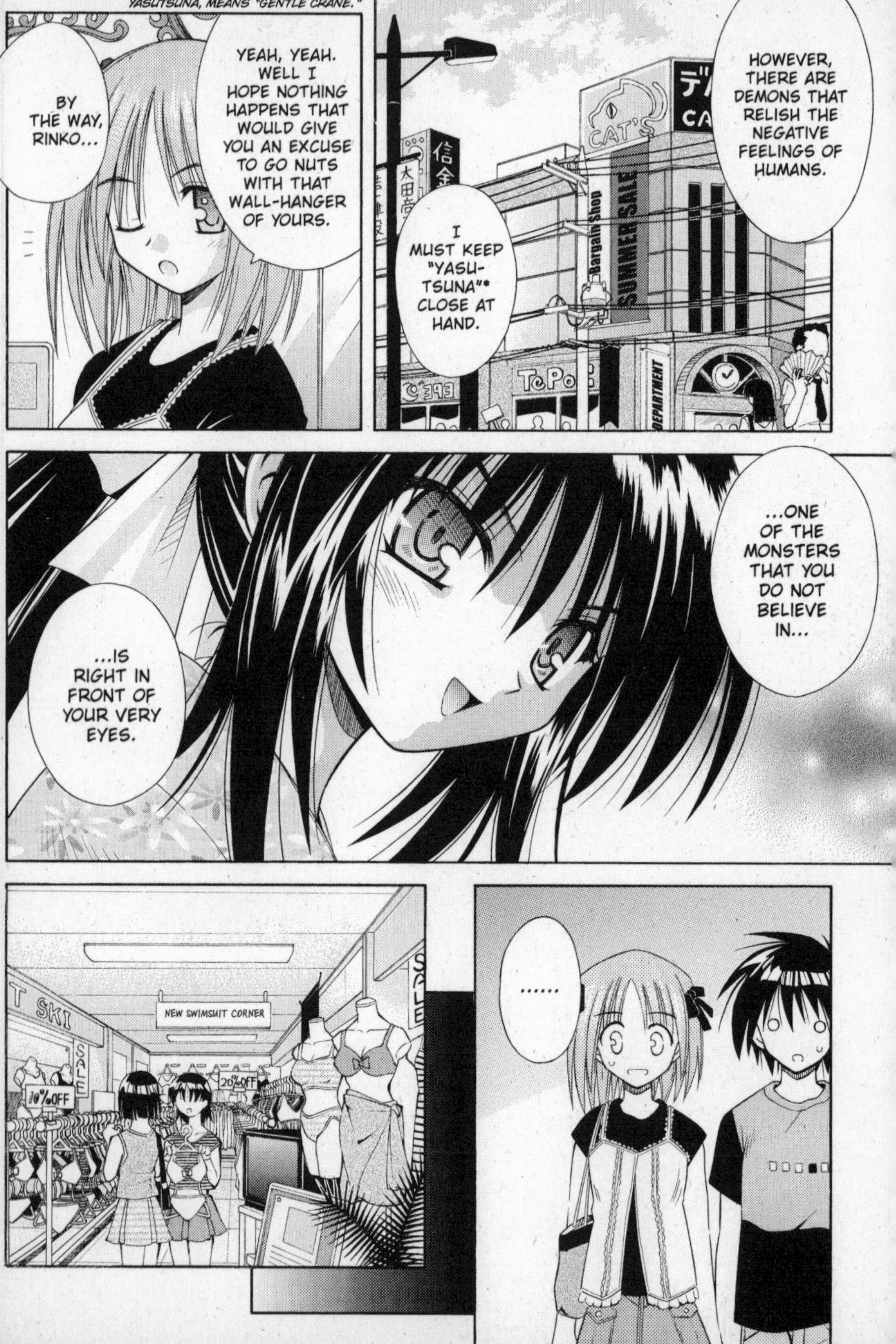
HOWEVER, THERE ARE DEMONS THAT RELISH THE NEGATIVE FEELINGS OF HUMANS.
I MUST KEEP "YASU-TSUNA"* CLOSE AT HAND.
CAT'S
Bargain Shop
SUMMER SALE
DEPARTMENT
YEAH, YEAH. WELL I HOPE NOTHING HAPPENS THAT WOULD GIVE YOU AN EXCUSE TO GO NUTS WITH THAT WALL-HANGER OF YOURS.
BY THE WAY, RINKO...
...ONE OF THE MONSTERS THAT YOU DO NOT BELIEVE IN...
...IS RIGHT IN FRONT OF YOUR VERY EYES.
......
NEW SWIMSUIT CORNER
SALE
20% OFF
10% OFF
SALE
*THE NAME OF HIMARI'S SWORD, YASUTSUNA, MEANS "GENTLE CRANE."

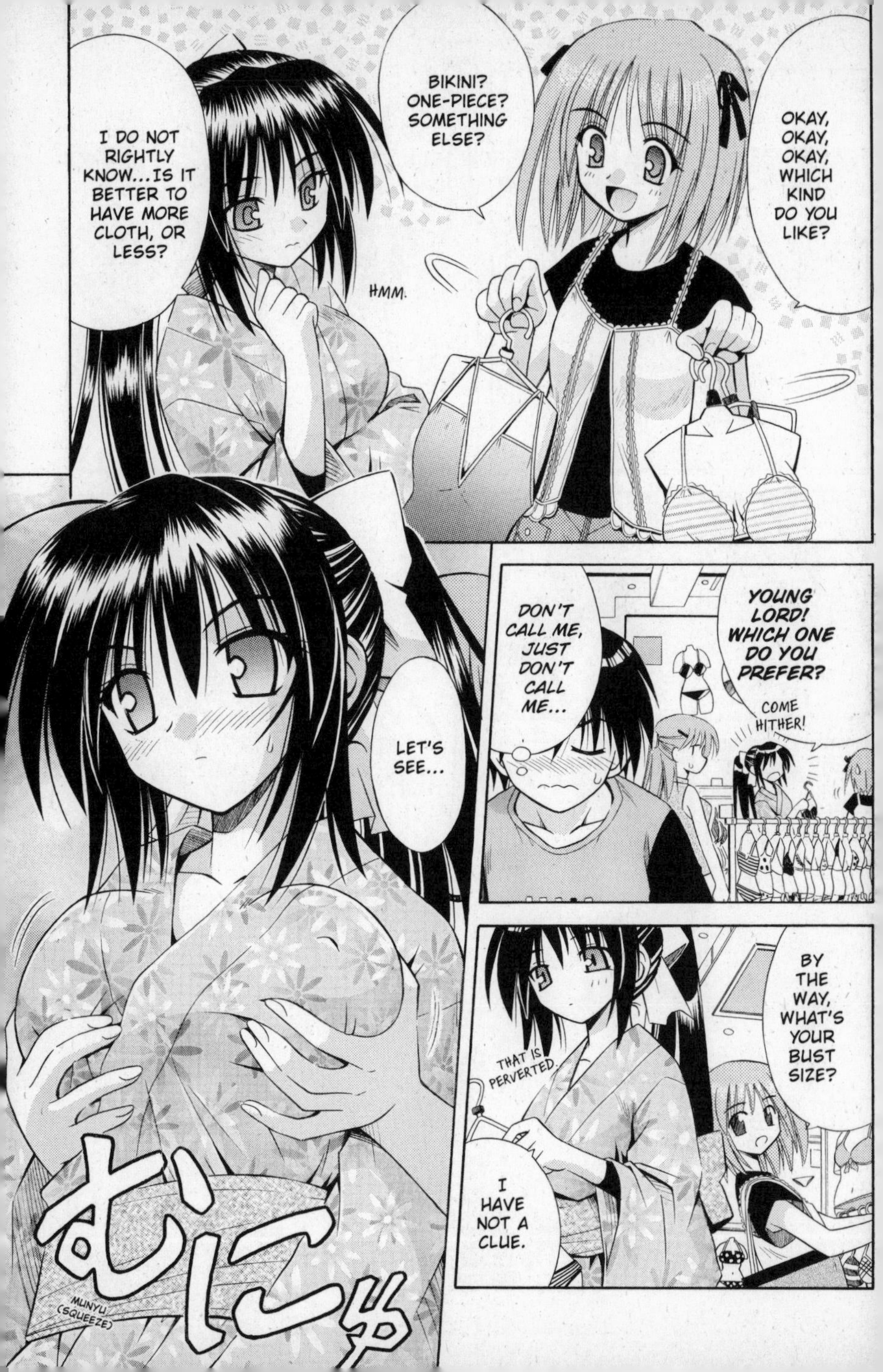
OKAY, OKAY, OKAY, WHICH KIND DO YOU LIKE?
BIKINI? ONE-PIECE? SOMETHING ELSE?
HMM.
I DO NOT RIGHTLY KNOW...IS IT BETTER TO HAVE MORE CLOTH, OR LESS?
YOUNG LORD! WHICH ONE DO YOU PREFER?
COME HITHER!
DON'T CALL ME, JUST DON'T CALL ME...
BY THE WAY, WHAT'S YOUR BUST SIZE?
THAT IS PERVERTED.
I HAVE NOT A CLUE.
LET'S SEE...
むにゅ
MUNYU (SQUEEZE)

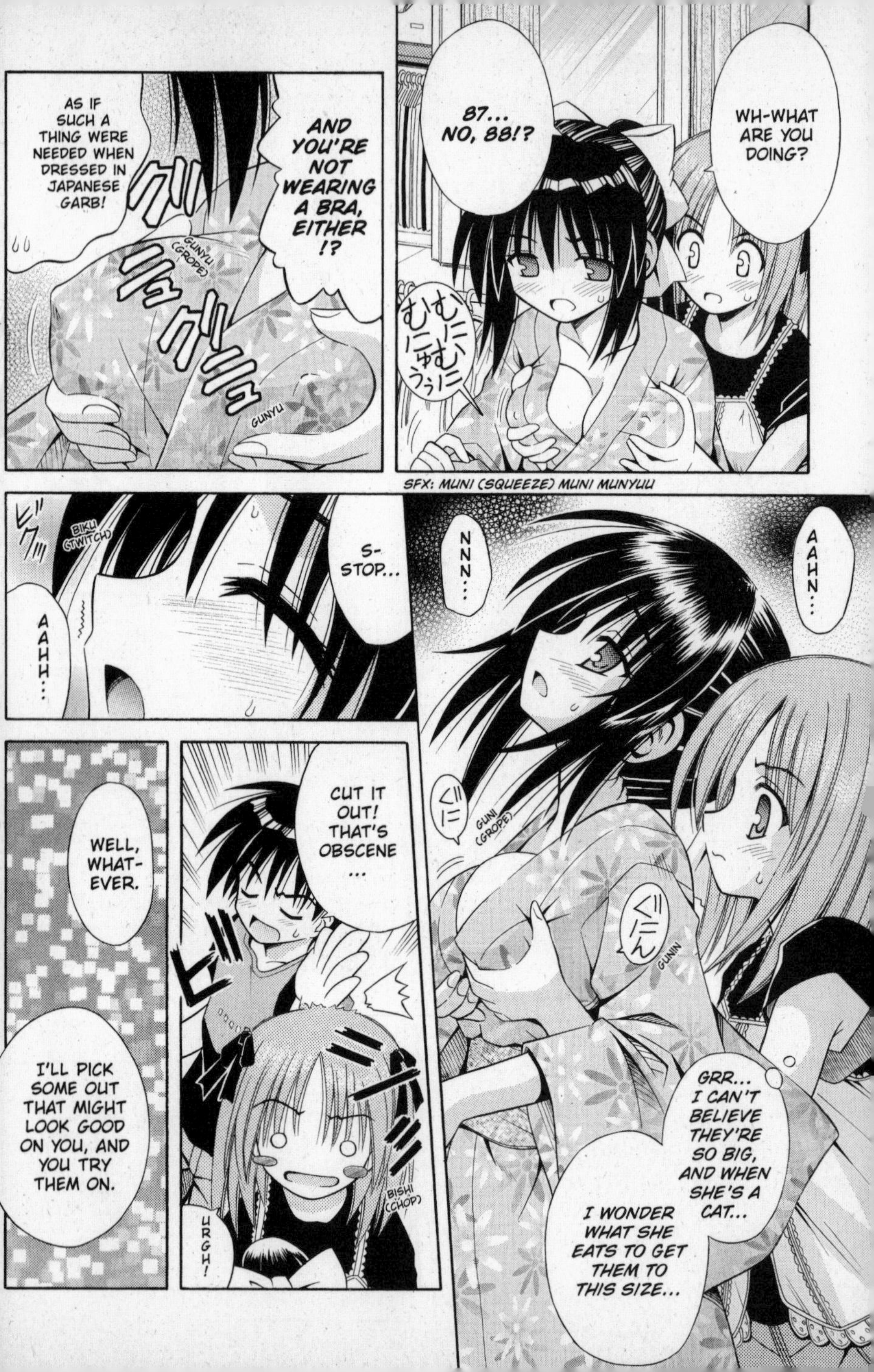
WH-WHAT ARE YOU DOING?
87... NO, 88!?
SFX: MUNI (SQUEEZE) MUNI MUNYUU
AND YOU'RE NOT WEARING A BRA, EITHER!?
AS IF SUCH A THING WERE NEEDED WHEN DRESSED IN JAPANESE GARB!
GUNYU (GROPE)
GUNYU
AAHN...
NNN...
GUNI (GROPE)
GUNIN
GRR... I CAN'T BELIEVE THEY'RE SO BIG, AND WHEN SHE'S A CAT...
I WONDER WHAT SHE EATS TO GET THEM TO THIS SIZE...
S-STOP...
BIKU (TWITCH)
AAHH...
CUT IT OUT! THAT'S OBSCENE ...
BISHI (CHOP)
URGH!
WELL, WHATEVER.
I'LL PICK SOME OUT THAT MIGHT LOOK GOOD ON YOU, AND YOU TRY THEM ON.

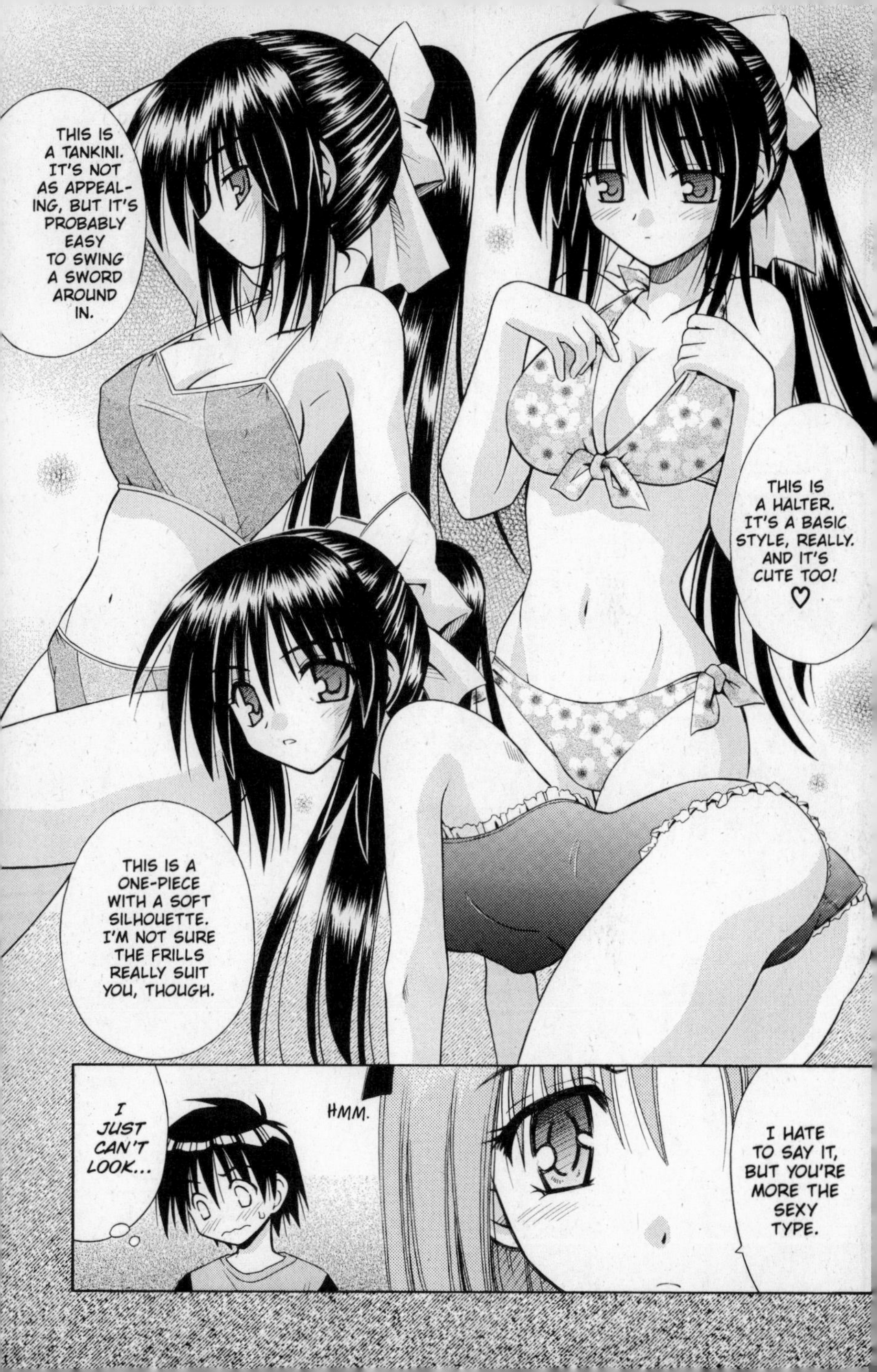
THIS IS A TANKINI. IT'S NOT AS APPEAL-ING, BUT IT'S PROBABLY EASY TO SWING A SWORD AROUND IN.
THIS IS A HALTER. IT'S A BASIC STYLE, REALLY. AND IT'S CUTE TOO! ♡
THIS IS A ONE-PIECE WITH A SOFT SILHOUETTE. I'M NOT SURE THE FRILLS REALLY SUIT YOU, THOUGH.
I HATE TO SAY IT, BUT YOU'RE MORE THE SEXY TYPE.
HMM.
I JUST CAN'T LOOK...

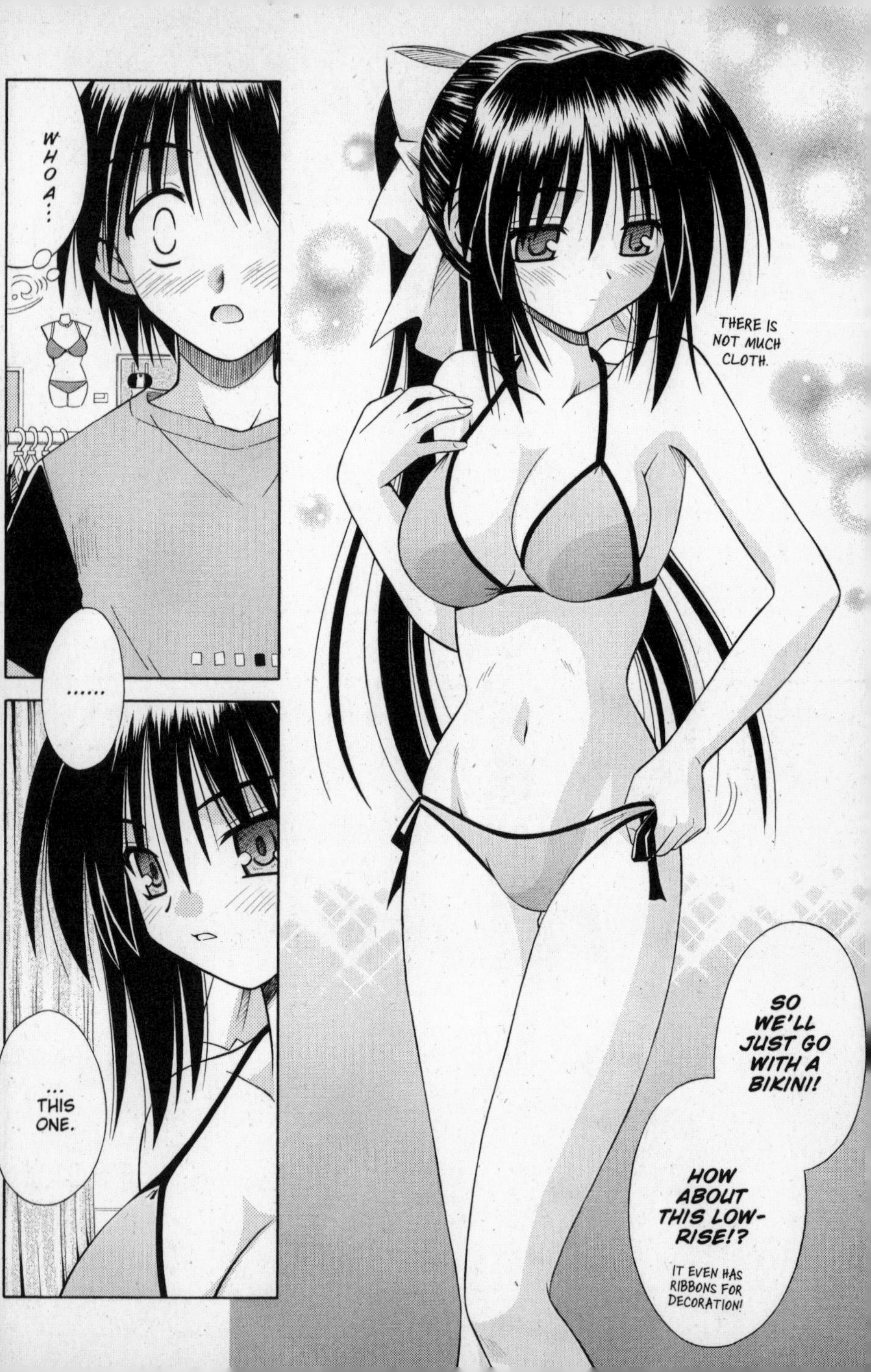
THERE IS NOT MUCH CLOTH.
SO WE'LL JUST GO WITH A BIKINI!
HOW ABOUT THIS LOW-RISE!?
IT EVEN HAS RIBBONS FOR DECORATION!
WHOA...
......
...THIS ONE.

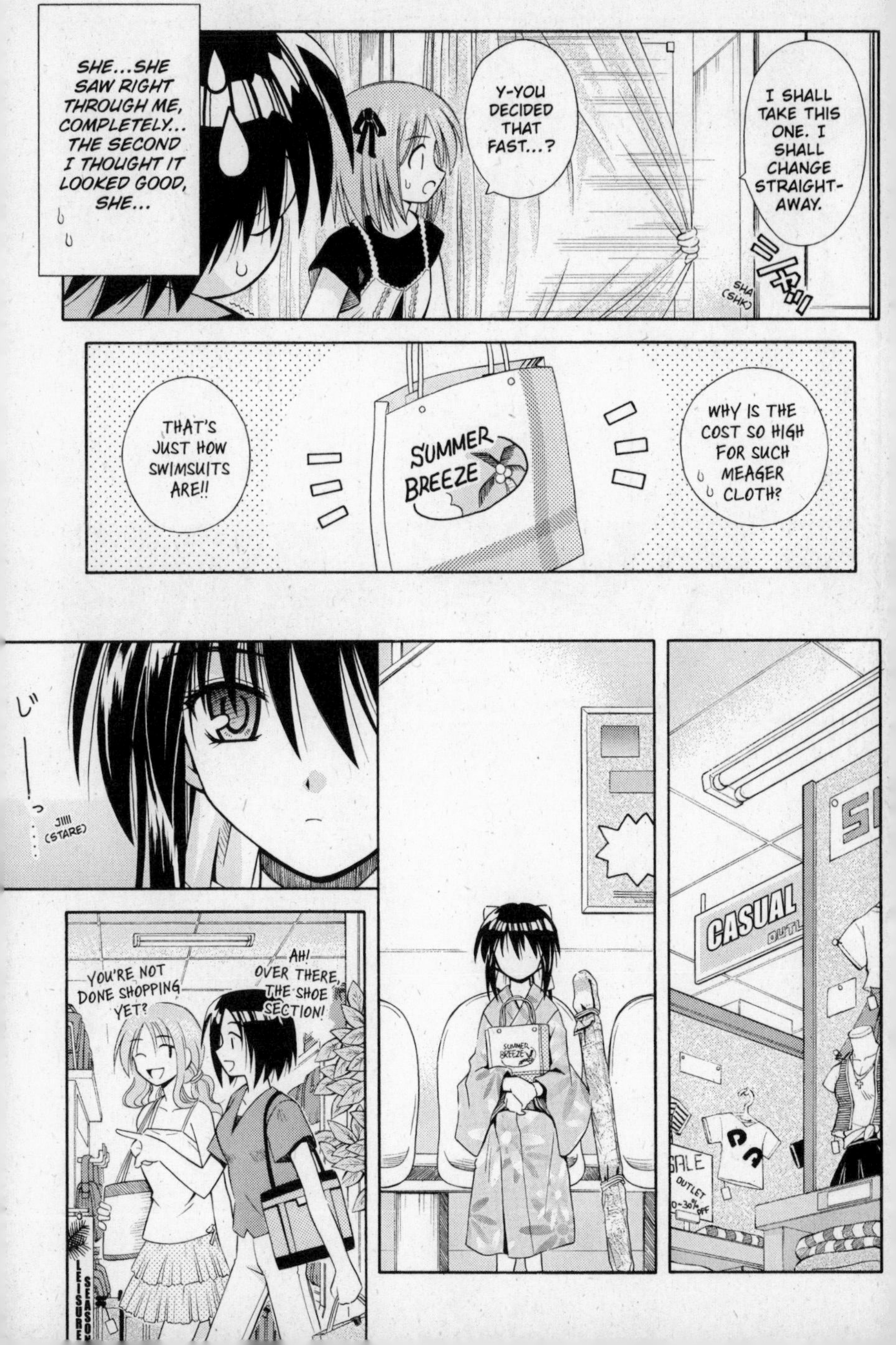
I SHALL TAKE THIS ONE. I SHALL CHANGE STRAIGHT-AWAY.
SHA (SHK)
Y-YOU DECIDED THAT FAST...?
SHE...SHE SAW RIGHT THROUGH ME, COMPLETELY... THE SECOND I THOUGHT IT LOOKED GOOD, SHE...
WHY IS THE COST SO HIGH FOR SUCH MEAGER CLOTH?
SUMMER BREEZE
THAT'S JUST HOW SWIMSUITS ARE!!
CASUAL
SALE
OUTLET
SUMMER BREEZE
JIIII (STARE)
AH! OVER THERE, THE SHOE SECTION!
YOU'RE NOT DONE SHOPPING YET?
LEISURE

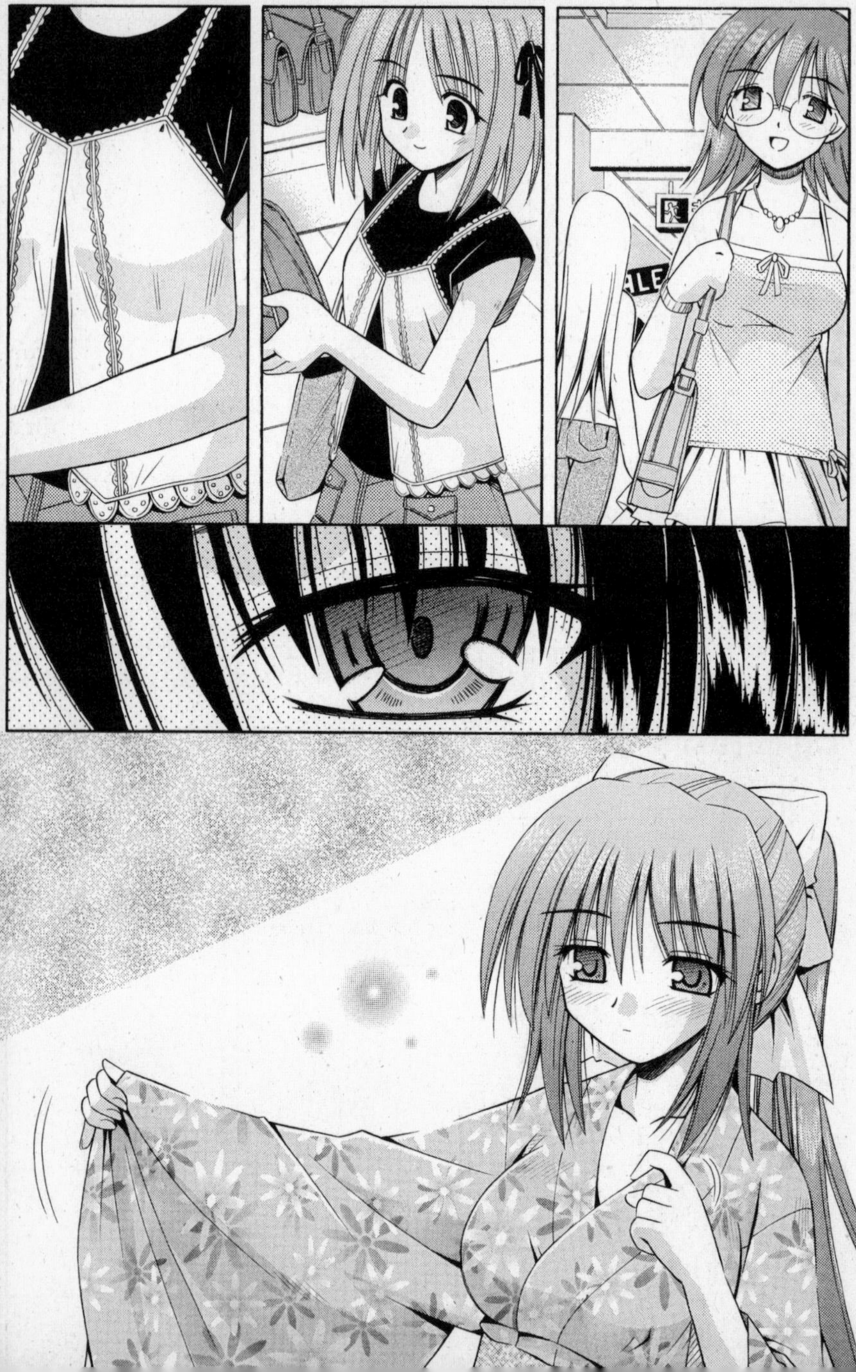

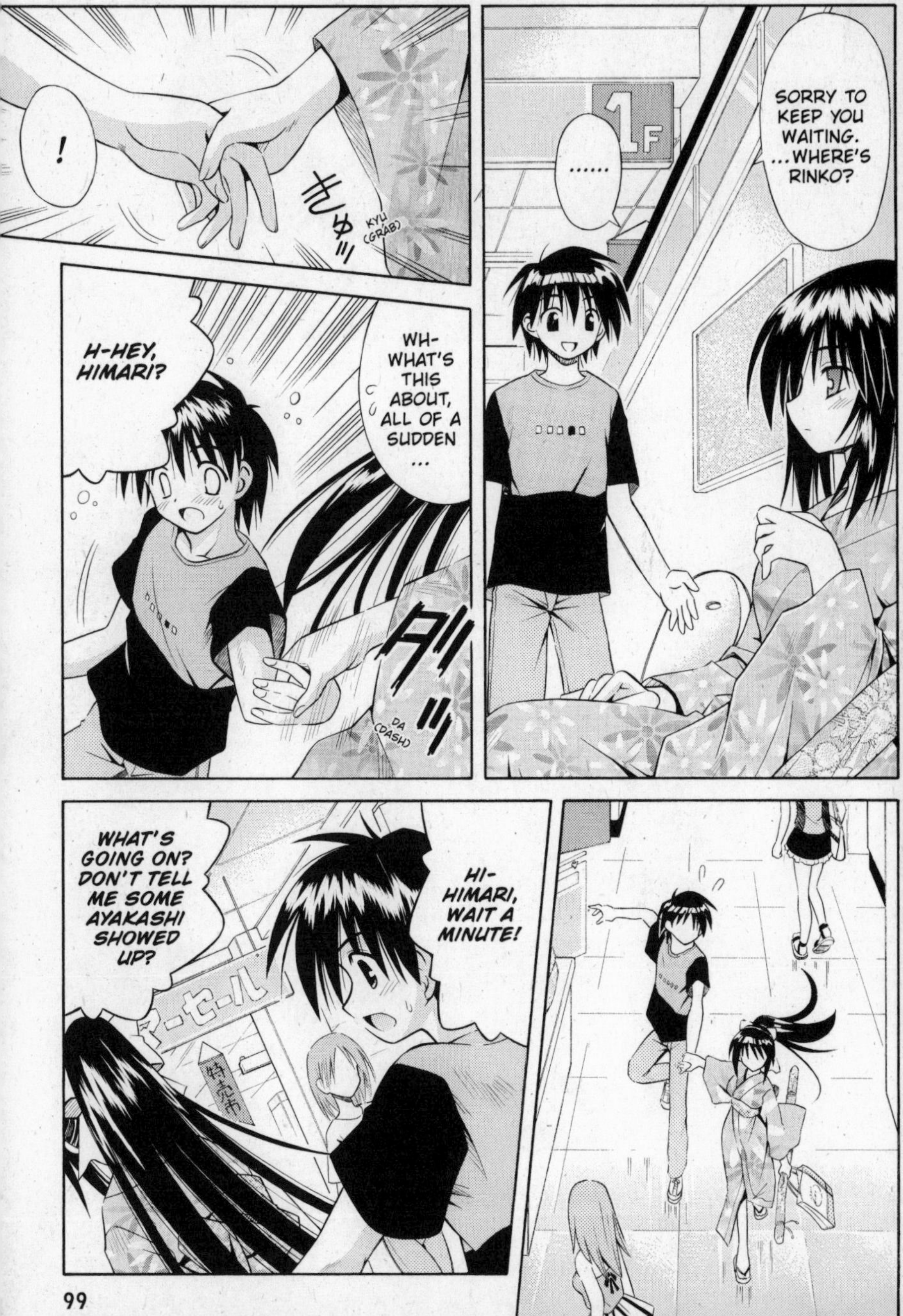
SORRY TO KEEP YOU WAITING. ...WHERE'S RINKO?
......
1F
!
きゅ
KYU (GRAB)
WH- WHAT'S THIS ABOUT, ALL OF A SUDDEN ...
H-HEY, HIMARI?
ダッ
DA (DASH)
HI- HIMARI, WAIT A MINUTE!
WHAT'S GOING ON? DON'T TELL ME SOME AYAKASHI SHOWED UP?

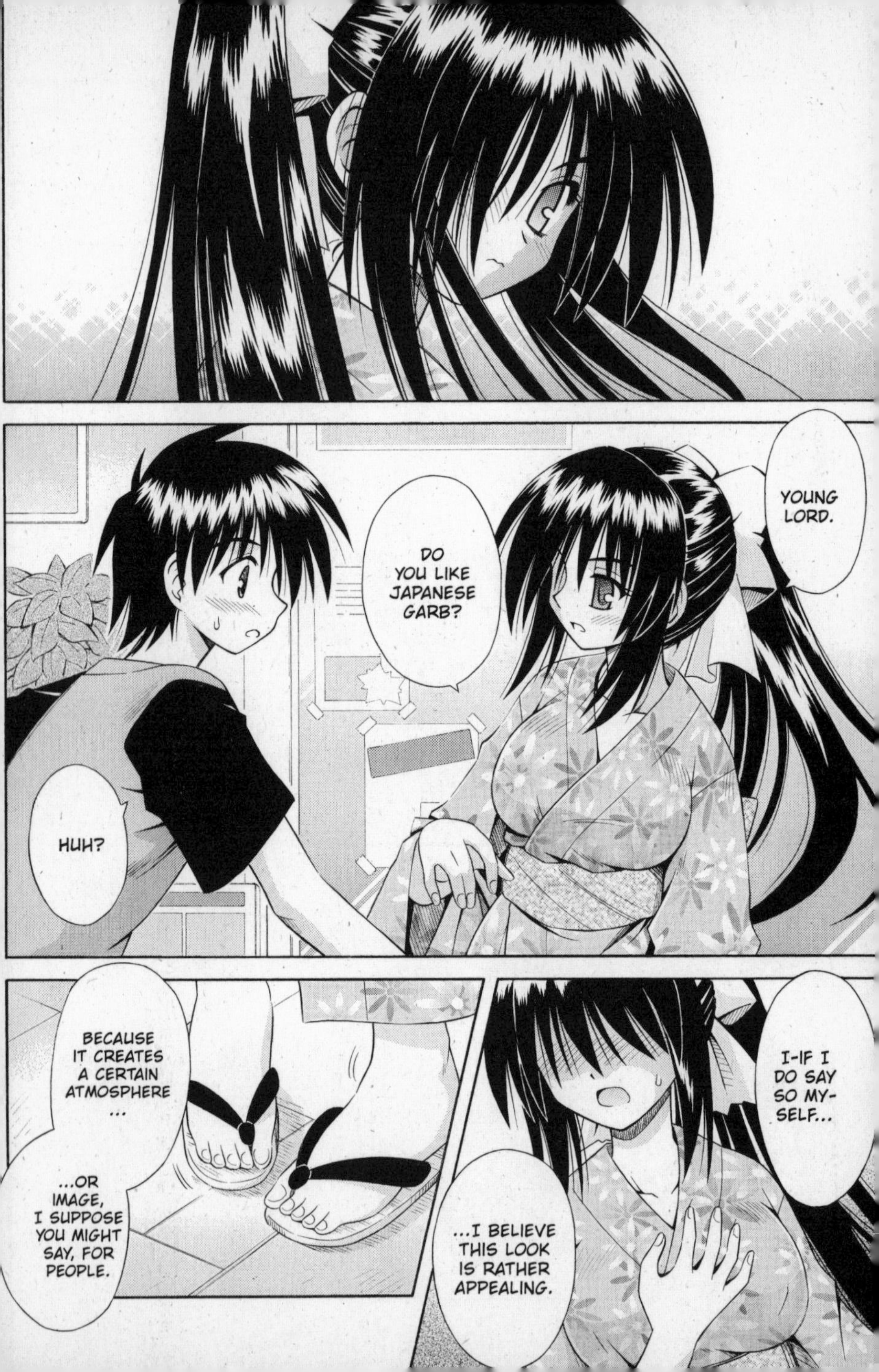
YOUNG LORD.
DO YOU LIKE JAPANESE GARB?
HUH?
I-IF I DO SAY SO MY-SELF...
...I BELIEVE THIS LOOK IS RATHER APPEALING.
BECAUSE IT CREATES A CERTAIN ATMOSPHERE ...
...OR IMAGE, I SUPPOSE YOU MIGHT SAY, FOR PEOPLE.

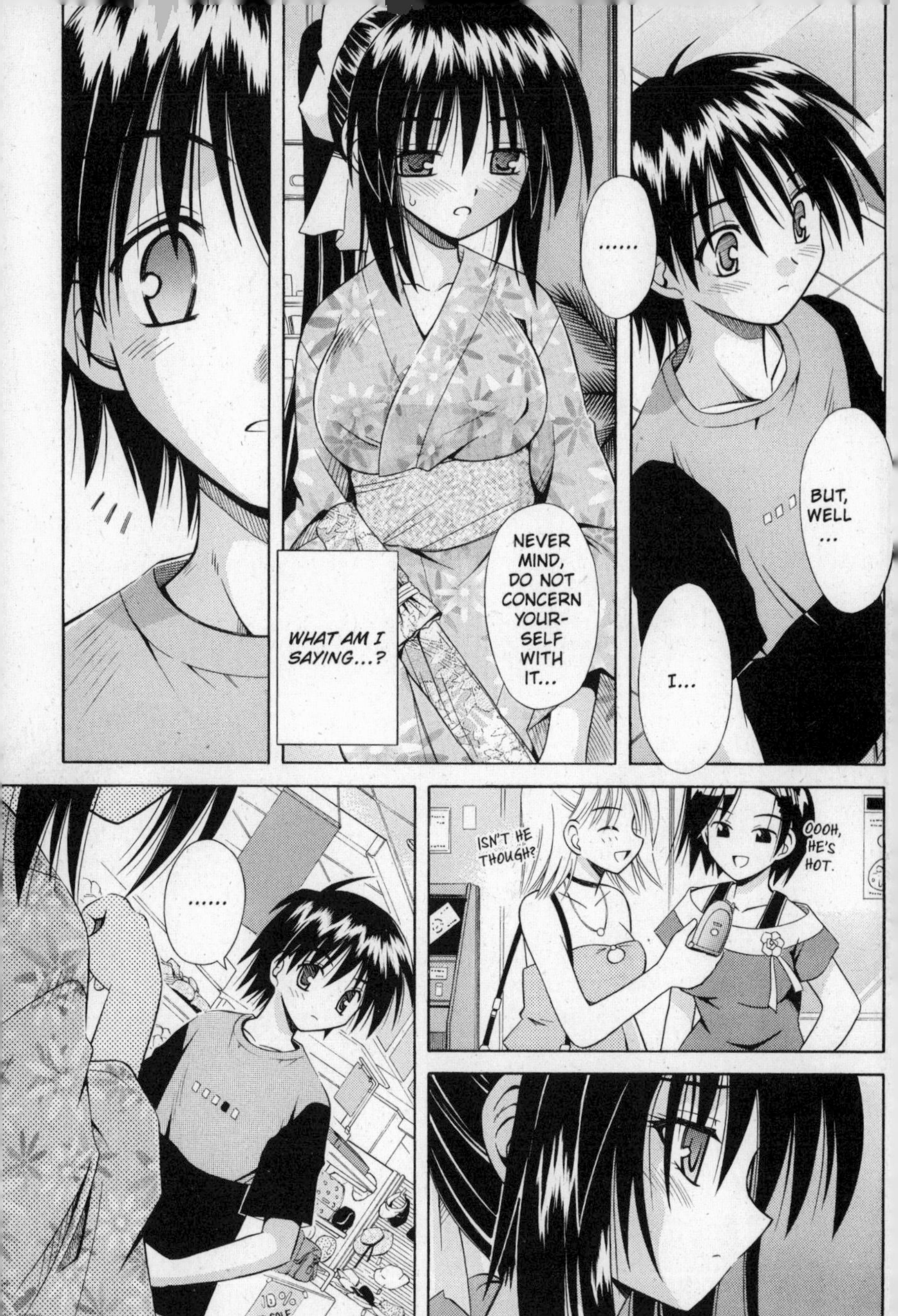
......
BUT, WELL ...
I...
NEVER MIND, DO NOT CONCERN YOUR-SELF WITH IT...
WHAT AM I SAYING...?
OOOH, HE'S HOT.
ISN'T HE THOUGH?
......
10% OFF SALE

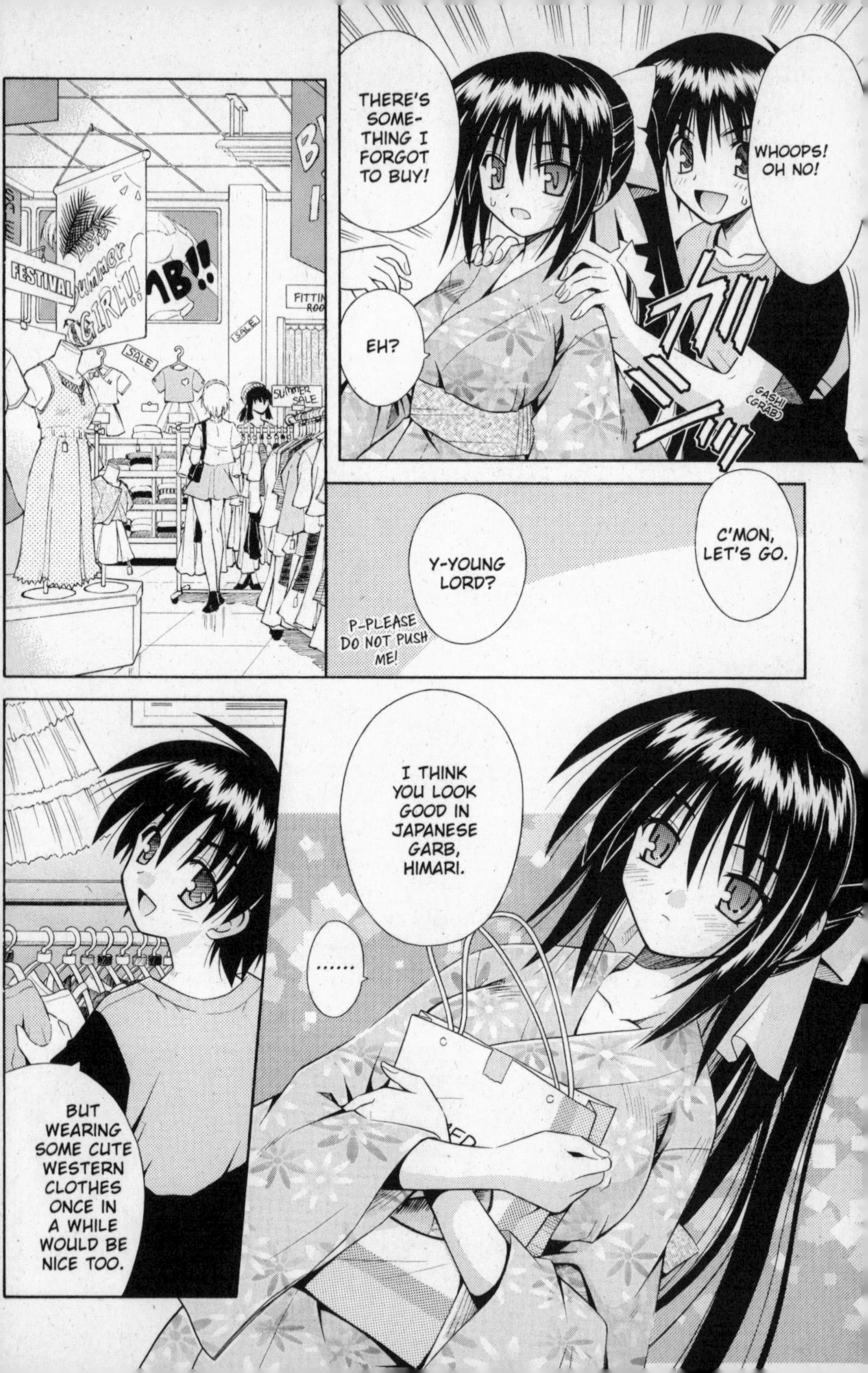
WHOOPS! OH NO!
THERE'S SOME-THING I FORGOT TO BUY!
EH?
GASHI (GRAB)
C'MON, LET'S GO.
Y-YOUNG LORD?
P-PLEASE DO NOT PUSH ME!
FESTIVAL
SALE
SALE
SUMMER SALE
I THINK YOU LOOK GOOD IN JAPANESE GARB, HIMARI.
....
BUT WEARING SOME CUTE WESTERN CLOTHES ONCE IN A WHILE WOULD BE NICE TOO.

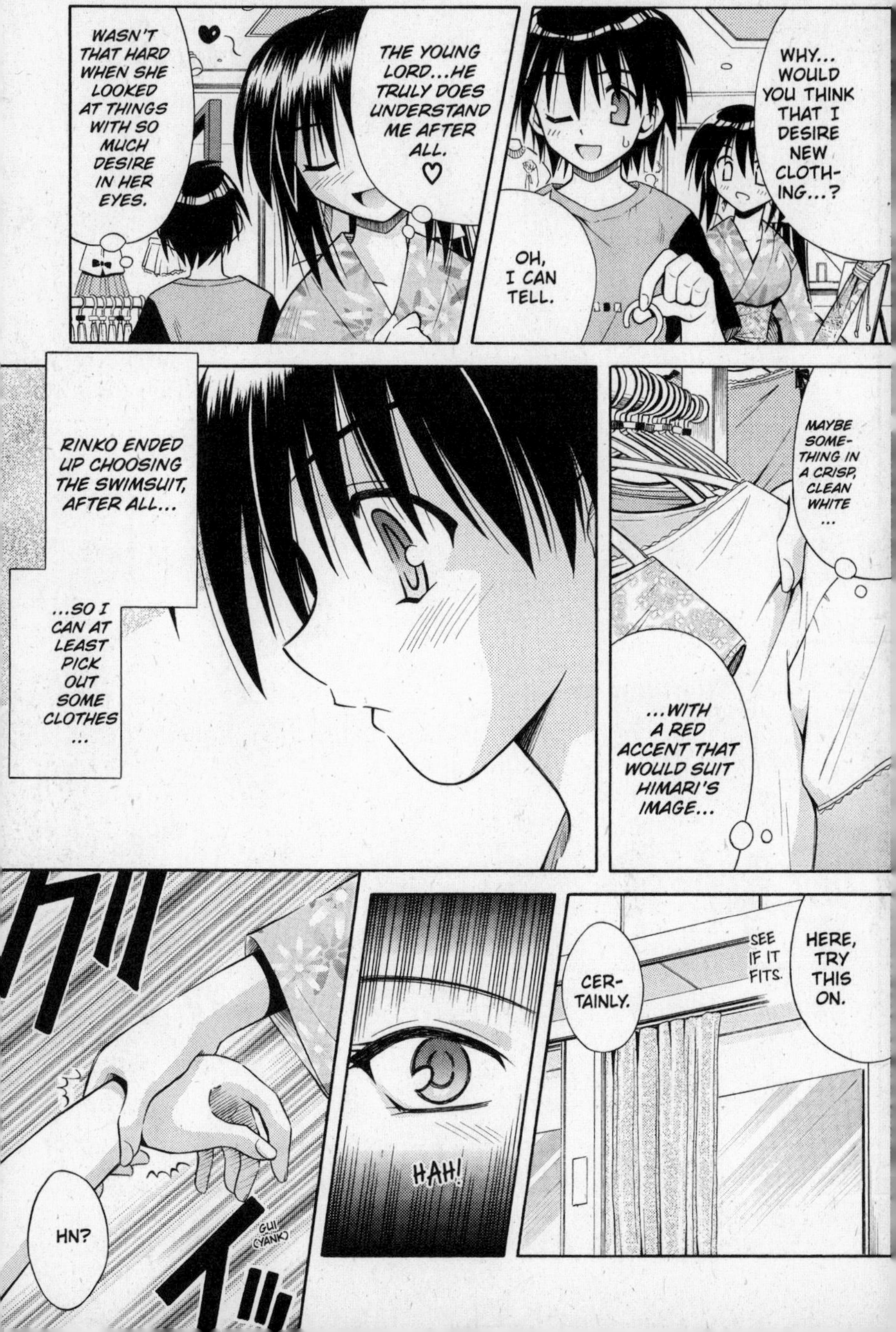
WHY... WOULD YOU THINK THAT I DESIRE NEW CLOTH-ING...?
OH, I CAN TELL.
THE YOUNG LORD...HE TRULY DOES UNDERSTAND ME AFTER ALL. ♡
WASN'T THAT HARD WHEN SHE LOOKED AT THINGS WITH SO MUCH DESIRE IN HER EYES.
MAYBE SOME-THING IN A CRISP, CLEAN WHITE...
...WITH A RED ACCENT THAT WOULD SUIT HIMARI'S IMAGE...
RINKO ENDED UP CHOOSING THE SWIMSUIT, AFTER ALL...
...SO I CAN AT LEAST PICK OUT SOME CLOTHES...
HERE, TRY THIS ON.
SEE IF IT FITS.
CER-TAINLY.
HAH!
HN?
GUI (YANK)

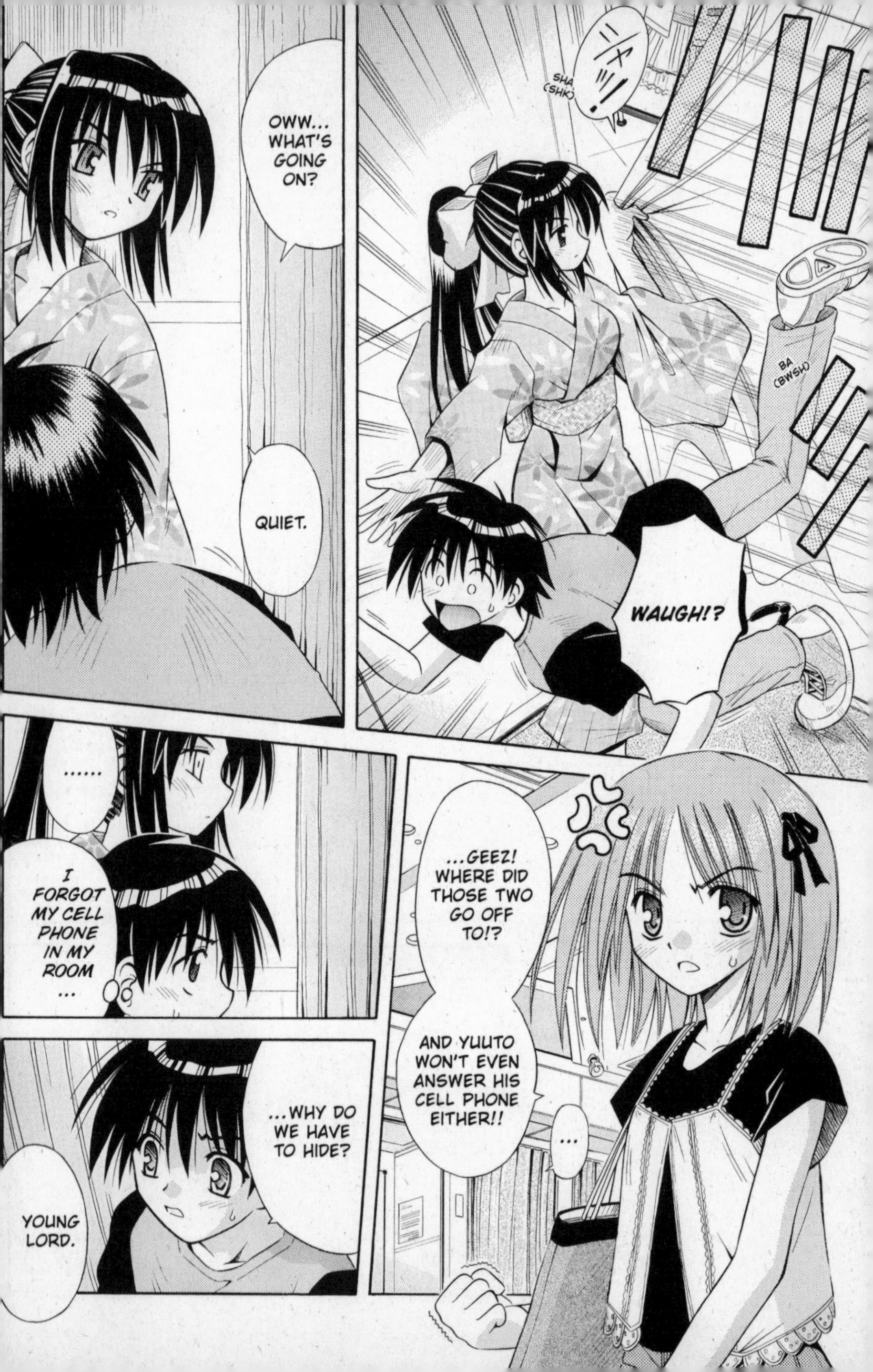
シャッ!!
SHA (SHK)
BA (BWSH)
WAUGH!?
OWW... WHAT'S GOING ON?
QUIET.
...GEEZ! WHERE DID THOSE TWO GO OFF TO!?
AND YUUTO WON'T EVEN ANSWER HIS CELL PHONE EITHER!!
...
......
I FORGOT MY CELL PHONE IN MY ROOM ...
...WHY DO WE HAVE TO HIDE?
YOUNG LORD.

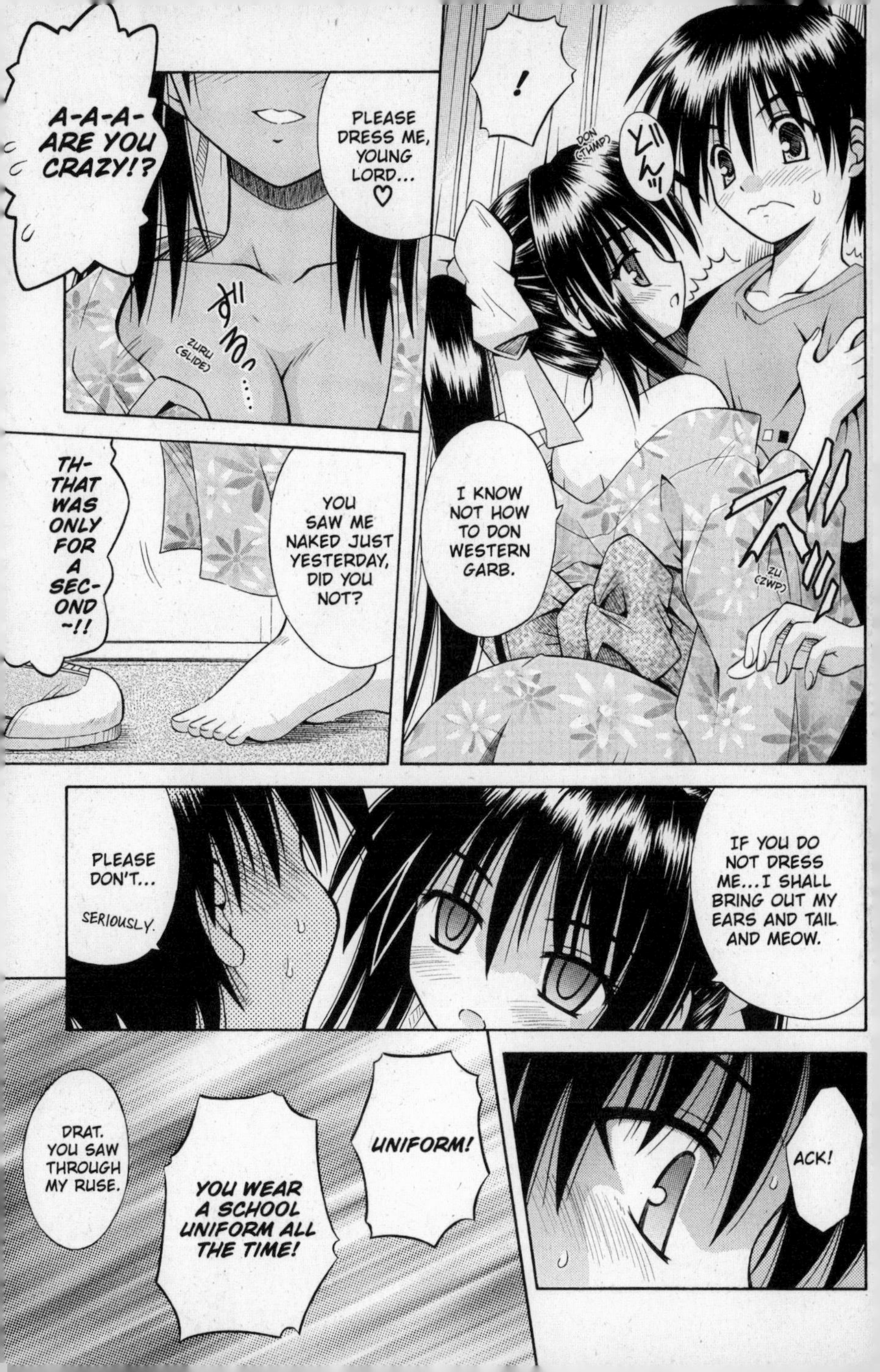
!
DON (THMP)
I KNOW NOT HOW TO DON WESTERN GARB.
ZU (ZWP)
PLEASE DRESS ME, YOUNG LORD... ♡
ZURU (SLIDE)
A-A-A-ARE YOU CRAZY!?
YOU SAW ME NAKED JUST YESTERDAY, DID YOU NOT?
TH-THAT WAS ONLY FOR A SEC-OND-!!
IF YOU DO NOT DRESS ME...I SHALL BRING OUT MY EARS AND TAIL AND MEOW.
PLEASE DON'T...
SERIOUSLY.
ACK!
UNIFORM!
YOU WEAR A SCHOOL UNIFORM ALL THE TIME!
DRAT. YOU SAW THROUGH MY RUSE.

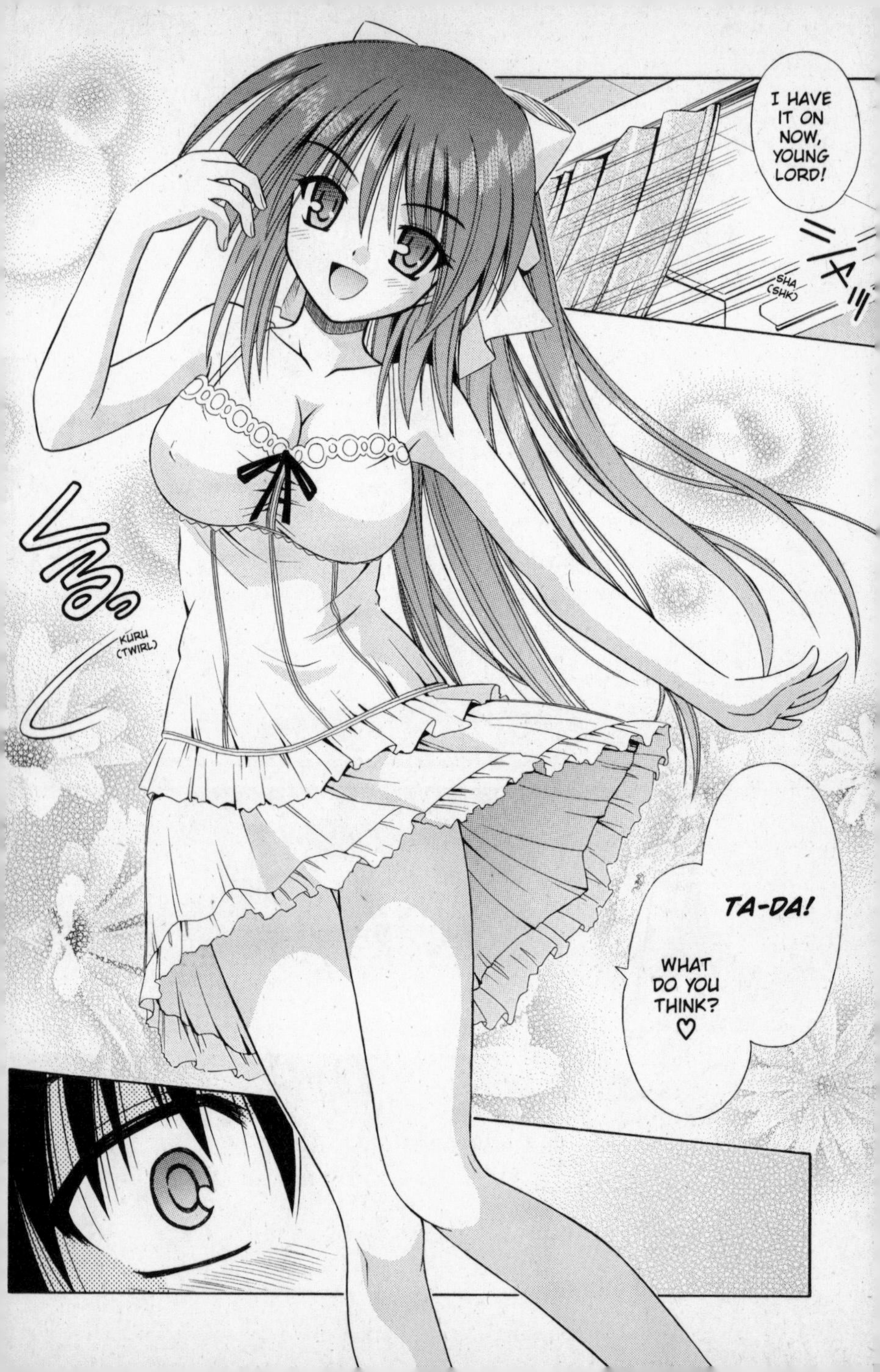
I HAVE IT ON NOW, YOUNG LORD!
SHA (SHK)
TA-DA!
WHAT DO YOU THINK? ♡
KURU (TWIRL)

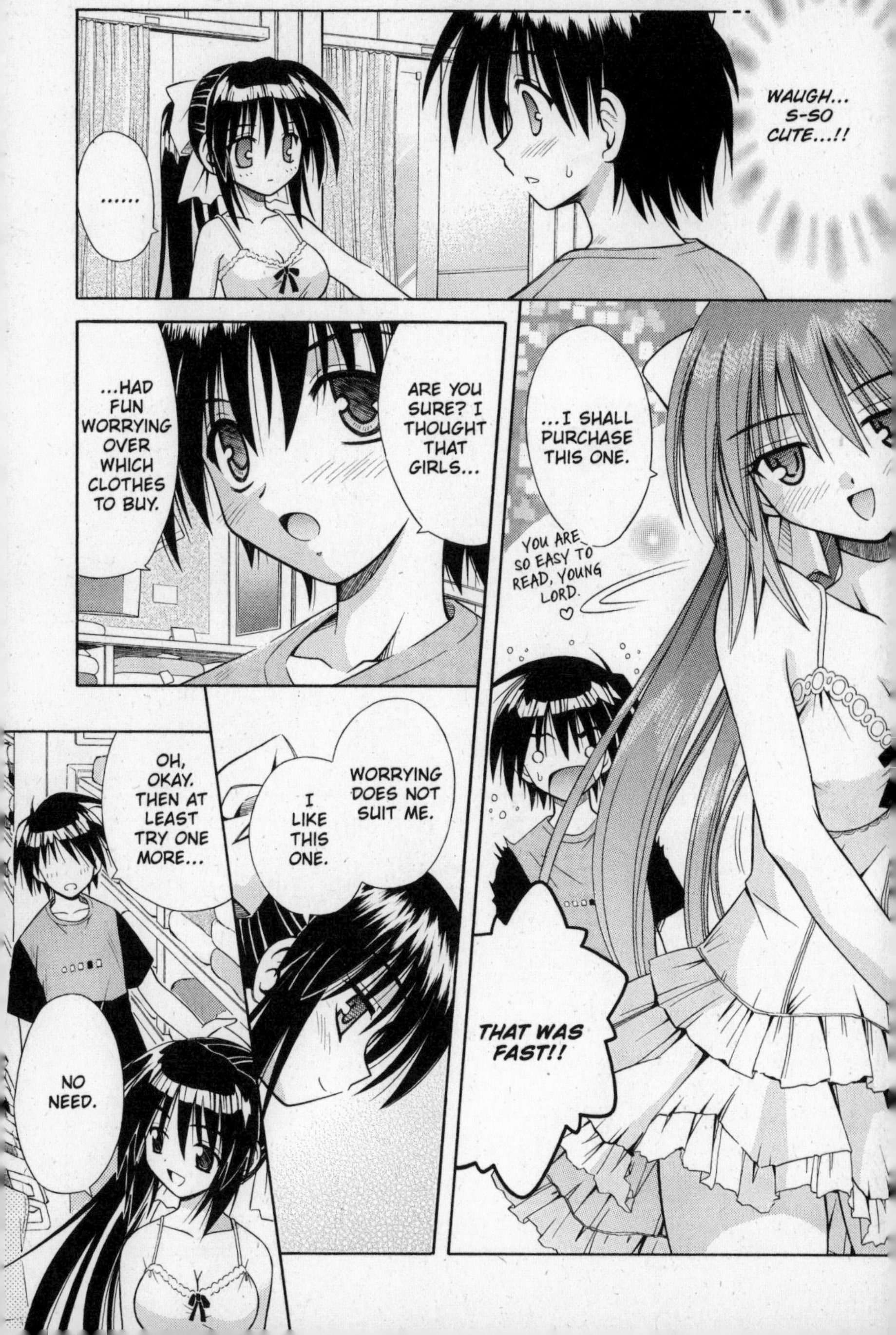
WAUGH... S-SO CUTE...!!
......
...I SHALL PURCHASE THIS ONE.
YOU ARE SO EASY TO READ, YOUNG LORD. ♡
THAT WAS FAST!!
ARE YOU SURE? I THOUGHT THAT GIRLS...
...HAD FUN WORRYING OVER WHICH CLOTHES TO BUY.
WORRYING DOES NOT SUIT ME.
I LIKE THIS ONE.
OH, OKAY. THEN AT LEAST TRY ONE MORE...
NO NEED.

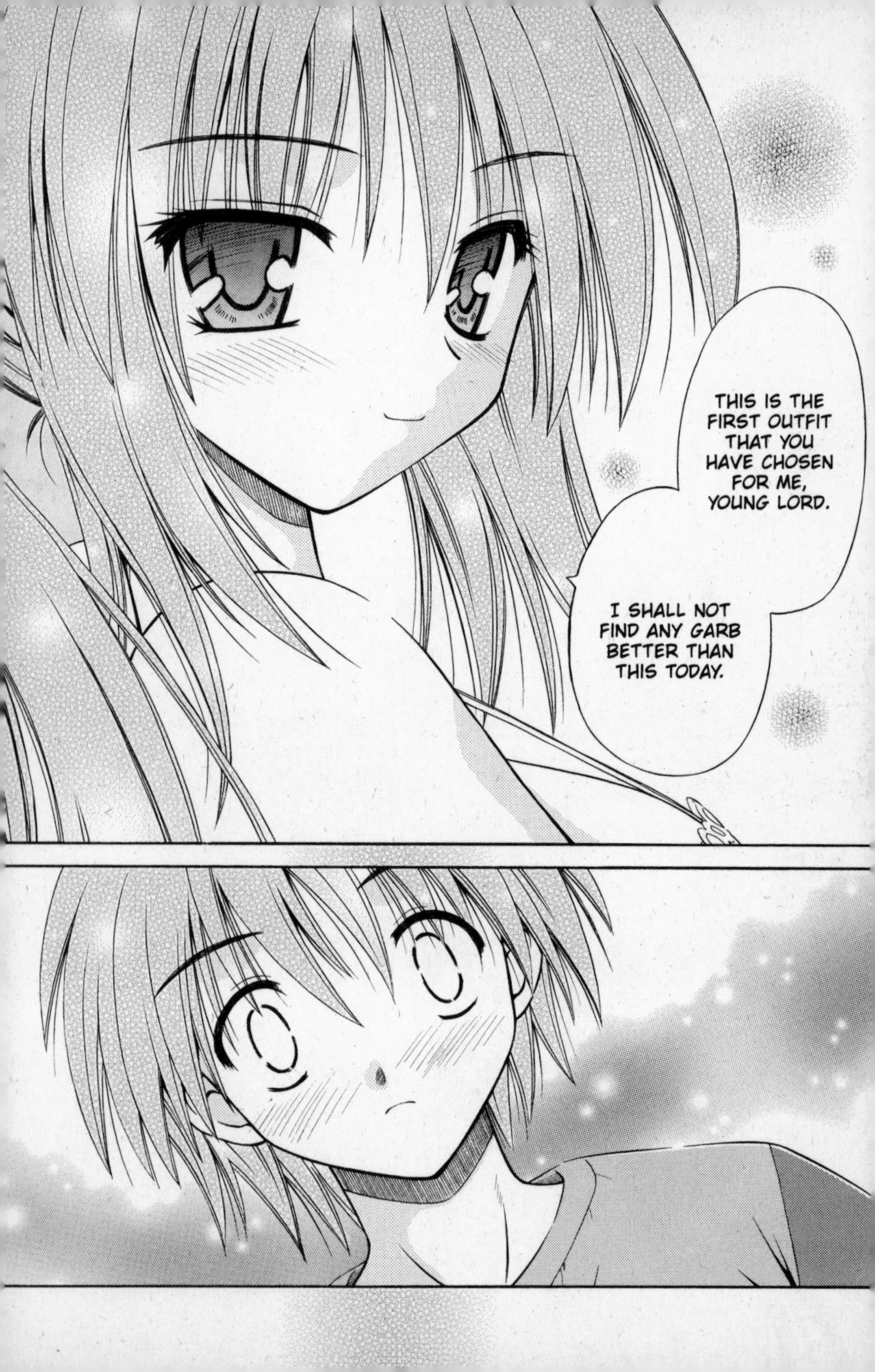
THIS IS THE FIRST OUTFIT THAT YOU HAVE CHOSEN FOR ME, YOUNG LORD.
I SHALL NOT FIND ANY GARB BETTER THAN THIS TODAY.

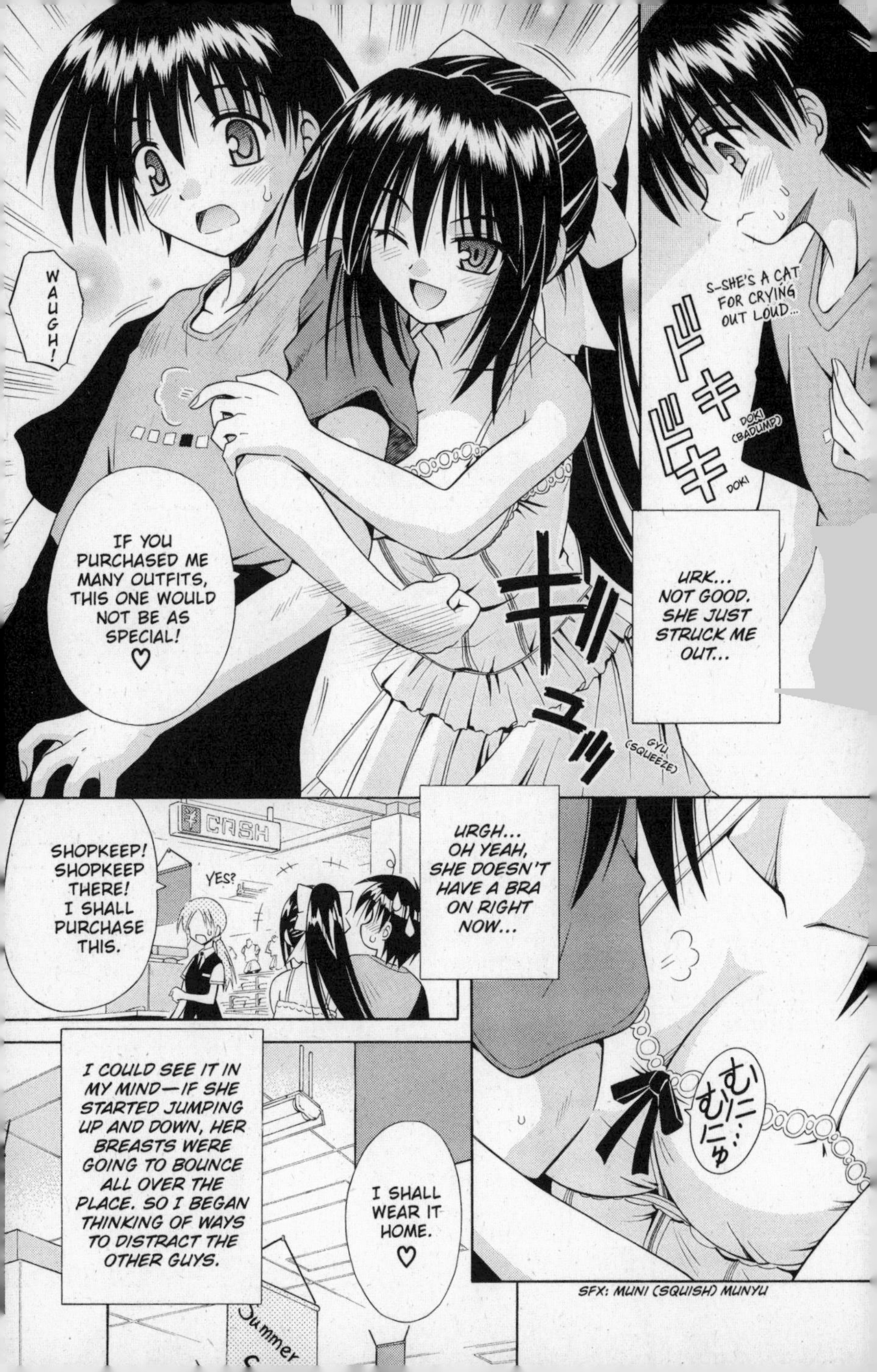
S-SHE'S A CAT FOR CRYING OUT LOUD...
ドキ ドキ
DOKI (BADUMP) DOKI
WAUGH!
IF YOU PURCHASED ME MANY OUTFITS, THIS ONE WOULD NOT BE AS SPECIAL! ♡
ギュッ
GYU (SQUEEZE)
URK... NOT GOOD. SHE JUST STRUCK ME OUT...
URGH... OH YEAH, SHE DOESN'T HAVE A BRA ON RIGHT NOW...
むに むにゅ…
SFX: MUNI (SQUISH) MUNYU
CASH
SHOPKEEP! SHOPKEEP THERE! I SHALL PURCHASE THIS.
YES?
I SHALL WEAR IT HOME. ♡
I COULD SEE IT IN MY MIND—IF SHE STARTED JUMPING UP AND DOWN, HER BREASTS WERE GOING TO BOUNCE ALL OVER THE PLACE. SO I BEGAN THINKING OF WAYS TO DISTRACT THE OTHER GUYS.
Summer

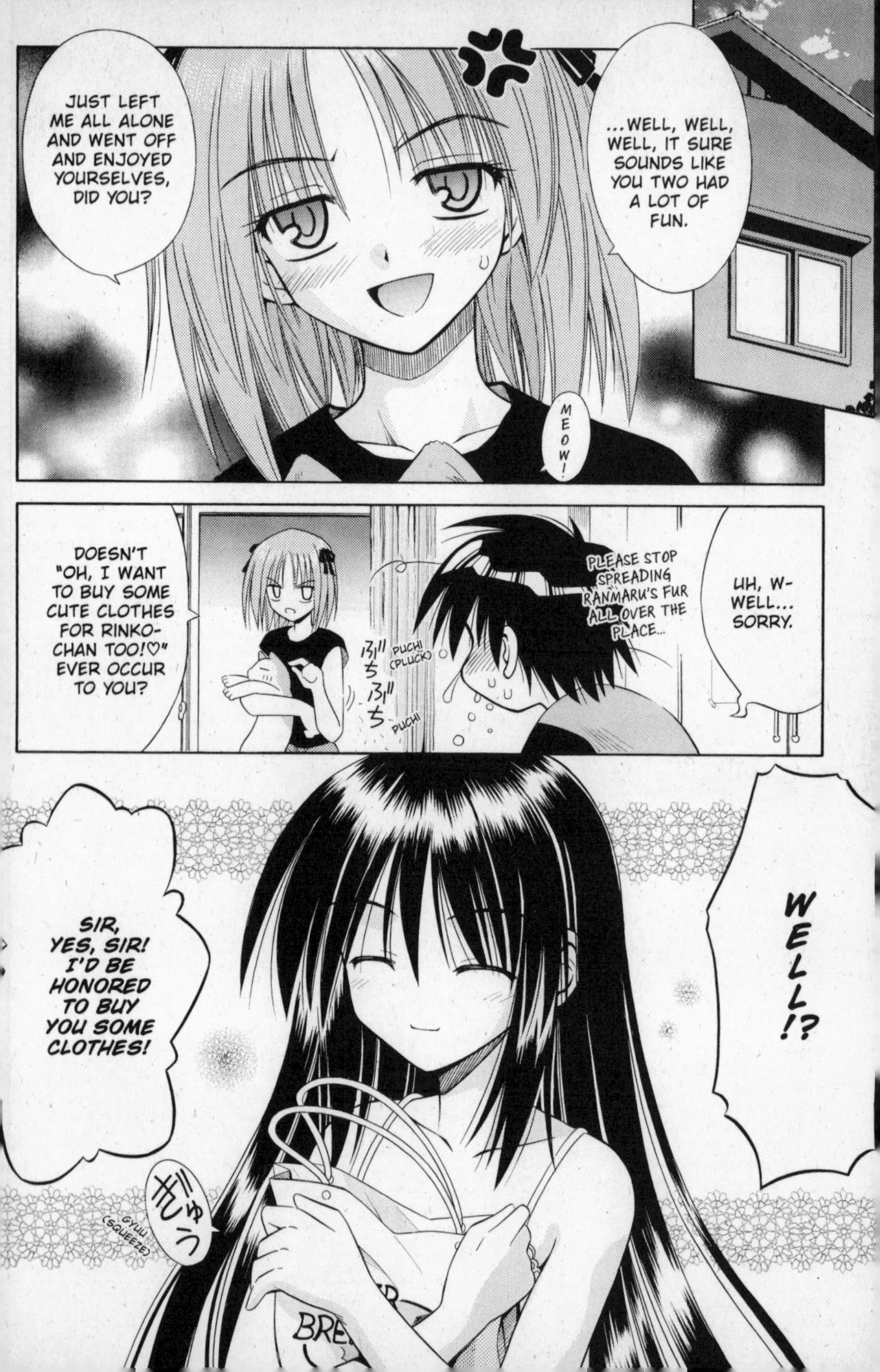
...WELL, WELL, WELL, IT SURE SOUNDS LIKE YOU TWO HAD A LOT OF FUN.
JUST LEFT ME ALL ALONE AND WENT OFF AND ENJOYED YOURSELVES, DID YOU?
MEOW!
UH, W-WELL... SORRY.
PLEASE STOP SPREADING RANMARU'S FUR ALL OVER THE PLACE...
ぷち PUCHI (PLUCK)
ぷち PUCHI
DOESN'T "OH, I WANT TO BUY SOME CUTE CLOTHES FOR RINKO-CHAN TOO!♡" EVER OCCUR TO YOU?
WELL!?
SIR, YES, SIR! I'D BE HONORED TO BUY YOU SOME CLOTHES!
ぎゅう GYUU (SQUEEZE)

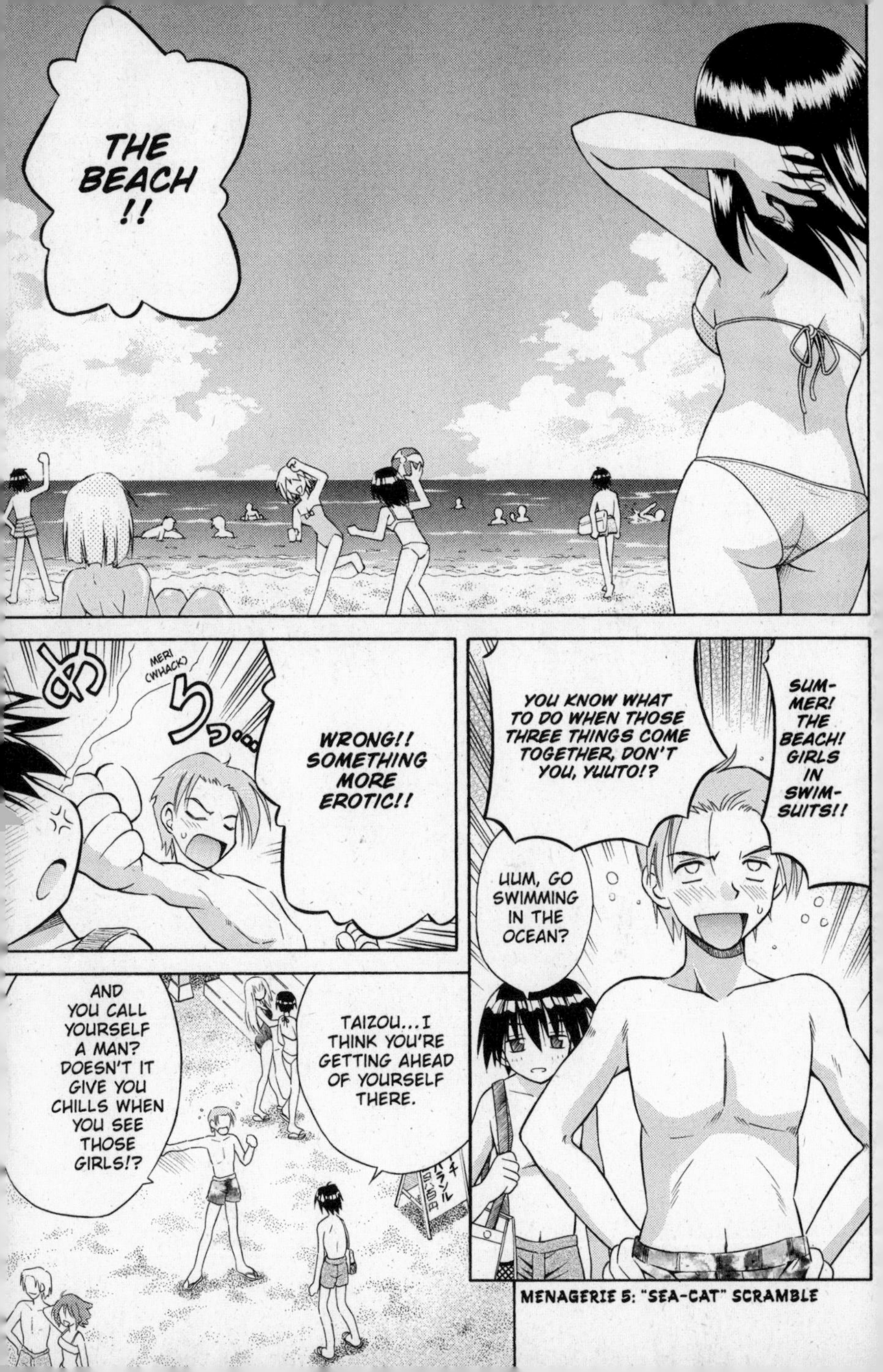
THE BEACH !!
SUM-MER! THE BEACH! GIRLS IN SWIM-SUITS!!
YOU KNOW WHAT TO DO WHEN THOSE THREE THINGS COME TOGETHER, DON'T YOU, YUUTO!?
UUM, GO SWIMMING IN THE OCEAN?
MERI (WHACK)
WRONG!! SOMETHING MORE EROTIC!!
TAIZOU...I THINK YOU'RE GETTING AHEAD OF YOURSELF THERE.
AND YOU CALL YOURSELF A MAN? DOESN'T IT GIVE YOU CHILLS WHEN YOU SEE THOSE GIRLS!?

MENAGERIE 5: "SEA-CAT" SCRAMBLE

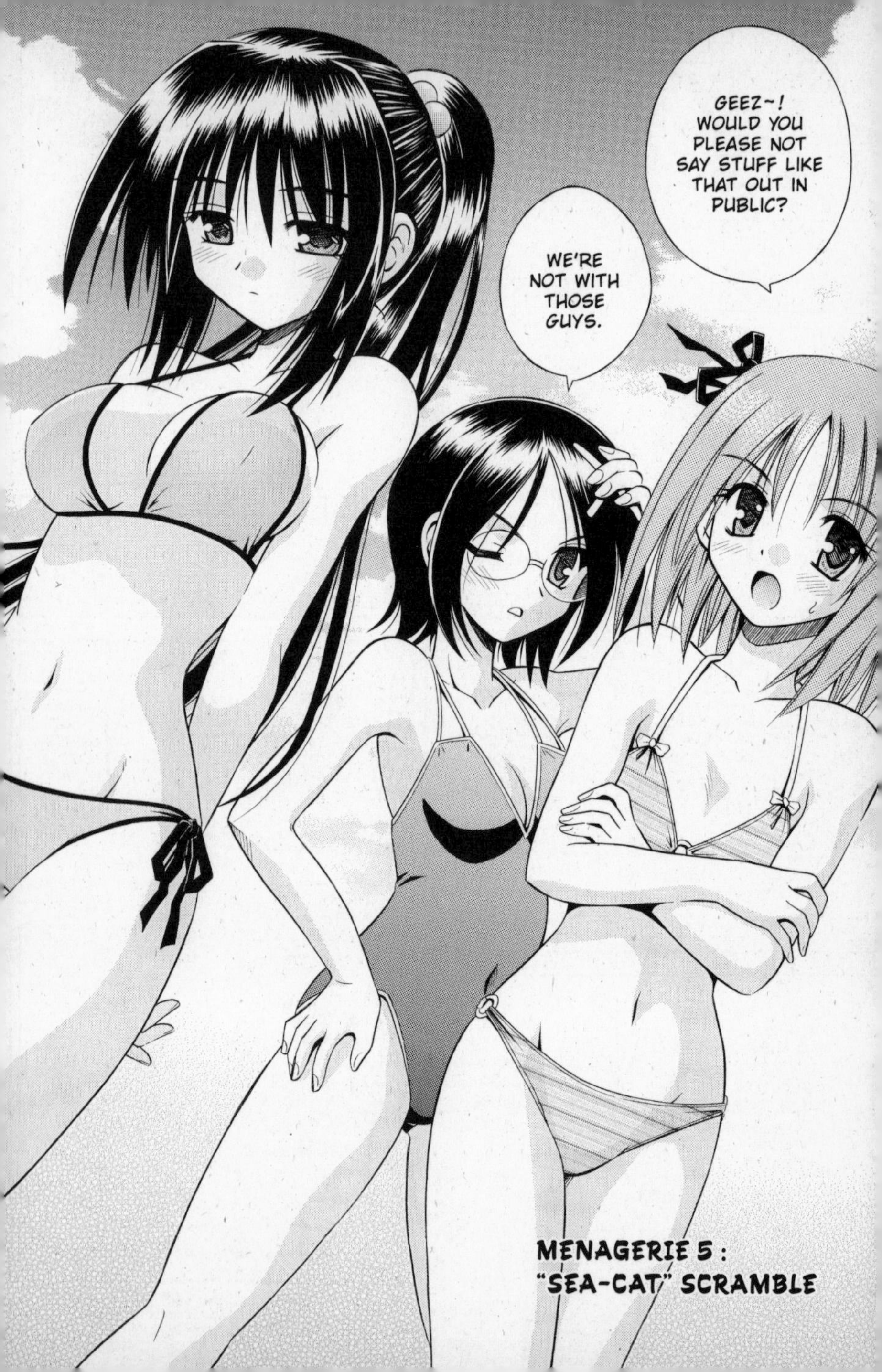
GEEZ~! WOULD YOU PLEASE NOT SAY STUFF LIKE THAT OUT IN PUBLIC?
WE'RE NOT WITH THOSE GUYS.
MENAGERIE 5 :
"SEA-CAT" SCRAMBLE

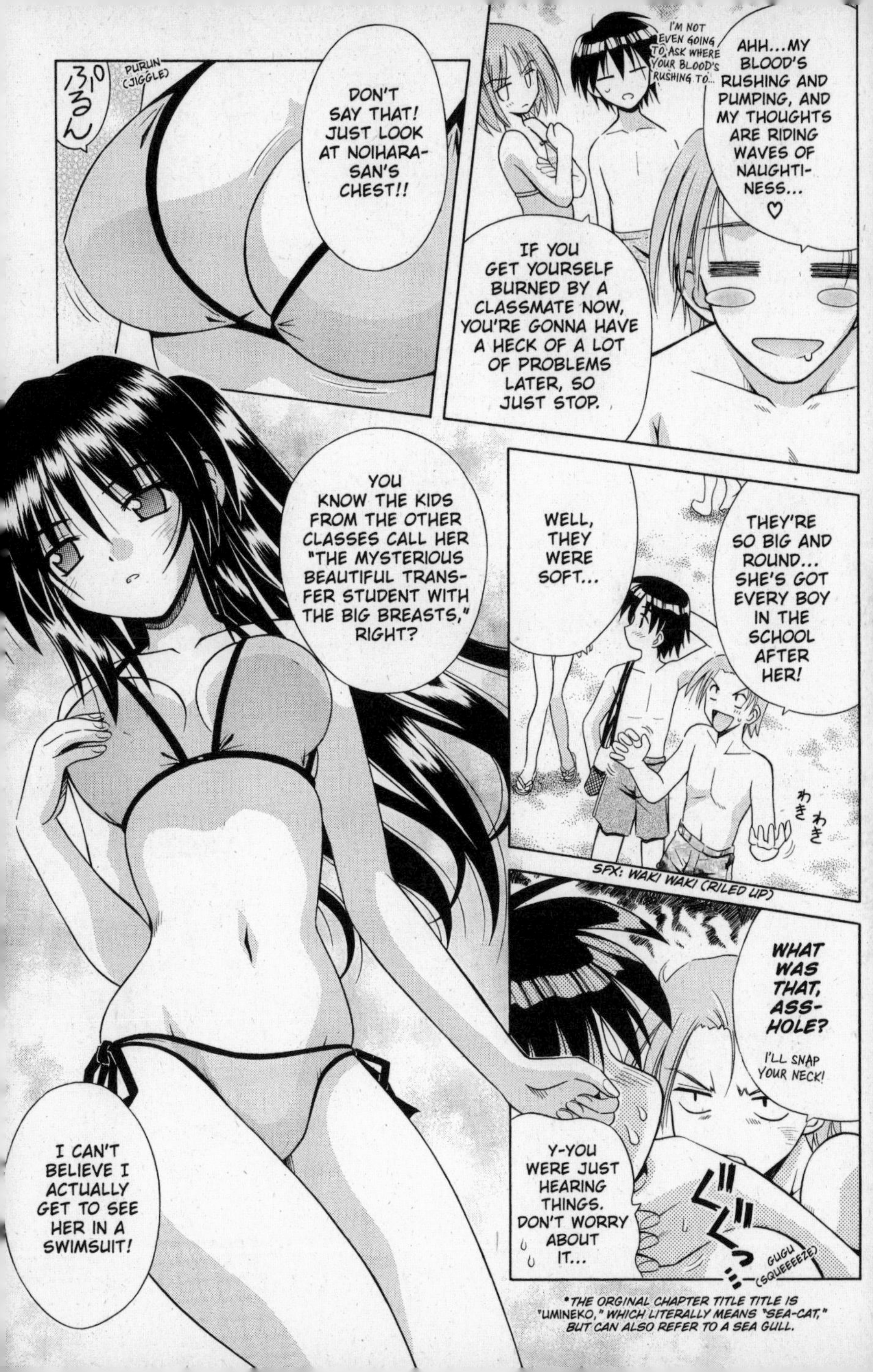
AHH...MY BLOOD'S RUSHING AND PUMPING, AND MY THOUGHTS ARE RIDING WAVES OF NAUGHTI-NESS... ♡
I'M NOT EVEN GOING TO ASK WHERE YOUR BLOOD'S RUSHING TO...
IF YOU GET YOURSELF BURNED BY A CLASSMATE NOW, YOU'RE GONNA HAVE A HECK OF A LOT OF PROBLEMS LATER, SO JUST STOP.
ぷるん
PURUN (JIGGLE)
DON'T SAY THAT! JUST LOOK AT NOIHARA-SAN'S CHEST!!
THEY'RE SO BIG AND ROUND... SHE'S GOT EVERY BOY IN THE SCHOOL AFTER HER!
WELL, THEY WERE SOFT...
わきわき
SFX: WAKI WAKI (RILED UP)
WHAT WAS THAT, ASS-HOLE?
I'LL SNAP YOUR NECK!
Y-YOU WERE JUST HEARING THINGS. DON'T WORRY ABOUT IT...
ぐぐっ
GUGU (SQUEEEEZE)
YOU KNOW THE KIDS FROM THE OTHER CLASSES CALL HER "THE MYSTERIOUS BEAUTIFUL TRANS-FER STUDENT WITH THE BIG BREASTS," RIGHT?
I CAN'T BELIEVE I ACTUALLY GET TO SEE HER IN A SWIMSUIT!

*THE ORGINAL CHAPTER TITLE TITLE IS "UMINEKO," WHICH LITERALLY MEANS "SEA-CAT," BUT CAN ALSO REFER TO A SEA GULL.

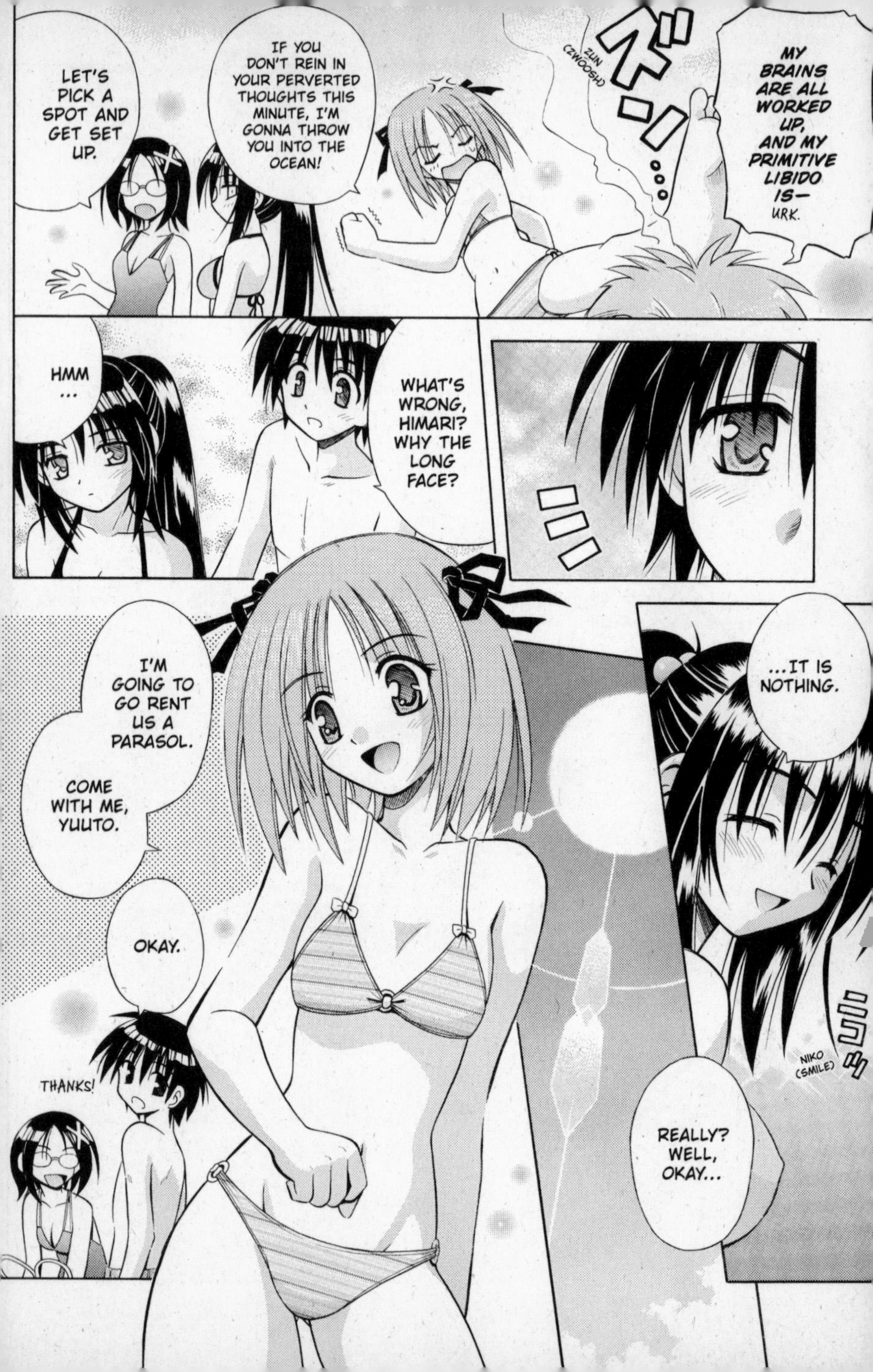
MY BRAINS ARE ALL WORKED UP, AND MY PRIMITIVE LIBIDO IS—
URK.
ZUN (ZWOOSH)
IF YOU DON'T REIN IN YOUR PERVERTED THOUGHTS THIS MINUTE, I'M GONNA THROW YOU INTO THE OCEAN!
LET'S PICK A SPOT AND GET SET UP.
WHAT'S WRONG, HIMARI? WHY THE LONG FACE?
HMM ...
...IT IS NOTHING.
NIKO (SMILE)
REALLY? WELL, OKAY...
I'M GOING TO GO RENT US A PARASOL.
COME WITH ME, YUUTO.
OKAY.
THANKS!

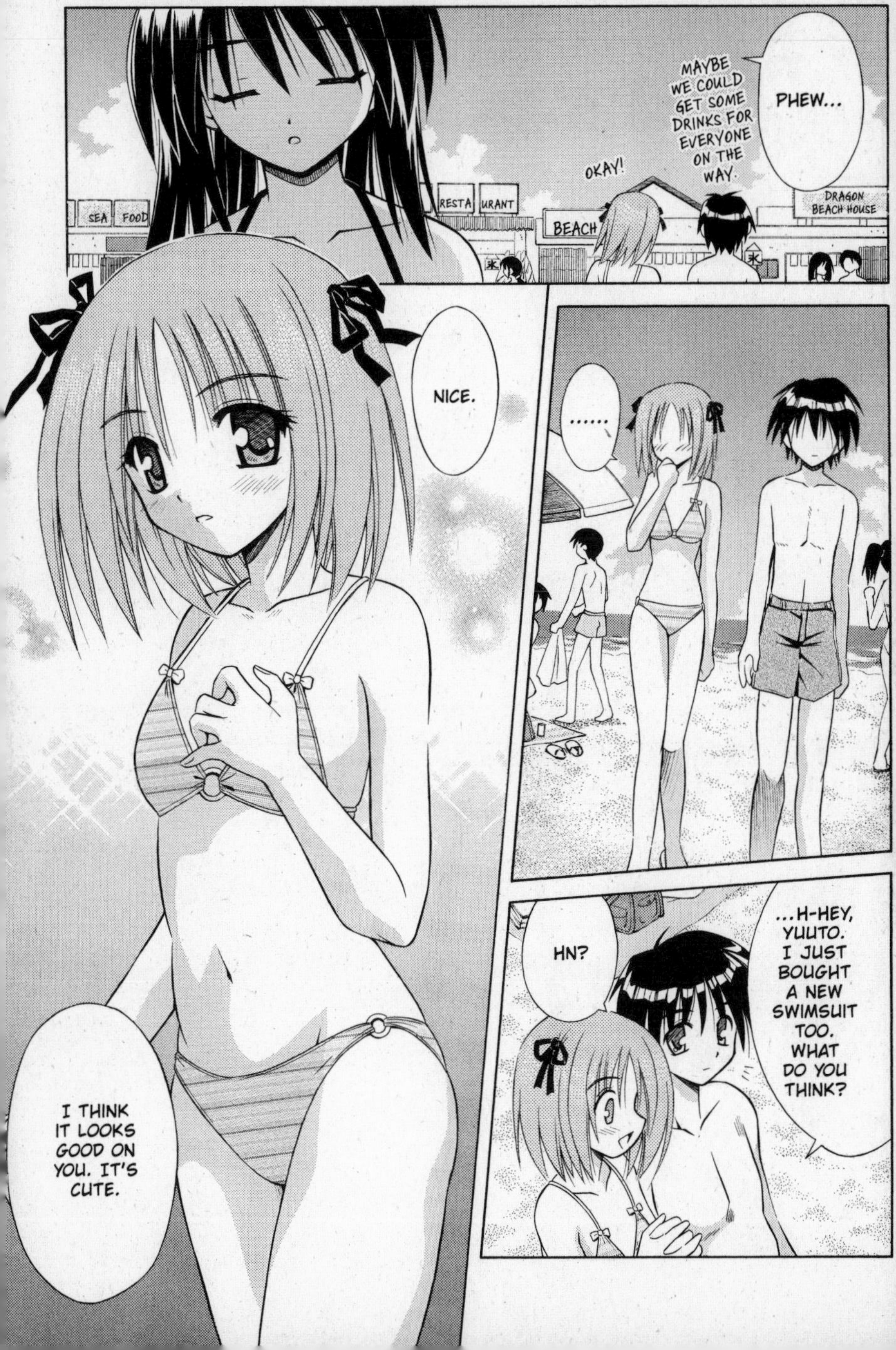
PHEW...
DRAGON BEACH HOUSE
MAYBE WE COULD GET SOME DRINKS FOR EVERYONE ON THE WAY.
OKAY!
BEACH
RESTA URANT
SEA FOOD
......
...H-HEY, YUUTO. I JUST BOUGHT A NEW SWIMSUIT TOO. WHAT DO YOU THINK?
HN?
NICE.
I THINK IT LOOKS GOOD ON YOU. IT'S CUTE.

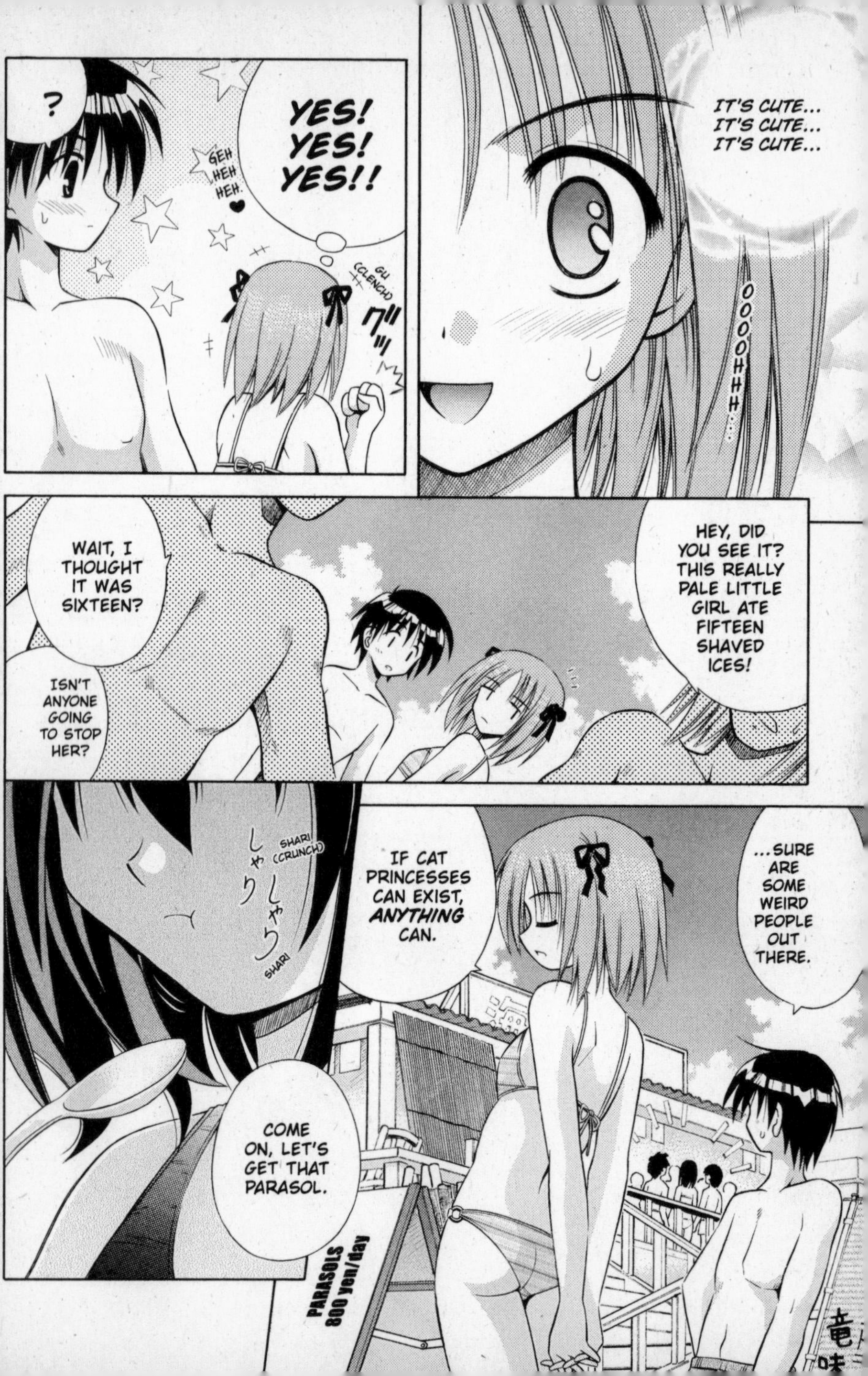
IT'S CUTE... IT'S CUTE... IT'S CUTE...
OOOOOHHHH...
?
YES! YES! YES!!
GEH HEH HEH. ♥
GU (CLENCH)
グッ
HEY, DID YOU SEE IT? THIS REALLY PALE LITTLE GIRL ATE FIFTEEN SHAVED ICES!
WAIT, I THOUGHT IT WAS SIXTEEN?
ISN'T ANYONE GOING TO STOP HER?
...SURE ARE SOME WEIRD PEOPLE OUT THERE.
IF CAT PRINCESSES CAN EXIST, **ANYTHING** CAN.
COME ON, LET'S GET THAT PARASOL.
PARASOLS 800 yen/day
しゃり SHARI (CRUNCH)
しゃり SHARI

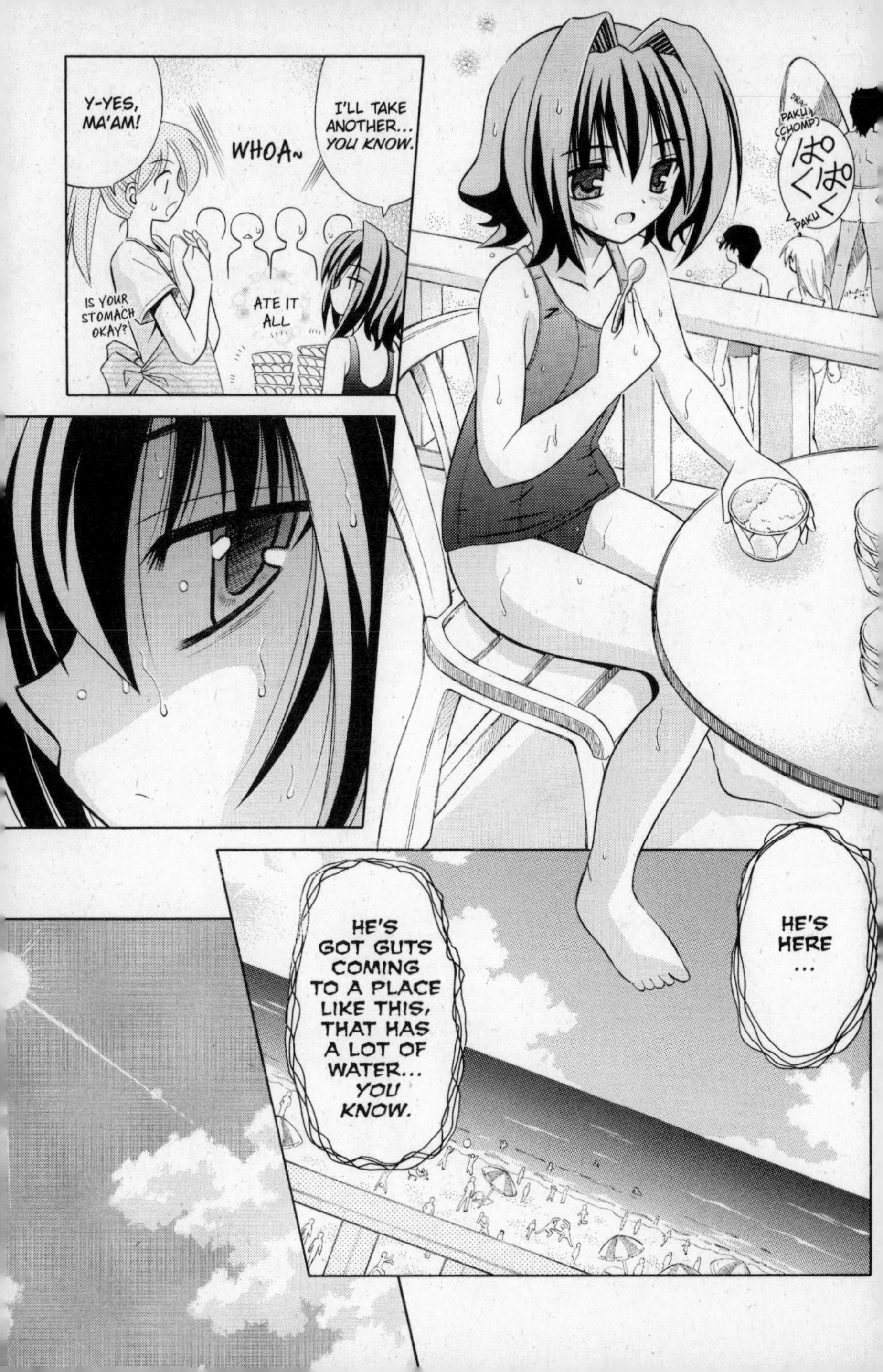
PAKU (CHOMP)
ぱくぱく
PAKU
I'LL TAKE ANOTHER... YOU KNOW.
Y-YES, MA'AM!
WHOA~
ATE IT ALL
IS YOUR STOMACH OKAY?
HE'S HERE...
HE'S GOT GUTS COMING TO A PLACE LIKE THIS, THAT HAS A LOT OF WATER... YOU KNOW.

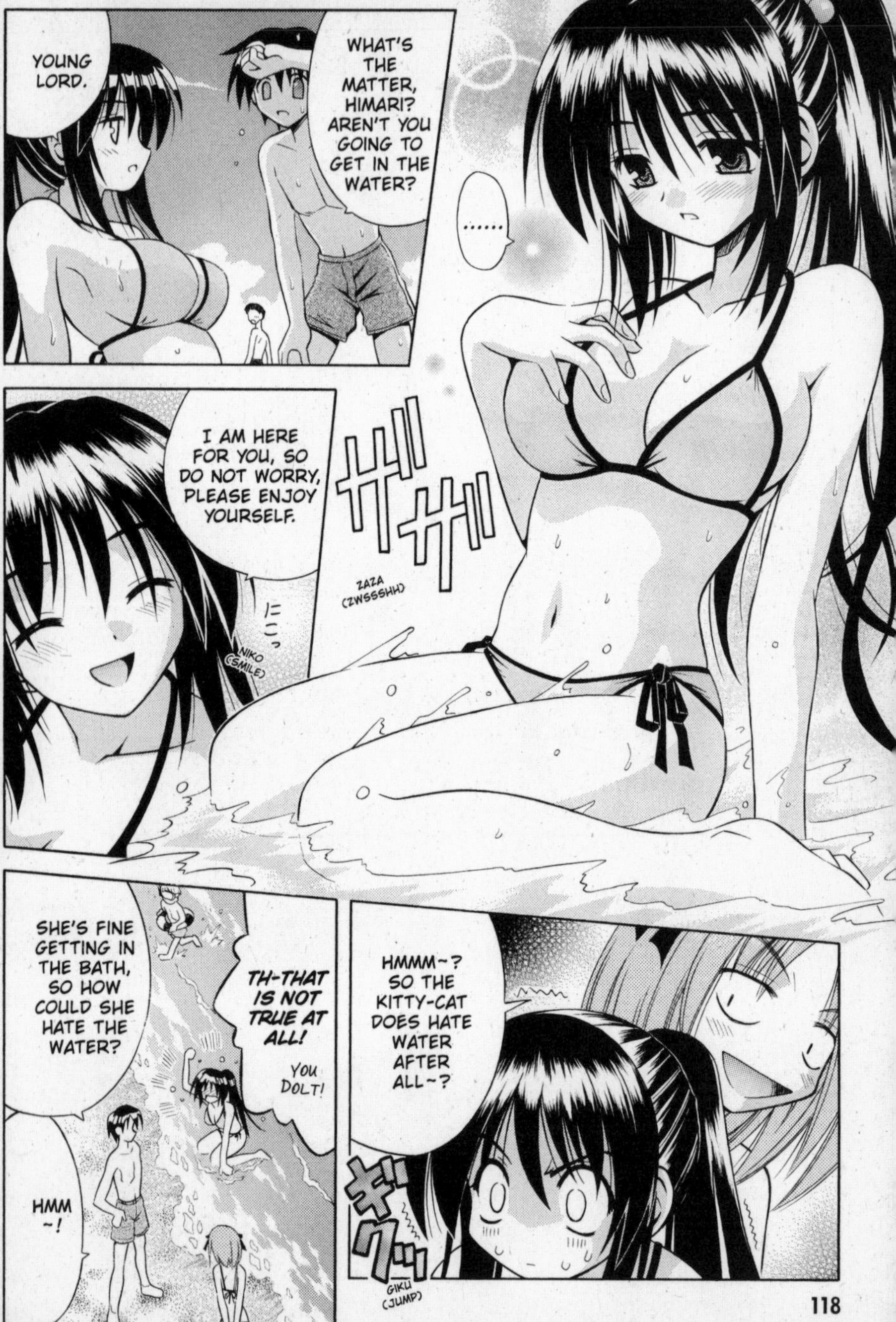
......
ザザ
ZAZA (ZWSSSHH)
WHAT'S THE MATTER, HIMARI? AREN'T YOU GOING TO GET IN THE WATER?
YOUNG LORD.
I AM HERE FOR YOU, SO DO NOT WORRY, PLEASE ENJOY YOURSELF.
にこっ
NIKO (SMILE)
HMMM~? SO THE KITTY-CAT DOES HATE WATER AFTER ALL~?
ギクッ
GIKU (JUMP)
TH-THAT IS NOT TRUE AT ALL!
YOU DOLT!
SHE'S FINE GETTING IN THE BATH, SO HOW COULD SHE HATE THE WATER?
HMM ~!

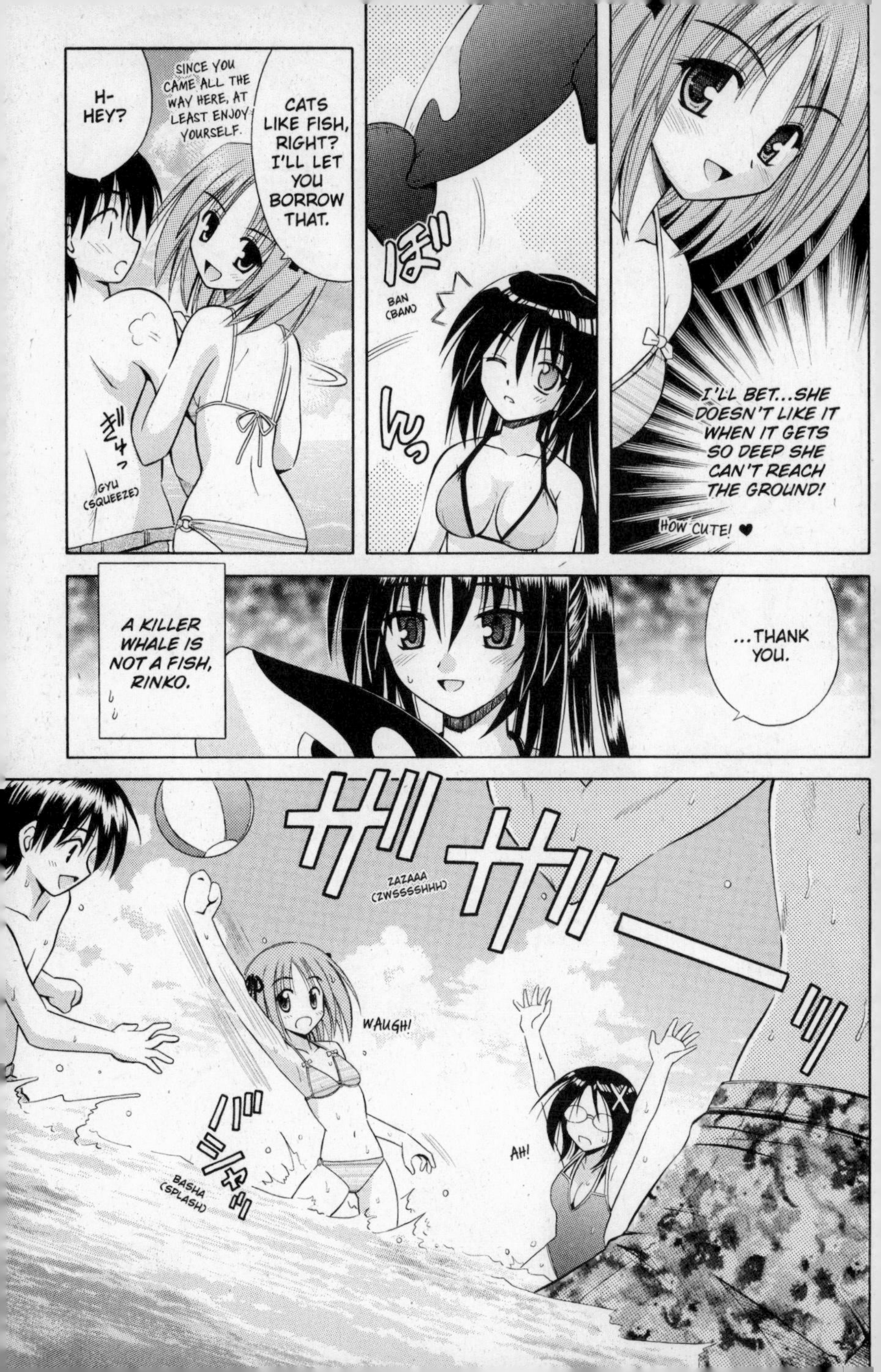
I'LL BET...SHE DOESN'T LIKE IT WHEN IT GETS SO DEEP SHE CAN'T REACH THE GROUND!
HOW CUTE! ♥
ぼ
BAN (BAM)
んっ
H-HEY?
SINCE YOU CAME ALL THE WAY HERE, AT LEAST ENJOY YOURSELF.
CATS LIKE FISH, RIGHT? I'LL LET YOU BORROW THAT.
ぎゅっ
GYU (SQUEEZE)
...THANK YOU.
A KILLER WHALE IS NOT A FISH, RINKO.
ザザァーッ
ZAZAAA (ZWSSSSHHH)
AH!
WAUGH!
バシャッ
BASHA (SPLASH)

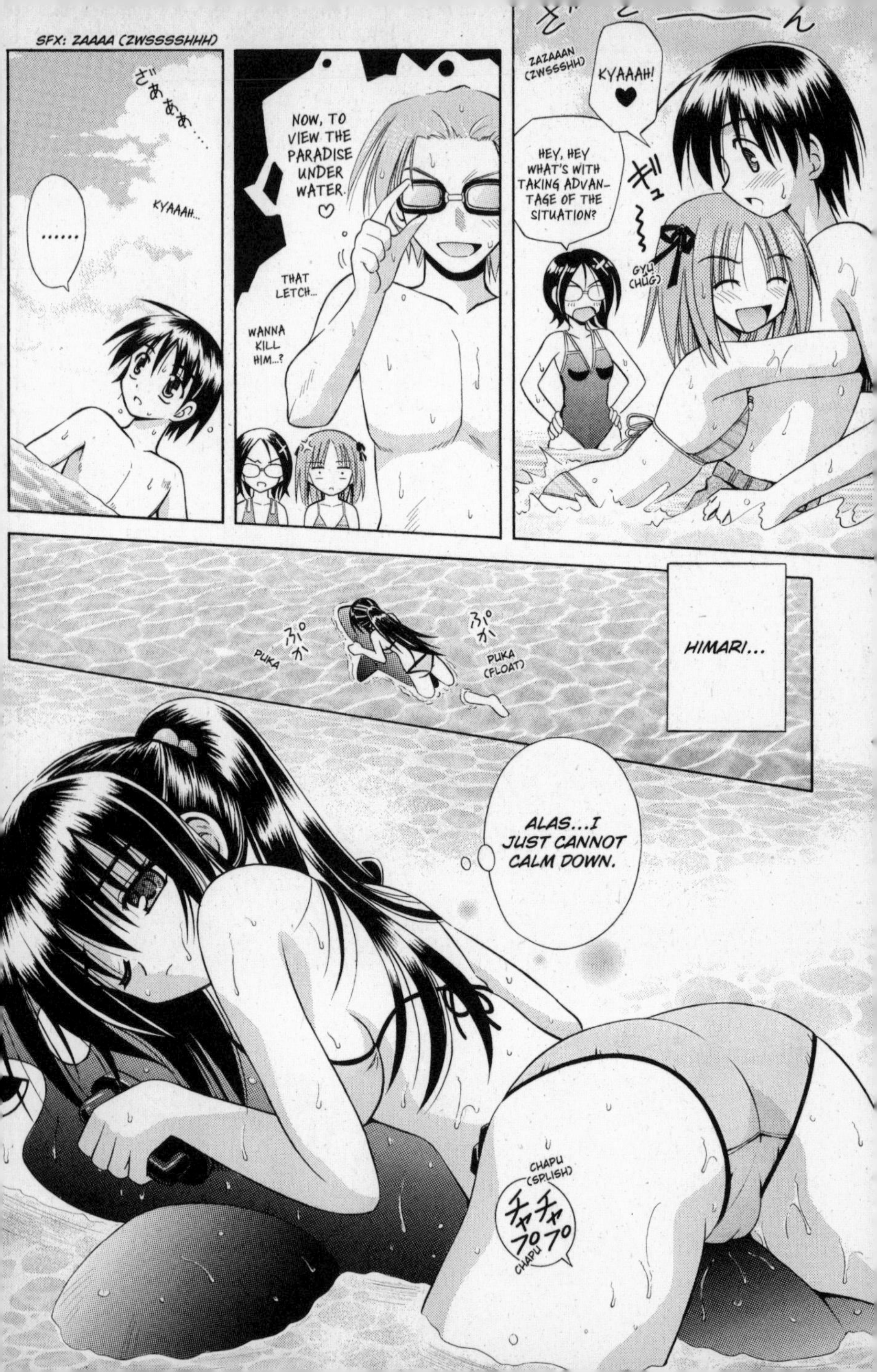
KYAAAH!
ZAZAAAN (ZWSSSHH)
HEY, HEY WHAT'S WITH TAKING ADVANTAGE OF THE SITUATION?
GYU (HUG)
NOW, TO VIEW THE PARADISE UNDER WATER.
THAT LETCH...
WANNA KILL HIM...?
SFX: ZAAAA (ZWSSSSHHH)
KYAAAH...
......
HIMARI...
PUKA (FLOAT)
PUKA
ALAS...I JUST CANNOT CALM DOWN.
CHAPU (SPLISH)
CHAPU

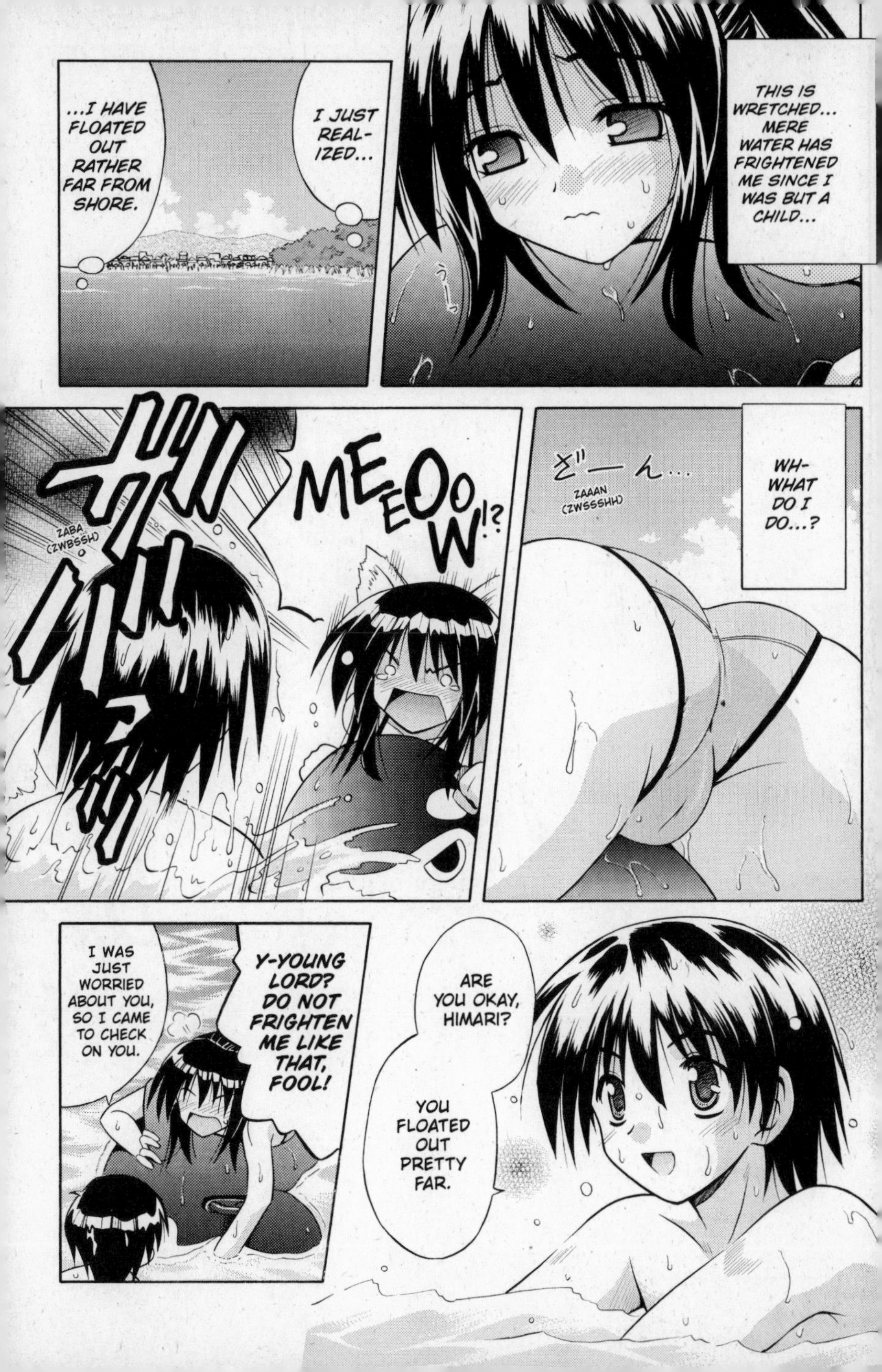
THIS IS WRETCHED... MERE WATER HAS FRIGHTENED ME SINCE I WAS BUT A CHILD...
I JUST REAL-IZED...
...I HAVE FLOATED OUT RATHER FAR FROM SHORE.
WH-WHAT DO I DO...?
ざーん…
ZAAAN (ZWSSSHH)
MEEOOW!?
ZABA (ZWBSSH)
ARE YOU OKAY, HIMARI?
YOU FLOATED OUT PRETTY FAR.
Y-YOUNG LORD? DO NOT FRIGHTEN ME LIKE THAT, FOOL!
I WAS JUST WORRIED ABOUT YOU, SO I CAME TO CHECK ON YOU.

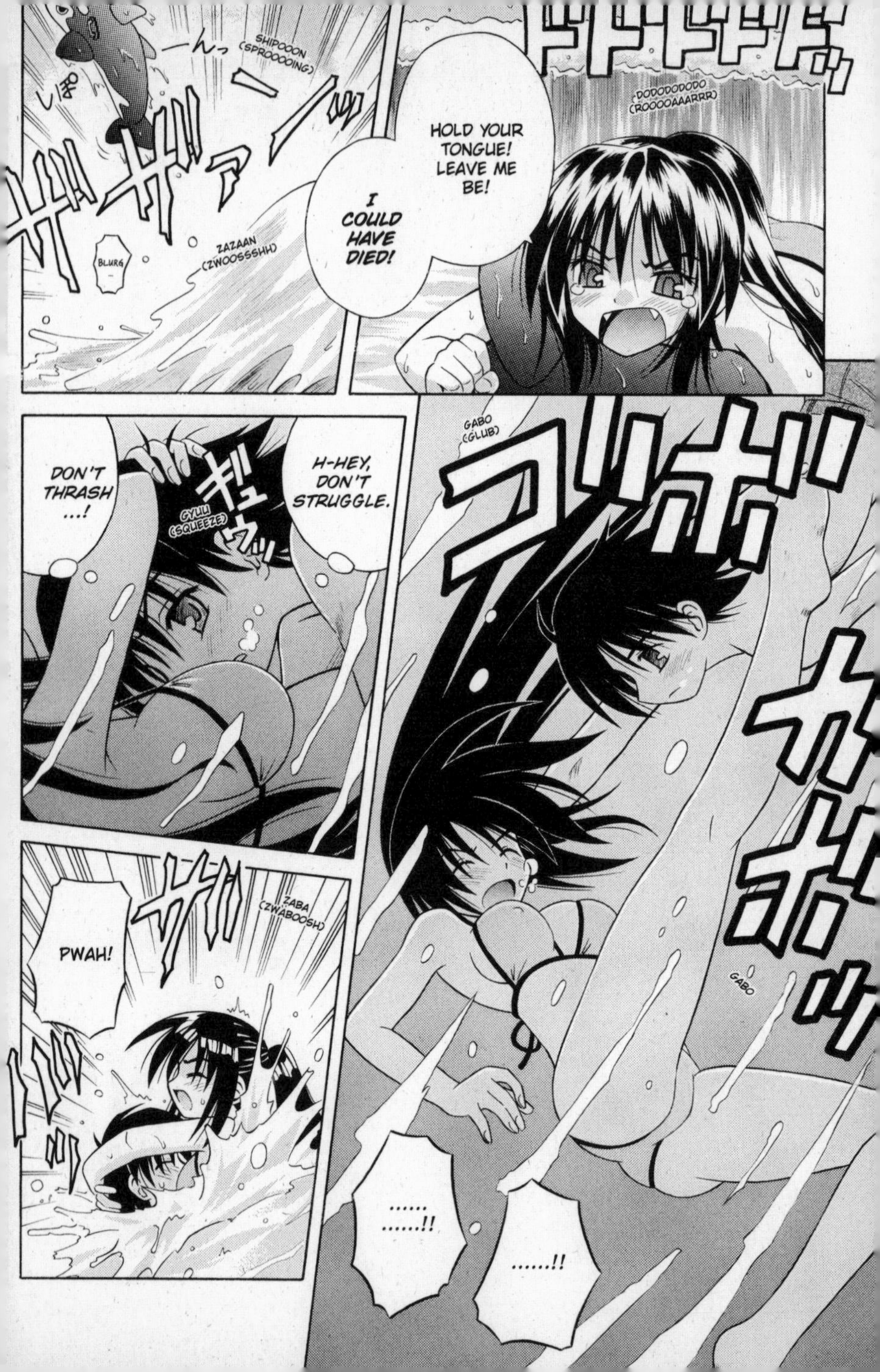

DODODODODO (ROOOOAAARRR)
HOLD YOUR TONGUE! LEAVE ME BE!
I COULD HAVE DIED!
SHIPOOON (SPROOOOING)
ZAZAAN (ZWOOSSSHH)
BLURG...
GABO (GLUB)
GABO
......!!
....!!
H-HEY, DON'T STRUGGLE.
GYUU (SQUEEZE)
DON'T THRASH ...!
ZABA (ZWABOOSH)
PWAH!

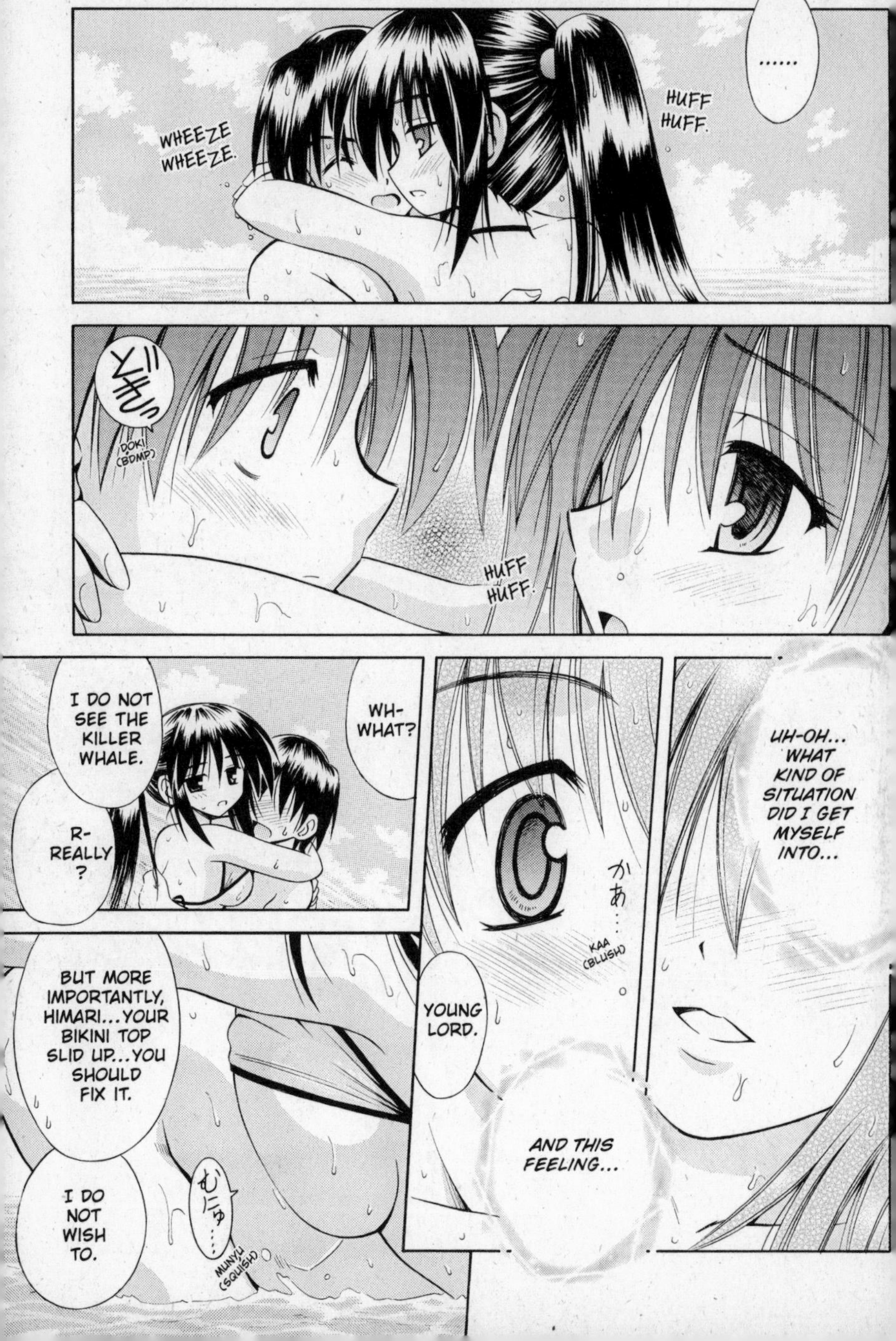
......
HUFF HUFF.
WHEEZE WHEEZE.
HUFF HUFF.
どきっ
DOKI (BDMP)
UH-OH... WHAT KIND OF SITUATION DID I GET MYSELF INTO...
AND THIS FEELING...
かあ...
KAA (BLUSH)
YOUNG LORD.
WH- WHAT?
I DO NOT SEE THE KILLER WHALE.
R- REALLY?
BUT MORE IMPORTANTLY, HIMARI...YOUR BIKINI TOP SLID UP...YOU SHOULD FIX IT.
I DO NOT WISH TO.
むにゅ...
MUNYU (SQUISH)

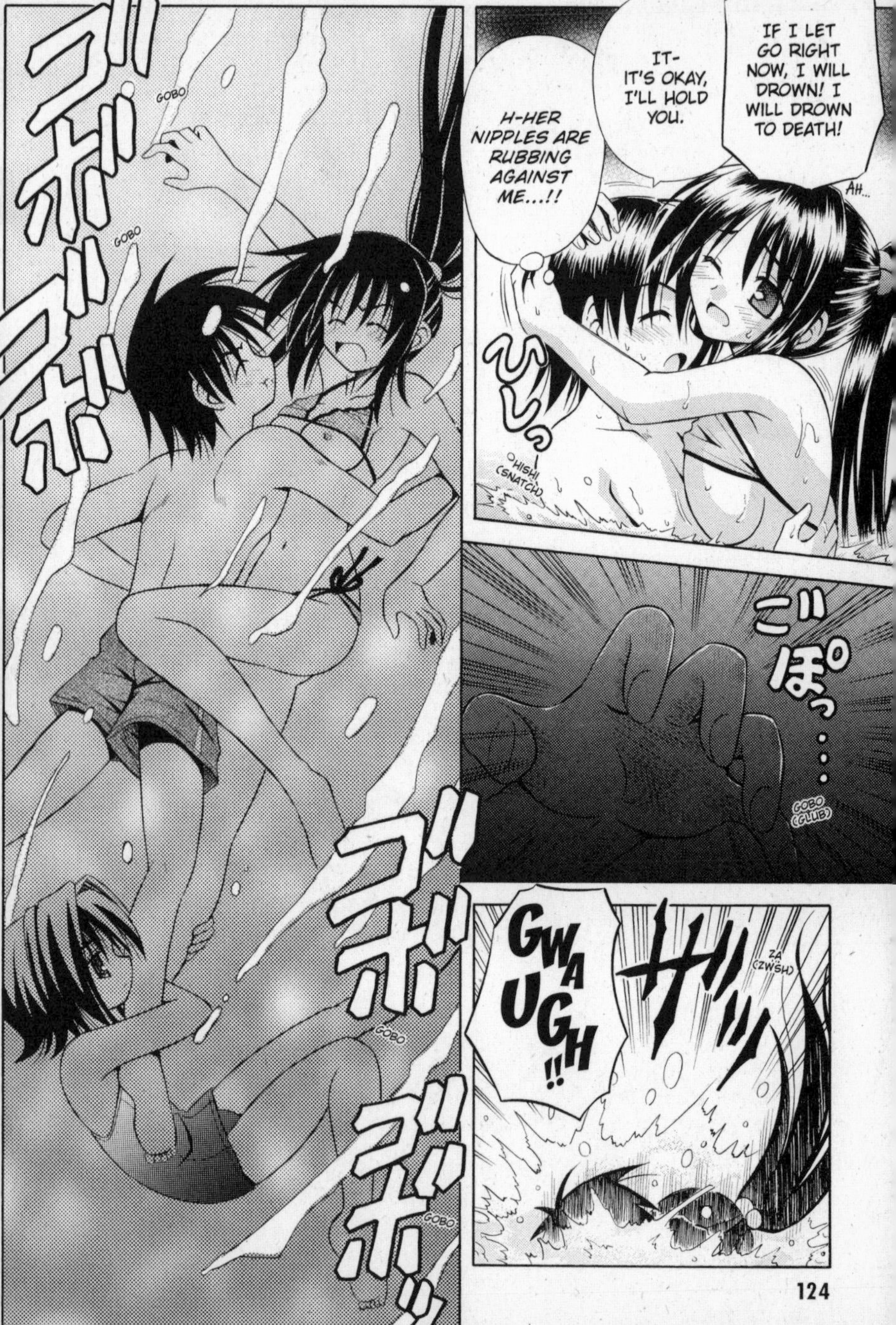
IF I LET GO RIGHT NOW, I WILL DROWN! I WILL DROWN TO DEATH!
IT- IT'S OKAY, I'LL HOLD YOU.
H-HER NIPPLES ARE RUBBING AGAINST ME...!!
AH...
ひしっ
HISHI (SNATCH)
ごぽっ…
GOBO (GLUB)
GWAUGH!!
ザッ
ZA (ZWSH)
ゴボゴボ
GOBO
GOBO
ゴボゴボッ
GOBO
GOBO

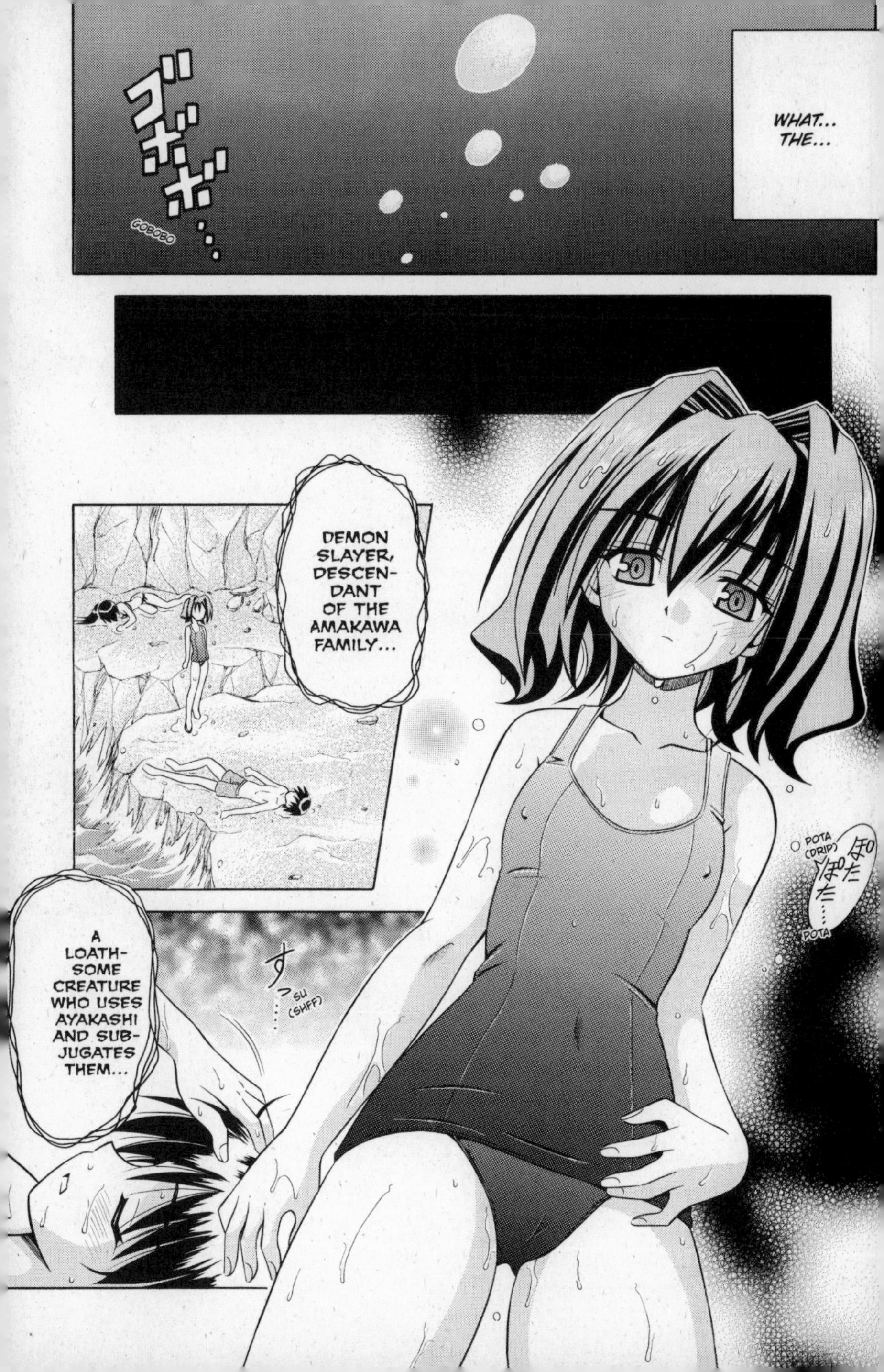
WHAT... THE...
ゴボボ・・・
GOBOBO
DEMON SLAYER, DESCENDANT OF THE AMAKAWA FAMILY...
ぽたぽた……
POTA (DRIP) POTA
すっ…
SU (SHFF)
A LOATHSOME CREATURE WHO USES AYAKASHI AND SUBJUGATES THEM...

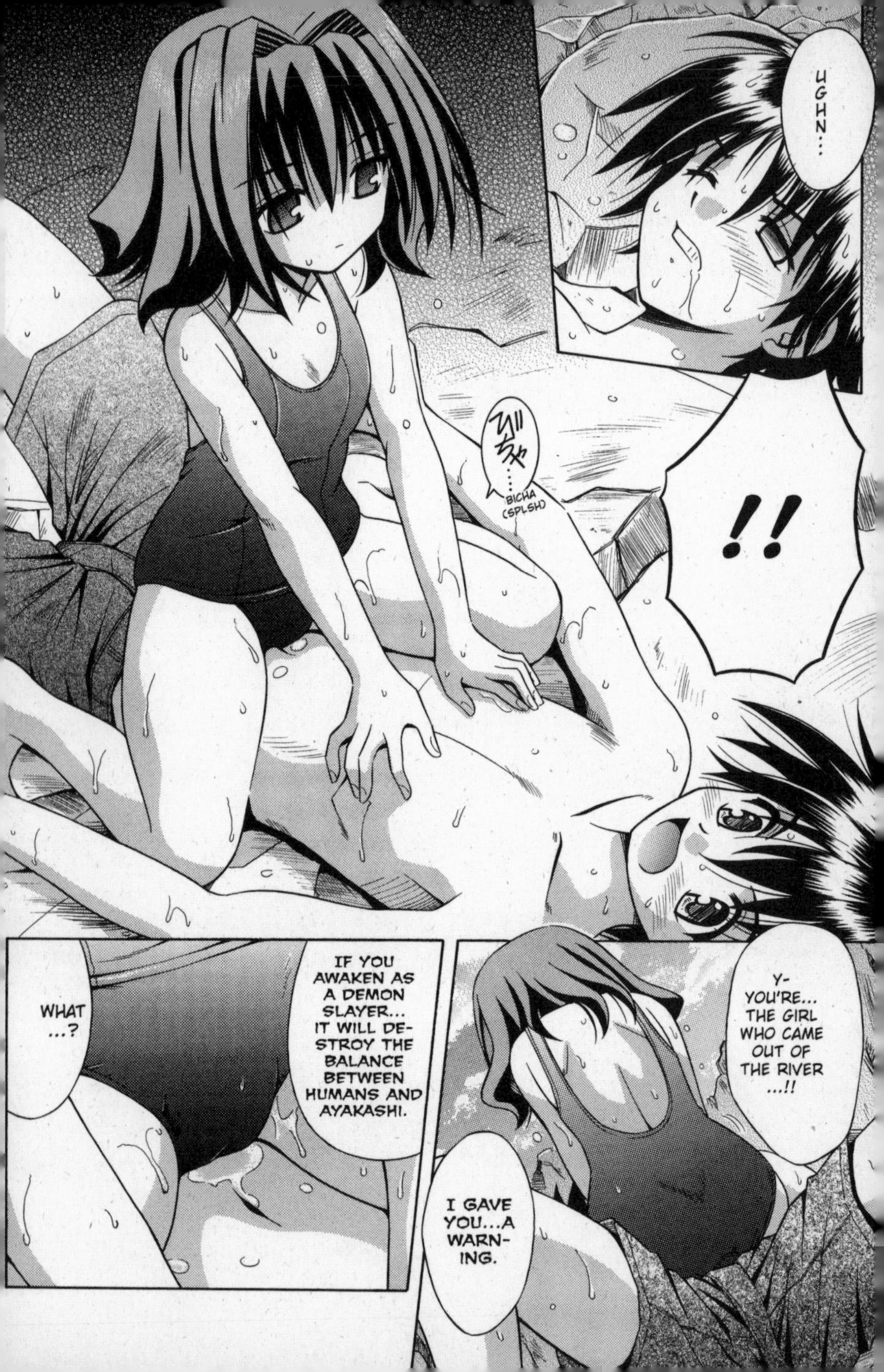
UGHN...
びちゃ…
BICHA (SPLSH)
!!
Y- YOU'RE... THE GIRL WHO CAME OUT OF THE RIVER ...!!
I GAVE YOU...A WARNING.
IF YOU AWAKEN AS A DEMON SLAYER... IT WILL DE-STROY THE BALANCE BETWEEN HUMANS AND AYAKASHI.
WHAT ...?

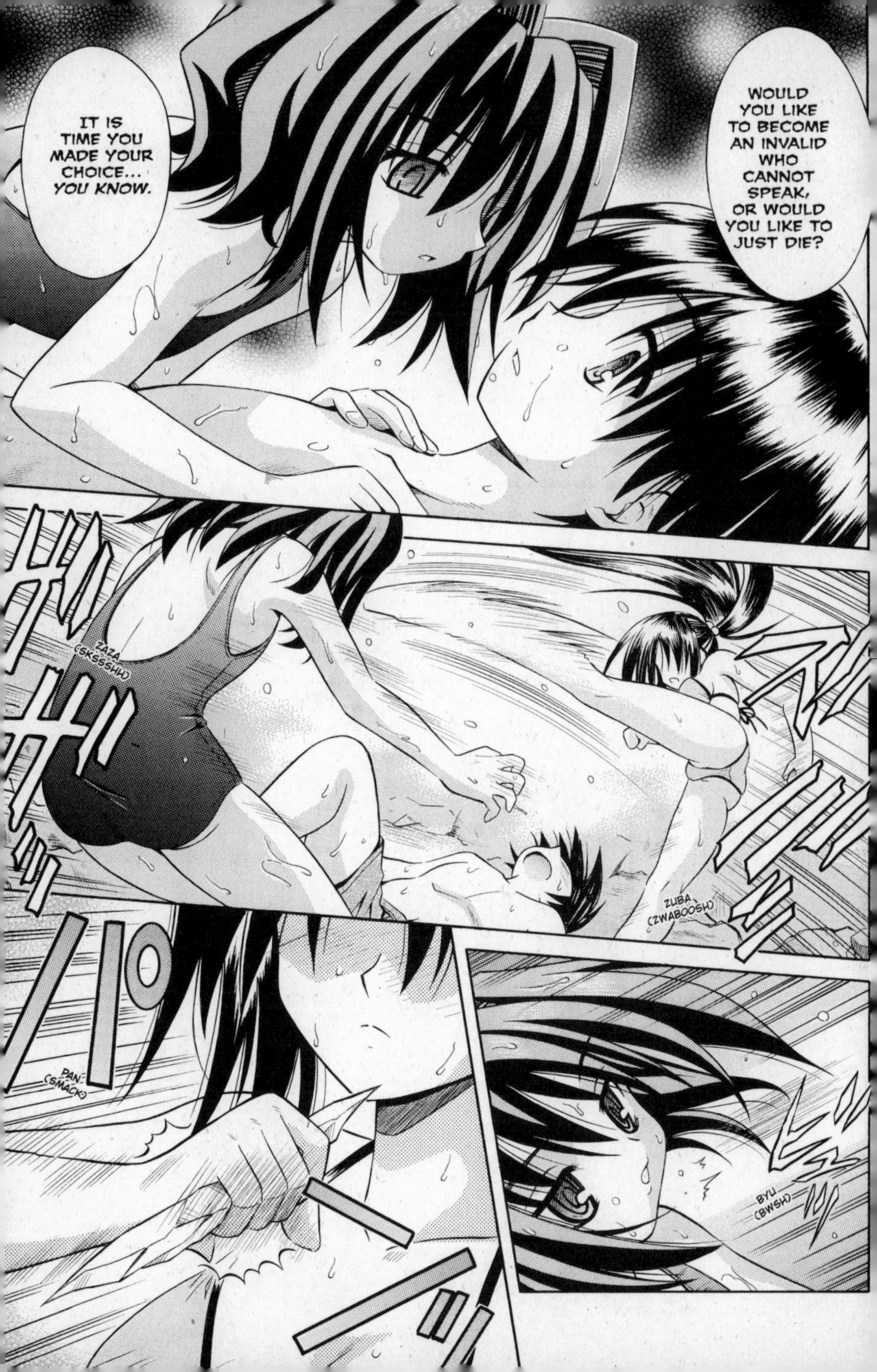
WOULD YOU LIKE TO BECOME AN INVALID WHO CANNOT SPEAK, OR WOULD YOU LIKE TO JUST DIE?
IT IS TIME YOU MADE YOUR CHOICE... YOU KNOW.
ZUBA (ZWABOOSH)
ZAZA (SKSSSHH)
BYU (BWSH)
PAN (SMACK)

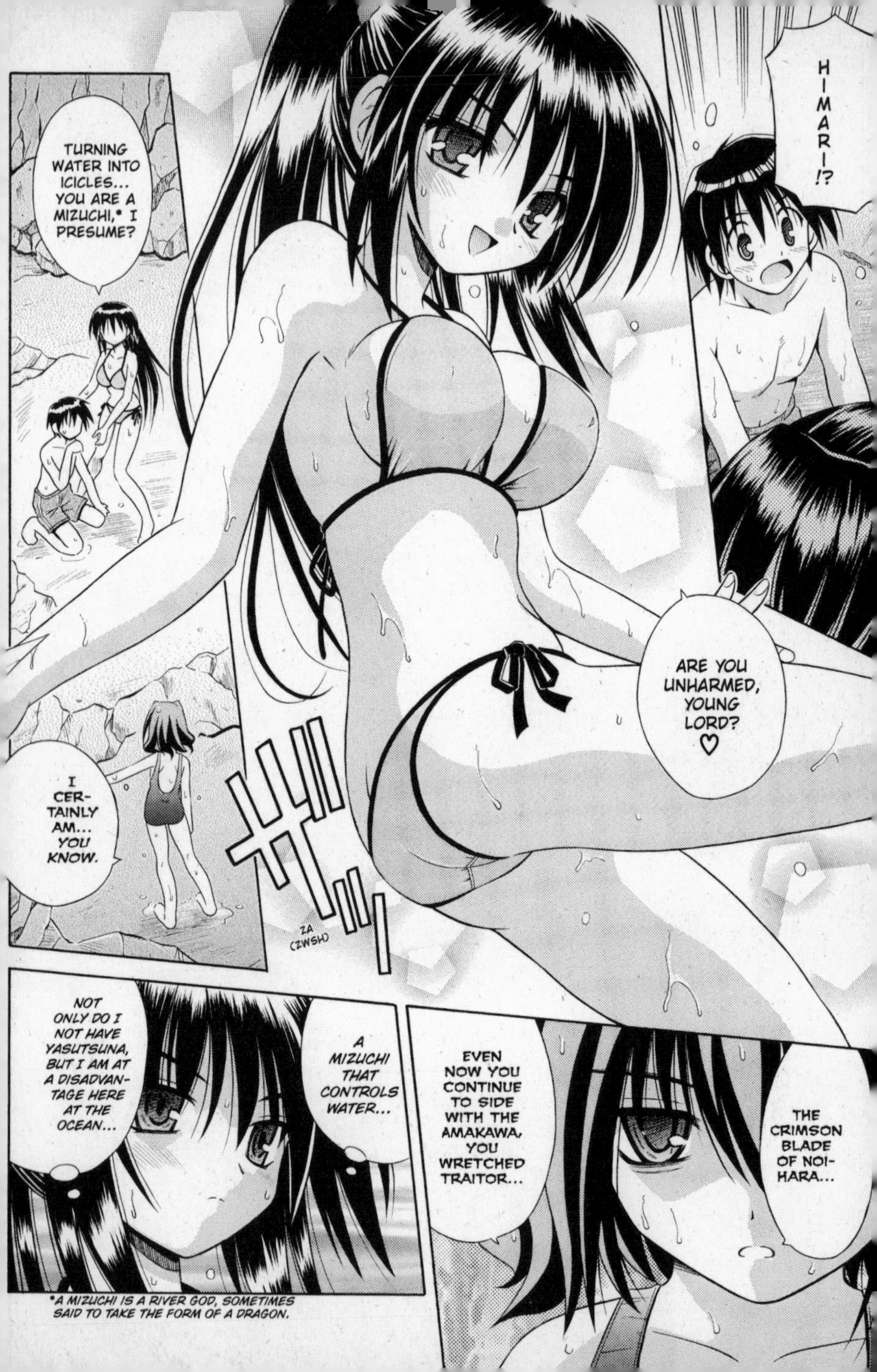
HIMARI!?
ARE YOU UNHARMED, YOUNG LORD? ♡
ZA (ZWSH)
TURNING WATER INTO ICICLES... YOU ARE A MIZUCHI,* I PRESUME?
I CER-TAINLY AM... YOU KNOW.
THE CRIMSON BLADE OF NOI-HARA...
EVEN NOW YOU CONTINUE TO SIDE WITH THE AMAKAWA, YOU WRETCHED TRAITOR...
A MIZUCHI THAT CONTROLS WATER...
NOT ONLY DO I NOT HAVE YASUTSUNA, BUT I AM AT A DISADVAN-TAGE HERE AT THE OCEAN...

*A MIZUCHI IS A RIVER GOD, SOMETIMES SAID TO TAKE THE FORM OF A DRAGON.

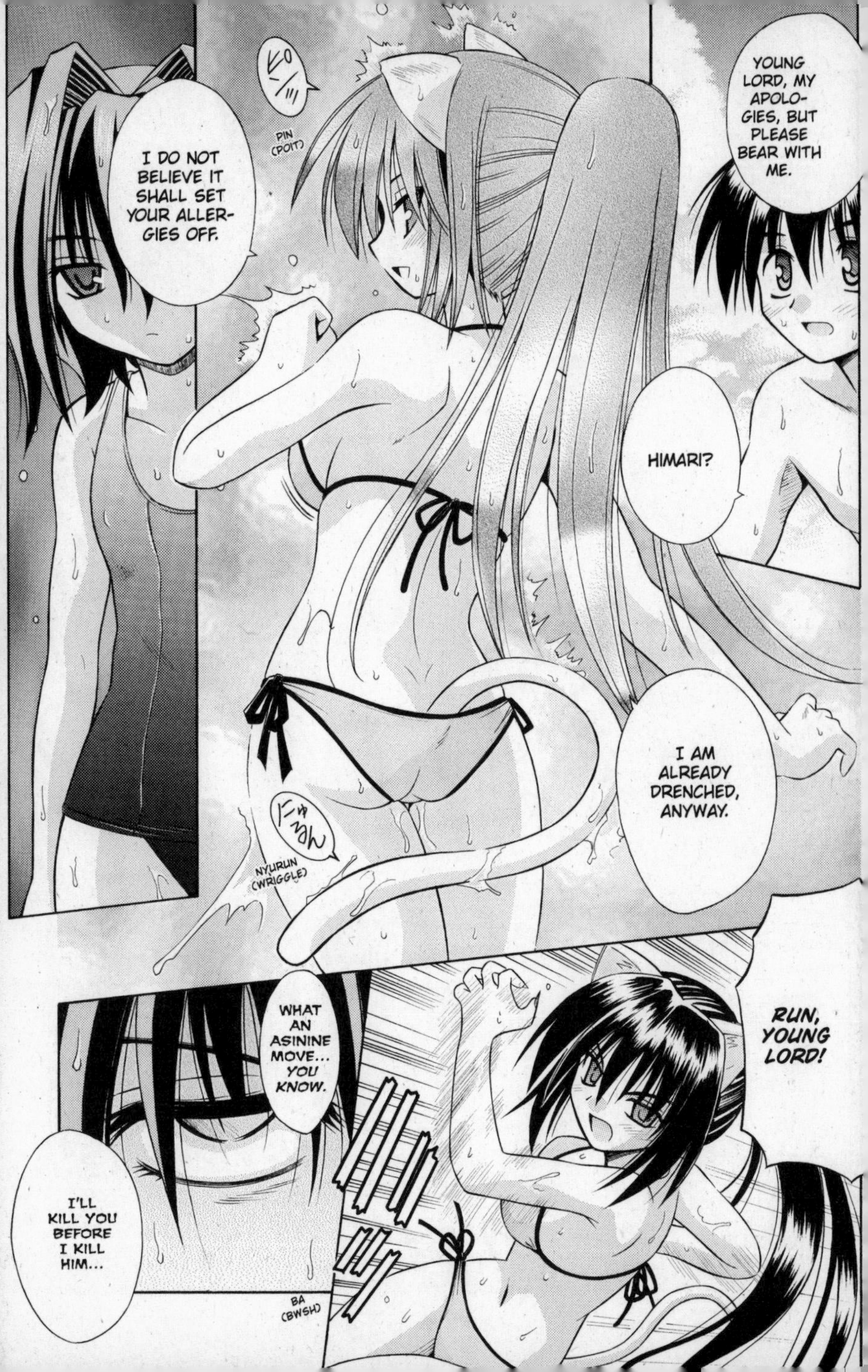
YOUNG LORD, MY APOLOGIES, BUT PLEASE BEAR WITH ME.
PIN (POIT)
I DO NOT BELIEVE IT SHALL SET YOUR ALLERGIES OFF.
HIMARI?
I AM ALREADY DRENCHED, ANYWAY.
にゅるん
NYURUN (WRIGGLE)
RUN, YOUNG LORD!
WHAT AN ASININE MOVE... YOU KNOW.
I'LL KILL YOU BEFORE I KILL HIM...
BA (BWSH)

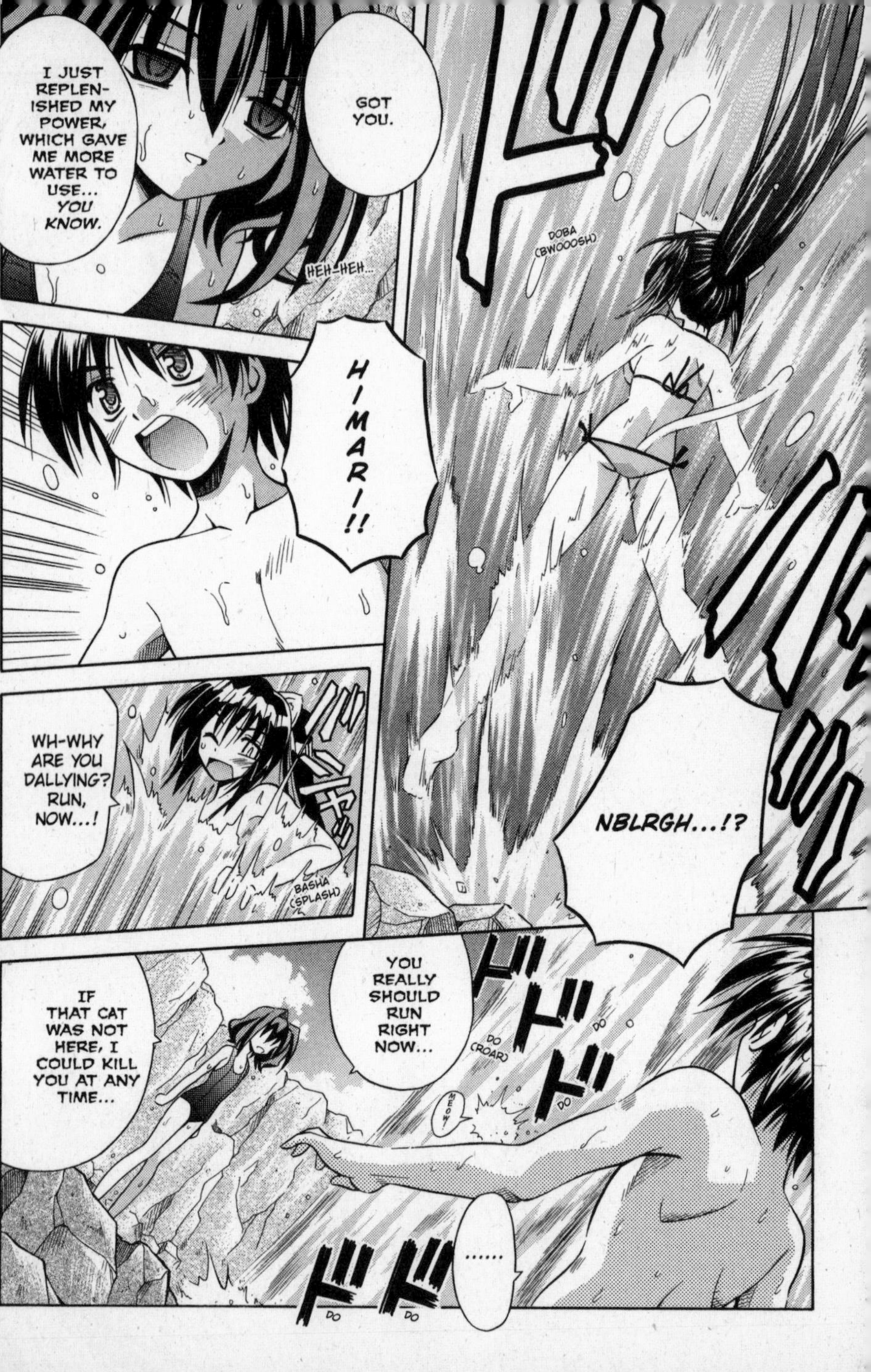
DOBA (BWOOOSH)
NBLRGH...!?
GOT YOU.
I JUST REPLENISHED MY POWER, WHICH GAVE ME MORE WATER TO USE... YOU KNOW.
HEH-HEH...
HIMARI!!
WH-WHY ARE YOU DALLYING? RUN, NOW...!
BASHA (SPLASH)
YOU REALLY SHOULD RUN RIGHT NOW...
DO (ROAR)
DO
DO
IF THAT CAT WAS NOT HERE, I COULD KILL YOU AT ANY TIME...
MEOW!
......
DO
DO

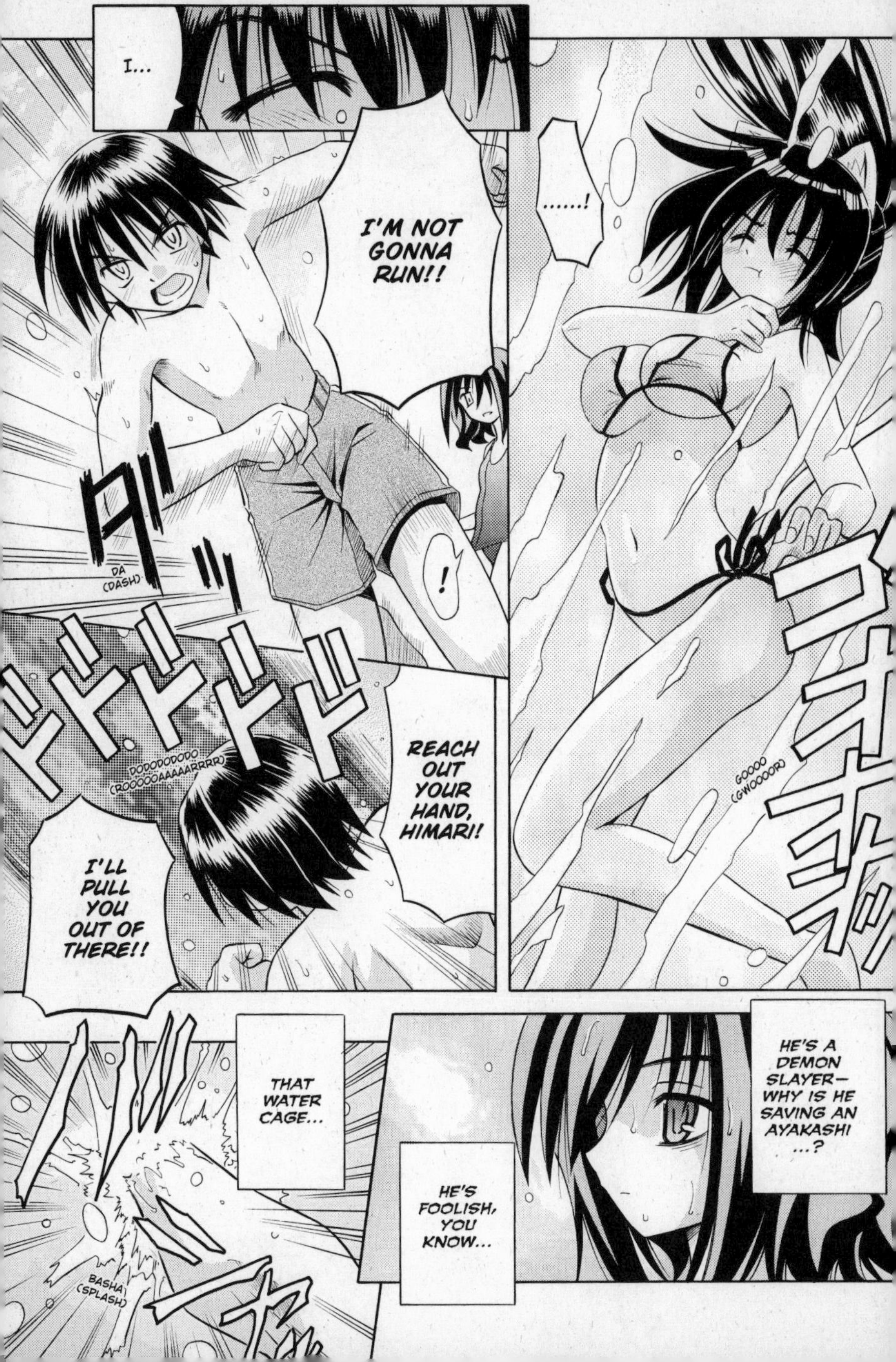
......!
GOOOO (GWOOOOR)
I...
I'M NOT GONNA RUN!!
!
DA (DASH)
REACH OUT YOUR HAND, HIMARI!
DODODODODO (ROOOOOAAAAARRRR)
I'LL PULL YOU OUT OF THERE!!
HE'S A DEMON SLAYER— WHY IS HE SAVING AN AYAKASHI ...?
HE'S FOOLISH, YOU KNOW...
THAT WATER CAGE...
BASHA (SPLASH)

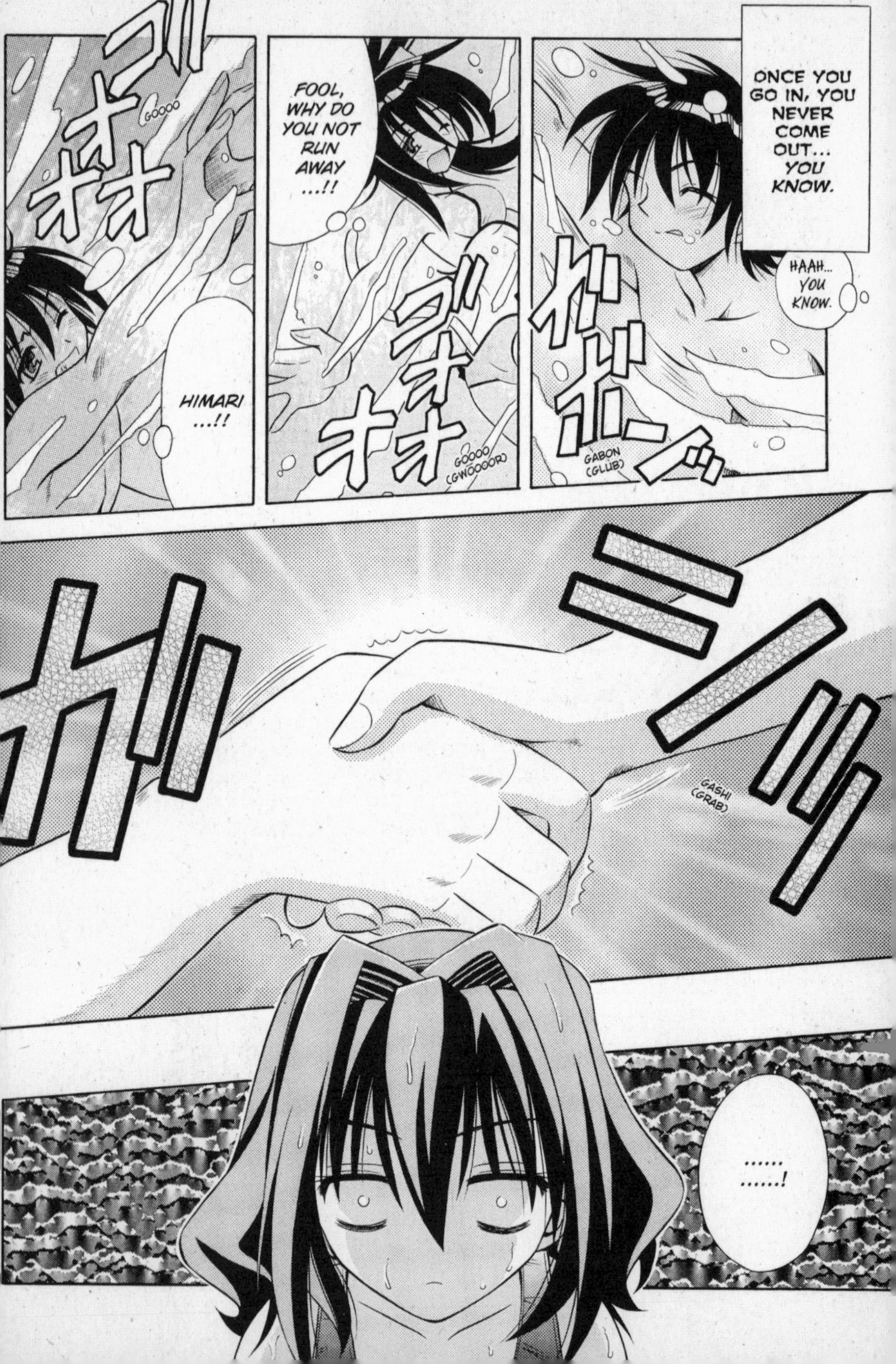
ONCE YOU GO IN, YOU NEVER COME OUT... YOU KNOW.
HAAH... YOU KNOW.
GABON (GLUB)
FOOL, WHY DO YOU NOT RUN AWAY ...!!
GOOOO (GWOOOOR)
GOOOO
HIMARI ...!!
GASHI (GRAB)
....!

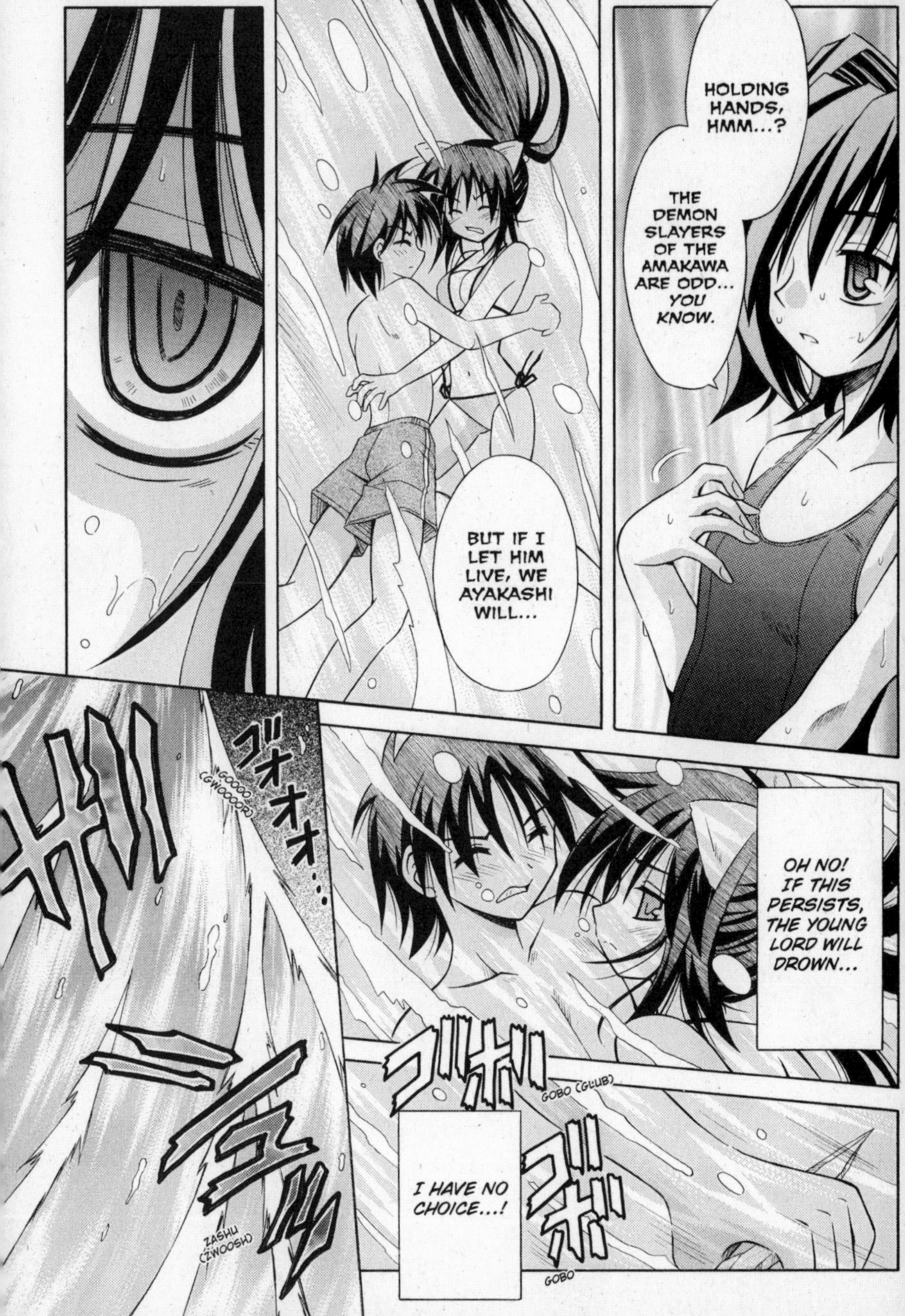
HOLDING HANDS, HMM...?
THE DEMON SLAYERS OF THE AMAKAWA ARE ODD... YOU KNOW.
BUT IF I LET HIM LIVE, WE AYAKASHI WILL...
OH NO! IF THIS PERSISTS, THE YOUNG LORD WILL DROWN...
ゴボ
GOBO (GLUB)
ゴボ
GOBO
I HAVE NO CHOICE...!
ゴォオオ…
GOOOO (GWOOOOR)
ZASHU (ZWOOSH)

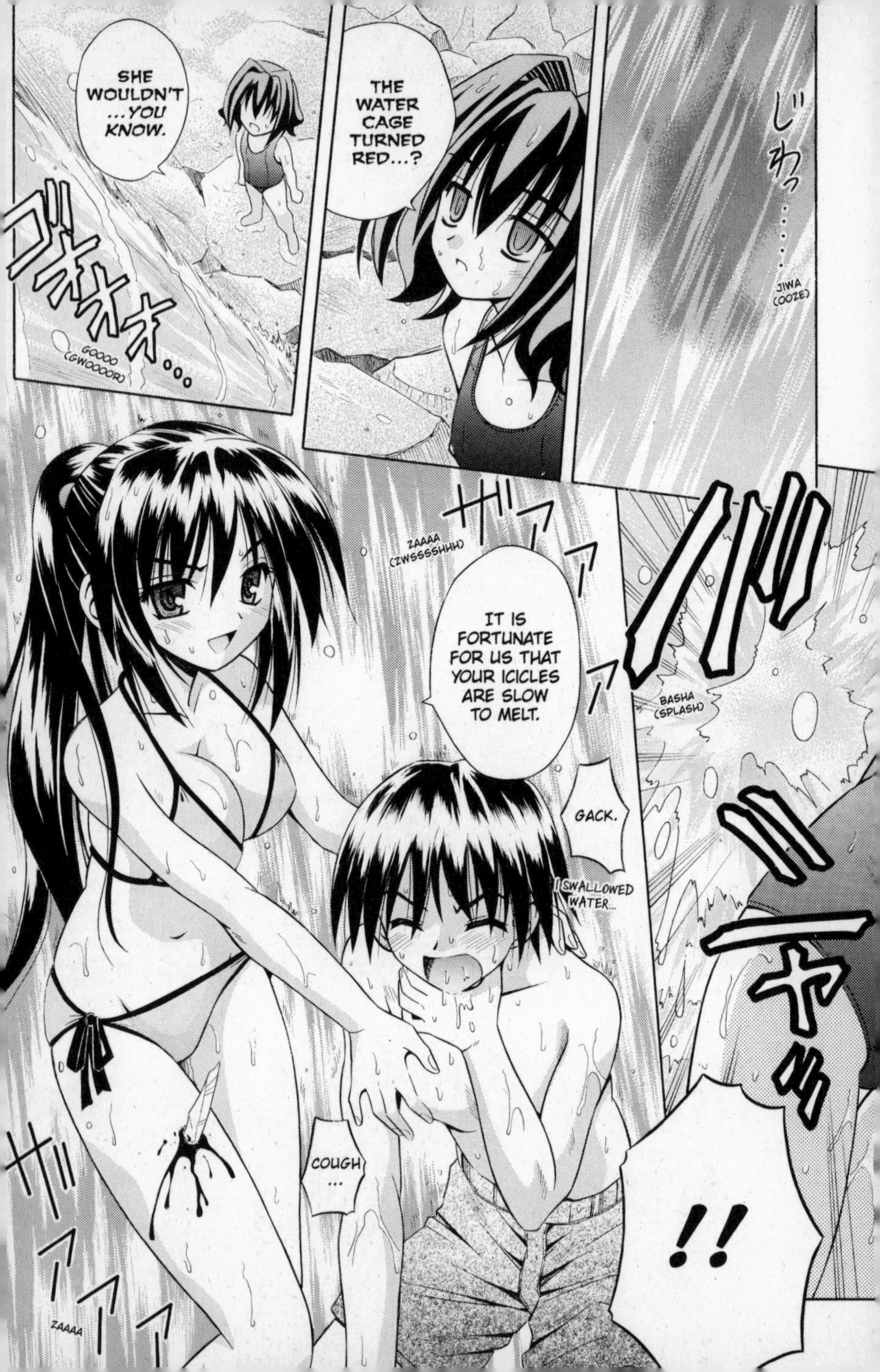

JIWA (OOZE)
THE WATER CAGE TURNED RED...?
SHE WOULDN'T ...YOU KNOW.
GOOOO (GWOOOOR)
BASHA (SPLASH)
!!
ZAAAA (ZWSSSSHHH)
IT IS FORTUNATE FOR US THAT YOUR ICICLES ARE SLOW TO MELT.
GACK.
I SWALLOWED WATER...
COUGH ...
ZAAAA

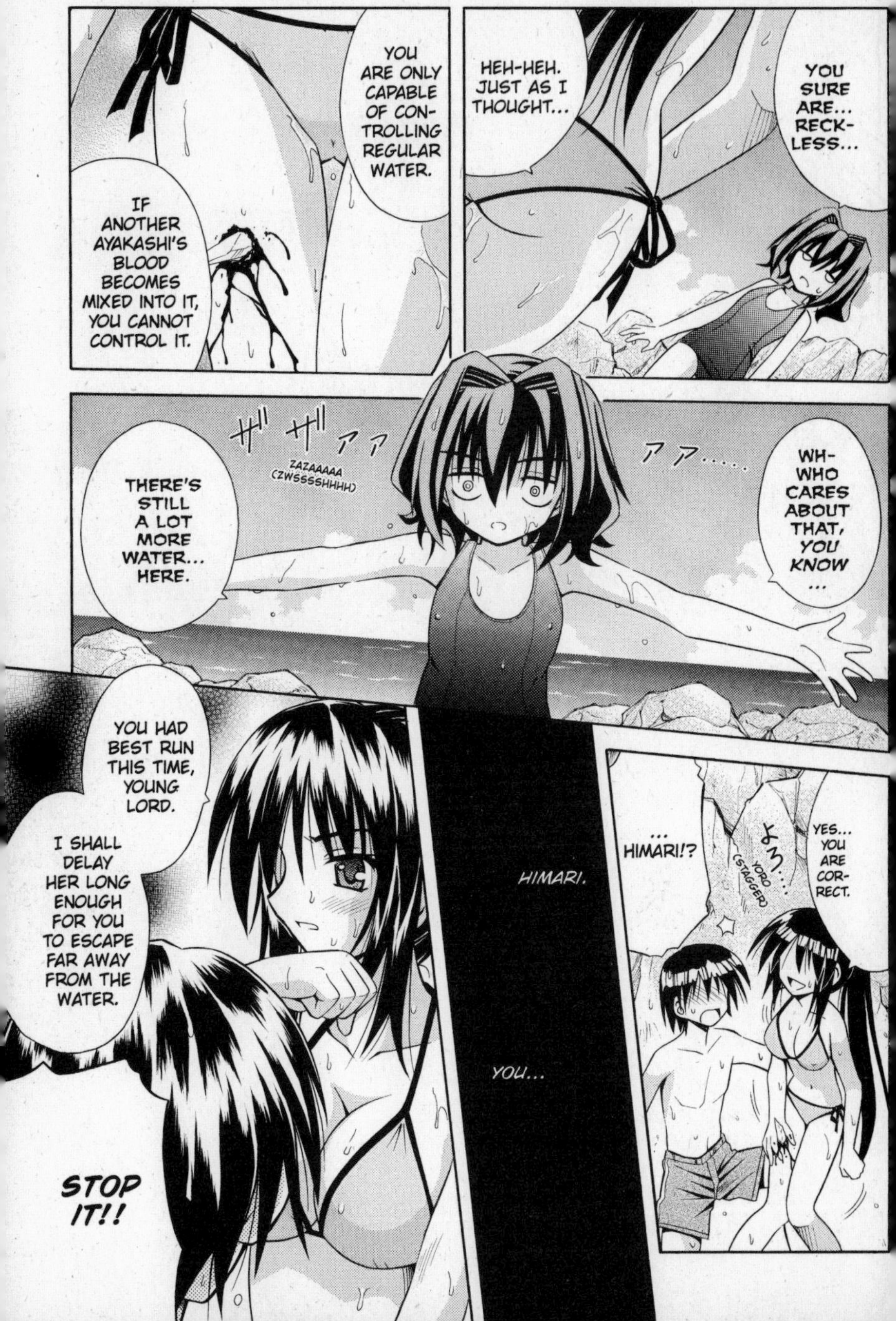
YOU SURE ARE... RECK-LESS...
HEH-HEH. JUST AS I THOUGHT...
YOU ARE ONLY CAPABLE OF CON-TROLLING REGULAR WATER.
IF ANOTHER AYAKASHI'S BLOOD BECOMES MIXED INTO IT, YOU CANNOT CONTROL IT.
WH-WHO CARES ABOUT THAT, YOU KNOW...
ザザアアアア.....
ZAZAAAAA (ZWSSSSHHHH)
THERE'S STILL A LOT MORE WATER... HERE.
YES... YOU ARE COR-RECT.
よろ...
YORO (STAGGER)
...HIMARI!?
HIMARI.
YOU...
YOU HAD BEST RUN THIS TIME, YOUNG LORD.
I SHALL DELAY HER LONG ENOUGH FOR YOU TO ESCAPE FAR AWAY FROM THE WATER.
STOP IT!!

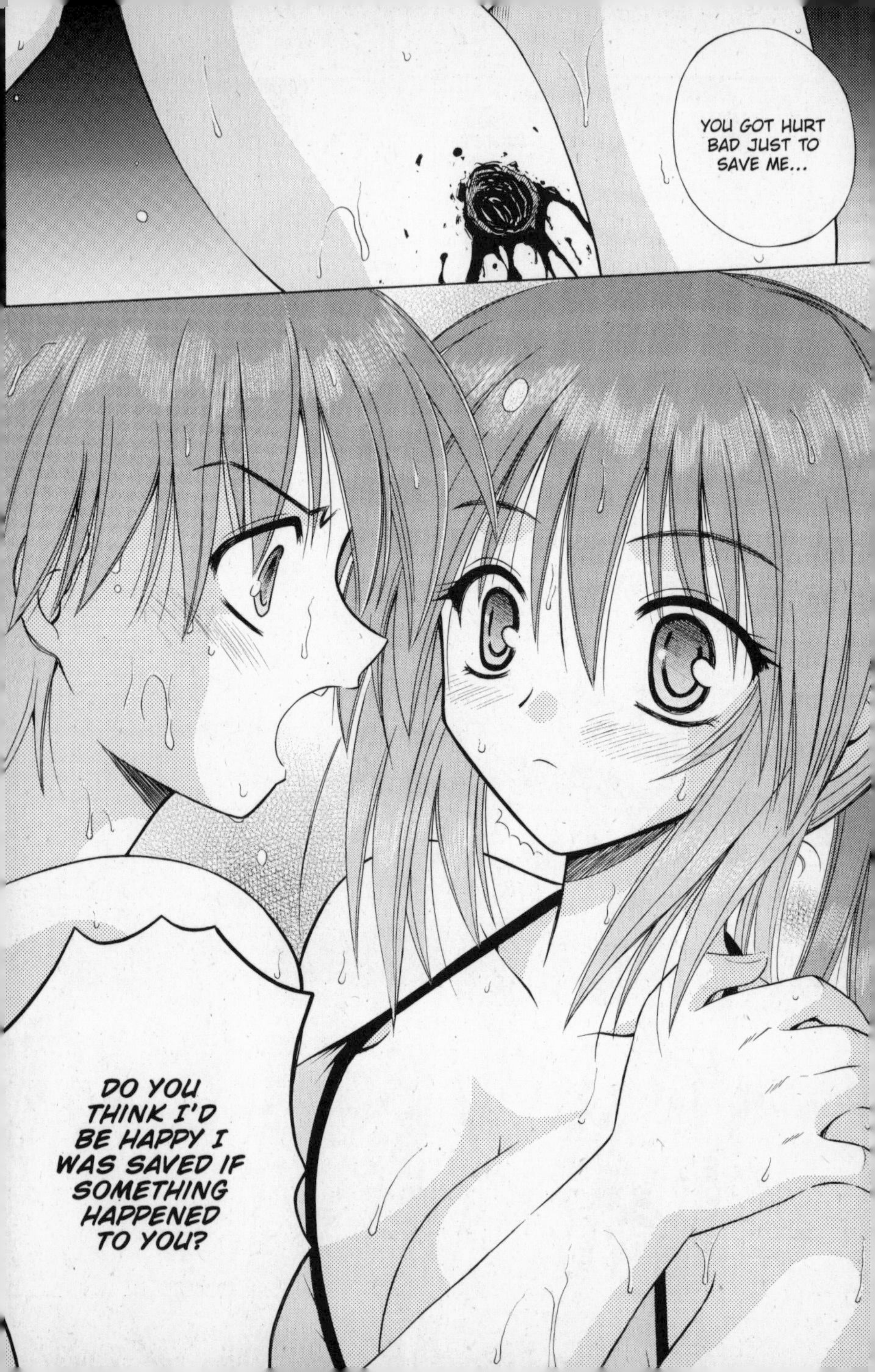
YOU GOT HURT BAD JUST TO SAVE ME...
DO YOU THINK I'D BE HAPPY I WAS SAVED IF SOMETHING HAPPENED TO YOU?

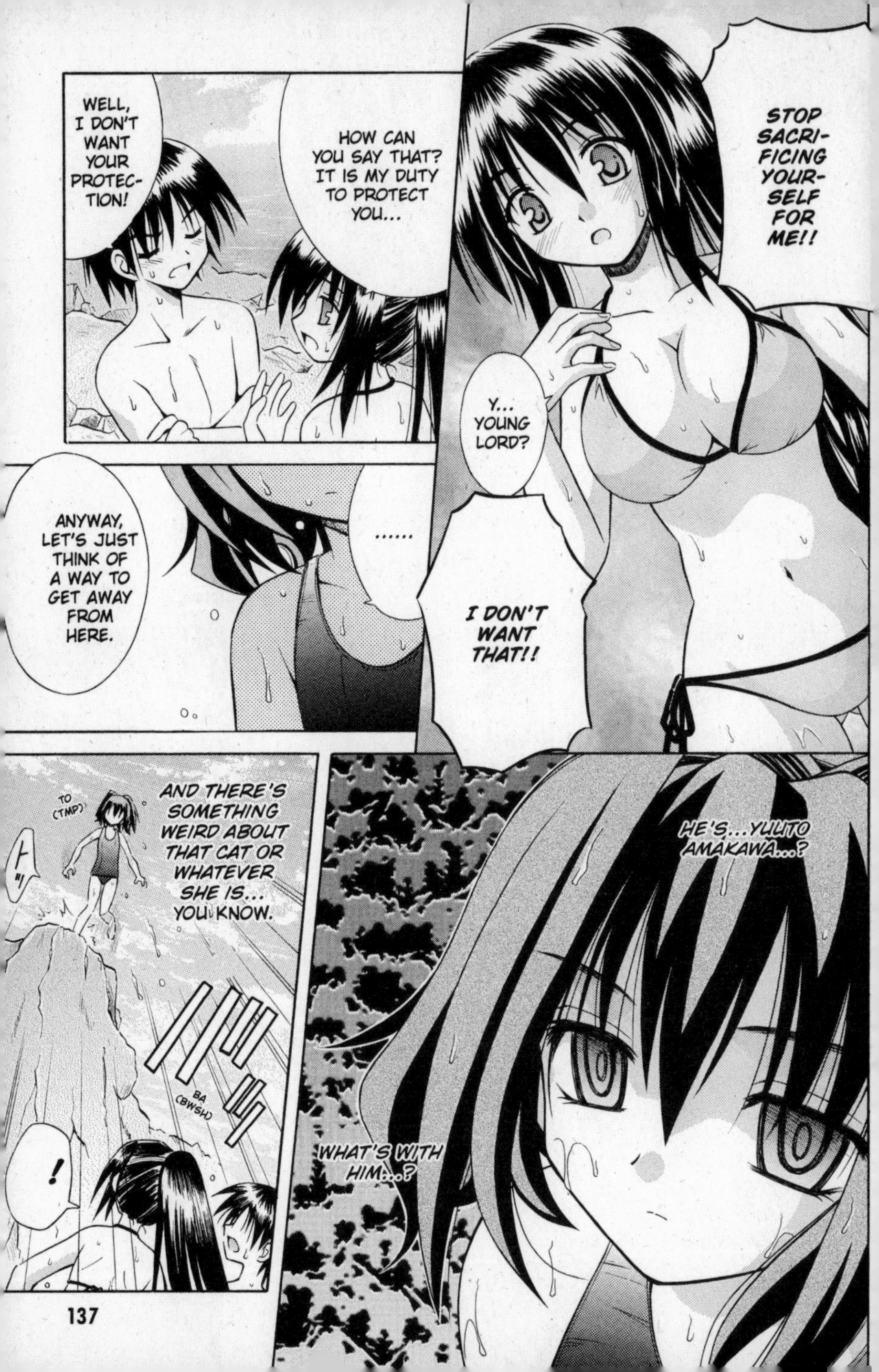
STOP SACRIFICING YOURSELF FOR ME!!
Y... YOUNG LORD?
I DON'T WANT THAT!!
HOW CAN YOU SAY THAT? IT IS MY DUTY TO PROTECT YOU...
WELL, I DON'T WANT YOUR PROTECTION!
......
ANYWAY, LET'S JUST THINK OF A WAY TO GET AWAY FROM HERE.
HE'S...YUUTO AMAKAWA...?
WHAT'S WITH HIM...?
AND THERE'S SOMETHING WEIRD ABOUT THAT CAT OR WHATEVER SHE IS... YOU KNOW.
TO (TMP)
BA (BWSH)
!

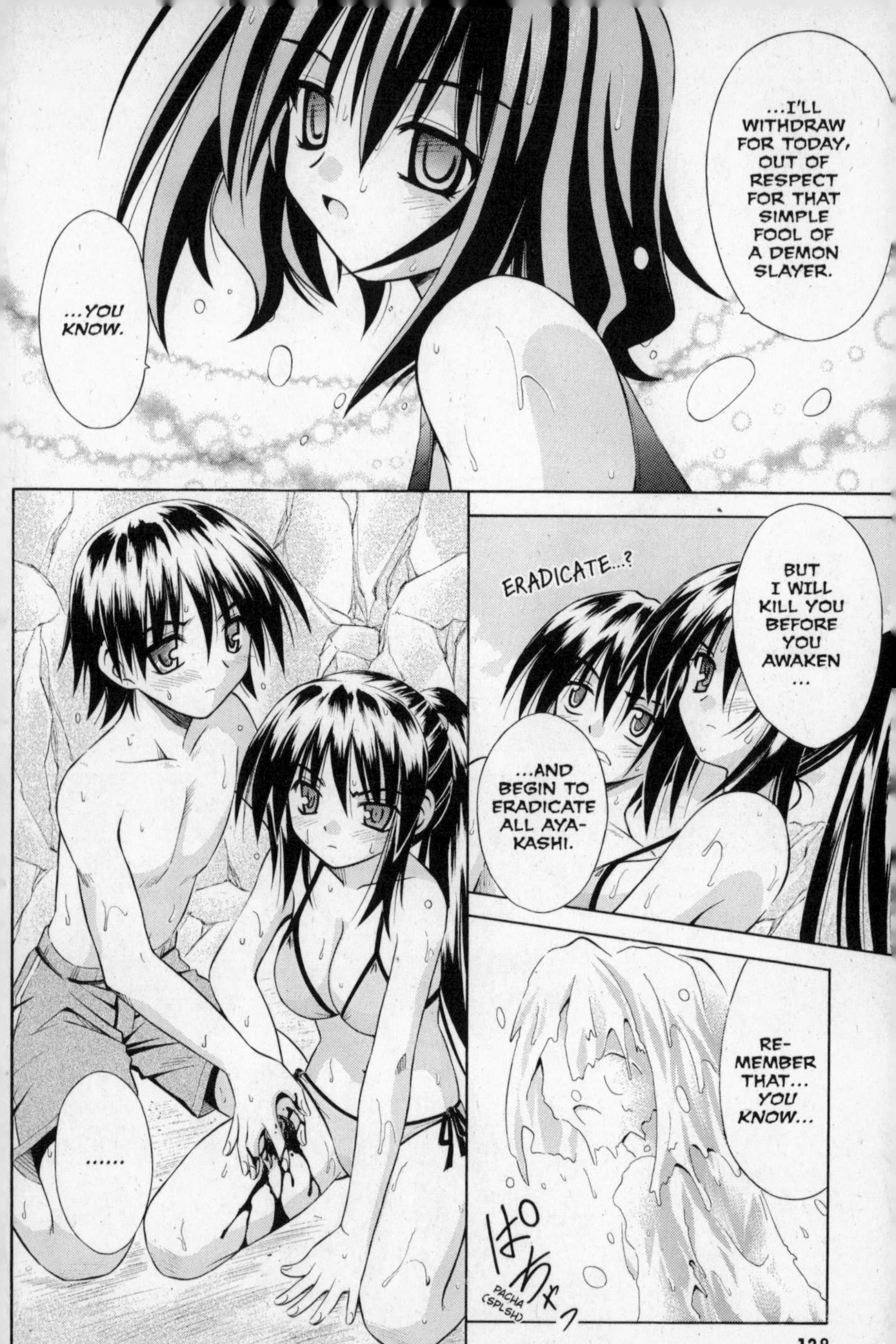
...I'LL WITHDRAW FOR TODAY, OUT OF RESPECT FOR THAT SIMPLE FOOL OF A DEMON SLAYER.
...YOU KNOW.
BUT I WILL KILL YOU BEFORE YOU AWAKEN ...
...AND BEGIN TO ERADICATE ALL AYA-KASHI.
ERADICATE...?
RE-MEMBER THAT... YOU KNOW...
ぱしゃっ
PACHA (SPLSH)
......

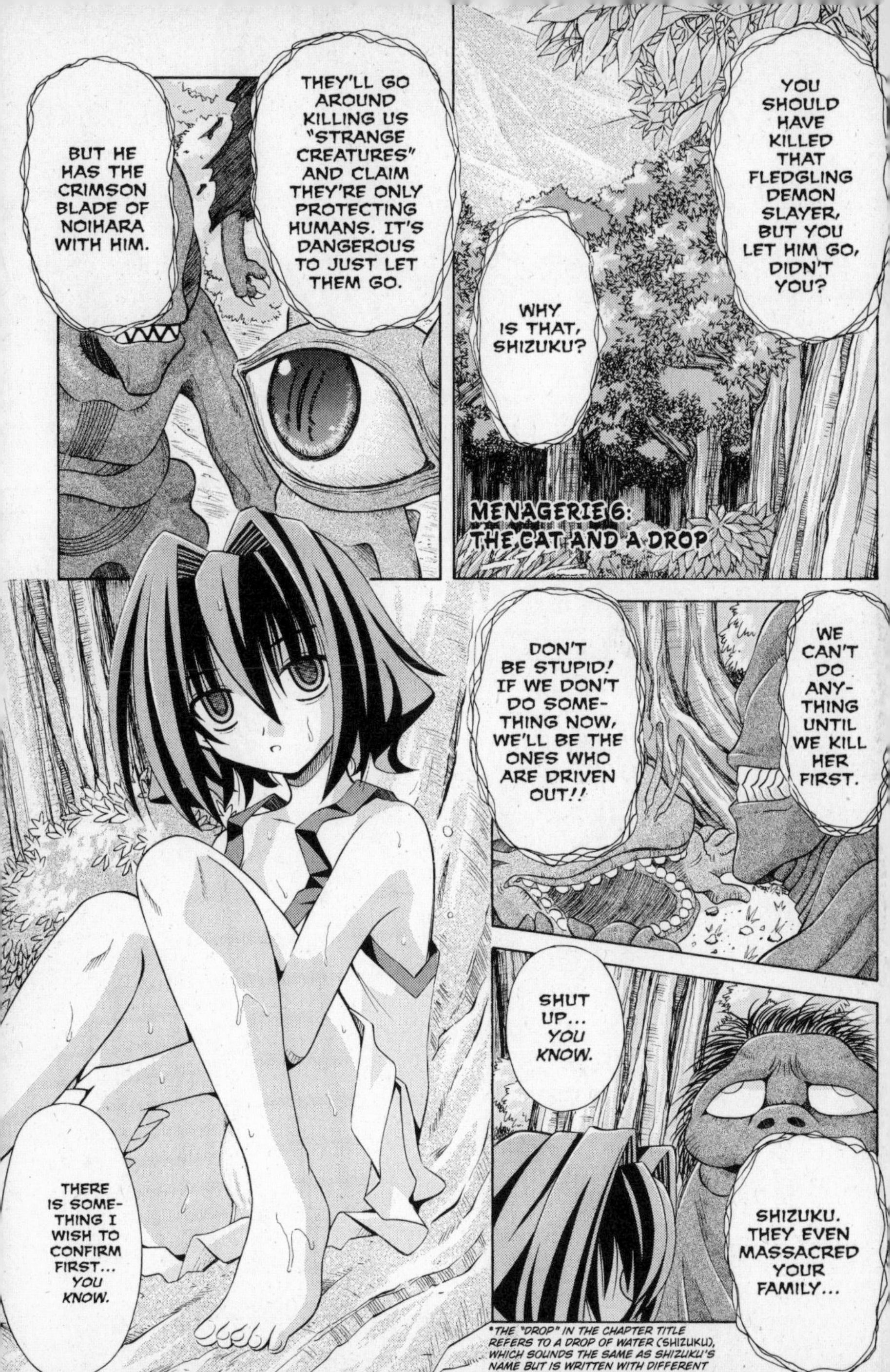
YOU SHOULD HAVE KILLED THAT FLEDGLING DEMON SLAYER, BUT YOU LET HIM GO, DIDN'T YOU?
WHY IS THAT, SHIZUKU?
MENAGERIE 6: THE CAT AND A DROP
THEY'LL GO AROUND KILLING US "STRANGE CREATURES" AND CLAIM THEY'RE ONLY PROTECTING HUMANS. IT'S DANGEROUS TO JUST LET THEM GO.
BUT HE HAS THE CRIMSON BLADE OF NOIHARA WITH HIM.
WE CAN'T DO ANY-THING UNTIL WE KILL HER FIRST.
DON'T BE STUPID! IF WE DON'T DO SOME-THING NOW, WE'LL BE THE ONES WHO ARE DRIVEN OUT!!
SHIZUKU. THEY EVEN MASSACRED YOUR FAMILY...
SHUT UP... *YOU KNOW.*
THERE IS SOME-THING I WISH TO CONFIRM FIRST... *YOU KNOW.*

THE "DROP" IN THE CHAPTER TITLE REFERS TO A DROP OF WATER (SHIZUKU), WHICH SOUNDS THE SAME AS SHIZUKU'S NAME BUT IS WRITTEN WITH DIFFERENT CHARACTERS.

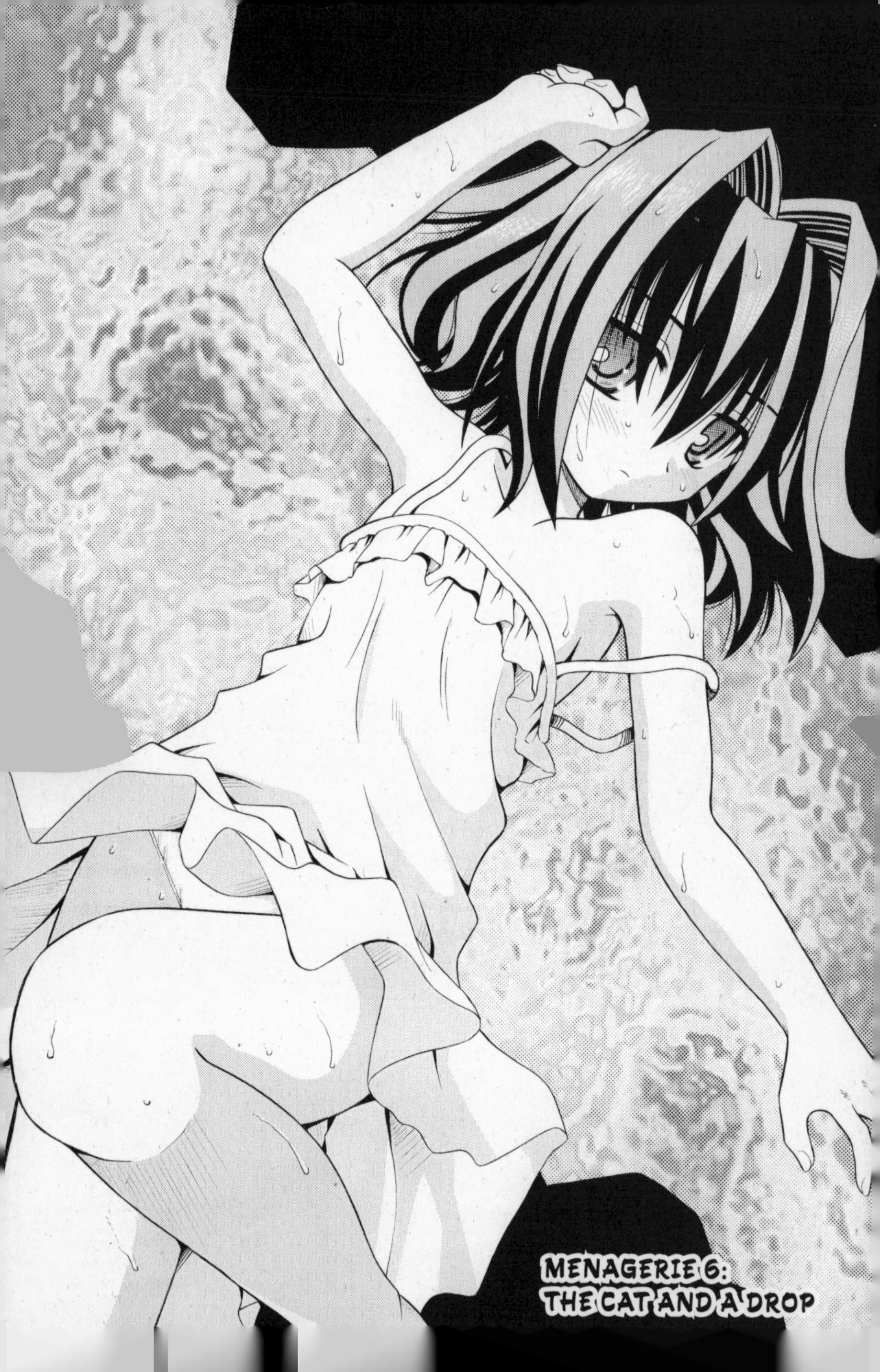
MENAGERIE 6:
THE CAT AND A DROP

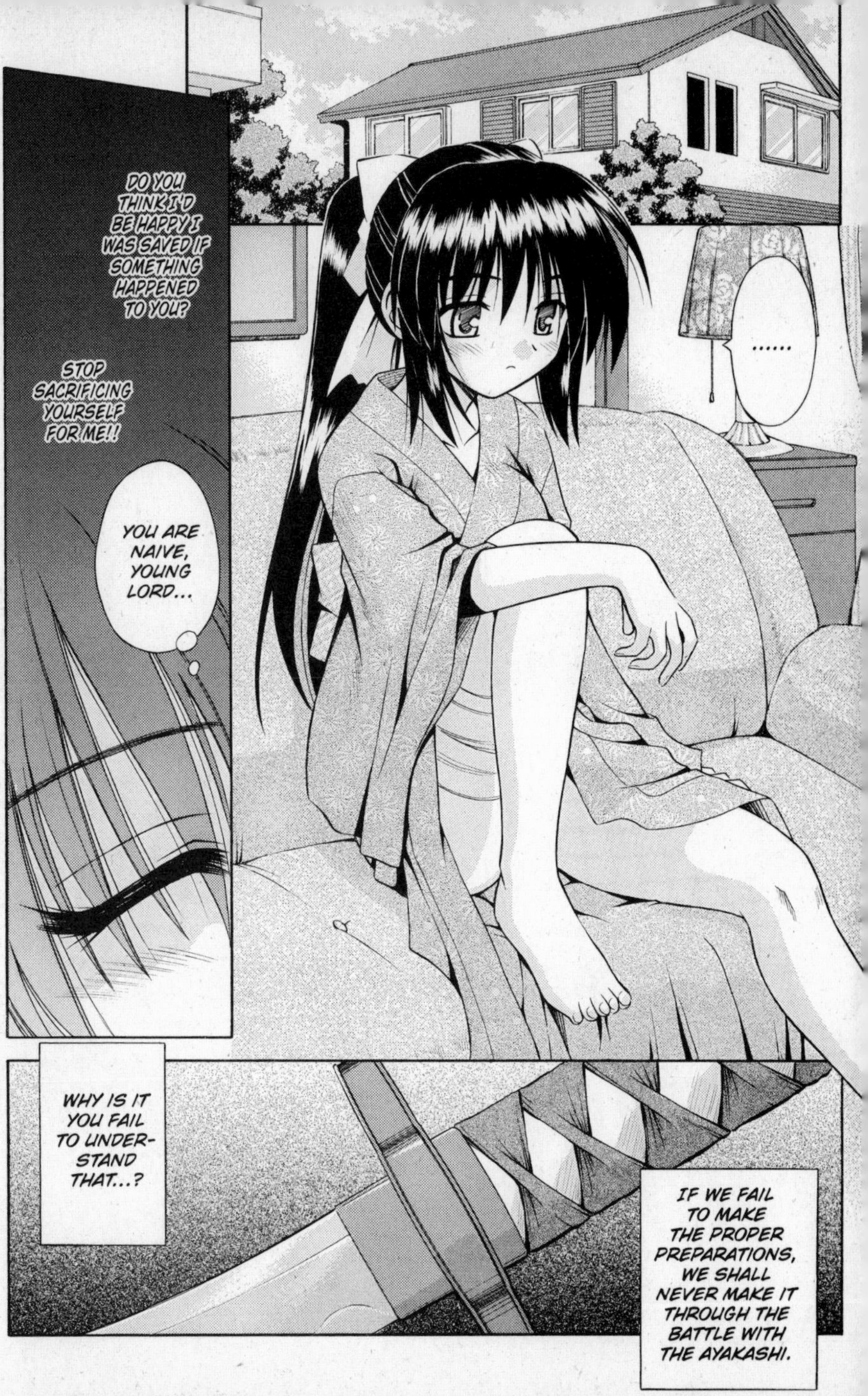
......
DO YOU THINK I'D BE HAPPY I WAS SAVED IF SOMETHING HAPPENED TO YOU?
STOP SACRIFICING YOURSELF FOR ME!!
YOU ARE NAIVE, YOUNG LORD...
WHY IS IT YOU FAIL TO UNDER-STAND THAT...?
IF WE FAIL TO MAKE THE PROPER PREPARATIONS, WE SHALL NEVER MAKE IT THROUGH THE BATTLE WITH THE AYAKASHI.

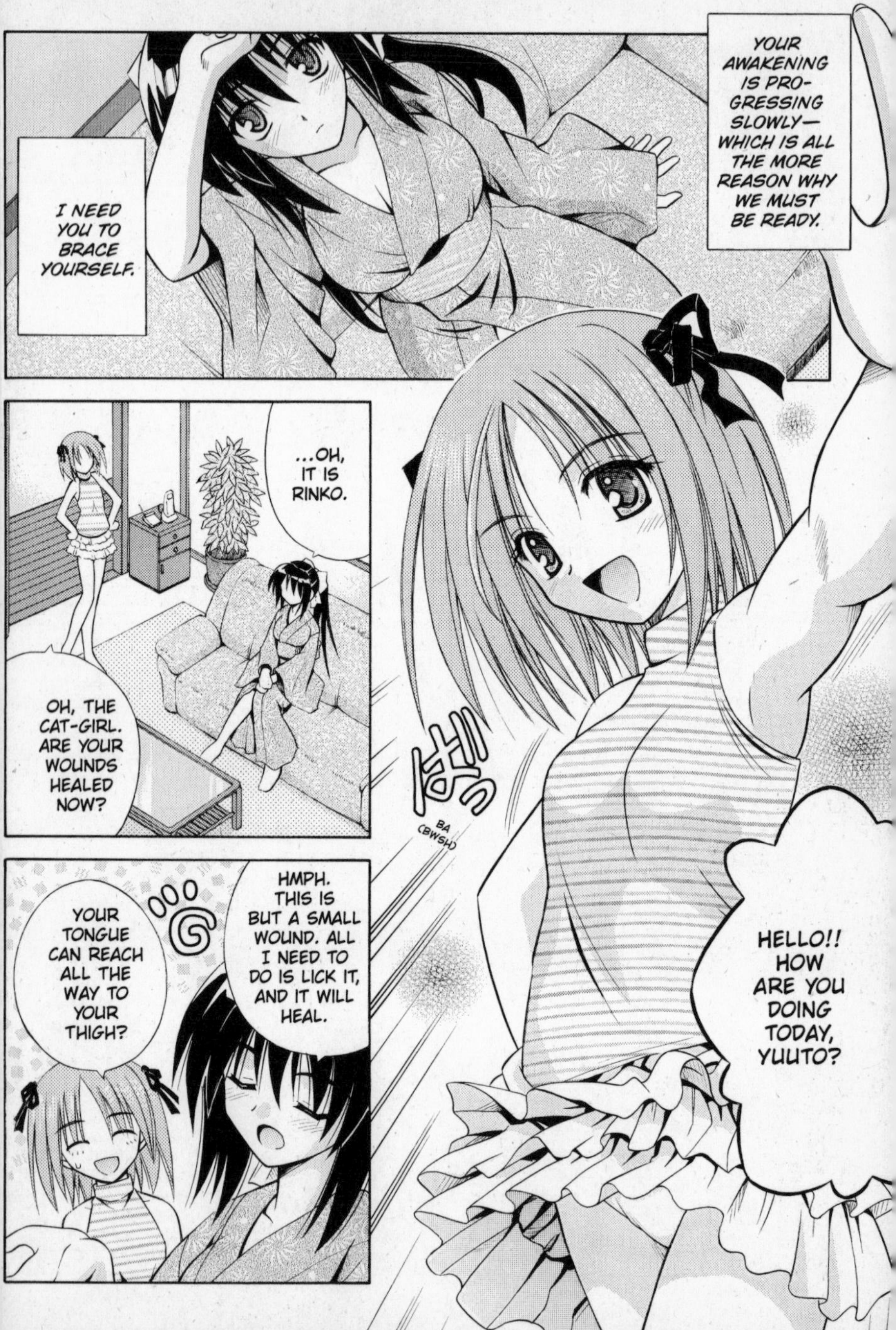
YOUR AWAKENING IS PRO-GRESSING SLOWLY—WHICH IS ALL THE MORE REASON WHY WE MUST BE READY.
I NEED YOU TO BRACE YOURSELF.
BA (BWSH)
HELLO!! HOW ARE YOU DOING TODAY, YUUTO?
...OH, IT IS RINKO.
OH, THE CAT-GIRL. ARE YOUR WOUNDS HEALED NOW?
HMPH. THIS IS BUT A SMALL WOUND. ALL I NEED TO DO IS LICK IT, AND IT WILL HEAL.
YOUR TONGUE CAN REACH ALL THE WAY TO YOUR THIGH?

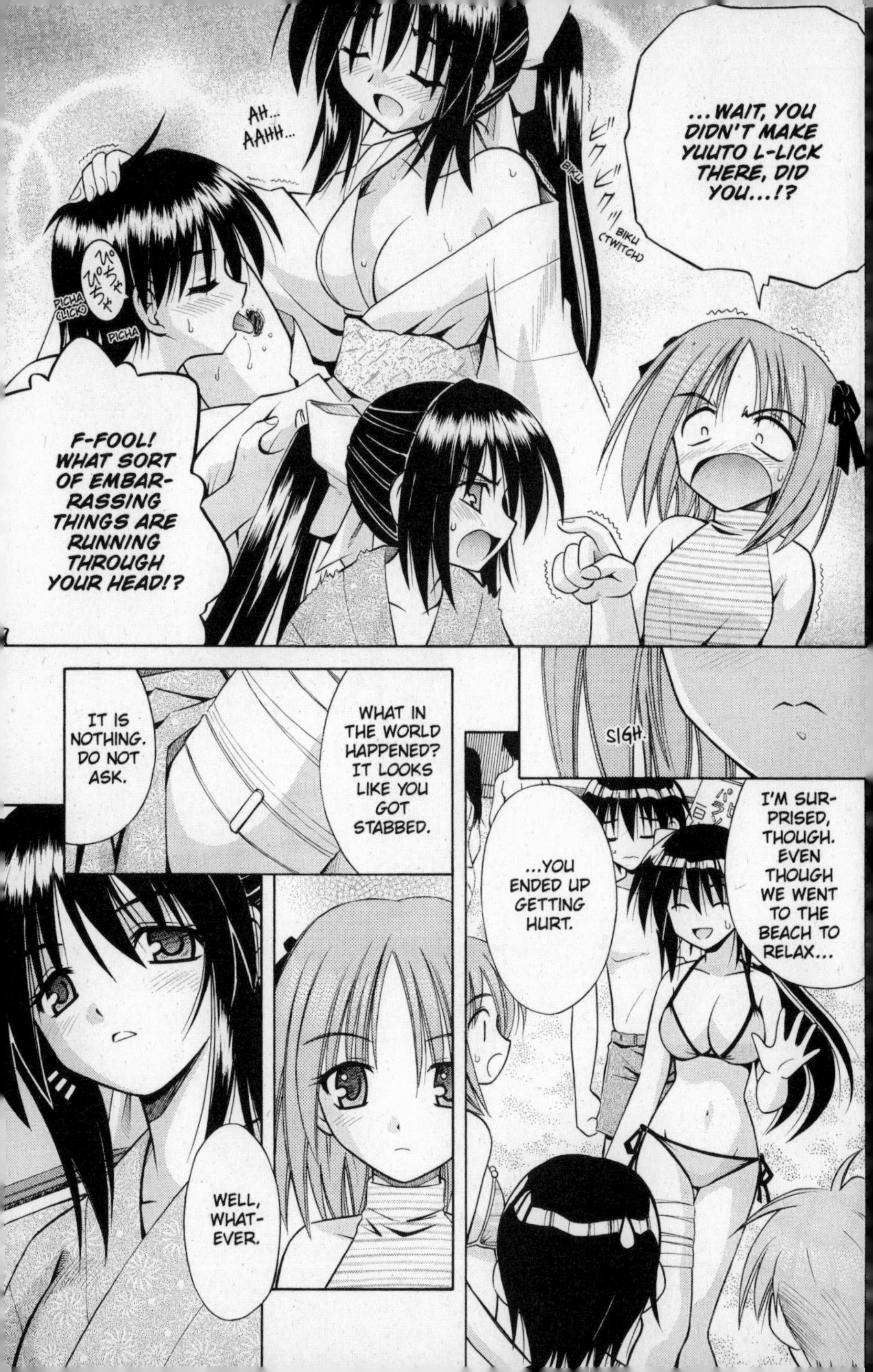
...WAIT, YOU DIDN'T MAKE YUUTO L-LICK THERE, DID YOU...!?
ビクビクッ
BIKU
BIKU (TWITCH)
AH... AAHH...
ぴちゃぴちゃ
PICHA (LICK)
PICHA
F-FOOL! WHAT SORT OF EMBARRASSING THINGS ARE RUNNING THROUGH YOUR HEAD!?
SIGH.
I'M SURPRISED, THOUGH. EVEN THOUGH WE WENT TO THE BEACH TO RELAX...
...YOU ENDED UP GETTING HURT.
WHAT IN THE WORLD HAPPENED? IT LOOKS LIKE YOU GOT STABBED.
IT IS NOTHING. DO NOT ASK.
WELL, WHATEVER.

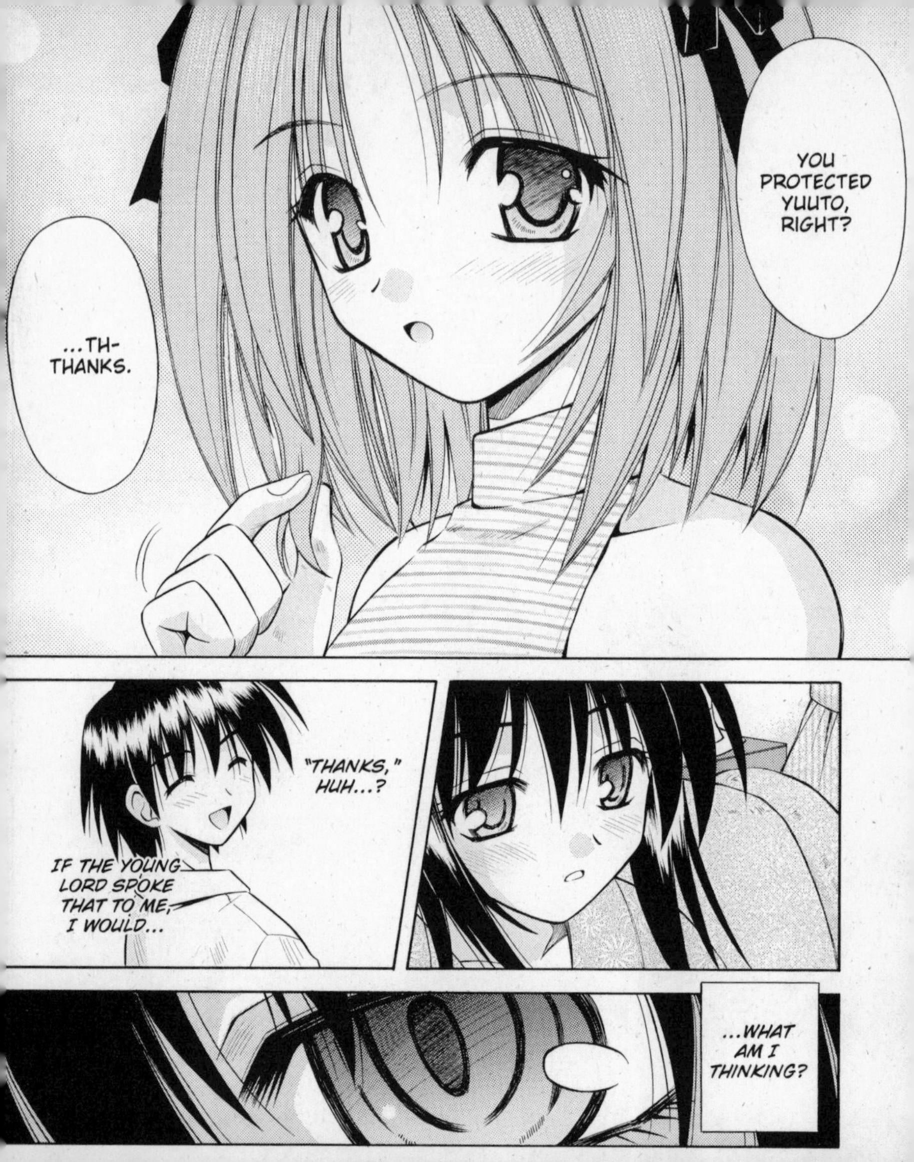
YOU PROTECTED YUUTO, RIGHT?
...TH-THANKS.
"THANKS," HUH...?
IF THE YOUNG LORD SPOKE THAT TO ME, I WOULD...
...WHAT AM I THINKING?

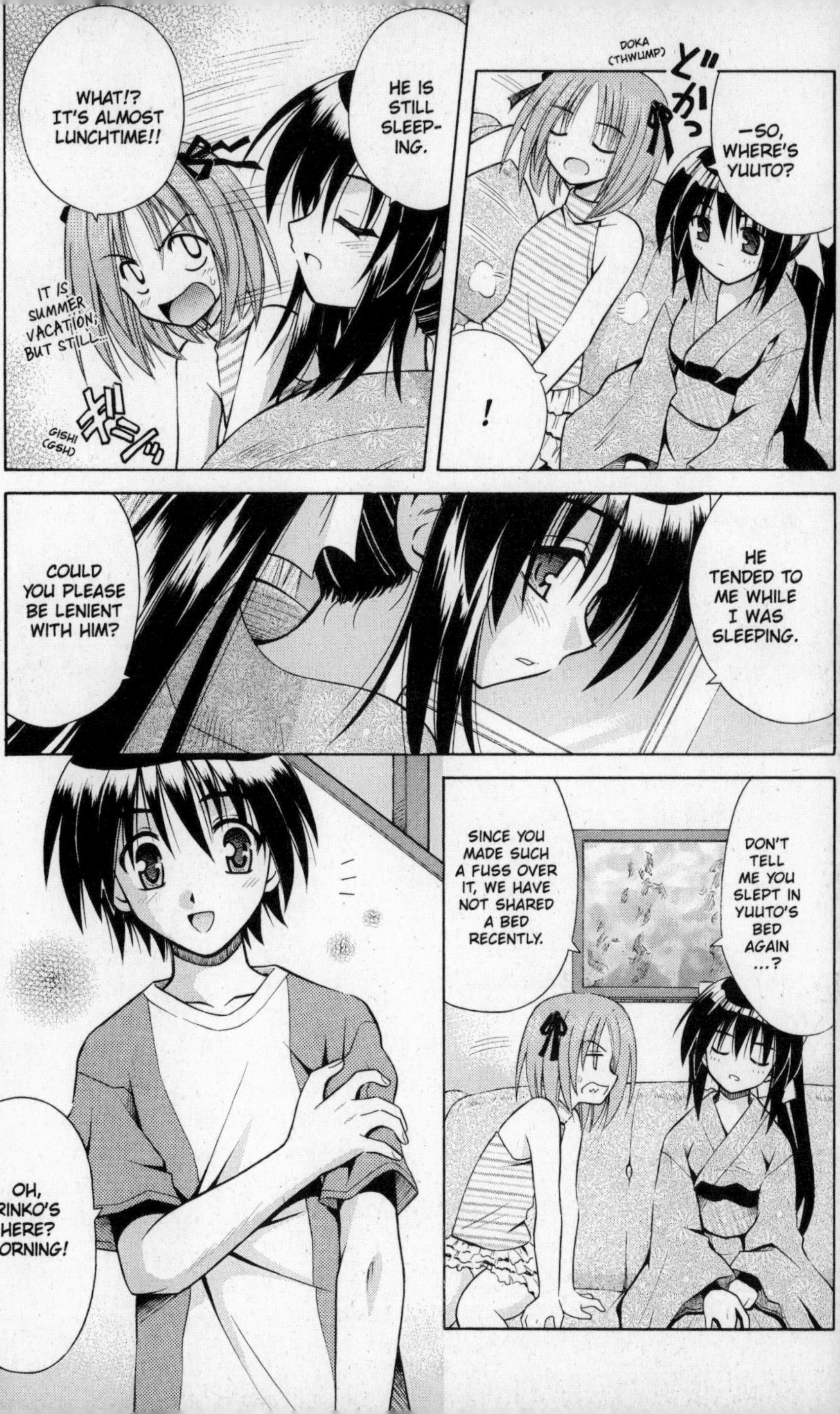
DOKA (THWUMP)
—SO, WHERE'S YUUTO?
!
HE IS STILL SLEEP-ING.
WHAT!? IT'S ALMOST LUNCHTIME!!
IT IS SUMMER VACATION, BUT STILL...
GISHI (GSH)
HE TENDED TO ME WHILE I WAS SLEEPING.
COULD YOU PLEASE BE LENIENT WITH HIM?
DON'T TELL ME YOU SLEPT IN YUUTO'S BED AGAIN ...?
SINCE YOU MADE SUCH A FUSS OVER IT, WE HAVE NOT SHARED A BED RECENTLY.
OH, RINKO'S HERE? MORNING!

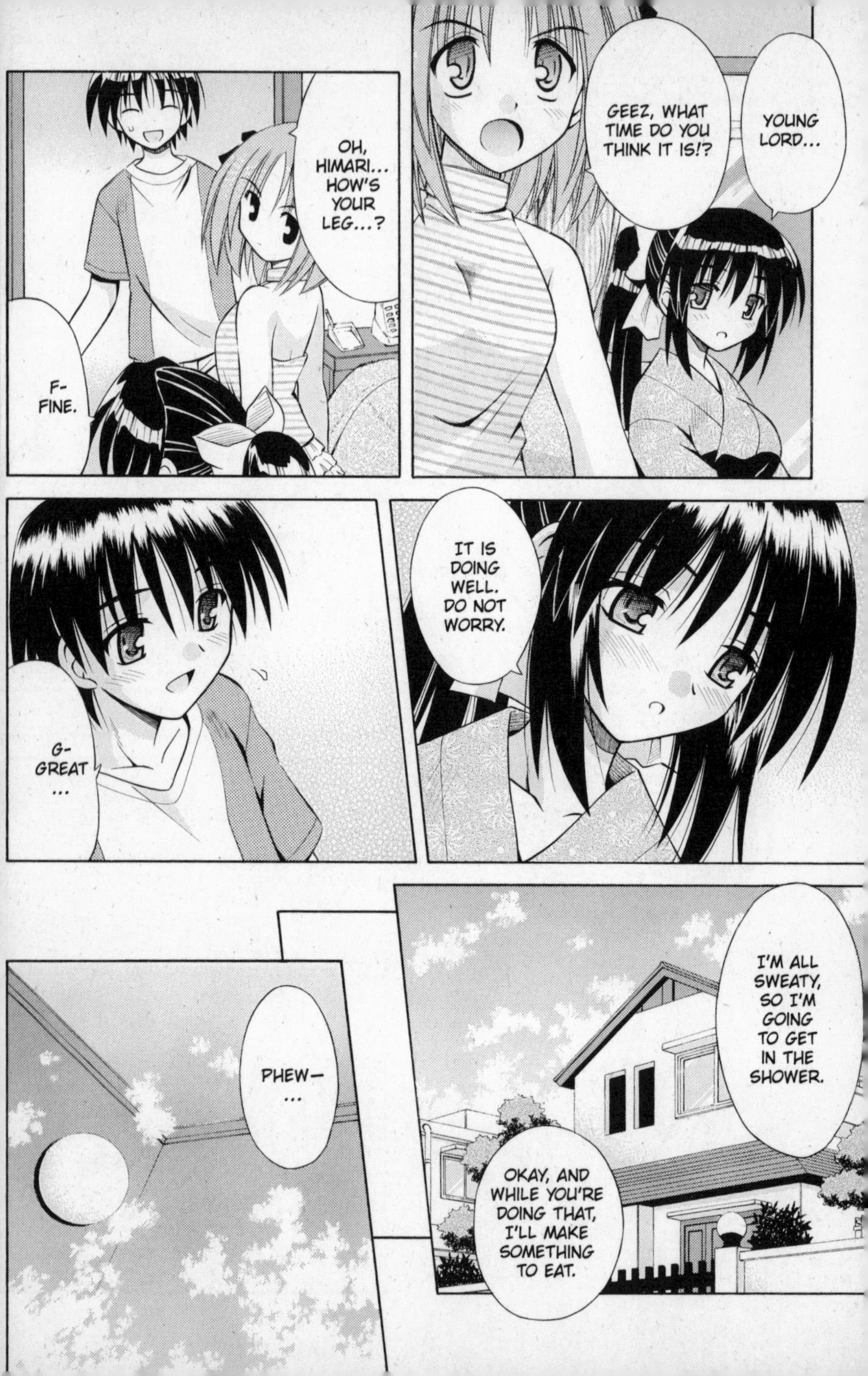
YOUNG LORD...
GEEZ, WHAT TIME DO YOU THINK IT IS!?
OH, HIMARI... HOW'S YOUR LEG...?
F-FINE.
IT IS DOING WELL. DO NOT WORRY.
G-GREAT...
I'M ALL SWEATY, SO I'M GOING TO GET IN THE SHOWER.
OKAY, AND WHILE YOU'RE DOING THAT, I'LL MAKE SOMETHING TO EAT.
PHEW—...

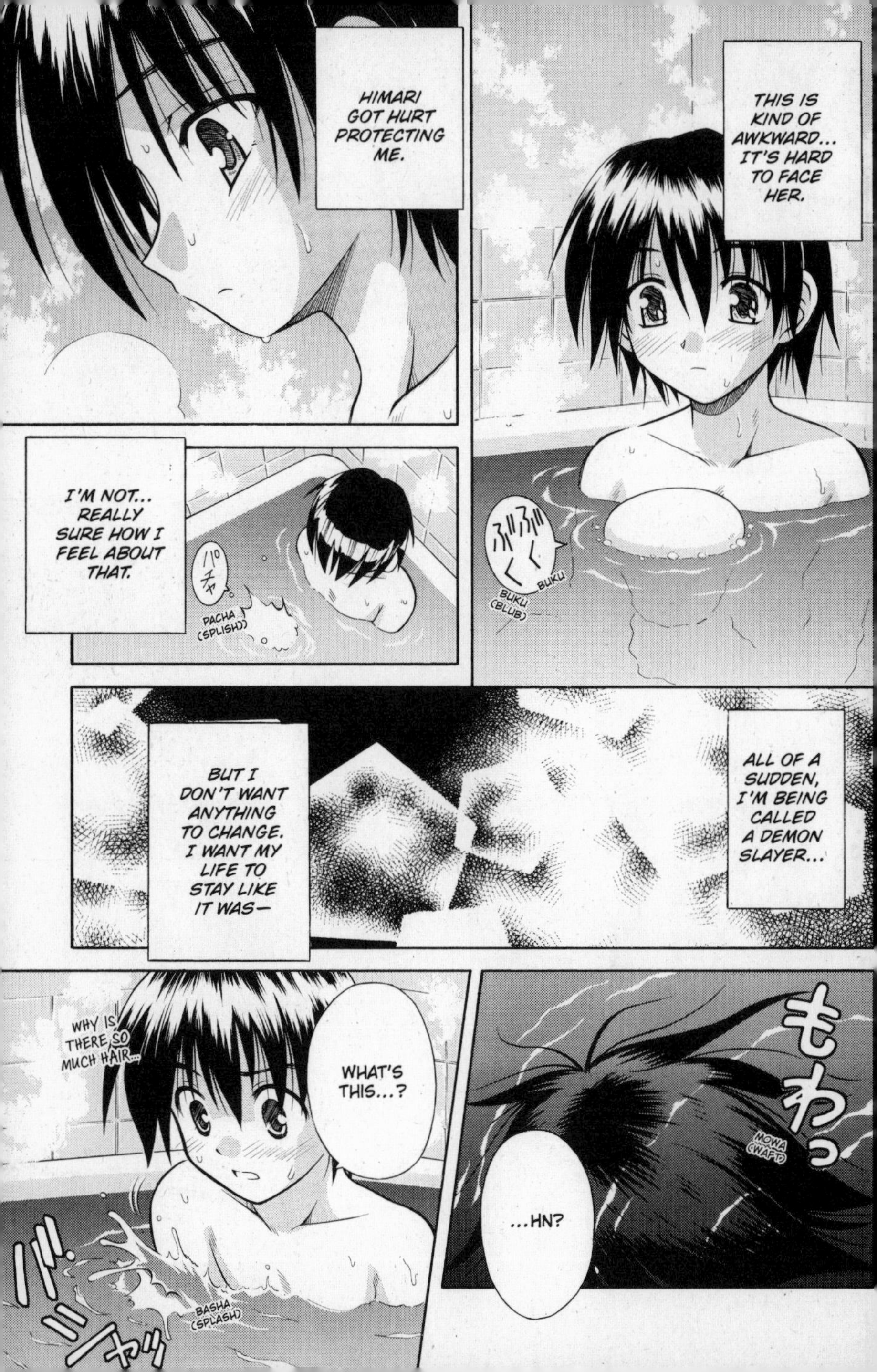
THIS IS KIND OF AWKWARD... IT'S HARD TO FACE HER.
ぶくぶく
BUKU BUKU (BLUB)
HIMARI GOT HURT PROTECTING ME.
I'M NOT... REALLY SURE HOW I FEEL ABOUT THAT.
パチャ
PACHA (SPLISH)
ALL OF A SUDDEN, I'M BEING CALLED A DEMON SLAYER...
BUT I DON'T WANT ANYTHING TO CHANGE. I WANT MY LIFE TO STAY LIKE IT WAS—
もわっ
MOWA (WAFT)
...HN?
WHAT'S THIS...?
WHY IS THERE SO MUCH HAIR...
バシャッ
BASHA (SPLASH)

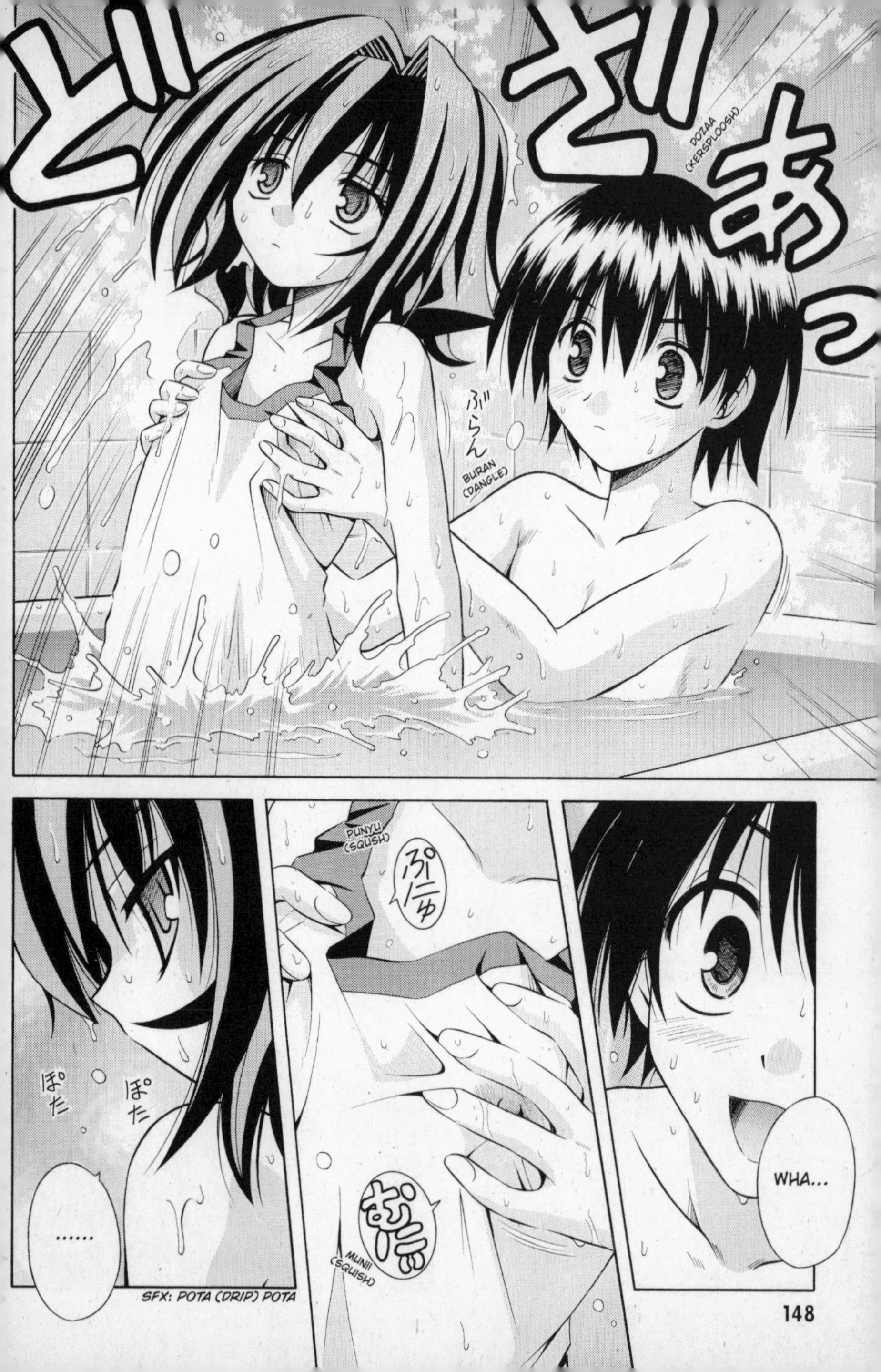
どざあっ
DOZAA (KERSPLOOSH)
ぶらん
BURAN (DANGLE)
WHA...
PUNYU (SQUISH)
ぷにゅ
MUNII (SQUISH)
ぽた ぽた
......
SFX: POTA (DRIP) POTA

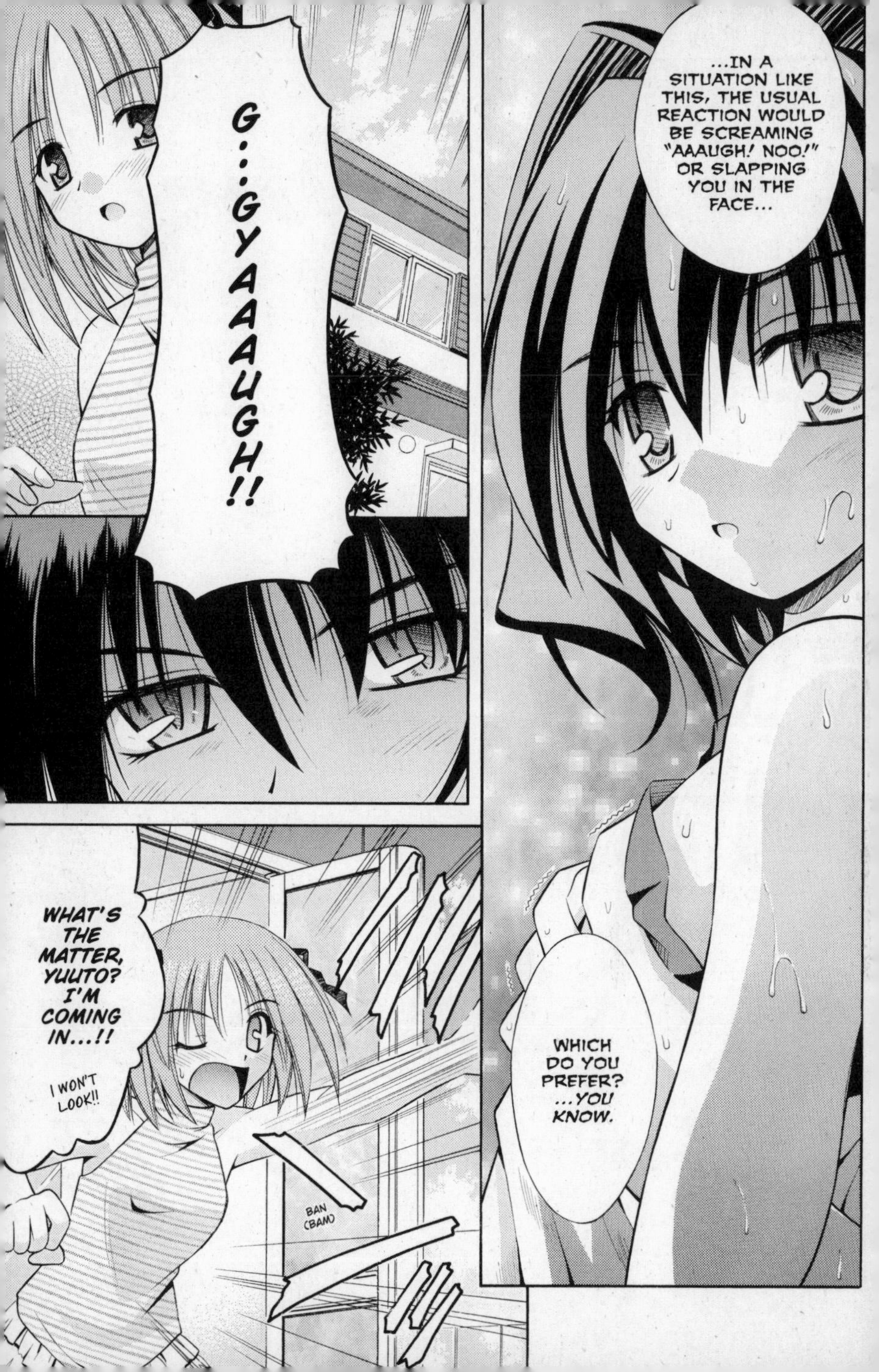
...IN A SITUATION LIKE THIS, THE USUAL REACTION WOULD BE SCREAMING "AAAUGH! NOO!" OR SLAPPING YOU IN THE FACE...
WHICH DO YOU PREFER? ...YOU KNOW.
G..GYAAAAUGH!!
WHAT'S THE MATTER, YUUTO? I'M COMING IN...!!
I WON'T LOOK!!
BAN (BAM)

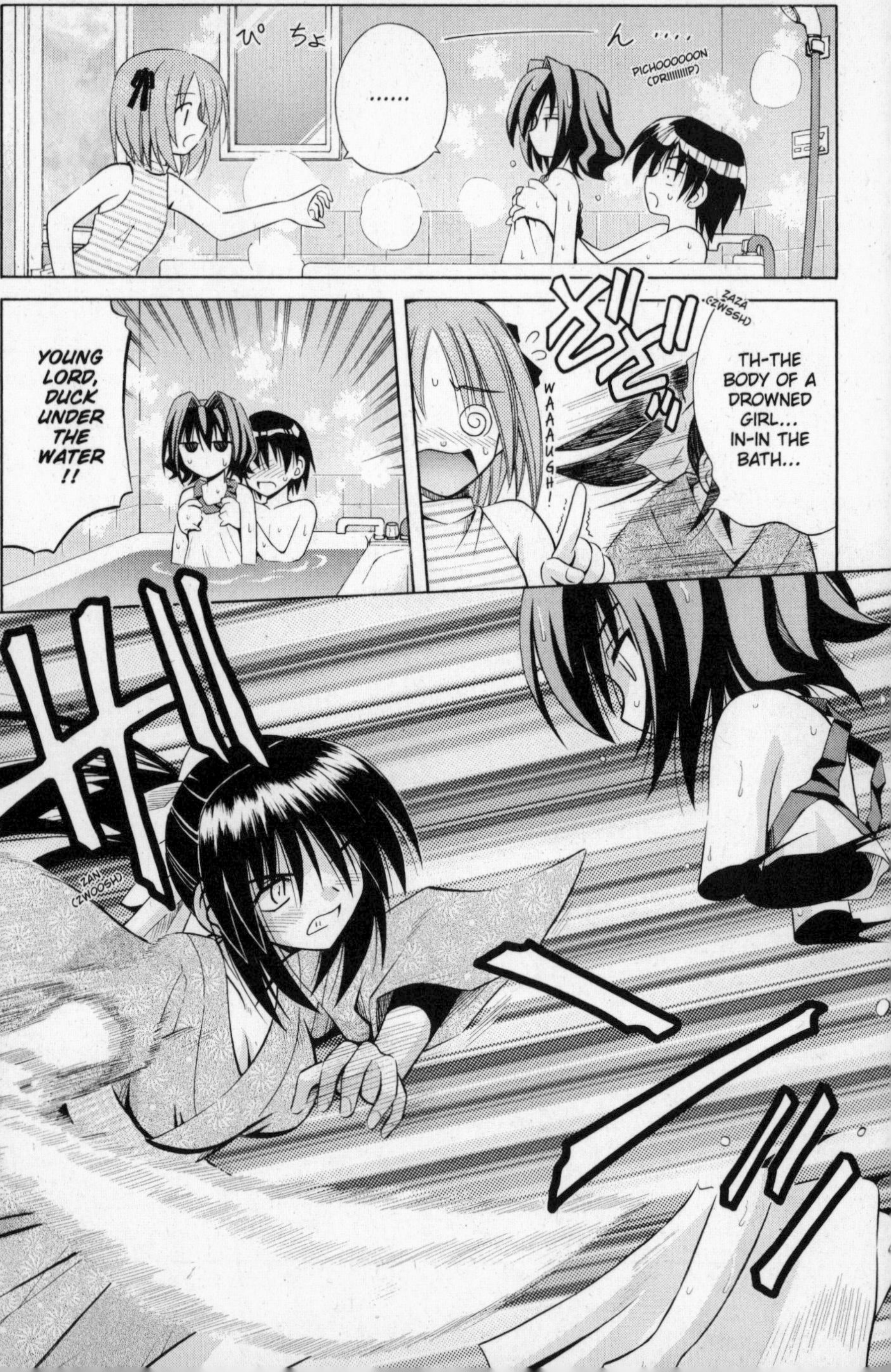
ぴちょ―――ん….
PICHOOOOOOON (DRIIIIIIIIP)
......
ZAZA (ZWSSH)
TH-THE BODY OF A DROWNED GIRL... IN-IN THE BATH...
WAAAAUGH!
YOUNG LORD, DUCK UNDER THE WATER!!
ZAN (ZWOOSH)

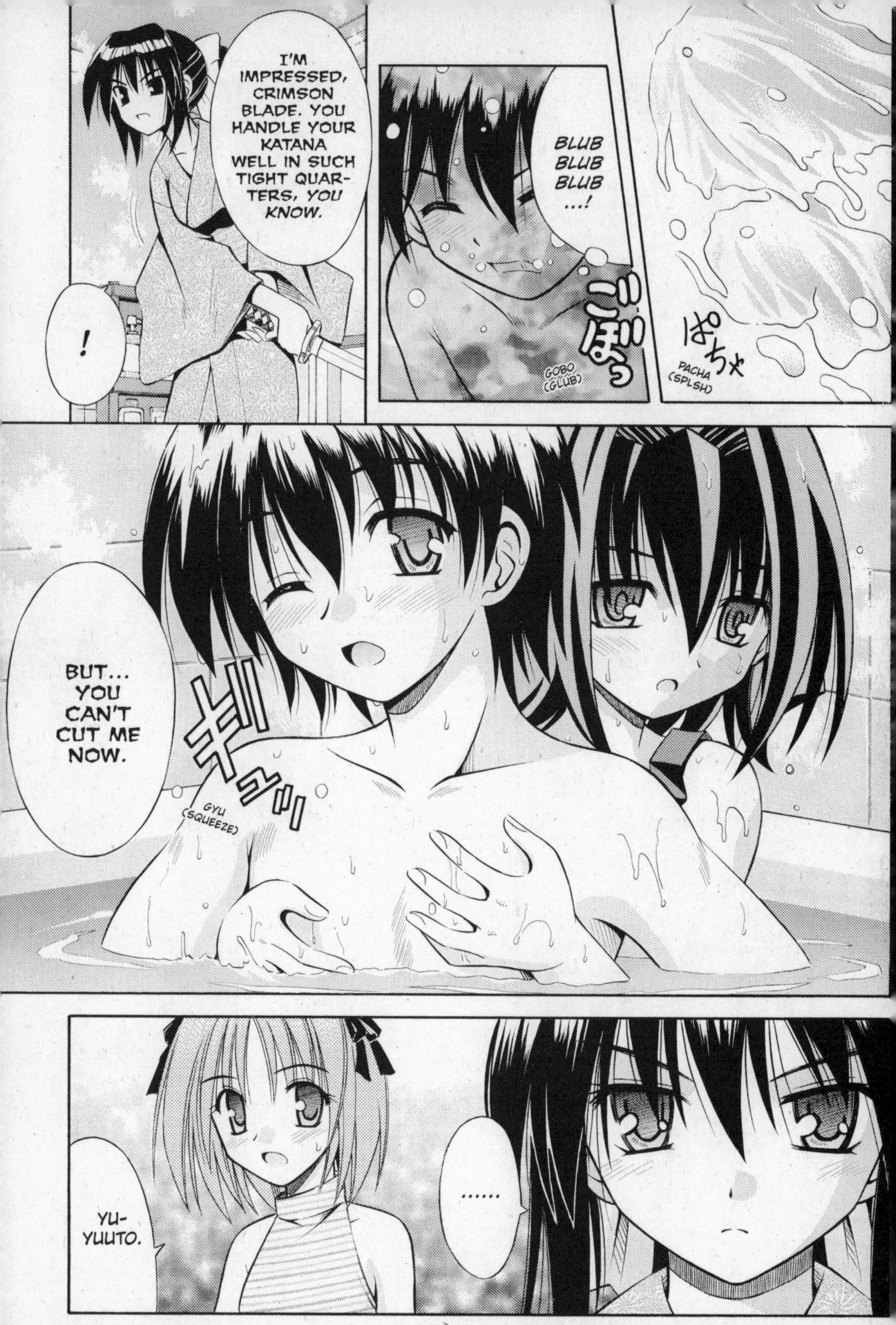
ぱちゃ
PACHA (SPLSH)
BLUB BLUB BLUB ...!
ごぼっ
GOBO (GLUB)
I'M IMPRESSED, CRIMSON BLADE. YOU HANDLE YOUR KATANA WELL IN SUCH TIGHT QUARTERS, YOU KNOW.
!
BUT... YOU CAN'T CUT ME NOW.
ギュッ
GYU (SQUEEZE)
......
YU-YUUTO.

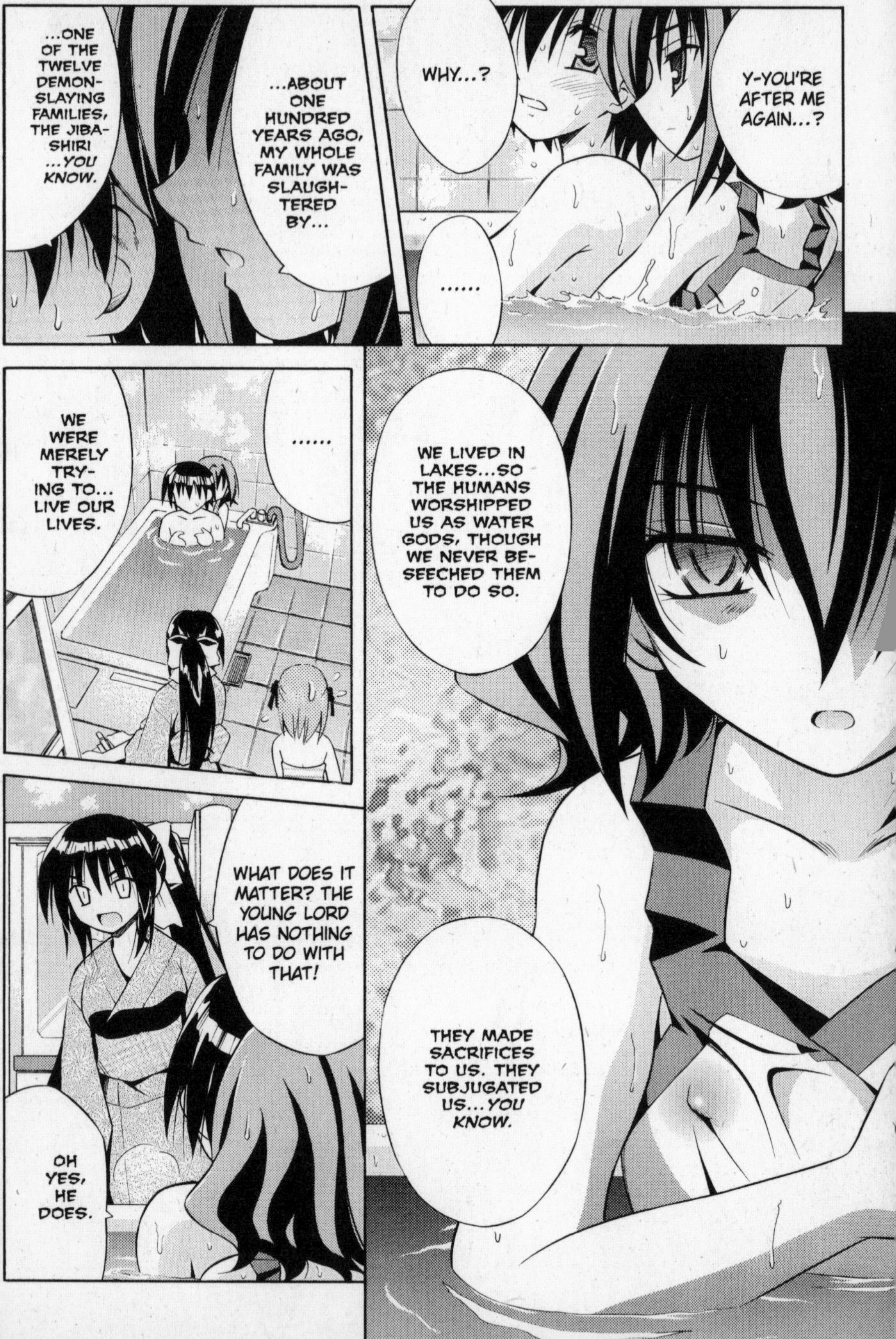
Y-YOU'RE AFTER ME AGAIN...?
WHY...?
......
...ABOUT ONE HUNDRED YEARS AGO, MY WHOLE FAMILY WAS SLAUGHTERED BY...
...ONE OF THE TWELVE DEMON-SLAYING FAMILIES, THE JIBASHIRI ...*YOU KNOW.*
WE LIVED IN LAKES...SO THE HUMANS WORSHIPPED US AS WATER GODS, THOUGH WE NEVER BESEECHED THEM TO DO SO.
THEY MADE SACRIFICES TO US. THEY SUBJUGATED US...*YOU KNOW.*
......
WE WERE MERELY TRYING TO... LIVE OUR LIVES.
WHAT DOES IT MATTER? THE YOUNG LORD HAS NOTHING TO DO WITH THAT!
OH YES, HE DOES.

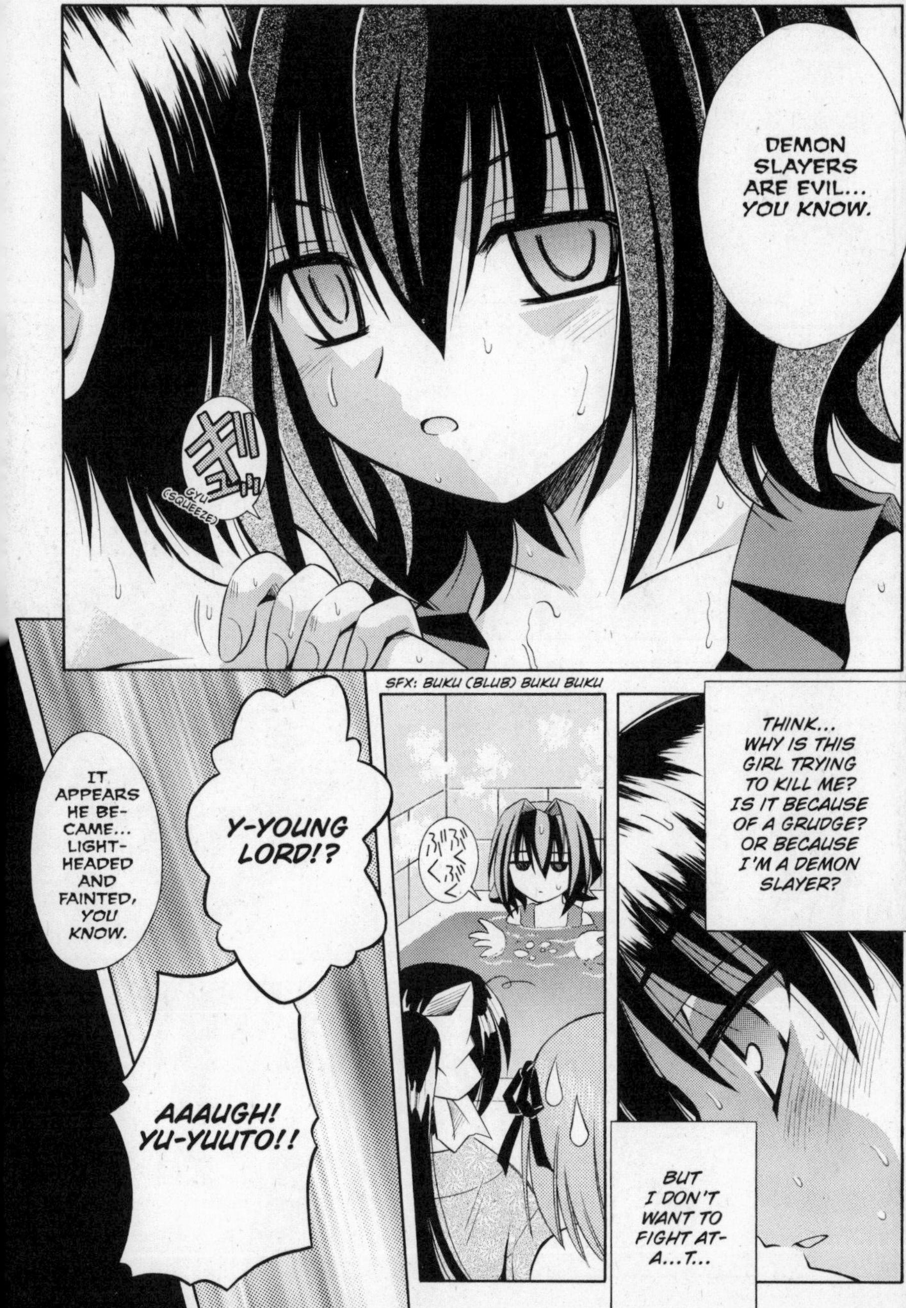
DEMON SLAYERS ARE EVIL... YOU KNOW.
GYU (SQUEEZE)
THINK... WHY IS THIS GIRL TRYING TO KILL ME? IS IT BECAUSE OF A GRUDGE? OR BECAUSE I'M A DEMON SLAYER?
BUT I DON'T WANT TO FIGHT AT-A...T...
SFX: BUKU (BLUB) BUKU BUKU
Y-YOUNG LORD!?
IT APPEARS HE BE-CAME... LIGHT-HEADED AND FAINTED, YOU KNOW.
AAAUGH! YU-YUUTO!!

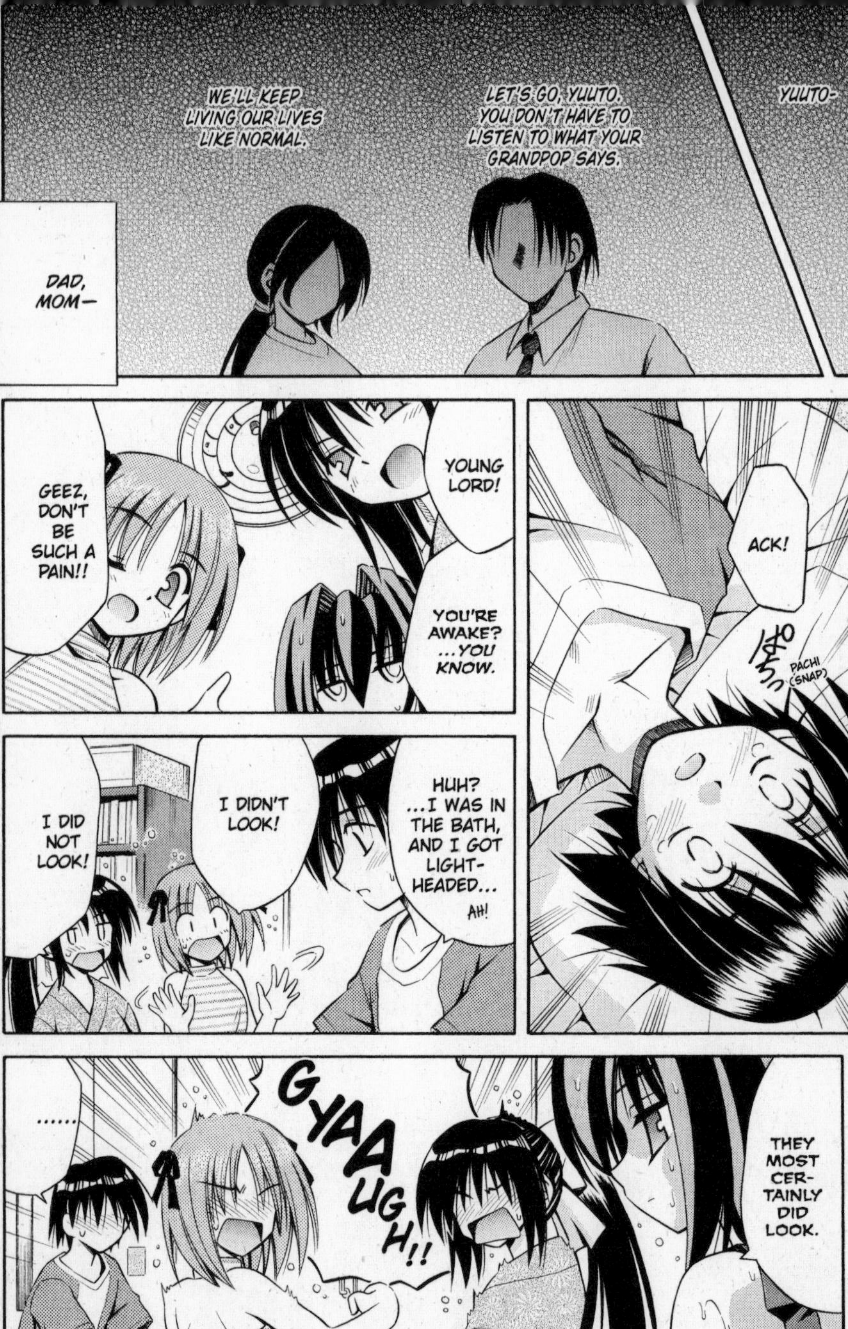
YUUTO-
LET'S GO, YUUTO. YOU DON'T HAVE TO LISTEN TO WHAT YOUR GRANDPOP SAYS.
WE'LL KEEP LIVING OUR LIVES LIKE NORMAL.
DAD, MOM—
ACK!
PACHI (SNAP)
YOUNG LORD!
YOU'RE AWAKE? ...YOU KNOW.
GEEZ, DON'T BE SUCH A PAIN!!
HUH? ...I WAS IN THE BATH, AND I GOT LIGHT-HEADED...
AH!
I DIDN'T LOOK!
I DID NOT LOOK!
THEY MOST CERTAINLY DID LOOK.
GYAAAUGH!!
......

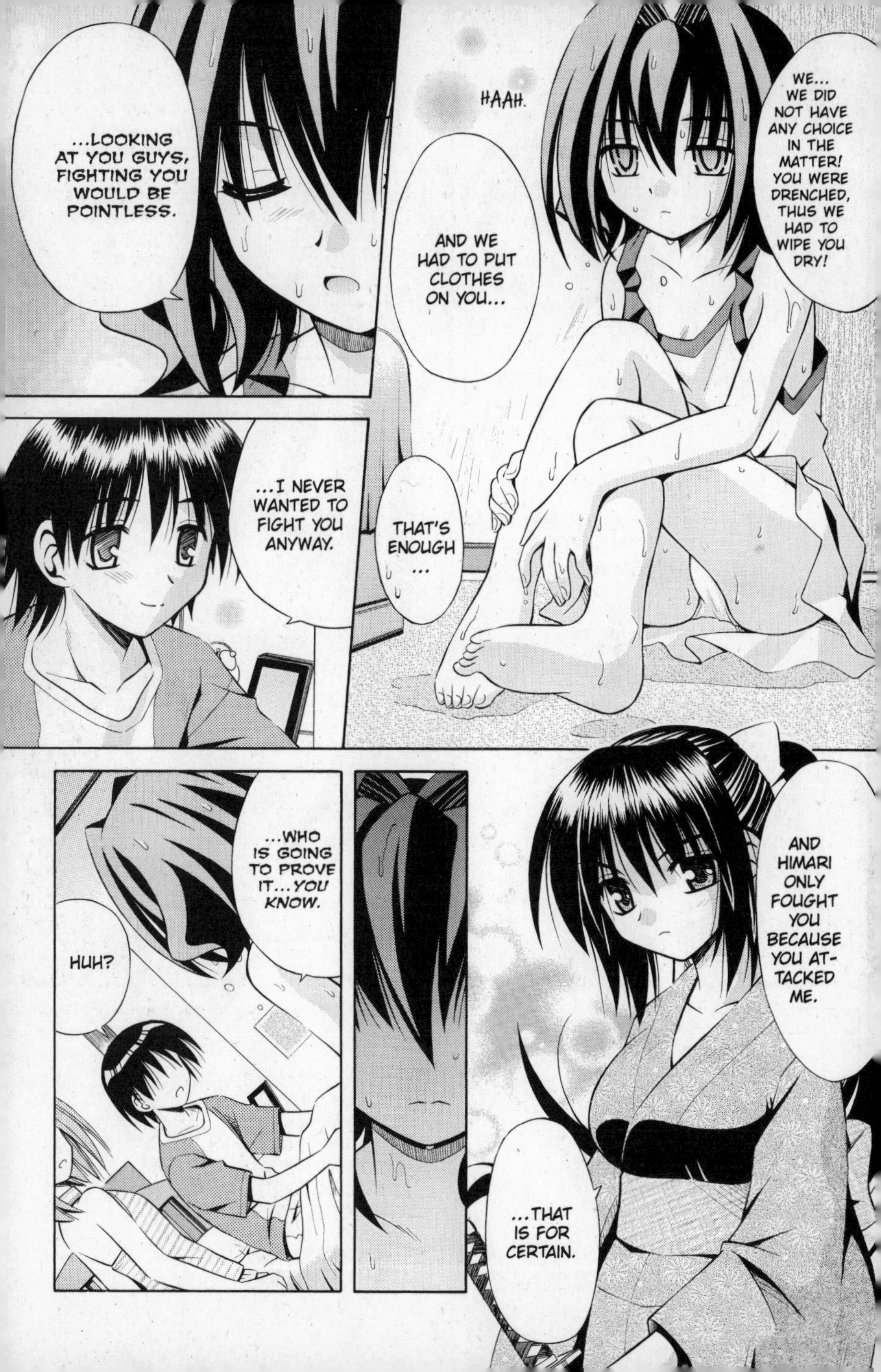
WE... WE DID NOT HAVE ANY CHOICE IN THE MATTER! YOU WERE DRENCHED, THUS WE HAD TO WIPE YOU DRY!
HAAH.
AND WE HAD TO PUT CLOTHES ON YOU...
THAT'S ENOUGH...
...LOOKING AT YOU GUYS, FIGHTING YOU WOULD BE POINTLESS.
...I NEVER WANTED TO FIGHT YOU ANYWAY.
AND HIMARI ONLY FOUGHT YOU BECAUSE YOU AT-TACKED ME.
...THAT IS FOR CERTAIN.
...WHO IS GOING TO PROVE IT... YOU KNOW.
HUH?

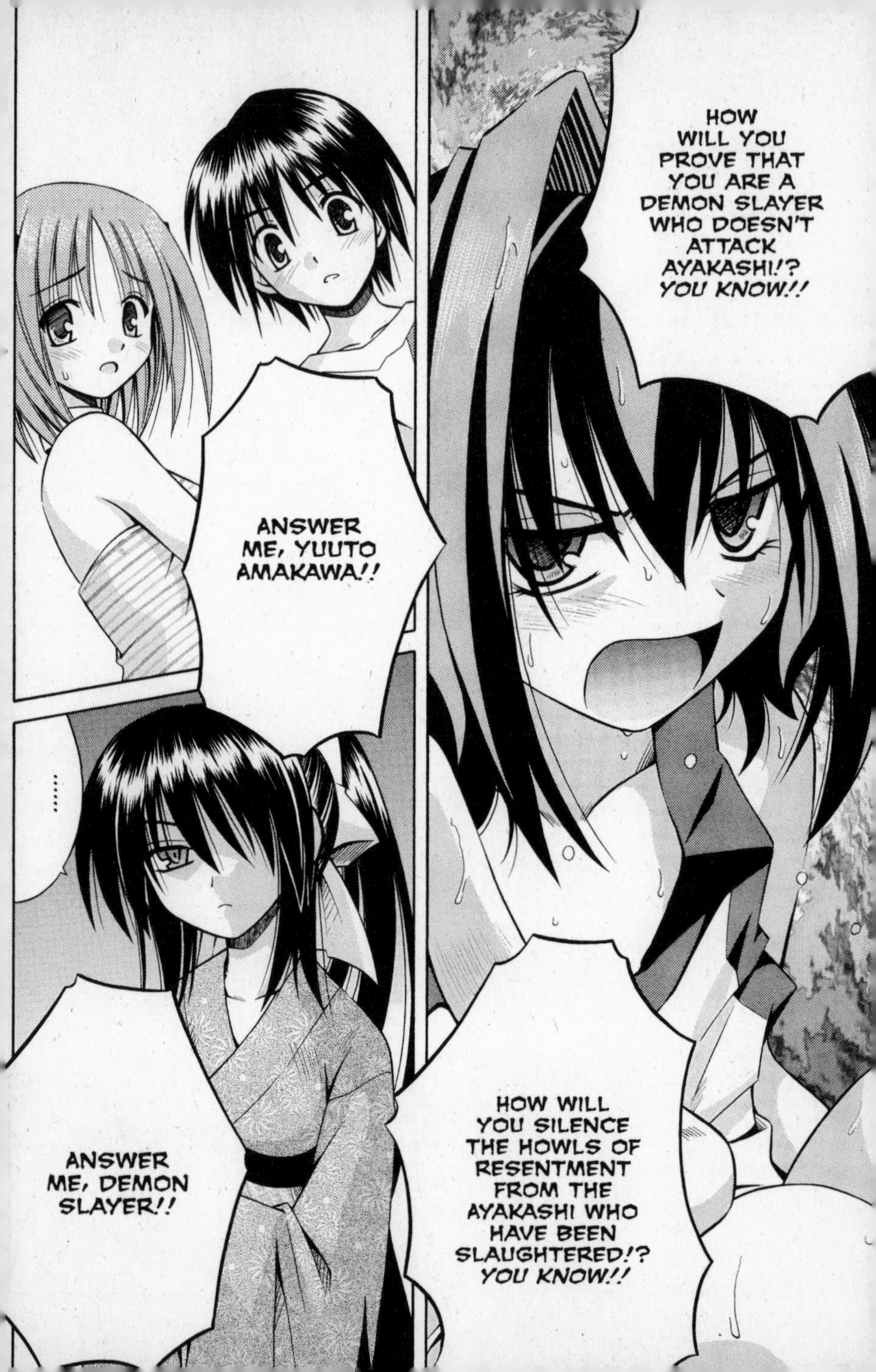
HOW WILL YOU PROVE THAT YOU ARE A DEMON SLAYER WHO DOESN'T ATTACK AYAKASHI!? YOU KNOW!!
HOW WILL YOU SILENCE THE HOWLS OF RESENTMENT FROM THE AYAKASHI WHO HAVE BEEN SLAUGHTERED!? YOU KNOW!!
ANSWER ME, YUUTO AMAKAWA!!
......
ANSWER ME, DEMON SLAYER!!

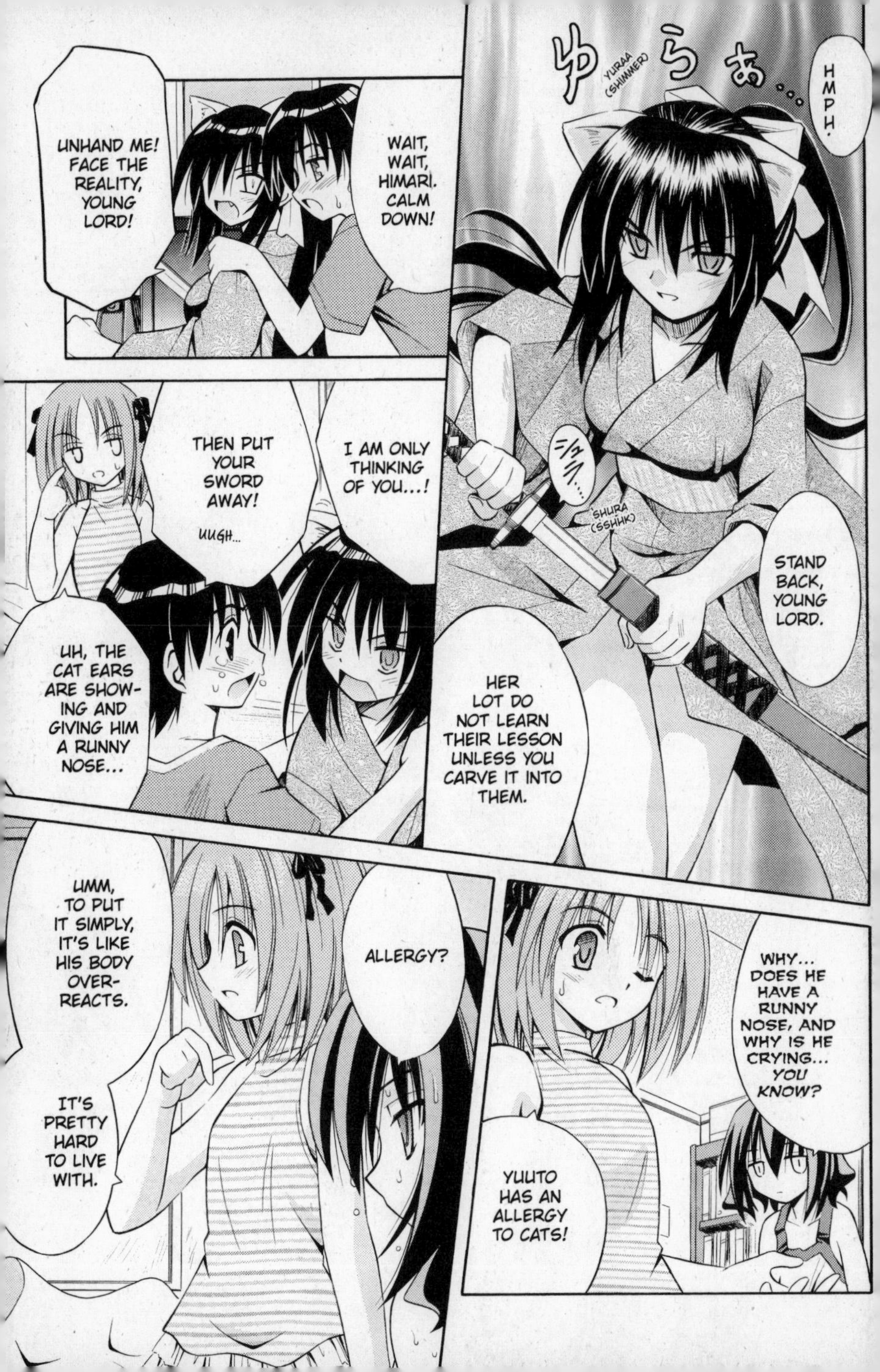
ゆらぁ…
YURAA (SHIMMER)
HMPH.
シュラ…
SHURA (SSHHK)
STAND BACK, YOUNG LORD.
HER LOT DO NOT LEARN THEIR LESSON UNLESS YOU CARVE IT INTO THEM.
WAIT, WAIT, HIMARI. CALM DOWN!
UNHAND ME! FACE THE REALITY, YOUNG LORD!
I AM ONLY THINKING OF YOU...!
THEN PUT YOUR SWORD AWAY!
UUGH...
UH, THE CAT EARS ARE SHOWING AND GIVING HIM A RUNNY NOSE...
WHY... DOES HE HAVE A RUNNY NOSE, AND WHY IS HE CRYING... YOU KNOW?
YUUTO HAS AN ALLERGY TO CATS!
ALLERGY?
UMM, TO PUT IT SIMPLY, IT'S LIKE HIS BODY OVER-REACTS.
IT'S PRETTY HARD TO LIVE WITH.

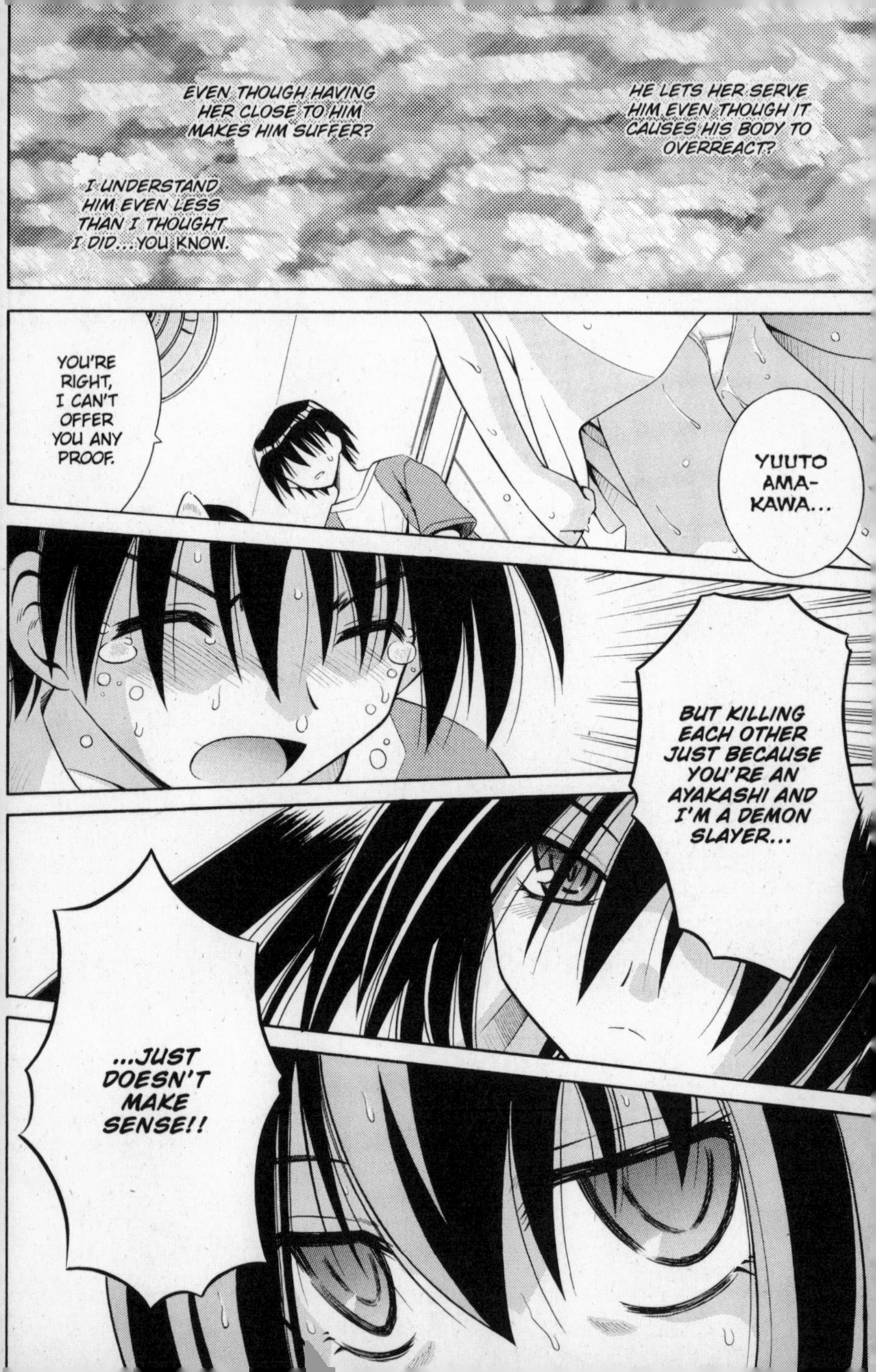
HE LETS HER SERVE HIM EVEN THOUGH IT CAUSES HIS BODY TO OVERREACT?
EVEN THOUGH HAVING HER CLOSE TO HIM MAKES HIM SUFFER?
I UNDERSTAND HIM EVEN LESS THAN I THOUGHT I DID... YOU KNOW.
YUUTO AMA-KAWA...
YOU'RE RIGHT, I CAN'T OFFER YOU ANY PROOF.
BUT KILLING EACH OTHER JUST BECAUSE YOU'RE AN AYAKASHI AND I'M A DEMON SLAYER...
...JUST DOESN'T MAKE SENSE!!

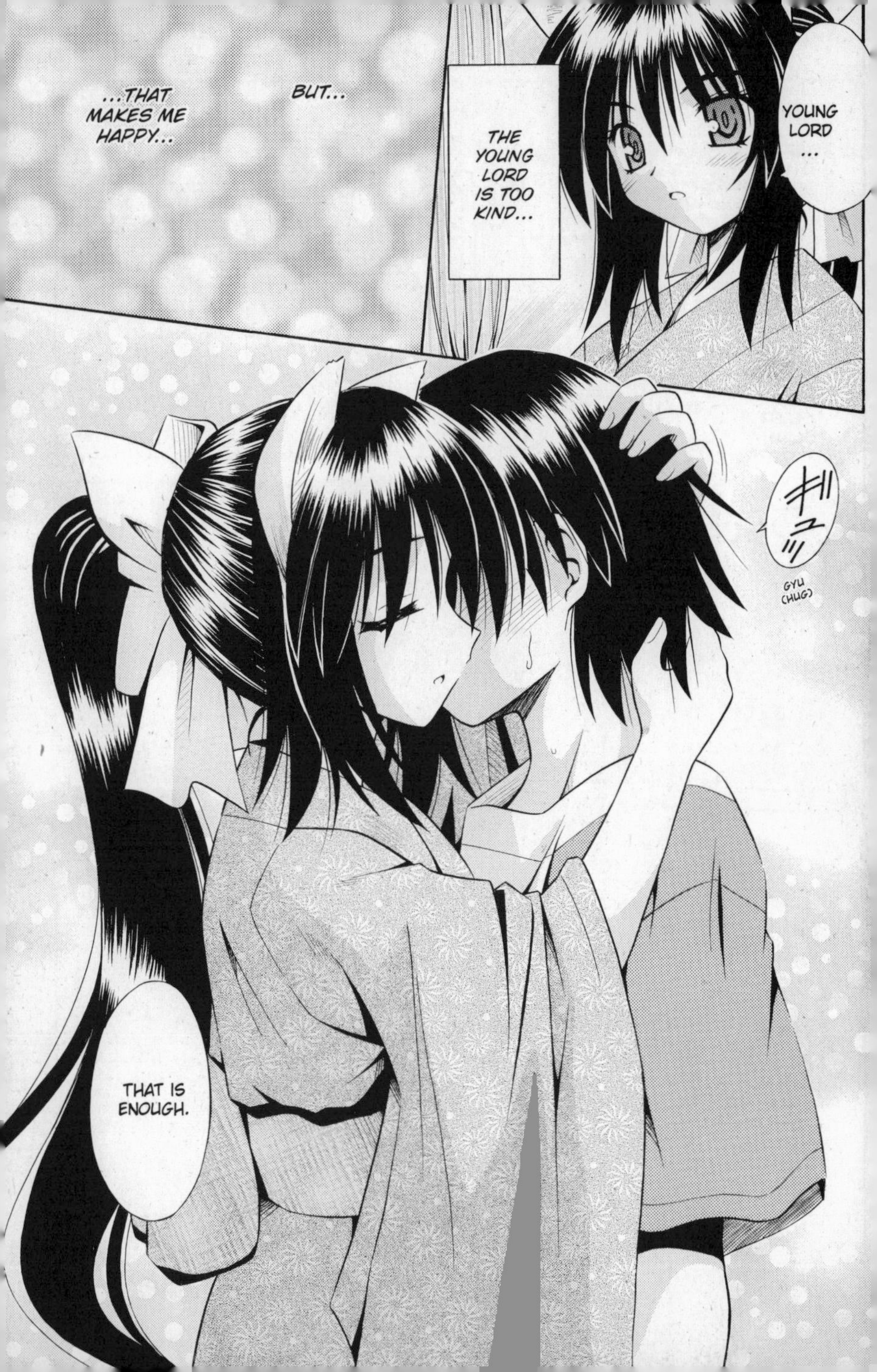
YOUNG LORD ...
THE YOUNG LORD IS TOO KIND...
BUT...
...THAT MAKES ME HAPPY...
ギュッ
GYU (HUG)
THAT IS ENOUGH.

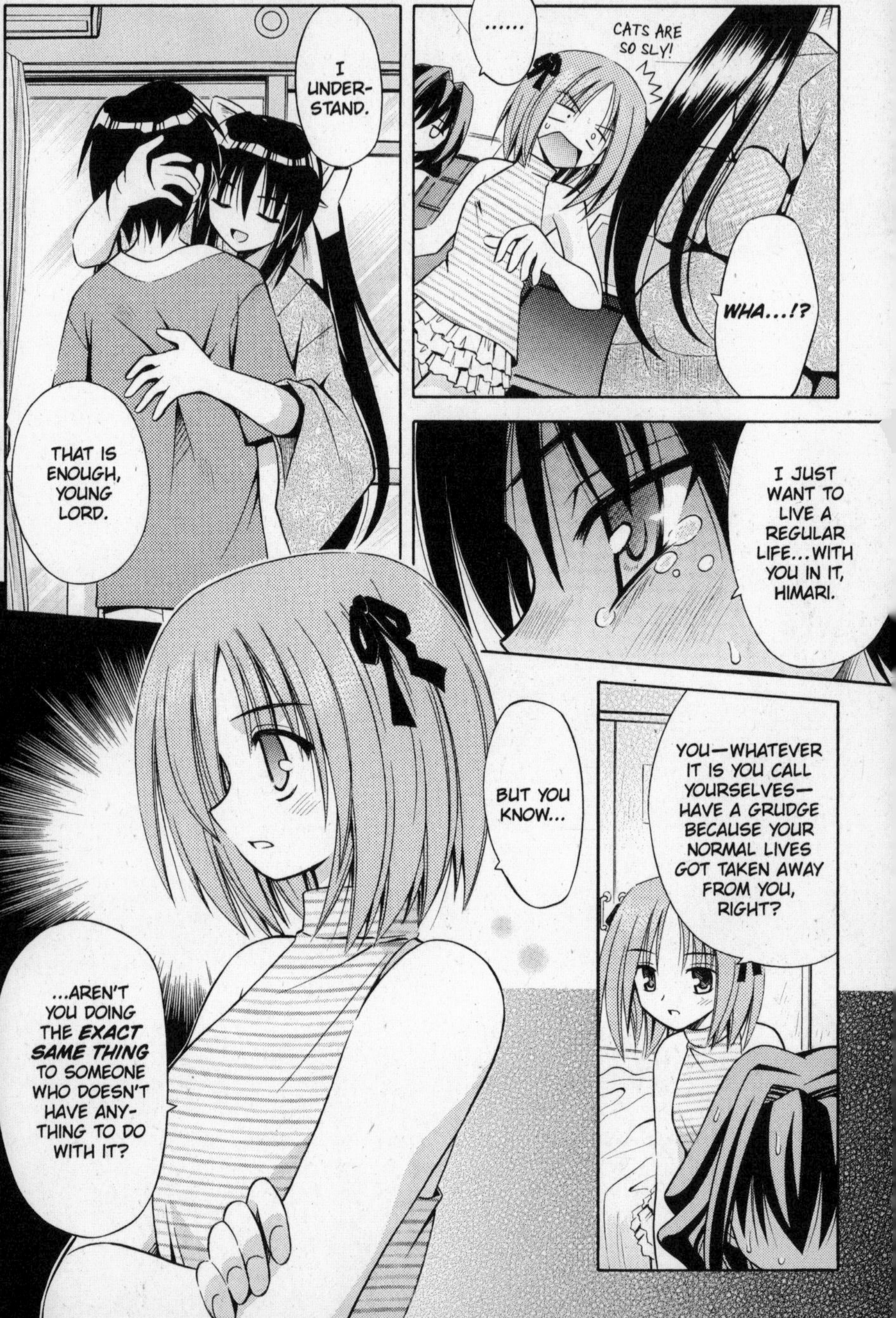
......
CATS ARE SO SLY!
WHA...!?
I JUST WANT TO LIVE A REGULAR LIFE...WITH YOU IN IT, HIMARI.
I UNDER-STAND.
THAT IS ENOUGH, YOUNG LORD.
YOU—WHATEVER IT IS YOU CALL YOURSELVES—HAVE A GRUDGE BECAUSE YOUR NORMAL LIVES GOT TAKEN AWAY FROM YOU, RIGHT?
BUT YOU KNOW...
...AREN'T YOU DOING THE ***EXACT SAME THING*** TO SOMEONE WHO DOESN'T HAVE ANY-THING TO DO WITH IT?

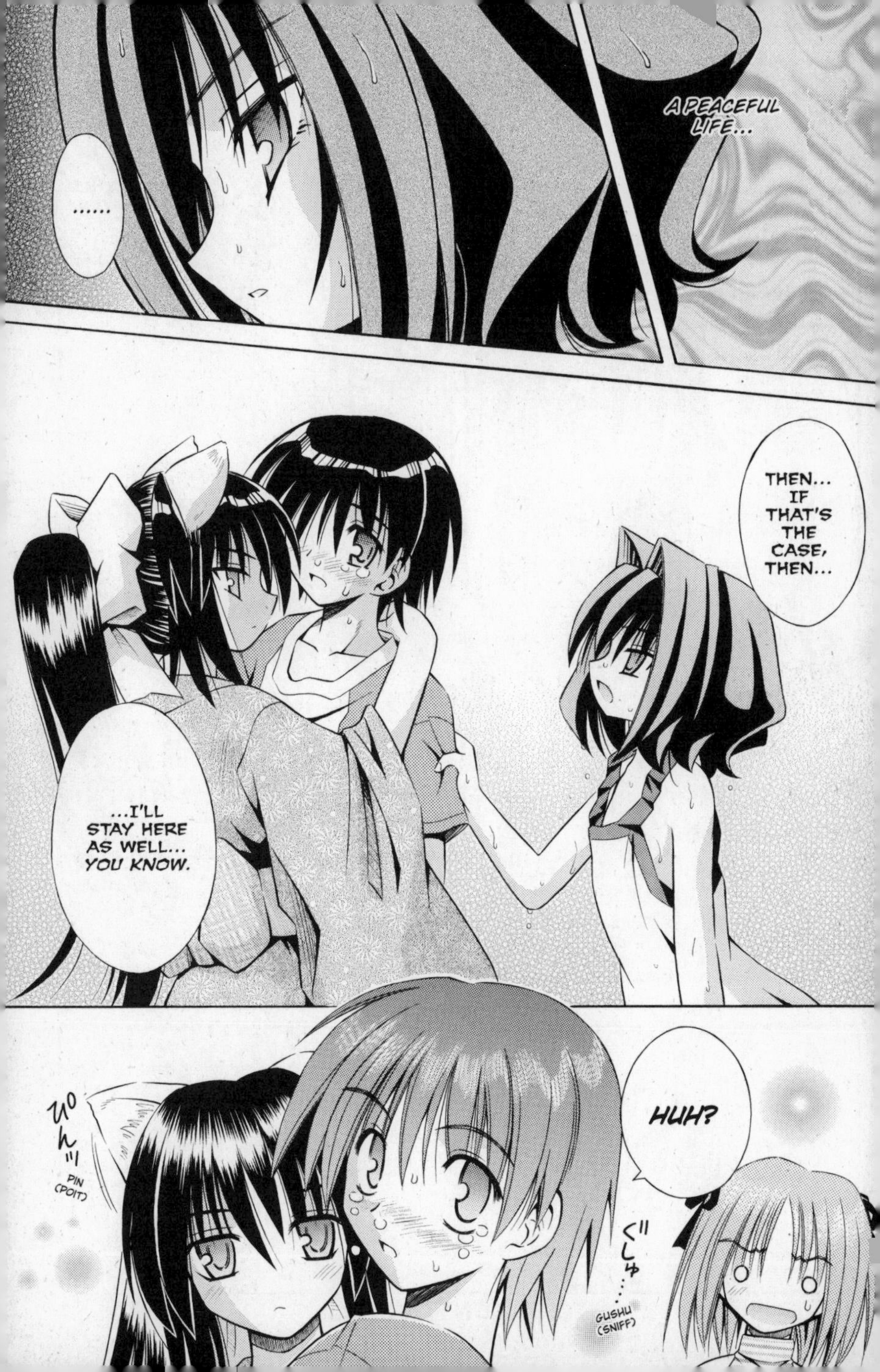
A PEACEFUL LIFE...
......
THEN... IF THAT'S THE CASE, THEN...
...I'LL STAY HERE AS WELL... YOU KNOW.
HUH?
ぐしゅ...
GUSHU (SNIFF)
ぴんッ
PIN (POIT)

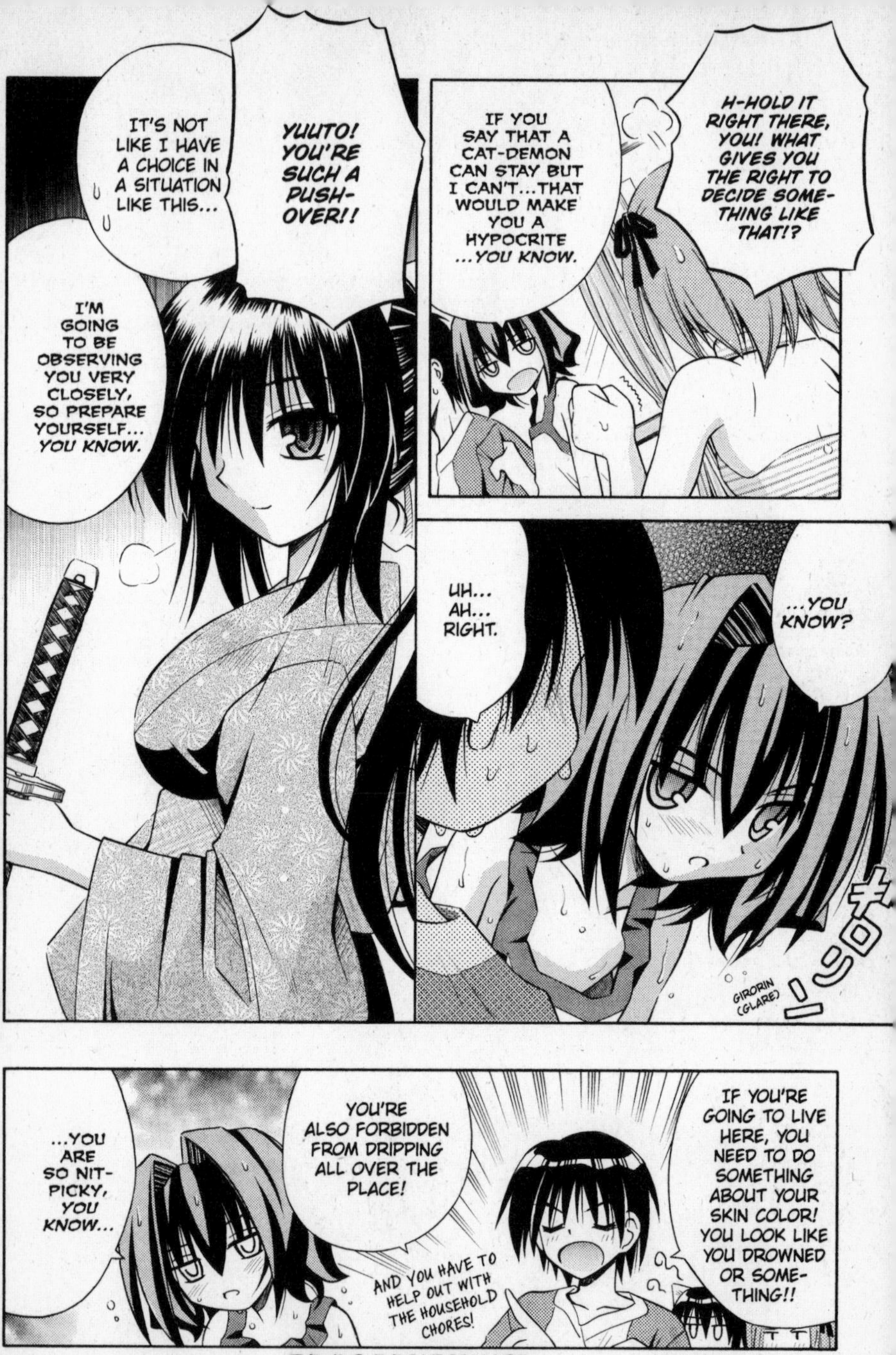
H-HOLD IT RIGHT THERE, YOU! WHAT GIVES YOU THE RIGHT TO DECIDE SOMETHING LIKE THAT!?
IF YOU SAY THAT A CAT-DEMON CAN STAY BUT I CAN'T...THAT WOULD MAKE YOU A HYPOCRITE ...YOU KNOW.
...YOU KNOW?
UH... AH... RIGHT.
GIRORIN (GLARE)
YUUTO! YOU'RE SUCH A PUSH-OVER!!
IT'S NOT LIKE I HAVE A CHOICE IN A SITUATION LIKE THIS...
I'M GOING TO BE OBSERVING YOU VERY CLOSELY, SO PREPARE YOURSELF... YOU KNOW.
IF YOU'RE GOING TO LIVE HERE, YOU NEED TO DO SOMETHING ABOUT YOUR SKIN COLOR! YOU LOOK LIKE YOU DROWNED OR SOME-THING!!
AND YOU HAVE TO HELP OUT WITH THE HOUSEHOLD CHORES!
YOU'RE ALSO FORBIDDEN FROM DRIPPING ALL OVER THE PLACE!
...YOU ARE SO NIT-PICKY, YOU KNOW...

TO BE CONTINUED...